Contesting Democracy

Contesting Democracy

Substance and Structure in
American Political History, 1775–2000

EDITED BY
Byron E. Shafer and Anthony J. Badger

 University Press of Kansas

Published by the University Press of Kansas (Lawrence, Kansas 66049), which was organized by the Kansas Board of Regents and is operated and funded by Emporia State University, Fort Hays State University, Kansas State University, Pittsburg State University, the University of Kansas, and Wichita State University

Library of Congress Cataloging-in-Publication Data

Contesting democracy : substance and structure in American political history, 1775–2000 / edited by Byron E. Shafer and Anthony J. Badger.
    p.   cm.
Includes index.
   ISBN 0-7006-1138-x (cloth : alk. paper) — ISBN 0-7006-1139-8 (pbk. : alk. paper)
   1. United States—Politics and government.   2. United States—Politics and government—Historiography.   3. Democracy—United States—History. 4. Political culture—United States—History.   I. Shafer, Byron E.   II. Badger, Anthony J.
   E183 .C765 2001
   320.973—dc21   2001002320

British Library Cataloguing in Publication Data is available.

Printed in the United States of America

10 9 8 7 6 5 4 3 2 1

For Hugh Davis Graham

CONTENTS

PREFACE

The essays that make up *Contesting Democracy* possess a single root, shared goals, a common general framework, sharply individualized analyses, and, in the end, some notably diverse conclusions. And each aspect of that introduction probably requires some further comment.

These essays initially grew from conversations—conversations that, as they so often do, became a friendly argument—between Tony Badger and me (Byron Shafer) about the current state of the study of political history in (and of) the United States. The essence of that argument, presented abstractly, met with quick and easy recognition from the political historians, themselves otherwise diverse, who cover in this book the entire history of an independent United States. Collectively, they were willing to undertake a joint project. Individually, they were willing to assume their suggested responsibilities within it.

They were willing to work additionally within a common framework, one emphasizing the interaction of policy substance and social structure in shaping politics. This was probably made easier by the fact that they were reassured about weighting that interaction according to the key elements of their own assigned time periods. We hope that the product allows the reader to follow common elements across American political history while reading its content in the distinctive fashion of its distinguished authors, who treat the main overlapping developments in notably different—indeed, often contrasting—ways.

Moving between the study of American political life as pursued in two related countries, Tony and I were struck by the easy acceptance in Britain of the importance of what one might call "large *P* politics"—the struggle to shape the outcomes of government and its centrality to the character of public life, even when those outcomes were not the central story of their time. What made this seem striking in our time was the joint perception of an effort to move away from this and toward what one might call "small *P* politics" in the contemporary United States, with its associated preference for the small, private, and idiosyncratic—a preference for disaggregation, even deviant cases, rather than for collectivity and dominant trends.

We were still able to generate argument out of those perceptions. I was willing to grant the presence of an abstracted "politics of everything," in the same way that there is an economics of everything, an anthropology of everything, a social structure of everything, and so on. I was less willing to credit the advantages of such a microfocus for studying the sweep (and interpretation) of political life. Tony was more tolerant—perhaps just more understanding—both of this perspective and of the work growing from it and more confident that it had to rejoin large *P* politics in the long run. Nevertheless, we both remained rooted in the latter. Or perhaps we just thought that it was not only more consequential, on balance, but also a lot more fun.

In any case, one reason for this peculiar disjunction seemed to be not just the absence of broad-gauge, recent histories of American politics with a large *P*. Rather, it seemed to be the absence of works that set out consciously to synthesize recent understandings of the evolution of American politics—now vastly expanded in its linkages between the shaping of governance and the underlying changes in American society, economy, and, indeed, polity. That might have been sufficient incentive to pursue such a project and even to recruit its cast of participants. But there was a second major aspect to our reading of contemporary political history of the United States, which we also set out to address.

We felt that much of the political history that met our mutual preference—large rather than small *P* politics—was still divided into two perversely distinct camps. One of these wrote political history through its substance, emphasizing great substantive issues, major substantive divisions, and grand substantive policies. The other wrote political history by way of its structural influences, emphasizing social and economic change, major societal cleavages, and the role of key intermediary organizations. We credited the utility of thinking in terms of both approaches. We just doubted the wisdom of treating them separately and often exclusively.

So, the second organizing notion for the chapters that follow was to seek a reunification of the focus on substance and structure as shaping influences on American political life. Rather than allow this to be mere exhortation to the various authors, however, we thought it essential to specify the immediate subaspects of such an approach. The trick here was to offer these with sufficient specificity that all the authors could at least nod toward each element, without having to sacrifice the essence of the political history of their assigned times, while constructing these subaspects with sufficient abstraction that the contextual elements of those times could still be slotted into overarching (and continuing) concerns.

What we settled on—my proposal, and Tony's agreement at a point when it was not yet clear that the other authors would be similarly comfortable—was another simple conceptual division, within the realms of substantive conflict and structural influence. First, we planned to urge the authors (at this point, still hypothetical), when isolating the main substantive conflicts of their assigned times, to be additionally mindful of a potential division between what could be called basically economic concerns—infrastructure, tariffs and taxation, divisible benefits, social welfare—and basically cultural concerns—national expansion and integration, rights and liberties, behavioral norms, and socialization into them.

Second, we urged the authors, when isolating the key structural influences of their times, to think in terms of a simple tripartite division: societal cleavages, the main divisions at the social base for politics, from which so much of political conflict springs; intermediary organizations, especially political parties and organized interests; and governmental structure itself, in both its electoral and its policy-making arrangements.

Somewhat to our surprise, everyone who was invited to participate agreed. Ron Formisano at the University of Florida, David Waldstreicher at Notre Dame University, Joel Silbey at Cornell University, Michael Holt at the University of Virginia, Peter Argersinger at Southern Illinois University, Richard Jensen of the University of Illinois at Chicago (emeritus), and Jim Patterson at Brown University all expressed a willingness to take up their assignments. Tony (at Cambridge University) and I (at Oxford University) thus found ourselves committed to the project in a new and practical way.

Moreover, and even more surprisingly, all these individuals agreed to another main element of the proposed organization—namely, that the particular chronological periods assigned to them would feature significant overlap. We reasoned that if the point of the project was to emphasize large *P* politics and to reunite policy substance and structural influence while doing so, this was sufficiently different from what we were reading elsewhere that it would be unwise to assume that the book would take on the same temporal contours as earlier works.

It was necessary, in effect, to permit the analysis to create the periods. And the only way to do this was to create significant temporal overlap in the assignments. None of the authors balked at this proposal, despite the fact that it almost demanded different interpretations of the same elements. That is, the same conflict or development might simply look different if it was cast as an inaugurating, a distinguishing, or a closing element of an extended historical era. We think the result is much more stimulating by virtue of these differences.

That result was first presented as a series of public lectures at Oxford and Cambridge in the fall of 1999. Those lectures were subsequently revised into the chapters that follow, with some further attention to the way they interact. The product aspires to be a comprehensive American political history, with a broad sweep and a determined synthesizing effort. It nevertheless displays significant internal interpretive differences: over the route to the establishment of an independent (and distinctively American) politics, over the central dynamics of the broad middle period that followed, over the main engines for the shift toward what we recognize as the modern world, and, inevitably, over what its inescapable contributions will be to some as-yet-unknown future.

Early on, Fred Woodward, director of the University Press of Kansas, encouraged us to "think no further" about who might publish such a venture. This left us free to think much further about the substance and structure of the project itself, and that has proved extremely liberating. Later on, Melinda Wirkus managed production, freelance editor Linda Lotz did the copyediting, and Alex Perkins at Cambridge created the index. We thank them all. Throughout, Hugh Davis Graham at Vanderbilt University enthused, queried, or criticized as the situation demanded. This is only the latest instance of that multifaceted support, and we dedicate the book to him.

— B. E. S.

INTRODUCTION

In April 1995, political historians crowded into a conference room at the annual convention of the Organization of American Historians (OAH). Responding to a call for the creation of a body designed to represent the interests of political history within the organization, they heard a panel of distinguished political historians talk about "The Future of Political History." This panel, gender-balanced and measured, included two of the contributors to this volume and painted an inclusive intellectual picture of an evolving political history, one that could embrace practitioners of social, cultural, and legal history as well.

Not all the platform speakers, however, felt that the panel was facing the practical facts. James T. Patterson spoke forcefully to the operational concerns of the audience, as several members made clear from the floor. These political historians believed that, far from being expanded, their field was becoming marginalized in the profession, even excluded from it. Back in the 1970s, social history had passed political history as the subfield producing the most doctoral dissertations, so that political historians were now outnumbered in their own departments. More seriously, senior chairs were no longer being replaced, and graduate students could not get jobs.

These scholars felt particularly betrayed by their professional organization. They searched in vain for sessions on political history at the annual meeting and found themselves invisible in the pages of the *Journal of American History,* which published articles that were far more likely to talk about washing machines and cinema than elections and public policy. In this, they were expressing concerns shared with diplomatic historians, who had long since founded their own organization, the Society for the History of American Foreign Relations, to compensate for what they believed was active exclusion from the OAH.

Their angst was reinforced by other concerns, especially that the discipline of history was becoming specialized to its own detriment. The more academic it became, the more distant it was from popular audiences, and political historians had always been an important part of this popular connection. The general public might still make history books into best-sellers, but these books were written by nonacademic historians. Apparently, academic historians could no longer manage a compelling national narrative. Instead, they retailed disparate histories of particular groups and of "constructed identities." They were not helped by the conversion of what had been, into the 1960s, largely a celebration of unprecedented economic growth, responsive if contentious government, and foreign policy triumphs into a negative account of oppression overseas and elite control at home.[1]

Their concerns were rooted in real developments. The creation of a new social history "from the bottom up"—the history of the inarticulate many, rather than the articulate few—gave agency to groups that were increasingly asserting their rights in the late 1960s and 1970s. The high politics of parties, campaigns, and elections had little evident relevance to the story of Italian women in Buffalo, textile workers in the Piedmont, or slaves on the Barrow plantation. And underneath, the liberal faith in government and politics celebrated by historians who had come of age in the 1940s and 1950s was eroded by Vietnam, Watergate, and stagflation.

Still, even in 1995, it was more difficult for a British observer to sympathize fully with the political historians' lament. It was not easy to picture prizewinners and holders of distinguished chairs such as Bill Leuchtenburg, Alan Brinkley, Laura Kalman, and James Patterson as marginalized outsiders or a persecuted minority. Moreover, the *Journal of American History* seemed a good deal more exciting and intellectually stimulating than the *English Historical Review.*[2]

In any case, the essays in this volume suggest that political history is alive and well. The inclusive vision of the optimistic speakers on the 1995 panel was not merely wishful thinking. Political history is not restricted simply to the story of partisan entities, election campaigns, and public officials. It uses many of the theoretical insights that social historians have mined for years and refuses to separate politics from society.

The durability of this history should not be surprising. Political historians have always borrowed richly from other disciplines. The work of the ethnocultural historians in the 1970s, for example, rescued nineteenth-century political history from the limited attractions of presidential politics in the Gilded Age and brought back from obscurity issues that had practical salience for real voters. Historians who had concentrated only on class determinants of voter preference and on economic issues now concentrated on religious determinants and cultural issues—Sunday blue laws, Prohibition, the teaching of foreign languages in schools—that spoke to the very essence of daily concerns in school, church, and club of late-nineteenth-century America, an emphasis that became even easier to embrace as cultural issues returned to prominence in late-twentieth-century politics.

Political history has gained additional sustenance from a revived interest in the state and in state building, as Bill Leuchtenberg predicted in his 1986 presidential address at the OAH.[3] Historical sociologists and political scientists formed the booming Politics and History Section of the American Political Science Association, launched the journals *Clio* and *Studies in American Political Development,* and debated state-centered and society-centered explanations of political and social change. What resulted was a much broader definition of what constitutes the state and its major players, a definition informed constantly by comparison with more highly developed European states. Moreover, this emphasis on the state could scarcely be said to mean a mere interest in elites; the twentieth-century fiscal state, with its war-making, taxing, and welfare roles, impacted everywhere on the daily lives of "the inarticulate many."

Other contributions are even more recent. In 1993, Hugh Davis Graham could still lament "The Stunted Career of Policy History." Traditional political history, he argued, was good at reconstructing the origins of public policy, the motivations of political leaders, the ensuing political controversies, and legislative successes. Yet not enough attention had been paid "to the open-ended process of implementation." The success of the *Journal of Policy History* demonstrates the healthy subsequent growth of Graham's initially sickly offspring, and the success of policy history needs little explanation.[4]

In the era of a rights revolution, the governmental policies that most affect the private sphere of ordinary Americans—on race, on schooling, on abortion—have all been determined far more by judges and bureaucrats than by politicians and elected officials. Likewise, policy history directly addresses a recurring theme of American politics in the post–New Deal era: the unanticipated consequences of reform and government action. Given the feminist, policy-centered activism of a younger generation of women's historians, it is not surprising that they have highlighted the gendered dimension of this social policy, particularly social welfare policy. The same awareness has highlighted the gendered nature of political discourse in a by-and-large male political world, whether that of the Federalists and Whigs or that of "Pitchfork" Ben Tillman.

Incorporation of the new social history has significantly widened definitions of the public sphere, the very definition of what is political. Robin Kelley defined infrapolitics as "the daily confrontations, evasive actions, and stifled thoughts that often inform organized political movements."[5] The location of such infrapolitics was to be found not just in the voting booth and legislature but also in the semipublic and semiprivate spaces of community and household, of workplace and public spaces. Such definitions give an active role to those who are usually seen as passive targets of the political process. One thus looks for political history in unusual places: in the social life of Chicago's industrial workers or in the price-checking activities of legions of housewives for the Office of Price Administration.

This widened definition has received its greatest stimulus from women's and African American history. Antebellum middle-class women may not have had the vote, but they exploited their domestic roles as moral exemplars to secure legitimacy for public participation in evangelical reform movements. Later, women reformers exploited that same domestic legitimacy to provide the driving force for the social justice reforms of Progressivism. African American women—as domestic servants after the Civil War, as potential voters in North

Carolina in the 1920s, and as bus riders in World War II Birmingham—have all been the focus of serious scholarship. In the process, they have inevitably come to be seen as shaping the wider political process.

An older style of political history still retains great popular resonance. Over fifty years ago, Thomas C. Cochran, a business historian, lamented the dominance in American historical writing of what he identified as "the presidential synthesis," which sliced up the study of American history into presidential terms of office, thereby distorting the analysis of long-term social, economic, and political change.[6] The insatiable demand for biographies of inhabitants of the White House nevertheless testifies to the continued resilience of that synthesis, reinvigorated by the University Press of Kansas through its series on presidential administrations. The study of the Coolidge administration by Robert H. Ferrell, distinguished diplomatic historian and biographer of Harry Truman, brings the number of presidents covered by this series to thirty-nine, with only Grant, Reagan, and Clinton awaiting interpretation.

Historians may question the utility of (yet more) presidential biographies. I myself have argued that biographies of Franklin D. Roosevelt do not and cannot tell us what we need to know about the New Deal, that is, its exact relationship to the immense transformation of American society in the second half of the twentieth century.[7] Others may lament a certain style of "Rotary Club" history. But few can deny the immense popular appeal of such an approach, whether measured by book sales, the rise of the History Channel, or the success of PBS documentaries. There is no apparent slowdown in the production of studies of Lincoln, and the biographical interest in FDR (despite my advice) shows little sign of diminishing. Just since 1992, Truman has been the subject of three massive biographies, totaling over 2,300 pages.

The presidential synthesis has encouraged other productive new scholarship, especially in the areas of policy history and state building, by energizing institutions with a concern for political history. Thus, although the Miller Center at the University of Virginia aims to build up the primary sources on modern American presidents, most notably by transcribing and editing thousands of hours of secret tapes from the Kennedy, Johnson, and Nixon administrations and by conducting oral history interviews with senior administration officials, it is also centrally concerned with economic policy and political and social reform.[8]

As has so often been the case in the past, the establishment of presidential libraries is the key to unlocking a wealth of scholarship that focuses on far more than presidential lives. Just as the proceedings of the conferences organized by the Johnson Library heralded new work on civil rights, the environment, and the economy, so the conference organized by Gary Fink and Hugh Davis Graham used the opening of the Carter Library "as a lens through which to view larger changes in American government and society during the second half of the twentieth century."[9] The conference planned for the University of California at Santa Barbara in March 2002 promises to do the same for the Reagan years.

The despair of those political historians in 1995 may have been exacerbated by developments particular to that time, including impatience with the demands of political correctness and (losing) fights for departmental resources. We certainly hope so, and we hope that this time is rapidly passing. We also hope that the essays in this volume, as indicators of the richness and scope of the current interest in political history, suggest a vibrant future for that subject.

—A. J. B.

Notes

1. In recapturing the sense of angst on the part of political historians, I have been immensely assisted by the discussions in James T. Patterson, "Americans and the Writing of Twentieth-Century History," in *Imagined Histories: American Historians Interpret the Past,* ed. Anthony Molho and Gordon S. Wood (Princeton, N.J., 1998); Mark Leff, "Revisioning U.S. Political History," *American Historical Review* 100 (June 1995): 829–53; and Steven M. Gillon, "The Future of Political History" (copy in the author's possession). I am additionally grateful for the comments of Jane Dailey, Steve Gillon, Jim Patterson, and Hugh Davis Graham.

2. The June 1995 issue of the *Journal of American History* had a picture of Mickey Mouse on the cover and contained articles on "the boy" in Puritan New England, celebrations and print culture in the early nation, the Open Door policy and China, and Walt Disney. The June 1995 issue of the *English Historical Review* appeared in its customary austere gray cover with unadorned text. It contained articles on six chapters of Henry II, crown patronage in Tudor England, Captain Edmond Wynne and the Irish famine, the Crusades, and German civil administration in the Soviet Union.

3. William E. Leuchtenberg, "The Pertinence of Political History: Reflections on the Significance of the State in America," *Journal of American History* 73 (1986): 585–600.

4. Hugh Davis Graham, "The Stunted Career of Policy History: A Critique and Agenda," *Public Historian* (1993): 14–33.

5. Robin Kelley, "We Are Not What We Seem: Rethinking Black Working-Class Opposition in the Jim Crow South," *Journal of American History* 80 (1993): 75–112.

6. Thomas C. Cochran, "The 'Presidential Synthesis' in American History," *American Historical Review* 53 (1948): 748–59.

7. Tony Badger, "The New Deal without FDR: What Biographies of Roosevelt Cannot Tell Us," in *History and Biography: Essays in Honour of Derek Beales,* ed. T. C. W. Blanning and David Cannadine (Cambridge, 1996), 243–65.

8. The Miller Center's first symposium on Progressivism has already occurred, the one on the New Deal is imminent, and one on the Great Society is planned. The first examines the efforts of Progressives to create "self-rule on a grand scale and break the hold of localist parties and courts that had dominated American politics for decades." The second examines the implications of the argument that "the new social contract heralded by Roosevelt marks the beginning of the so-called

1. State Development in the Early Republic
Substance and Structure, 1780–1840

Ronald P. Formisano

Issues of periodization—of the temporal division most appropriate to an understanding of American political history—surface with the beginning of American politics and hence with the opening chapter of any synthesis. An automatic, regular, temporal cut would have defined this opening period from roughly 1775 to 1820, as the editors of this volume initially suggested. Yet such key developments as mass political parties and a new political culture need to be picked up by at least the 1790s and followed into the 1830s. It is not just, or even mainly, political parties and political culture, however, that underline the need to push the period's demarcations ahead in time, but rather the importance of focusing on the broad theme of American political development during the early Republic.

For this, I focus mainly on the development of the nation-state, with an emphasis on *state*.[1] I argue that the issue of state power—how much government, and with what degree of capacity for action—pervaded the major ideological and partisan conflicts of the early Republic and conditioned the party battles of the Federalists and the Republicans, as well as the sectional and partisan struggles that came later. Although slavery cast a shadow on this debate in the Federal and Jeffersonian eras, after 1816 the defense of slavery increasingly underlay this axial question, a condition that begins to explain why the federal government, after a period of state formation launched by the Federalists and partially sustained by the Jeffersonians, remained relatively undeveloped up to the Civil War.

Important beginnings had been made, but, for reasons examined later, central state formation had been slowed, even stalled, by the 1830s and 1840s.[2] A distinction between *state* and *nation* thus needs to be made at the outset. Although the line between them is sometimes blurred in reality, my concern here is principally with the state rather than with the nation, or the "imagined community." The nation as the locus of communal subjective identity developed parallel to the growth of the state—indeed, preceded it—and grew at different rates in different regions, as did the public sphere of citizen (and noncitizen) participation. The development of neither the imagined community nor the public sphere, however, is of primary concern here.[3]

* * *

The (Statist) Balance in the Revolutionary Era

[handwritten margin note: → practice of giving a centralized government control over economic planning and policy]

The American Revolution created a distinctive political culture within which the development of the state would take place. It was a culture marked by traditions of popular participation, a relatively widespread sense of efficacy among the citizenry, and, most consequentially, a deep-seated fear of power. Kevin Phillips, following Linda Colley and David H. Fischer, recently called the attention of a popular audience to the extraordinary political "assertiveness of ordinary Englishmen—and English*women*" during the eighteenth century, which was "a staple of wry continental comment from the tracts of Montesquieu to the operas of Mozart." Popular participation in Britain was remarkable compared with that on the European continent, but in British North America, there flourished an "even more democratic and participatory politics."[4] During the Revolution, ordinary men and woman engaged in meetings, tavern gatherings, crowd and mob actions (some organized by gentlemen and some not), parades and demonstrations, and military service in the Revolutionary War itself. Largely encouraged by native elites, the number of participating middling and ordinary Americans expanded, and, as significantly, so did their sense of efficacy.[5]

The Revolution's potential promise of independence for such dependent classes as women and African Americans would be unrealized. Yet the enlargement of the public sphere during the Revolution was real and had roots in the remarkable economic development of the colonies during the eighteenth century, which contributed to a "broad diffusion of an expansive sense of self-worth throughout the independent, mostly land-owning, adult male population." It had also been prepared by the habits of a colonial politics that, while routinely conducted by the few at the top of society, "invariably contained a latent potential for widespread popular mobilization." Although the colonies had experienced no common political life before 1765, two different ideas of empire formed on each side of the Atlantic, and the clash between them "turned into revolution when the settlers formed their common resistance to Britain by providing themselves with an historical-mythological identity, allowing them to declare themselves a people."[6]

The Revolution originated most immediately in Great Britain's efforts to tighten the administration of its colonial empire following the French and Indian War and in the elimination of France from competition for control of North America. From 1765 to 1775, however, Britain replaced Catholic France as the threatening power, limiting opportunity for many American interest groups. A broad, cross-class coalition of merchants and artisans, speculators and settlers, southern planters (many in debt to British merchants) and yeomen supported the rebellion against Britain. Remaining loyal were royal and proprietary officials, Anglican ministers, some merchants, and backcountry farmers and subcultures at odds with patriot landowners and cultural groups. Revolutionary

leadership, in contrast, came primarily from gentlemen and middle-class lieutenants who were steeped in the English radical or "country" tradition. That tradition had helped inculcate an intense distrust of power, especially executive
power, and the belief in power's ability to threaten liberty, which to Americans
meant the defense of property or the pursuit of opportunity.

The populist phase of the Revolution unleashed high levels of participation,
with political initiatives often taken by publics operating "out-of-doors," sometimes expressing anti-aristocratic and anti-elite resentments. In 1789, David
Ramsay observed that the conflict with England "gave a spring to the active
powers of the inhabitants, and set them on thinking, speaking, and acting far beyond that to which they had been accustomed."[7] This populist phase also produced innovative state constitutions that reflected the prevailing fear of executive tyranny. Governors and upper houses lost power to lower houses, and the
latter delegated much to local governments. The Pennsylvania Constitution of
1776, with its weak executive, unicameral legislature, and embrace of popular
ratification by all adult white males, has been taken to epitomize the era, but
other state constitutions (Vermont excepted) did not depart from the prevailing
assumption among most gentlemen and elites that government should mirror
the social hierarchy.

Hence, "stake-in-society" thinking also persisted, and several new state constitutions contained property qualifications for officeholding and voting. The
commitment to property-based citizen rights was so strong that in 1776 the New
Jersey Constitution enfranchised all adult inhabitants with £50 of property; its
framers realized that this would allow unmarried women (who qualified) to
vote, which they did until 1807, when their suffrage became a casualty of partisan politics. Yet to whatever degree constitutions diverged in fashioning hierarchical politics, they converged in emanating the pervasive distrust of power
and in fashioning mechanisms to control it.[8]

The centrifugal forces released by the Revolution continued into the 1780s
and bedeviled the confederation of states that had stumbled to victory over the
British but whose 1781 Articles of Confederation had not given that government—that quasi-state—the power to enforce its decisions, to levy taxes, or to
deal in a unified way with foreign powers. The situation worsened with an economic downturn in the two years following peace, 1783–1785, as British goods
flooded into the country and specie poured out. A chain reaction of called debts
and merchant failures and lost jobs ensued. American leaders had looked forward to free trade with the arrival of independence, but the British erected mer-
cantilist barriers, closing the British West Indies to American shippers and prohibiting or placing high duties on the import of American staples to Britain. The
states individually failed at retaliation, thus strengthening the economic nationalists pushing for congressional power over trade, who were aided by
Spain's closing the Mississippi to U.S. commerce.

Increasingly, the nationalists or proto-federalists who wanted to reform the Articles articulated a broad "pro-developmental vision" that included encouragement of native manufactures as well as "an expanding oceanic commerce."[9] For these things, they needed a state with "energy." The confederation government grew more insolvent instead, so that by 1786, seven states had issued some form of paper money, North Carolina and Rhode Island recklessly so. When Rhode Island tried to force creditors to accept the new paper, many merchants closed their shops and went into hiding, prompting riots. Rhode Island became a byword among the nationalists for democratic tyranny that threatened the very foundations of commercial society.

So too did the insurgency of desperate farmers burdened by debts and taxes in western and central Massachusetts, which became known, under the auspices of the nationalist elite, as Shays's Rebellion. In 1786–1787, Daniel Shays was just one of many local leaders of widespread and decentralized disturbances characterized by traditional crowd actions aimed at closing courts in several counties to prevent foreclosures. The Massachusetts disturbances were only the most spectacular of the protests that rippled through the backcountry from New Hampshire to South Carolina. This self-described "Regulation," though often armed, contained no radical agenda. Conservative elites cooking constitutional reform would nevertheless turn "Shayism" and "Generalissimo Shays" into useful weapons to influence public opinion. If Daniel Shays had not existed, the federalists would have invented him. In a sense, they did, in that they created the myth that the Massachusetts Regulation possessed a single leader and posed a threat to property and social order. The construction of Shays formed part of a broad reaction against the popular politics of the 1770s and 1780s, and the sense of crisis helped promote the nationalist elite's agenda.[10]

A rump group of constitutional reformers met at Annapolis in September 1786 and then issued a call for a convention that would consider wholesale revamping of the government. In the next weeks and months, they and allies superbly manipulated their construction of the events in Rhode Island and Massachusetts. A sense of crisis percolated, in part real, in part manufactured. The following spring in Philadelphia, the reformers crafted a constitution that would enable the creation of a more effective central government than had been possible under the Articles. Based on an ideal of balanced government with separation of powers, the constitution above all sought to protect liberty from power.

It did incorporate two major compromises: one between large and small states, resulting in bicameralism, and a second protecting slavery and recognizing it in all but name, particularly through the counting of three-fifths of all slaves for purposes of representation. Slaves were counted for tax purposes, and the delegates regarded slavery as a "distracting question" rather than a moral issue, though the question of ending the slave trade did spark sharp debate. That too brought a compromise, giving Congress the power to end the trade no sooner than 1808.

Most importantly, perhaps, the constitution reserved to the states all powers not specifically enumerated for Congress, thus creating a hybrid government of dual sovereignty that amounted to a standing invitation to contest the federal government's power.[11] The American nationalists had accomplished a marvelous feat, solving the difficult problem of the locus of sovereignty by rooting it theoretically in the people. In practice, however, the ambiguity of dual sovereignty constituted one necessary—though not sufficient—cause of the Civil War. It would nourish states' rights and disunionist movements from the 1790s through the 1850s, most potently the Southern rights movement that became Southern nationalism.[12]

The constitution's creators differed little in their expectation that gentlemen would continue to rule throughout the land, as they made clear through such mechanisms as the indirect election of senators and the president. The lower orders would continue to give deference to "the elevated classes of the community." The new Republic would be—and this was hardly a matter of self-conscious debate or reflection—a white men's republic.[13] Women's inclusion was not considered, though the founders' construction of women played an important role in their thinking about political life. Historians of gender have argued that the "Founding Fathers" used a "grammar of manhood" that defined citizenship according to manly virtues in opposition to womanhood, a discourse that excluded from the body politic not only women, African Americans, and Indians but also disorderly white men who were not fit for citizenship. Although American leaders had themselves engaged in a revolution against patriarchal authority, they saw themselves as a new kind of benevolent patriarchy—"enlightened paternalists"—that would care for the interests of dependent groups excluded from their "fraternity of citizenship."[14]

The fight over ratification during 1787–1788, however, took place primarily among the included, though not entirely, judging by the number of "disorderly" white men who took part in popular demonstrations. The nationalists called themselves federalists, thereby stealing their opponents' name and adding to the advantages of wealth, status, resources, and influence they already enjoyed. "The *better sort*," said one anti-federalist, "have means of convincing those who differ from them." The "better sort" were also better organized and controlled most of the newspapers. Urban and commercial farming areas tended to support the constitution, as did most merchants, especially shipowning merchants, professional men, and mechanics and other small tradesmen. Anti-federalism tended to be strong in the backcountry, but some prominent wealthy men who feared loss of power in their own local fiefdoms also opposed the constitution, as did "agrarian-minded" gentlemen. Similarly, some farmers and rural areas supported it.[15]

Historians have found a strong tendency for division on the constitution along cosmopolitan versus localist lines. Thus, experience in the Continental army, proximity to General Washington, service in Congress, education, or simply better access to communication even below the patriciate made for a cosmopolitan outlook, while localists were attached to their regions, states, or smaller units in remote areas. Although the ratification struggle created an intense and passionate ideological conflict, in which the crowd traditions of the revolutionary era were revived, at most 20 percent of adult white males voted in the elections for delegates to the state ratifying conventions. Many nonvoters simply may not have paid much attention; others may have thought the war already lost.[16] Thus the cosmopolitans or centrists won, but the impulses fueling anti-federalism would animate a broader and more powerful oppositional coalition by the end of the 1790s.

The central issue would be to what extent and in what manner the federal government would actually function as a central state. It quickly fused with the persisting dilemma of relations with Britain, as centralizers and Anglophiles coalesced as a "court" party of "Federalists," the party of "energy" in government. Against them rose a "country" party of "Republicans," the party of "liberty," which reacted against the Federalist creation of a vigorous central state.[17] "I am not a friend to very energetic government," Jefferson said; "it is always oppressive." He and his allies would also oppose alliance with or (as they saw it) subservience to Great Britain. The French Revolution of 1789 and France's radicalization after 1793 would vastly complicate matters, as would the resumption of twenty years of war between Britain and France. Centrifugal forces and threats posed by European powers on the seas and the North American continent itself created genuine doubt among many members of the early national generation that the United States—the "experiment," as Washington and his contemporaries often referred to it—would survive as a nation.[18]

State Formation Under the Constitution

Within two years of the launching of the new government in 1789, under the aegis of President George Washington, a highly self-conscious state and nation builder, it became clear that two different visions of the good society had been temporarily united in the constitutional project. James Madison of Virginia, though regarded as the document's architect, had seen it as a means, along with westward expansion, of preserving the "republican revolution" and an agrarian society. Alexander Hamilton, however, the new secretary of the treasury, wanted the nation to emulate Great Britain in its path to stability and national greatness. Madison and Thomas Jefferson, secretary of state in the new administration, saw the constitution as the means by which the United States "could avoid the European curses of professional armed forces, persistent public debts, powerful executives, and other instruments . . . that Hamilton associated with effective statehood."[19]

In the early 1790s, Hamilton brought forward his proposals of funding, assumption, and a national bank, by which wealthy and influential men would be tied to the new government. Hamilton also proposed an unprecedented excise tax on distilled spirits, along with governmental aid to native manufactures. By 1792, the Federalists had also nationalized the militia and created an army of 5,000, laying the groundwork for a national military establishment and stimulating republican fears of militarism. Madison and Jefferson objected to paying off Continental and state debts in a manner that discriminated against many ordinary citizens and certain states (such as their Virginia) and generally feared a British-like financial system of influence and corruption.[20]

Although this split in the earlier constitutional coalition over economic policy initiated the movement toward the first political parties, partisan groupings among the political classes did not become immediately coherent. Yet as James Huston observed, a core set of economic issues, largely encompassed by Hamilton's program, remained basic to the contending "ideology and values" of all nineteenth-century political parties, as did the basic issue of the power of the central government over the economy.[21]

Attitudes toward England and France also became increasingly salient as political formations reacted to the French Revolution. At first, all Americans welcomed the events of 1789 and were flattered by the existence of a new and sympathetic, even imitative, republic. But the execution of Louis XVI, the backfiring of the French ambassador's mission to influence American opinion in 1793 (in the Citizen Genet affair), and the Terror of 1793–1794 all undercut sympathy for France, as well as for the homegrown and newly organized Democratic Republican Societies—short-lived clubs of progressives who admired French principles.[22]

At the same time, relations with England still rankled, because the former mother country treated the United States as an inferior, refusing to evacuate military posts in the Northwest and imposing new restrictions on American shipping. New England shippers wanted to ply a neutral trade with Britain and France, but the latter (as a former ally) expected special consideration, or at least that the United States not knuckle under to British demands. From 1793 to 1815, as the two European powers fought, the United States maneuvered to maintain its interests and neutral rights. Throughout, foreign policy decisions agitated American politics, until the new nation fought a second war with England, and the European wars ended serendipitously with Napoleon's defeat.

During 1794–1795, a "republican interest" began to become more defined and self-conscious in opposition to the court party of the emerging Federalists. The fight over the Jay Treaty, particularly, hardened partisan blocs in Congress and led to elites mobilizing popular demonstrations against and for the treaty. Republicans denounced it as commercial subservience to Britain, while Federalists defended it by pointing to British agreements to evacuate the Northwest and to pay reparations for ship and cargo seizures of 1793–1794, as well as to a new accord with Spain reopening the Mississippi and New Orleans. Merchants who traded with Britain's enemies, however, gravitated to the opposition.

During 1794, too, the Federalists had shown how far they would go in pursuing an energetic government. Farmers in the Pennsylvania backcountry, mostly Scotch-Irish, had rebelled against Hamilton's excise tax on liquor with vigilante violence against revenue agents and cooperating farmers. As they had earlier in responding to the Massachusetts "Regulations" of 1786–1787, the "friends of order," this time led by Washington and Hamilton, created another specter of elites manipulating ordinary people for sinister goals, while using the occasion to discredit the newly formed Democratic Republican Societies that were criticizing the government's "unwarranted accumulation of power."

Washington sent an army of some 13,000 militiamen, larger than any American force in the Revolution, to squash the Whiskey Rebellion. Though it met no resistance, Hamiltonians relished the government's symbolic show of authority, while the republican interest gained new adherents in the backcountry, especially among non-English cultural groups. At the same time, the Federalist nation builders enjoyed additional success elsewhere on the frontier, in their efforts to combat Indian tribes. There, the federal government "turned the corner" by 1796, "triumphing over its Imperial and Indian rivals" and cementing its legitimacy among and control over the settlers.[23]

Political factions of "notables" contested and determined the 1796 presidential election, with a sectional distribution of electoral votes giving John Adams victory over Thomas Jefferson (who would in these preparty days serve as vice president), a victory that reflected the fact that the northern states still had a slightly larger number of votes than their southern counterparts. During Adams's administration, public opinion at first turned against the Republicans, due to the quasi-war with France and the French attempt to leverage shakedown money from the United States in the XYZ affair. But the "High Federalists," led by the still-influential Hamilton, would push the government to reach too far toward statism, creating a navy department, building ships, and authorizing a new 10,000-man army. Striking at their domestic opponents, congressional Federalists pushed through the Alien and Sedition Acts, limiting free speech, the press, and the activities of aliens, but in fact taking aim at the growing opposition movement of Jefferson and Madison.[24]

Federalist nativism in the 1790s also expressed itself in court decisions and laws that defined political allegiances "heavily in terms of birthplace [thereby hoping] to compel obedience to the U.S. government and to curb the influx of foreign-born Jeffersonian voters." The High Federalists even proposed that only the native born should be citizens. In contrast, Jeffersonian Republicans championed "policies encouraging immigration, including expansive expatriation, naturalization, and voting rights. Hence they became more the party of consensually based democratic citizenship, the self-proclaimed party of 'the people,' though only for whites."[25]

The Federalist conception of society as organic, hierarchic, and deferential had several paradoxical consequences, including a more welcoming posture toward women (elite, native) in at least an informal public role. Far more than Republicans, Federalist orators "acknowledged and encouraged women's political potential." Both first parties, as Rosemarie Zagarri revealed, paid far more attention to women than historians have realized. But it was the putative conservatives (like the Whigs later in the nineteenth century) who, more socially secure and adhering to a tradition of positive rights rooted in community and civic virtue, were "more progressive concerning women." The Republicans, as a challenging group, not only were radical for the time but also conceived of society as composed of individuals pursuing their private interests, and they conceived of freedom "in a narrow legalistic sense that protected the individual's rights from intrusion by the state." The negative liberalism of these Republicans extended to white males, not to dependent groups such as women and nonwhites.[26]

Another consequence of the Federalists' "particularly organic and hierarchical" conception of society was their intense anti-partyism. The Federalists thought of themselves not as an *administration* but rather as *the government* or simply *government*. The notion of legitimate opposition had not yet taken hold. Of necessity, "the republican interest" defended its organizing outside of government, but members too shared their opponents' assumption that victory meant conversion or elimination of the opposition. The factional groupings leading into 1800 are thus best regarded as parties of notables or "quasi-parties"; years ago, Roy F. Nichols aptly labeled them "antipower associations."[27]

From the mid-1790s, the moral passion and ideological tension of politics raged at fever pitch. The Federalists, especially the Congregational clergy of New England, had been associating Jefferson and Republicanism with French irreligion, atheism, and immorality. Jefferson and Madison, for their part, truly believed that Hamilton was a monarchist and a militarist and saw the Alien and Sedition Acts as unconstitutional partisan warfare abetting "the progress of evil," as Madison put it in the Virginia Resolutions, asserting the rights of states to reject unconstitutional acts of Congress.[28]

In 1798–1799, however, the Federalists split over the issue of war with France and even more over Hamiltonian demands for a new army of unprecedented size and permanence. Adams and moderate Federalists in Congress resisted the High Federalist clamor for war and for a standing army over which Hamilton would wield great control. As the Federalists self-destructed, the Republicans appealed to the many groups the Federalists had alienated by their exercise of state power. Even at that, the election was close, and Adams actually ran stronger in 1800 than he had in 1796, losing to Jefferson by sixty-five to seventy-three electoral votes.[29]

The pattern of electoral votes showed a clear sectional polarity: all thirty-nine New England votes for Adams versus all forty-one southern votes as well as all seven western votes for Jefferson.[30] In a nation with a population of some 5.3 million spread along 1,200 miles of coastline and reaching hundreds of miles into the interior, Jefferson's 1800 victory can be regarded, as I suggested some years ago, as a successful example of the "mobilization of the periphery" against a core or center perceived to be overbearing and hegemonic. In their aggressive efforts to create a nation-state, the Federalists had alienated many groups occupying political, geographic, economic, status, or cultural peripheries in American life. But the Federalists had also "transformed trans-Appalachia from a potential source of revenue, disunion, and chaos into a region of genuine revenue, growing external security, and increasing loyalty to the United States of America."[31]

In 1800, regions, communities, groups, and individuals constituting the center of economic, cultural, and institutional life for the nation as a whole tended to vote Federalist, while the periphery supported Jefferson and the Republicans. The center did not encompass only the urban or cosmopolitan, nor did the periphery include all that was rural or local. Yet in important ways, the division continued the court-country and local-cosmopolitan dichotomies of the eighteenth century. Group alignments had shifted considerably since the Revolution, but an overarching rough division still pitted central networks of traditional authority against peripheral challengers, newcomers, dissenters, and outsiders who wished to be included in, protected from, or just left alone by the central establishment. "Energy in government" rallied the faithful of the center; "'anarchy' was their fear. 'Economy' was the slogan of the periphery, 'consolidation' and 'aristocracy' their bugaboos."[32]

In New England, support for Federalism tended to reflect both a positive orientation toward central government power and the allegiance of commercially and culturally dominant centers, especially those associated with the Congregational clergy. In Massachusetts, for example, the countinghouses, merchants, and lawyers of Boston and of wealthy Essex County were the eastern core of Federalism, while the prosperous merchants, farmers, and authoritarian clergy of the Connecticut River Valley, known as "River Gods," led Federalism's western stronghold. There, and in eastern Massachusetts as well, Congregational orthodoxy and Federalism marched hand in hand.

Republican votes came most heavily from peripheral areas—the islands, Cape Cod, the Berkshire Mountains, and the newly settled district of Maine. These areas contained ethnic diversity and numerous dissenting religious groups, as well as freethinkers and "Nothingarians." (Daniel Shays's hometown of Pelham in central Massachusetts was of Scotch-Irish background and strongly Jeffersonian.) But Republicans also included merchants who traded with France, lawyers and other professionals, entrepreneurs, and small manufacturers—elites or rising elites who tended to be outsiders.[33]

In Virginia, the pattern was reversed, with the dominant Republican elites producing leaders for the national periphery, while at home they represented the core of cultural and economic hegemony—the center. "The Federalist opposition," according to William Shade, "was rooted in the now peripheral areas that desired the Constitution in 1788 and would support John Quincy Adams in the 1820s." Towns also tended to be Federalist, and in 1800, Adams won half the votes of Virginia's two emerging cities, Richmond and Norfolk. But the Jeffersonian Republicans dominated most tidewater and especially central and southern piedmont counties: tobacco culture, slaveholding, and Republican strength went together. "The Jeffersonians in the Old Dominion were the party of the planter gentry and represented the interests of eastern conservatives."[34]

Unlike the situation in New England and the middle states, old-stock English ancestry was associated with the Jeffersonian state establishment, while the culturally marginal Scotch-Irish tended to be Federalist; Federalist counties contained twice as many Presbyterians as Republican counties did. As in the North, however, Germans tended to be Republicans, especially where they confronted the Scotch-Irish, as did Baptists. Thus, the agrarian-minded planter gentry of Virginia, dominant at home, represented the periphery in national affairs—but a periphery that occupied the central government after 1800 and managed to exert a powerful influence over its development long after 1824.

State Development Under the Opposition

The argument that the partisan warfare of the 1790s and later "produced 'the nation' as contestants tried to claim true American nationality and the legacy of the Revolution" has been restated by David Waldstreicher in perhaps its most imaginative and persuasive form to date. William Chambers, Robert Wiebe, and other historians had earlier noted the nationalizing function of party conflict, and this thesis is more attractive if the "nation" is considered in terms of identity and nationalism, but not necessarily with regard to the nation-state.[35] "Energy in government" and the Federalist program had been officially rejected in the "revolution of 1800." It was true, as will be seen shortly, that the "Republican Ascendancy" eventually moved far toward Federalist statism by 1816. Further, in several states, political parties as well as state governing capacity expanded in the early nineteenth century. Yet if one focuses attention on the development of national political *parties* through 1816—parties that served a limited nationalizing function—one must conclude that the case is one of "de-development." That is, after 1800, party development on the national level atrophied, while it was not until after 1816 that state development encountered adversity.[36]

Even the nation as an imagined community confronted formidable obstacles, as most Americans "still lived in a world of small scale and scarcity. People, goods, and information moved slowly." Although a market-based economy was coming into being, many elements of "an older barter economy [were still] imbedded in the social structure of many communities." In addition, Americans were a heterogeneous people; about half were of English descent, whereas some of the other (quite culturally diverse) half did not speak English. "American English" itself was a language still becoming, and dialects and meanings of words differed across regions. One historian of the language concluded that "the name of the nation spoke unity, but the evidence [up to 1850] does not bear out this assertion."[37]

Yet it can be argued that both the imagined community and a public sphere grew during the first decades of the nineteenth century, though the former more so in the North than in the South. Space does not permit further pursuit of these corollary themes, but it is relevant to note the assertion of political scientist Anne Norton that the idea of the sanctity of national union "was foreign to the South, where political union was regarded as an expedient and perhaps sentimental measure. The South was therefore a stranger to the campaigns to encourage both institutional consolidation and subjective national allegiance, which were common in the North throughout the antebellum period."[38]

Meanwhile, the new nation-state, though not drastically scaled back, was reduced after 1800 and at the same time maintained. Ever since Henry Adams took revenge on behalf of his illustrious ancestors by writing an irony-laced history of the Jefferson and Madison administrations, historians have recognized that the Jeffersonian Republicans, controlling the government for more than a quarter century of peace and war, gradually adopted some of the centralizing policies of their opponents. Jefferson appeared to shift sharply away from statism, beginning with his personal style—dressing casually, walking and riding horseback around Washington, and forgoing the impressive coach and six used by his Federalist predecessors. More importantly, he achieved repeal of the excise tax, cut back the army and navy, replaced some top Federalist officials with deserving Republicans, began to pay off the national debt, and reduced the Federalist-dominated judiciary.

Famously, he put aside his strict constitutionalism to purchase Louisiana from Napoleon, doubling the country at a stroke and opening a huge expanse to the western settlement so desired by Republican leaders. Yet—and here were the real initial moves toward statism—he also worked with the national bank and realized that "we can never get rid of [Hamilton's] financial system." And although Jefferson did indeed approve legislation reducing the army in 1802, that law also made the Army Corps of Engineers separate from the artillery and established a military academy—whereas Federalists had fervently sought to make a military establishment self-perpetuating.[39]

Jefferson and his successors went on to pursue a cautious, conciliatory patronage policy, appointing carefully selected Republicans to minimize partisan bitterness and even keeping or appointing moderate Federalists.[40] A longer-run irony would be the way the Louisiana territory helped make the nation more urban and commercial. In the short run, Republican attempts to pursue free trade floundered during the intensification of the Napoleonic Wars after 1806, and as efforts at economic warfare by Jefferson and Madison failed, elements of their party moved to promote manufacturing and development, particularly at the state level.[41]

The War of 1812 decisively pushed the Republicans to a statist agenda. At its end, lifted by a high tide of nationalist sentiment that gave the imagined community new symbols of itself, Republicans advocated a second national bank (which Madison had allowed to expire in 1811), tariffs, internal improvements, a stronger navy, and other Federalist measures.[42] With the end of the long foreign policy crisis, during which disunionist sentiment peaked in New England among the Federalists that Harlow Sheidley labeled "sectional nationalists," Federalism on the national level as well as sectionalism collapsed—the first permanently, the second temporarily.[43]

Although some ill feelings persisted in the Era of Good Feelings, the immediate postwar era following the "Second War of Independence" also constituted the apex of southern nationalism. This short-lived nationalism, which flourished among southern political leaders before the panic of 1819 and the Missouri controversies, depended largely on one pivotal circumstance: the southern slaveholders' sense of security derived from the long reign of the Virginia dynasty. According to a study devoted exclusively to the presidential politics of this era, contests for "the first place" were so dominated by Virginians "that they can be described . . . as the 'Virginia game.'"[44] Holding office for twenty-four years, Virginia's political elite reshaped the rules of the game to ensure their hegemony, which meant, in terms of state development, the periphery's continued occupation of the central government.

That home government, it needs to be emphasized, was a "small institution, small almost beyond modern imagination." In 1802, the official members of the government community over which Jefferson presided numbered 291, with Congress actually larger than the administrative apparatus based in Washington. In *The Federalist,* No. 27, Hamilton had written, "A government continually at a distance and out of sight can hardly be expected to interest the sensations of the people." Nichols once called attention to the "overlooked truth . . . that for years few really had any interest in the federal government save the Virginians, their Clintonian rivals, and a few die-hard Federalists."[45]

With limited functions and few favors to bestow or powers to exercise, national government attracted far less attention from citizens than state governments did. When Andrew Jackson took office in 1829, twenty-seven years later, the headquarters establishment had just barely doubled, to 625 persons, with 40 percent of the growth due to an increase in legislators and 41 percent due to an increase in the staffs of the Treasury Department and Post Office. By Jackson's time, however, interest in the government's *patronage* had reached a fever pitch among the political classes. Out in the country, for example, there were almost 8,000 post offices, and these "spoils of office," along with other government posts, helped energize a more intense and widespread competition with regard to winning control of that government.[46]

From 1804 to 1820, the situation was much different. When Jefferson took power, he expected that with the "monarchists" routed, the Republicans would rule as one big party. He did not expect a national two-party competition, still unrealized, to continue and assumed that the Republican Party would eventually wither away. Jefferson was correct in assuming that Federalism would become insignificant at the national level. But within the states, Jeffersonian foreign policy revived Federalist opposition, and partisan competition ran at high levels up to 1812. Indeed, the decision for war that year would spring in part from the desire of Madison and his allies to preserve the Republican establishment, as much as from the other reasons historians have debated (the Indian threat on the frontier, land hunger, maritime rights, national integrity, and so on).

Still, in the presidential contests, the Federalists amounted to little more than a minor factor. Moreover, the national political arena remained confined to the notables and their lieutenants during the years up to 1824, a time that Michael J. Heale termed the era of "The Mute Tribune," when presidential candidates did not campaign for office or communicate directly with the voters. Indeed, they had to appear uninterested and not to work on their own behalf.[47] The essence of the "Virginia game" was that Virginia capitalized on its unity in the federal arena and took advantage of the factionalism that prevailed in the large middle states, particularly New York—the state whose electoral votes in 1800 (engineered by Aaron Burr) had made Jefferson president. Between 1800 and 1820, the most significant challenge to Virginia came in 1812 from another Republican, New Yorker De Witt Clinton, who had inherited from his uncle George Clinton, former governor and vice president, the ambition to gain the first place in the land. Throughout the period, electoral votes displayed a marked sectional polarity, as they had in 1800, yet the Virginia dynasty concerned itself less with Federalist adversaries and more with middle-state allies and rivals.[48]

In 1800, Virginia could claim first rank among the states in population, wealth, and political distinction. By 1820, the Empire State had surpassed the Old Dominion in the first two categories, but not in political preeminence. Not coincidentally, the congressional attempt to admit Missouri without slavery—igniting the most ferocious sectional controversy to date—originated in New York among Republicans and was sustained by them and their allies. Thus, the movement to restrict slavery from Missouri was a kind of surrogate presidential politics and was even more about how national power—statist power, however much there would be—would be managed.

The panic of 1819 and the collapse of the economy simultaneously raised the general question of the national government's powers and, by provoking considerable resentment against the Bank of the United States in the South and West, sharpened the issue of federal and state governments' relations to banks. Old Republicans who embraced states' rights orthodoxy, as well as a new breed of populist politicians, blamed the bank, the tariff, and other governmental interventions for the economic dislocations.[49] Yet economic issues seemed to have little to do with the major challenge to Virginia rule, coming in the form of an attack on slavery extension during the Missouri controversies. Moreover, it came at a time when the Virginia political elite was already moving sharply away from postwar nationalism to embrace states' rights.

Before leaving office, Madison had actually vetoed the ambitious bill of 1816 providing for internal improvements, with its implicit agenda of national planning. More importantly, the Virginia planters were reacting to a potent burst of judicial nationalism coming from the Supreme Court. In three cases, *Martin v. Hunter's Lessee* (1816), *McCulloch v. Maryland* (1819), and *Cohens v. Virginia* (1821), the Marshall Court asserted its own power and that of Congress over both state legislatures and state courts. *McCulloch* upheld the power of Congress to charter the Bank of the United States and denied the right of a state (Maryland) to tax it. (Ten days before the decision, the House had rejected a bill to repeal the bank's charter.) Together with second thoughts about recent "consolidationist" trends, this moved "Virginia's Old Republicans [to spark] a states' rights revival that swept over the lower South during the 1820s."[50]

The threat to slavery implicit in the Court's decisions became linked in the minds of Virginia's leaders with the sudden attempt in 1819 to restrict slavery from Missouri. After coming to believe that the Missouri restriction sprang from a conspiracy to revive Federalism—an erroneous conclusion—the Virginians passionately opposed the compromises put forth during the three Missouri controversies of 1819–1821. "Nine-tenth's of the commonwealth's Jeffersonian elite, through their votes either in Congress or in the (Virginia) assembly, denied the constitutionality of congressional interference with slavery in the territories."[51]

An End to State Development

The significance of these events was that even though the Virginia dynasty ended in the next presidential election, the swing of Virginia and the South back to states' rights would constrict nation-state development as the southern periphery continued to dominate the central government indirectly. Consider the evidence for that domination assembled by historian Leonard Richards: slaveholders occupied the presidency for fifty of seventy-two years, from Washington to Lincoln; slaveholders were Speakers of the House for forty-six of those years, and the only Speakers to serve more than two terms (three of them) were from slaveholding states; slaveholders served as chairs of Ways and Means for forty-eight years; and in the case of Supreme Court appointees, nineteen were southerners, fifteen northerners.[52]

Southerners accounted for these discrepancies by boasting of their superiority to northern politicians. Northerners too sometimes gave southerners credit for producing strong leaders. But the keys to southern power, as some northerners saw it, "were regional unity, parity in the Senate, and the three-fifths clause of the Constitution. Alone, each was important; together, they were a formidable combination."[53]

In all the important sectional fights of the antebellum period, northerners divided more, but they compromised more as well. The free states always seemed to send enough "doughfaces" to Congress, that is, northern men who voted with the South on crucial tests and thus ensured southern victory. In 1820, the eccentric Virginian John Randolph had so named the eighteen northerners who broke ranks to admit Missouri while not one southerner defected. His shrill voice dripping with contempt, Randolph said that he had known that these men would give way. "They were scared at their own dough faces! . . . We had *them,* and if we wanted *three* more, we could have had them: yes, and if *these* had failed, we could have had three more of these men."[54] Similarly, in 1836, sixty northerners went along with the gag rule on anti-slavery petitions, compared with eight southerners who took the northern position.

Besides doughfaces, Richards points out, the South benefited from "rotten boroughs" created by the three-fifths clause. The 1787 provision became an almost meaningless tax provision, "seldom enacted into law," or poorly enforced when it was. But with gerrymandering by state legislatures, that provision created what Richards calls the "spoils of slave representation." Thus, in 1800, two Lees served in Congress. Silas Lee of Maine, which was then part of Massachusetts, represented 58,000 free citizens, well above the state average of 33,000 per district. "Lighthorse" Harry Lee of Virginia represented a Tidewater district with 19,000 slaves and only 14,000 whites, well below the state average of 23,000 per district. Although seldom noted by historians, the three-fifths rule, as much as Aaron Burr's politicking in New York, had won the 1800 election for Jefferson.[55]

Thus the South, with slightly more than half the free population of the North, could block any legislation in the House. The slaveholding states could also mobilize to check any energizing tendencies of the central government. The Missouri controversies thus originated as an attack on southern and specifically Virginian dominance. Far from being a "Federalist plot," the attempt to admit Missouri to the Union without slavery was launched from New York and sustained by New York Republicans and their allies chafing under "Virginia rule."[56] It was an early attempt to reverse or moderate the southern periphery's domination of the center.

By 1824, the Republican caucus—Republican congressmen meeting to select presidential candidates—was in disarray, and the Virginians recognized the necessity of stepping aside. Almost by accident, these and other circumstances brought to the presidency the leading nationalist of the day, and one of the few: John Quincy Adams. Although Adams and Henry Clay, his secretary of state, espoused economic nationalism, which Clay touted as the "American system," they were given scant opportunity by congressional opponents to engage in much more than nationalist rhetoric.

When the deliberately unpolitical Adams called in his first annual message for vigorous action by the government, including an expanded system of roads and canals, creation of a Department of the Interior and a national university, financing of exploration and science, a new naval academy, and a uniform system of weights and measures, his political enemies launched a campaign to demonize Adams's vision of "liberty by design." With their sights set on the 1828 presidential election, Adams's opponents used his exhortation to national purpose to rekindle all the fears of the periphery—southern, western, and northern interior—and several Republican factions came together in Congress to defeat most administration measures. John Tyler, the future president, called the message "a direct insult upon Virginia."[57]

From 1825 to 1828, the periphery mobilized again and used anti-statist appeals against a presumed threat from a hegemonic center. The "Adams Republicans" stood for economic nationalism in 1828, whereas the opposing coalition of Republicans that brought Tennessee slaveholder Andrew Jackson to the presidency stood primarily for opposition to such an agenda and any purposeful state building. The Jacksonians, who did not yet call themselves Democrats, represented another successful mobilization of the periphery like that of 1800: southern based and pro-slavery. In 1828, Jackson received 92 percent of the electoral votes of the slave states, compared with 49 percent of the nonslave states. The electoral map shows Adams's support cramped into the corner comprising New England, eastern New York, New Jersey, and part of the Chesapeake basin. All else reaching west and south, except for pockets of nonconformity, was Jackson territory.[58]

During the 1830s, mass political parties formed and became institutionalized in a manner not achieved by the Federalists or the Republicans. The Democrats and Whigs—the former rapidly, the latter unevenly—would come to accept party organization as a positive good, and a new ethos of partyism would prevail, along with extensive organization of the electorate, which was soon mobilized into partisan "armies." Parties in the electorate and in legislatures would interact with parties as campaign engines to an unprecedented extent.[59] These new parties—and their political culture—were made possible by the convergence of several interconnected changes in social behavior and material conditions. Transportation and communication revolutions were creating the technical capacity for mass organizations to function in the 1820s and 1830s. Simultaneously, the market revolution plus religious revivals energized increasing numbers of men and women to enter the public sphere, or at least made them receptive to reform movements and contests over public values, which helped to moralize politics and added to mass politicization.[60]

In this new political culture, great ideological battles once again convulsed the country, over programs for both economic and moral improvement. As in the 1790s, a national bank and protective tariffs took center stage, although this time, a powerful evangelical movement interacted with economic change to help polarize the population. Increasingly, the Jacksonian Democrats advocated limited government and states' rights and generated a populist appeal by denouncing monopolies, corporations, and special privileges for the wealthy few. Culturally, the laissez-faire approach of these Democrats appealed to ethnic outsiders and religious minorities, notably Irish Catholics, who increasingly became a reference group in American politics.

In contrast, the Whigs favored governmental activism to promote economic development and, at the state level, moral improvement. Whigs tended to see the nation as "a single moral community." Hence, in several states, powerful evangelical Protestant movements allied with Whiggery, or sometimes provided the basis for reformist splinter groups and third-party movements—notably nativist and anti-slavery movements.[61] Once again, as with the first parties, divergent postures on state authority and community morality influenced party attitudes toward women. By 1840, it was evident that Whigs welcomed women into the public sphere far more than Democrats did and that Whigs offered an ideal of feminine civic duty—"Whig womanhood"—providing further proof of their superior morality, as well as a view of family life different from that of the Democrats. Whigs preferred "a model of gentle, virtuous authority" that would slowly, over decades, translate into a vision of benevolent government. Democrats, in contrast, tended to describe expansions of government power as usurpations of the rights of white men.[62]

The details of these substantive divisions, and their structural bases, are treated in subsequent chapters. But I want to stress that, as in the 1790s, the overarching question was, how much government? And I want to call attention to the way the new parties, particularly the Jacksonian or Democratic Republicans (soon to be Democrats), plus southern opponents of "consolidation" functioned together to inhibit state development. Slaveholders exercised much control over policy making in Congress and over presidents through their influence in the major parties, particularly the Democratic. The impact of this on the development (or nondevelopment) of the American state is becoming more appreciated by historians.

Take the case of internal improvements. Despite conventional images of the Adams administration as favoring internal improvements but unable to get congressional approval and of Jackson as opposing internal improvements, political scientist Steven Minicucci has shown that the Adams-Jackson years (1825–1837) *together* constituted an "era of internal improvements," when spending reached levels unattained from 1789 to 1824 or from 1838 to 1860. Spending on improvements rose sharply during Adams's administration and actually increased after 1829, although Jackson shifted it away from eastern canals to roads and rivers, especially in the West. But after the panic of 1837, funds dried up. When they were available again, disbursements for internal improvements remained at much lower levels, with only a brief recovery in 1851–1852.

Why? Minicucci explains that congressional promoters of improvements failed to adjust to a new era dominated by mass parties. Additionally, however, he identifies "obstructionist Democratic presidents" as important in keeping appropriations low, and although the Democratic Party on the whole was only weakly opposed to improvements, the party leadership "took great pains not to offend, and even to favor, key partners in the old South." Indeed, "the core opponents of the policy were in fact concentrated in the old tidewater South. At least one of these, John Randolph . . . tied the power to construct improvements to the power to abolish slavery."[63] Thus, the case of internal improvements illustrates directly how the southern periphery's influence limited the exercise of state power.

Participation in the new nation had been high from the beginning, but initially only in state contests.[64] From the late 1820s, elections at all levels engaged citizens as social movements, third parties, and a party system mobilized the world's first mass electorate. Despite the emergence of strong parties, the central state did not become powerful, and it can be argued that not only the southern periphery's influence but also the new party system itself worked to weaken the state, independently of what John Quincy Adams called "the Sable Genius of the South."

In 1829, the Jacksonian Republicans entered office after raising exaggerated fears about the expansion of the central government under Adams, and thereafter they proceeded to restrict the scope of federal action (while at the same time strengthening the executive). An important part of this process, as Richard John has argued, was that "the Jacksonians transformed the American postal system from the central administrative apparatus of the American state into a wellspring of the mass party." Since the Post Office Act of 1792, the postal system had played an important role in providing a central state presence in many citizens' lives, fostering political participation and helping to create a national market, as well as a national public sphere. During the administration of Postmaster General John McLean (1823–1829), the postal system began to develop into an institution with the potential to strengthen the administrative state. But, as John points out, the postal agency's centralizing and secularizing tendencies made enemies, including Sabbatarians and slaveholders, and the Jacksonian Democrats soon subordinated the postal system to patronage and party building.

John's story thereafter becomes one of central state regression, with, for example, most dismissals taking place in the best-served sections of the country—New England and the Northwest—where the Democratic Party was weakest, in order to strengthen the Democracy in those regions. In general, with the creation of patronage-oriented mass parties preceding the establishment of civil service procedures to recruit a bureaucracy, "politicians were able to gain access to patronage for party building" rather than for state building.[65]

The focus here has been on <u>circumstances that slowed, even stalled, central state building once it had begun</u>. But it cannot be denied that the national government—all three branches—promoted economic development, land distribution, exploration, westward expansion, the transportation and communications revolutions, and other processes that helped to create, directly and indirectly, the nation as well as the state. A recent study of the U.S. Army's success in maintaining national sovereignty over the borderlands concluded that "not all of the organizing programs put forward by centrally-minded elites during the generation after the War of 1812 failed."[66]

After 1812, too, the Army Corps of Engineers contributed significantly to national development by building internal improvement networks as systematically as possible in a climate of logrolling and democratic opportunism.[67] Indeed, during the early republic, nationalism flourished (relatively) in branches of government least susceptible to popular politics, notably the Supreme Court and the executive bureaucracy, especially in the secretary of state's conduct of foreign policy. Voluntary associations, such as Freemasonry at least until 1830, attracted cosmopolitan men who were highly political and contributed to nationalizing trends. Moreover, the public sphere expanded significantly after 1816, with women participating in public and even partisan affairs both in the North and, remarkably, in parts of the South.[68]

That expanded sphere would significantly influence the course that national politics took in the 1840s and 1850s. To repeat a point made at the outset, the distinction between state and nation is often blurred in reality. The nation's collective memory, that repository of "those potent mental images that float within the minds of Americans singly and collectively," grew despite the stunting of the state.[69] The period from the Revolutionary War to Manifest Destiny and the Mexican War was prolific in the creation of symbols of nationhood, of collective identity, and of mythic transition, and these inevitably served the state in the long run as capital in the bank of civil religion.

Acknowledgments

I am indebted for critical readings of this essay to Jeffrey S. Adler, Richard R. John, and Byron E. Shafer.

Notes

1. By the term *development*, I mean to suggest growth, but also, following Green-stone, "change, contingency, and the impact of causal forces in reshaping a po-litical or social order. The concept draws on the powerful intuition that no fea-ture of human experience, including language itself, is exempt from change and transformation." J. David Greenstone, "Political Culture and American Political Development: Liberty, Union, and the Liberal Bipolarity," *Studies in American Po-litical Development* 1 (1986): 1.

2. Though I do not pursue this theme here, state governments to varying degrees continued to develop infrastructures after the War of 1812, a story that can be fol-lowed in many individual state studies and generally in Robert H. Wiebe, *The Opening of American Society: From the Adoption of the Constitution to the Eve of Dis-union* (New York, 1984), 194–252.

3. Key works on these concepts are Benedict Anderson, *Imagined Communities: Re-flections on the Origin and Spread of Nationalism*, rev. ed. (London, 1991); E.J. Hobs-bawm, *Nations and Nationalism since 1780: Programme, Myth, Reality* (Cambridge, 1990); Wilbur Zelinsky, *Nation into State: The Shifting Symbolic Foundations of American Nationalism* (Chapel Hill, N.C., 1988); Jurgen Habermas, *The Structural Transformation of the Public Sphere: An Inquiry into a Category of Bourgeois Society*, trans. Thomas Burger (Cambridge, Mass., 1989); and Craig Calhoun, ed., *Haber-mas and the Public Sphere* (Cambridge, Mass., 1991). For a review of literature di-rectly relevant to my purpose, see Richard R. John, "Governmental Institutions as Agents of Change: Rethinking American Political Development in the Early Republic, 1787–1835," *Studies In American Political Development* 11 (fall 1997): 347–80.

4. Kevin P. Phillips, *The Cousins' Wars* (New York, 1999), 516, 517; M.J. Heale, *The Making of American Politics, 1750–1850* (London, 1977), 31–33; Linda Colley, *Britons: Forging the Nation, 1707–1837* (New Haven, Conn., 1992); David Hackett Fischer, *Albion's Seed: Four British Folkways in America* (New York, 1989).

5. For a stirring narrative of the first phases of the Revolution in Massachusetts as a populist, collective enterprise, see David Hackett Fischer, *Paul Revere's Ride* (New York, 1994); see also David W. Conroy, *In Public Houses: Drink and the Revo-lution in Authority in Colonial Massachusetts* (Chapel Hill, N.C., 1995). Although after 1765 "an epidemic of rioting broke upon the American scene," it contained a low level of violence. Paul A. Gilje, *Rioting in America* (Bloomington, Ind., 1996), 35–59. Regarding women's expanded sphere of thought and action during the Revolution, see Mary Beth Norton, *Liberty's Daughters: The Revolutionary Experi-ence of American Women, 1750–1800* (Boston, 1980), 195–227.

6. Jack P. Greene, *Pursuits of Happiness: The Social Develoment of Early Modern British Colonies and the Formation of American Culture* (Chapel Hill, N.C., 1988), 195, 200; Tiziano Bonazzi, "Men, Like Flowers or Roots, Being Transplanted, Take after the Soil Wherein They Grow: Reflections on Alterity and Politics Regarding the Ori-gins of the United States of America," in *Multiculturalism and the History of Inter-national Relations from the 18th Century to the Present*, ed. Pierre Savard and Brunello Vigezzi (Milan, 1999), 26. Bonazzi sees the origin of the United States as "not part of the history of the fulfillment of liberty. Rather it belongs to the his-tory of the system of European states and the dynamics underlying its historical development" (27).

7. Gordon S. Wood, *The Creation of the American Republic, 1776–1787* (Chapel Hill, N.C., 1969); Ramsay quoted in Joseph J. Ellis, *After the Revolution: Profiles of Early American Culture* (New York, 1979), x. A recent neo-progressive view of popular politicization that summarizes much of the literature is Michael A. McDonnell, "Popular Mobilization and Political Culture in Revolutionary Virginia: The Failure of the Minutemen and the Revolution from Below," *Journal of American History* 85 (December 1998): 946–98. Ellis anticipated to a degree Wood's later book *The Radicalism of the American Revolution* (New York, 1992).

8. Calvin Jillson, "Patterns and Periodicity in American National Politics," in *The Dynamics of American Politics: Approaches and Interpretations,* ed. Lawrence C. Dodd and Calvin Jillson (Boulder, Colo., 1994), 32; M.J. Heale, *The Making of American Politics, 1750–1850* (London, 1977), 37–40; Judith Apter Klinghofer and Lois Elkis, "The Petticoat Electors: Women's Suffrage in New Jersey, 1776–1807," *Journal of the Early Republic* 12 (summer 1992): 159–93. For example, North Carolina required assemblymen to own 100 acres and senators 300 acres; New York allowed only £1,000 freeholders to vote for senators and governor—about one-third of adult white males.

9. Lance Banning, "Political Economy and the Creation of the Federal Republic," in *Devising Liberty: Preserving and Creating Freedom in the New American Republic,* ed. David Thomas Konig (Stanford, Calif., 1995), 24–26, 30; Heale, *Making of American Politics,* 50–51. Banning's view is admittedly almost neo-Beardian: "Of all the forces pushing toward reform, none was stronger than the movement for a federal power over commerce. At the Federal Convention, the determination of delegates to make America a single market—and to make that market safe for private property and private contracts—seems beyond dispute" (27). The nationalists also wanted a government capable of evicting the British from their trading posts and forts in the Northwest, where their presence increased Indian intransigence to American advance.

10. Banning, "Political Economy," 29–30; Heale, *Making of American Politics,* 51–52; Ronald P. Formisano, "Teaching Shays/The Regulation," *Uncommon Sense: A Newsletter Published by the Omohundro Institute of Early American History and Culture* 1 (winter 1998): 24, 26–35; John L. Brooke, "A Deacon's Orthodoxy: Religion, Class, and the Moral Economy of Shay's Rebellion," in *In Debt to Shays: The Bicentennial of an American Rebellion,* ed. Robert Gross (Charlottesville, Va., 1993), 206; Forrest McDonald, *E Pluribus Unum: The Formation of the American Republic, 1776–1790* (Boston, 1965), 135–54; Conroy, *In Public Houses,* 310–13.

11. Heale, *Making of American Politics,* 54–56; Banning, "Political Economy."

12. Among the many works that might be mentioned here, one recent one is Paul Finkleman, *Slavery and the Founders: Race and Liberty in the Age of Jefferson* (Armonk, N.Y., 1996).

13. By 1840, the "white men's republic" would become a tyrannically uniform "white man's democracy." James Brewer Stewart, "Response," in "SHA Roundtable: Racial Modernity," *Journal of the Early Republic* 18 (spring 1998): 234.

14. Heale, *Making of American Politics,* 60; Mark E. Kann, *A Republic of Men: The American Founders, Gendered Language, and Patriarchal Politics* (New York, 1998), 1, 3; Jay Fliegelman, *Prodigals and Pilgrims: The American Revolution against Patriarchal Authority, 1750–1800* (Cambridge, 1982); Jan Lewis, "'Of every age sex & condition': The Representation of Women in the Constitution," *Journal of the Early Republic* 15 (fall 1995): 359–87. For analysis of the Constitution as a "patriarchal legal text," see Joan Hoff, *Law, Gender, and Injustice: A Local History of U.S. Women* (New York,

1991), 22–23; see Gordon S. Wood, *Radicalism of the American Revolution* (New York, 1993), 145–68, regarding paternalists. Zagarri has argued that although male elites managed to circumvent the extension of natural rights principles to women at the time of the Revolution, in the long run, natural rights ideology worked (and was invoked) to subvert women's exclusion. Rosemarie Zagarri, "The Rights of Man and Woman in Post-Revolutionary America," *William and Mary Quarterly*, 3d ser., 55 (April 1998): 203–30.

15. Heale, *Making of American Politics*, 44–47, quotation at 63; Banning, "Political Economy," 27; Simon P. Newman, "Principles or Men? George Washington and the Political Culture of National Leadership, 1776–1801," *Journal of the Early Republic* 12 (winter 1992): 477–507; Paul A. Gilje, *Road to Mobocracy* (Chapel Hill, N.C., 1987), 97–99. The phrase "agrarian minded," in contrast to "commercial minded," is from Lee Benson, *Turner and Beard: American Historical Explanation Reconsidered* (Glencoe, Ill., 1960), 216–18; McDonald, *E Pluribus Unum*, 189–208.

16. The contest over the Constitution was not over "economic fundamentals. It did not pit capitalists against anti-capitalists, modern liberals against classical republicans, or progressive against conservative economic interests" (Banning, "Political Economy," 39).

17. The court-country cleavage has been described by many historians. See William Nisbet Chambers, *Political Parties in a New Nation: The American Experience, 1776–1809* (New York, 1965), and Stanley Elkins and Eric McKitrick, *The Age of Federalism* (New York, 1993), 19–24, who drew liberally from John M. Murrin, "The Great Inversion, or Court versus Country: A Comparison of the Revolutionary Settlements in England (1688–1721) and America (1776–1816)," in *Three British Revolutions: 1641, 1688, 1776*, ed. J. G. A. Pocock (Princeton, N.J., 1980), 368–453.

18. Thomas Jefferson, Paris, to James Madison, December 20, 1787, in John P. Kaminaki and Gaspare J. Saladino, eds., *The Documentary History of the Ratification of the Constitution*, vol. 9, *Ratification of the Constitution by the States: Virginia* [2] (Madison, Wis., 1990), 252; James D. Richardson, ed., *The Messages and Papers of the Presidents*, vol. 1 (Washington, D.C., 1903), 53.

19. Banning, "Political Economy," 19–21, Jefferson quotation, 39; Drew R. McCoy, *The Elusive Republic: Political Economy in Jeffersonian America* (Chapel Hill, N.C., 1980); Newman, "Principles or Men?"

20. Federalist military goals were perceived as interwoven with the other elements of Hamilton's nation-building agenda: Richard H. Kohn, *Eagle and Sword: The Federalists and the Creation of the Military Establishment in America, 1783–1802* (New York, 1975), 128–38, 278, 289, 299. Since the 1690s, England had financed its war with a funding system tied to a national debt, reliable revenues, a sinking fund, the Bank of England, and chartered corporations that purchased vast amounts of the debt in exchange for commercial privileges. Banning, "Political Economy," 20–21; see also, Colley, *Britons*.

21. James L. Huston, *Securing the Fruits of Labor: The American Concept of Wealth Distribution* (Baton Rouge, 1998), 221. Two other continuities identified by Huston are the struggle between individualism and community, and that "one party represented dynamic economic growth and the other either cautioned wariness or denied the need for change" (221).

22. By the end of the 1790s, "the example of France was to become a negative reference in American political culture." James M. Banner, Jr., "France and the Origins of American Political Culture," *Virginia Quarterly Review* 64 (fall 1988): 656–57.

23. Thomas P. Slaughter, *The Whiskey Rebellion: Frontier Epilogue to the American Revolution* (New York, 1986), 165–66; Matthew Schoenbachler, "Republicanism in the Age of Democratic Revolution: The Democratic-Republican Societies of the 1790s," *Journal of the Early Republic* 18 (spring 1998): 243, 254. "The land and the freedom it endowed passed to the whites, and the Indians gradually became their dependents—subject to all the humiliations" of that status. Alan Taylor, "Land and Liberty on the Post-Revolutionary Frontier," in Konig, *Devising Liberty*, 107.

24. Richard P. McCormick, *The Presidential Game: The Origins of American Presidential Politics* (New York, 1982), 50; for an emphasis on "ordinary American" inclusion in the politics of the 1790s, see Simon P. Newman, *Parades and the Politics of the Street* (Philadelphia, 2000); for a different view, see Peter Thompson, *Rum, Punch, and Revolution: Taverngoing and Public Life in Eighteenth-Century Philadelphia* (Philadelphia, 1999), 180–81, 202–3.

25. Rogers M. Smith, "Constructing American National Identity: Strategies of the Federalists," in *Federalists Reconsidered*, ed. Doron Ban-Atar and Barbara Oberg (Charlottesville, Va., 1998), 23, 38; Robert Kelley, *The Cultural Pattern In American Politics: The First Century* (New York, 1979), 114, 126–27.

26. Rosemarie Zagarri, "Gender and the First Party System," in Ban-Atar and Oberg, *Federalists Reconsidered*, 119, 121, 131–33; for differences among Federalists that seem to have been forgotten in present scholarship, see David Hackett Fischer, *The Revolution in American Conservatism: The Federalist Party in the Age of Jeffersonian Democracy* (New York, 1965), 2–17, 33–49.

27. John L. Brooke, *Heart of the Commonwealth: Society and Political Culture in Worcester County, Massachusetts, 1713–1861* (Cambridge, Mass., 1989), 262; Roy F. Nichols, *The Invention of American Political Parties: A Study of Political Improvisation* (New York, 1967), 213; Richard Hofstadter, *The Idea of a Party System: The Rise of Legitimate Opposition in the United States, 1780–1840* (Berkeley, Calif., 1969); Ronald P. Formisano, "Deferential-Participant Politics: The Early Republic's Political Culture, 1789–1840," *American Political Science Review* 68 (June 1974): 473–87. The Federalists had even sought to prevent southern and western congressmen (Republicans, of course) from sending circular letters to their constituents because they were broadcasting partisan opposition. Noble E. Cunningham, Jr., ed., *Circular Letters of Congressmen to Their Constituents 1789–1829: 1st Congress to 9th Congress 1789–1807* (Chapel Hill, N.C., 1978), 1: xxxvii–xl. The complex evolution of Federalist anti-partyism in one state is traced in Donald J. Ratcliffe, *Party Spirit in a Frontier Republic: Democratic Politics in Ohio, 1793–1821* (Columbus, 1998), 3–4, 60–61, 63–64, 133–35, 190–92, 195–201.

28. Sharp observes that historians have agreed that Federalists and Republicans were sincere about their fears regarding the threat posed by the other, and they have agreed that the rivals shared a consensus about republican government. Sharp argues that both propositions cannot be true unless, as he points out, Republicans and Federalists "failed to recognize that they *shared* a consensus." James Roger Sharp, *American Politics in the Early Republic: The New Nation in Crisis* (New Haven, Conn., 1993), 8.

29. Regarding the Federalist split over the standing army and war with France, see Kohn, *Eagle and Sword*, 259–73; for background, see Don Higginbotham, "The Federalized Militia Debate: A Neglected Aspect of Second Amendment Scholarship," *William and Mary Quarterly*, 3d ser., 55 (January 1998): 39–58.

30. Historians justly give credit to Aaron Burr's political organization and skills in

carrying New York for Jefferson in 1800, but the Hamilton-Adams rift was so severe that Adams probably "never stood a chance of gaining the state's 12 electoral voters," which Hamilton tightly controlled. Adams learned two months before the polls opened that "Hamilton says that you will not have a vote in N[ew] York *in any event*" (quoted in Kohn, *Eagle and Sword*, 271). Maryland and Delaware split eight to five, and the mid Atlantic went twenty to seven for Jefferson.

31. Ronald P. Formisano, *The Transformation of Political Culture: Massachusetts Parties, 1790s–1840s* (New York, 1983), 7. Andrew R. L. Cayton, "Radicals in the 'Western World': The Federalist Conception of Trans-Appalachian North America," in Ban-Atar and Oberg, *Federalists Reconsidered*, 95–96. The Federalists' use of the army and distribution of patronage in trans-Appalachia led to a double-edged reaction: demonstrating the power of the national government and attaching people to the United States, while at the same time "alienating people from the national government." Andrew R. L. Cayton, "'Separate Interests' and the Nation-State: The Washington Administration and the Origins of Regionalism in the Trans-Appalachian West," *Journal of American History* 79 (June 1992): 45, 47, 50, 66.

32. Formisano, *Transformation of Political Culture*, 149–50.

33. Ibid., 149–70; Brooke, *Heart of the Commonwealth*, 243–63. New England was the heartland of the ethnically English, but in the culturally diverse middle states, the larger non-English cultural groups (Scotch-Irish, Germans, Dutch) tended to be Republican, while English-stock Quakers tended to be Federal. Although old established families were frequently Republican, especially Scotch-Irish Presbyterians, high-status cultural and religious groups usually supported Federalists. This meant too that middle- and lower-class dependents of influential men adhered to Federalism. For analysis of the social bases of Federalist and Republican support generally, see Ronald P. Formisano, "Federalists and Republicans—Parties, Yes, System No," in *The Evolution of American Electoral Systems*, ed. Paul Kleppner et al. (Westport, Conn., 1981), 60–66; Fischer, *Revolution in American Conservatism*, 201–26; Kelley, *Cultural Pattern in American Politics*, 115–27.

34. William G. Shade, *Democratizing the Old Dominion: Virginia and the Second Party System, 1824–1861* (Charlottesville, Va., 1996), 115–17, quotations, 116, 117.

35. David Waldstreicher, *In the Midst of Perpetual Fetes: The Making of American Nationalism, 1776–1820* (Chapel Hill, N.C., 1997), 9, also 201–16; Wiebe, *Opening of American Society*, 112–19, 123; Chambers, *Political Parties in a New Nation*.

36. McCormick, *Presidential Game*, 76. Waldstreicher has encountered criticism on other grounds, notably that the public sphere in which his nationalism flourished "may well have been [in part because of sources selected] the province of a relatively small group of men and an even smaller group of 'respectable' women who shared similar values"; indeed, "it is possible that the 'imagined community' of the early republic was a mile wide and an inch deep." Andrew R. L. Cayton, "We Are All Nationalists, We Are All Localists," *Journal of the Early Republic* 18 (fall 1998): 526, 527. The term "Republican Ascendency" comes from George Dangerfield, *The Awakening of American Nationalism, 1815–1828* (New York, 1965), 103–4.

37. Jack Larkin, *The Reshaping of Everyday Life, 1790–1840* (New York, 1988), xv, 3–4, 5; James A. Henretta, "The 'Market' in the Early Republic," *Journal of the Early Republic* 18 (spring 1998): 304; David Simpson, *The Politics of American English, 1776–1850* (New York, 1986), 3–4, quotation, 9; regarding literacy and newspapers, see Larkin, *Reshaping of Everyday Life*, 35–36.

38. Anne Norton, *Alternative Americas: A Reading of Antebellum Political Culture* (Chicago, 1986), 28; Charles S. Sydnor, *The Development of Southern Sectionalism, 1819–1848* (Baton Rouge, 1948).

39. McCoy, *The Elusive Republic*; Banning, "Political Economy," 47; Richard Hofstadter, *The American Political Tradition* (New York, 1948), 35. Federalist and Republican differences regarding the Corps of Engineers reflected their divergent approaches to nation building. Todd Shallat, *Structures in the Stream: Water, Science, and the Rise of the U.S. Army Corps of Engineers* (Austin, Tex., 1994), 118–19.

40. Kohn, *Eagle and Sword*, 303; Martin Shefter, *Political Parties and the State: The American Historical Experience* (Princeton, N.J., 1994), 64–65; see Jeffrey L. Pasley, "Matthew Livingston Davis' Notes from the Political Underground" (unpublished manuscript), regarding Jefferson's resistance to partisan approaches emanating from lower-status partisan operatives.

41. Wiebe, *Opening of American Society*, 194–204, is particularly useful in describing states' exercise of power; William J. Novak, *The People's Welfare: Law and Regulation in Nineteenth-Century America* (Chapel Hill, N.C., 1996).

42. Banning, "Political Economy," 47–48; Waldstreicher, *In the Midst of Pepetual Fates*, 257–62. A still valuable account of postwar sentiment is Dangerfield's *Awakening of American Nationalism*, 1–71.

43. Harlow W. Sheidley, *Sectional Nationalism: Massachusetts Conservative Leaders and the Transformation of America, 1815–1836* (Boston, 1998).

44. McCormick, *Presidential Game*, 76–77.

45. James Sterling Young, *The Washington Community, 1800–1828* (New York, 1966), 28, 31, 33; Nichols, *Invention of American Political Parties*, 246–47; Formisano, *Transformation of Political Culture*, 16–17.

46. The Jackson administration's support of the attempt by New Hampshire Jacksonians to politicize the Portsmouth branch of the Bank of the United States became one of the precipitants of the bank war. Donald B. Cole, *Jacksonian Democracy in New Hampshire, 1800–1851* (Cambridge, Mass., 1970), 102–28.

47. M. J. Heale, *The Presidential Quest: Candidates and Images in American Political Culture, 1787–1852* (London, 1982), 21; Formisano, "Federalists and Republicans," 40–43.

48. McCormick, *Presidential Game*, 76–77; see Formisano, "Federalists and Republicans," 39, regarding the distribution of electoral votes, and 40–41, regarding the various movements at play in presidential politics in 1808, 1812, and 1816; see also, Norman Risjord, "Election of 1812," in *History of American Presidential Elections, 1789–1968*, 3 vols., ed. Arthur Schlesinger, Jr., and Fred L. Israel (New York, 1971), 1:249, 252–57, 259.

49. For a synthesis of the economic results of the 1819 panic and its connection to politics and society (within an interpretive framework very different from that presented here), see Charles G. Sellers, *The Market Revolution: Jacksonian America, 1815–1846* (New York, 1991), 131–71.

50. Shade, *Democratizing the Old Dominion*, 228. The impact of the Court's decisions was perhaps heightened because of the hegemonic position of lawyers and courts as articulators of republican culture. Robert A. Ferguson, *Law and Letters in American Culture* (Cambridge, Mass., 1984), 20–24.

51. Shade, *Democratizing the Old Dominion*, 231. "The two-year debate over Missouri forced upon the Virginia gentry the stark realization of their diminishing significance in the political arena that they had once believed to be their own. What is more, their honor had been called into question. The restrictionists posed the pos-

sibility that the Old Dominion itself lacked a republican government because it acquiesced in the continuation of the peculiar institution that the Yankees had moved to extinguish" (233–34).

52. Leonard Richards, *The Slave Power: The Free North and Southern Domination, 1780–1860* (Baton Rouge, 2000), 8–10, 61–62, 94. While stressing sharp divisions among Southerners, William W. Freishling recognized a similar pattern in *The Road to Disunion: Secessionists at Bay* (New York, 1990); see also, David M. Potter, *The South and the Concurrent Majority* (Baton Rouge, 1972).

53. Richards, *Slave Power*, 26. During the Civil War, the average Johnny Reb would boast that he could lick any three—or more—Yanks. James M. McPherson, *For Cause and Comrades: Why Men Fought in the Civil War* (New York, 1997).

54. Randolph quoted in Glover Moore, *The Missouri Controversy, 1819–1821* (Lexington, Ky., 1953), 104. I use the text from Richards, *Slave Power*, 85–86, which differs slightly from Moore.

55. The discussion of "rotten boroughs" is in Leonard Richards, "The Question of Slaveholder Domination" (unpublished paper in my possession), 13–14, 15, 17, 20; Richards otherwise discusses the effects of the three-fifths clause extensively in *Slave Power*, 32–46, 49–51. For Federalist complaints regarding the clause, see also James M. Banner, Jr., *To the Hartford Convention: The Federalists and the Origins of Party Politics in Massachusetts, 1789–1815* (New York, 1970), 101–9.

56. The standard account of the controversies differs from the interpretation offered here. Moore, *Missouri Controversy*, had some second thoughts about the controversy in 1970, as reflected in "The Missouri Controversy One Hundred and Fifty Years Later" (unpublished paper). My version in based on extensive reading of secondary and primary sources. A similar view can be found in Freishling, *Road to Disunion*, 144–54, and Robert P. Forbes, "Slavery and the Meaning of America, 1819–1837" (Ph.D. diss., Yale University, 1994).

57. John Lauritz Larson, "Liberty by Design: Freedom, Planning, and John Quincy Adams' American System," in *The State and Economic Knowledge: The American and British Experience*, ed. Mary C. Furner and Barry Supple (Cambridge, 1990), 73–102. Larson argued that Adams's design represented the founders' vision and was not necessarily unpopular (75, 89–96). Formisano, *Transformation of Political Culture*, 17; Richards, "Question of Slaveholder Domination," 25; Tyler quoted in Shade, *Democratizing the Old Dominion*, 85; Lynn Hudson Parsons, *John Quincy Adams* (Madison, Wis., 1998), 179–81; Sydnor, *Development of Southern Sectionalism*, 193–95.

58. The southern periphery's influence in the Midwest can be seen in Nicole Etcheson, *The Emerging Midwest: Upland Southerners and the Political Culture of the Old Northwest, 1787–1861* (Bloomington, Ind., 1996).

59. Ronald P. Formisano, "Deferential-Participant Politics: The Early Republic's Political Culture, 1789–1840," *American Political Science Review* 68 (June 1974): 473–87; Hofstadter, *Idea of a Party System*.

60. Formisano, *Transformation of Political Culture*, 15–22, 173–244.

61. Kelley, *Cultural Pattern in American Politics*, 141–84; Daniel Walker Howe, "The Evangelical Movement and Political Culture in the North during the Second Party System," *Journal of American History* 77 (March 1991): 1216–39; also suggestive is Major L. Wilson, "The 'Country' Versus the 'Court': A Republican Consensus and Party Debate in the Bank War," *Journal of the Early Republic* 15 (winter 1995): 619–47. Regarding the market revolution *not* creating the party

coalitions, see, for example, Daniel S. Dupre, *Transforming the Cotton Frontier: Madison County, Alabama, 1800–1840* (Baton Rouge, 1997). Holt's book on the Whig Party endorses the argument here regarding the basic difference between the parties—namely, their "conflicting philosophies about the proper role of *both* state and national governments." Democrats portrayed themselves as committed to hard money, anti-banking, anti-corporation, and negative government. Whigs believed in "positive action" by the government, especially in hard times, and also in regulating social behavior. Michael P. Holt, *The Rise and Fall of the American Whig Party: Jacksonian Politics and the Onset of the Civil War* (New York, 1999), 64, 66, 67, 68. Although Whigs rallied primarily from 1833 to 1835 in opposition to executive power, the underlying issue had to do with President Jackson's assertion of executive power regarding the scope of government and specifically his destruction of the national bank (23–34). See also Shade, *Democratizing the Old Dominion*, 189–90.

62. Elizabeth R. Varon, *We Mean to Be Counted: White Women and Politics in Antebellum Virginia* (Chapel Hill, N.C., 1998); Rebecca Edwards, *Angels in the Machinery: Gender in American Party Politics from the Civil War to the Progressive Era* (New York, 1997), 17; Stephanie McCurry, *Masters of Small Worlds: Yeoman Households, Gender Relations, and the Political Culture of the Antebellum South Carolina Low Country* (New York, 1995); Ronald P. Formisano, "The 'Party Period' Revisited," *Journal of American History* 86 (June 1999): 144, 147, 149.

63. Steven D. Minicucci, "Internal Improvements and the Union, 1790–1860" (paper presented at the American Political Science Association annual meeting, Atlanta, September 1–4, 1999), 27, 29, 30; Shallat, *Structures in the Stream*, 153. Besides the desire of leaders not to offend key partners in the Old South, Minicucci stresses equally that the party "had yet to master the use of particularistic benefits as a party-building tool" (29). For a parallel analysis of the impact of southern elites on the formation of national welfare policy in the twentieth century, see Russell L. Hanson, "Liberalism and the Course of American Social Welfare Policy," in Dodd and Jillson, *The Dynamics of American Politics*, 132–59; Jill S. Quadugno, *The Transformation of Old Age Security* (Chicago, 1988).

64. The Early Democratization Project at the American Antiquarian Society contains the most complete set of election returns for the early Republic.

65. See Richard R. John, *Spreading the News: The American Postal System from Franklin to Morse* (Cambridge, Mass., 1995), 206, 4–5, 15, 37, 53, 56, regarding the transformation of the system into a patronage engine. The last quotation is from Shefter, *Political Parties and the State*, 14. After the Civil War, the state began to claim some government jobs for a merit-based civil service, ironically through the very dynamic of party alternation in power that had expanded the spoils system in the first place. Ari Hoogenboom, *Outlawing the Spoils, 1865–1883* (Westport, Conn., 1963). The expansion of government jobs, however, meant little or no proportional decrease in offices controlled by parties until later. An 1842 congressional report deploring the effects of party patronage practices but confessing an inability to devise an acceptable remedy sounds eerily similar to complaints about the campaign finance system today; regarding the 1842 report, see McCormick, *Presidential Game*, 204–5.

66. Samuel Watson, "United States Army Officers Fight the 'Patriot War': Responses to Filibustering on the Canadian Border, 1837–1839," *Journal of the Early Republic* 18 (fall 1998): 519.

67. Forest G. Hill, *Roads, Rails, and Waterways: The Army Engineers and Early Trans-portation* (Norman, Okla., 1957). According to Hill, the General Survey Act of 1824 was "an effort to institute national planning of a system of internal improvements" (37). Military armories, of course, played an important role in the development of mass production. Merritt Roe Smith, *Harpers Ferry Armory and the New Technology: The Challenge of Change* (Ithaca, N.Y., 1977). Shallat, *Structures in the Stream*, conveys the sense that any partisan debates over the Corps of Engineers were really about the role and scope of government power.
68. Freemasons claimed that they were nonpartisan, but in any case they were highly political. Steven C. Bullock, *Revolutionary Brotherhoods, Freemasony, and the Transformation of the American Social Order, 1730–1840* (Chapel Hill, N.C., 1996), 220–38; Formisano, "The 'Party Period' Revisited," 93–120.
69. Wilbur Zelinsky, *Nation into State: The Shifting Symbolic Foundations of American Nationalism* (Chapel Hill, N.C., 1988), 19.

2. The Nationalization and Racialization of American Politics

Before, Beneath, and Between Parties, 1790–1840

David Waldstreicher

R ecent scholarship on the early United States depicts the emergence, by 1800, of a national popular political culture in a distinctly partisan and participatory mode. In this work, the polity of the early Republic appears less as a holding ground for "deference" or a premodern set of priorities than as a seedbed for the modern "democracy" that emerged in full force during the Jacksonian era. Some go even further, arguing that emerging Federalist and Jeffersonian parties actually shut down some of the more participatory, and thus democratic, aspects of revolutionary and postrevolutionary politics.[1]

Such arguments do not mesh well with an earlier scholarly consensus that equated democracy with mass political parties and dated both developments decades later, during the 1820s and 1830s. The result is that we now have two stories about democratization. That American historians do not even notice that parallel stories of democratization are being told about both eras suggests the continuing power of the traditional narrative, which divides political history—and U.S. history generally—at about 1815 or 1820.[2]

Two larger interpretive modes make it difficult, even illogical, to conceive of 1790 to 1840 as a coherent political era. One is a "new political history" focused on the development of party systems or formations. The other is a new social and cultural history devoted to the invention and struggles of social groups. Not at all mutually exclusive, political and sociocultural histories written since the 1970s have deepened our understanding of particular locales, group formation of all kinds, and everyday life in public and private. The focus on parties, locales, and groups, however, has limited the comprehension of national politics. Even while artfully triangulating the story of class, ethnic, religious, gendered, and even regional social formations in particular places, many scholars have left the story of national politics to others, sometimes while continuing to accept the periodizations set by national politics.[3]

Nationalization and Racialization as Organizing Concepts

The neglect of national politics—of narratives that connect social trends to political change on extended, variable, and interlocking scales in terms of space and in a sustained manner in terms of time—has also led to a striking divorce of structure from substance in political history. The resulting gap has been filled largely by political scientists and legal scholars, who have learned to devour sophisticated social and cultural histories as the new raw materials not only for theorizing and model building about American politics but also for the kinds of historical analysis that can make sense of extended periods. Many of these important studies look specifically to law, to the state, or to particular political institutions as structures that exist in dialectical relationship to policy, or to the substance of politics.

Drawing inspiration from this "new institutionalism," Richard R. John has argued that federal state-building during the first decades after ratification of the Constitution actually set the stage for the rise of "mass parties" during the Jacksonian era.[4] Such a possibility alters the periodization of change; it may also transform the very basis of a political history centered around the rise of parties. Too often, the rise of a two-party system has been assumed to be the summum bonum of "political development" in America. That narrative of party formation, particularly of the rise of a mature second party system, will always reduce the earlier Republic (1789–1815) into a mere prologue to the "party period," separating that era from both the revolutionary experience that informed it and the great democratization that supposedly followed.[5]

This, I believe, is the story and emphasis needing correction. What if, instead of beginning with what was, we have learned, not (yet) there—a fully developed two-party "system" or partisan "political era"—we focused on what was there and how it shaped subsequent developments? Here I take inspiration from a series of works that see race and racial formation at the center of American political and social development.[6] Historians Alexander Saxton, William W. Freehling, John Ashworth, Eric Foner, Robert P. Forbes, and Matthew Jacobson, along with political scientists Michael Goldfield, Rogers M. Smith, and Paul Frymer, have begun the process of reinterpreting racial conflict as not merely a crucial content or substance of American political history but a key structuring factor, a "mainspring" of American politics, in Goldfield's words.[7] Such a perspective issues a potent challenge to explanations of early U.S. political history that do not consider blacks and Indians to be subjects of political history when they were not voting citizens.

National politics was always more than elections, and it always mattered deeply to slaves, free blacks, natives, and other ordinary people, no matter how many of them voted or expressed deep loyalty to a party. Moreover, the actions, as well as the status, of slaves, free blacks, natives, and racially marked immigrants regularly drew the attention of citizens and became a fulcrum of partisan identity formation.[8] National politics emerged from the American Revolution and was given its outlines by the Constitution in a specific era of continuing imperial (which is to say, colonial and postcolonial) conflict. Because questions of

race and nationality, in the form of Indian wars, forced and voluntary migra-
tions, slavery and abolition, and diasporic politics, were extralocal and ultimately imperial or postcolonial questions, such a perspective reminds us that
the new political history's focus on parties in states and counties can obscure as
much about American politics as it reveals.

In order to describe more accurately the national, international, and racial
substance of U.S. politics, I partially break with the tradition of defining party
structures and ideologies as the substance of political culture and instead stress
that the emergence of particular cultural forms—such as nationalist celebrations,
presidential styles, and minstrelsy—can tell us just as much about American
politics. National cultural forms assumed special importance in this era of expansion and migration. Moreover, party (or, more broadly, political group) formation arose in tandem with extrapartisan activity in the streets of the new nation, especially during the crucial decades of mass politicization, the 1790s and
the 1830s. Only by conceiving of early U.S. politics as truly federal, even as cosmopolitan—as a dialectic of the local, the state, the national, as well as the international—can the complex relationship between evolving substance and al-
terations in party structure be grasped and given its due.

Understanding this dialectic requires a reassessment of the problem of American nationalism and a nationalistic political culture during the era of its initial
diffusion and elaboration.[9] Within a certain nationalist consensus, statesmen and
ordinary folk experimented with partisan structures and democratized their
public life and politics. The uncertain governmental future and literal geographic
shape of the nation compelled the attention of more and more people, encouraging successive attempts at coalition building. Nationalist, localist-regionalist,
and imperialist-expansionist visions reinforced one another, creating what I referred to elsewhere as a series of nationalist regionalisms, which were often
elaborately reasoned visions of federal union and the proper role of state and national governments.[10] Within each version of nationalism, enemies of union, republican government, and other legacies of the Revolution (such as both slavery and anti-slavery, peace and war with Indians) were repeatedly identified at
home and abroad.

Most importantly, the very question of who counted as a legitimate American subject continually reoccupied the center of political controversy, and the results of such struggles periodically altered the legal structures as well as the ideological substance of politics. Ultimately, the fights over nationalization and
democratization inspired extrapartisan activism even as the second party system came into being. By 1840, American politics stood ready to implode over
its greatest strengths, as race occupied the vital center of the greatest national
partisan campaign yet seen. Racialization presupposed nationalization. In important ways, racism proved to be democratic nationalism's crucial supplement,
only to emerge in the end as its Achilles' heel.[11]

Attending to the nationalization and racialization of American politics during the period under consideration thus helps explain the causes and outcomes of key political events, including the outbursts of violence—both wars and riots—that revealed the limits of partisanship as well as the ultimate ends of political action.[12] Positing a twinned process of political nationalization and racialization also provides a framework for understanding the collision of two mass parties with the proliferating groups of activists who looked outside the system for redress.[13] Nationalization and racialization laid the ground beneath the mediating activities of parties, set the context for the emergence of new parties, and provided core meanings for the battles between them.

Postcolonialism: The Coming of a National Politics

The new nation could not have been imagined as a relatively expansive and federal union had it not been for the British imperial nationalism the colonists first embraced and then, deciding that they were unequal members, used to invent the first postcolonial nation. In the process, Americans experimented profoundly with forms of government on the local and federal levels, especially during the late 1770s and 1780s. But this experimentation with forms, and the theoretical as well as practical changes it signaled, has so absorbed our attention that we have neglected the continuing postcolonial, and simultaneously imperial, substance of early U.S. politics.[14]

The unsettled nature of early politics from the revolutionary era through the 1830s is evident in the periodic and structural violence that marked this political order: skirmishes with the natives, contests on the high seas, slave rebellions, and rural as well as urban riots. American politics remained imperial precisely to the extent that it revolved around at least the partial integration of far-flung, generally subject peoples in an Atlantic economy—integrations that were predicated on slave trading, settler skirmishes with natives, and the triangular wars for the North American empire.[15] Battles over the status of the formerly and presently enslaved that rocked the public sphere in the 1830s should be seen as more unfinished postcolonial business.

During the Atlantic phase of early American politics, successful battles for empire provided the occasion and the template for reinventing, and then enlarging, the colonies as a federal republic. In each of these conflicts from the Seven Years' War to the War of 1812, Native Americans were major participants whose victories and defeats allowed for further expansion into the interior—expansion that set the stage for the next imperial war. Although some Americans such as Benjamin Franklin had come to wish that the United States would be an empire with a difference, eradicating slavery and treating the Indians fairly if firmly, the very nature of the national revolution and the war for independence as imperial ventures reinforced fears of republican decline and acted as a catalyst to strengthen the national government as well as a pattern of more committed, organized attention to national politics.

The new nation's "crisis of integration," then, followed from that of the British Empire, permitting grand dreams of continental domination, but also the characteristically imperial problem of rival empires and (unequal) domestic subjects such as Indians, slaves, and white inhabitants of the politically unorganized frontiers.[16] In this respect, the partial elimination of slavery in the North during this period emerged as a profound problem, insofar as it made certain kinds of agreement over population and economy—the first requirements of empire—virtually impossible, as the ambiguities of the Constitution on this question make apparent. Deep disagreement emerged in the first Federal Congress over even discussing the issue of slavery, with lower-south representatives sounding much like their fire-eating progeny some two generations later, seizing upon localism to begin, however tentatively, a states' rights tradition.

Men of the middle states—including Virginia—emerged as the swing voters in this geopolitics, sympathetic to slavery's gradual termination but unwilling to risk a fragile union for this kind of progress.[17] Such developments look like more than a sidebar—an unfortunate problem or paradox in the development of a liberal political tradition—in the wake of recent studies that demonstrate how important the threat of slave uprisings had been in getting Virginia and South Carolina to join the Revolution in the first place.[18]

Similarly, Indian wars, including a wave of efforts by tribes at creating their own relatively far-flung unions, contributed to an emerging East-versus-West axis of politics in those states that stretched outward from the seaboard so rapidly from the 1750s. It is easy to forget that the first time American armed forces mobilized after the Constitution, they marched westward not just to pacify war-making natives but also to pacify frontiersmen angry about taxes and their lack of protection against said Indians by the federal government. The Madisonian theory of federal union sought to evade such characteristic imperial problems, problems that the British imperial government had tried but failed to solve with limitations on the slave trade and westward migration.

For all its departures, the new U.S. politics would be deeply shaped by the same limitation that had doomed Anglo-American empire: its difficulty in attaching "excluded and dominated groups to the polity," whether violently or constitutionally.[19] Most of all, however, American national politics remained Atlantic and "neocolonial" in orientation because of crucial continuities in the economy. British "dumping" of manufactured goods in the immediate aftermath of independence only served as the first reminder that the postcolonial situation often has much in common with the colonial one. Americans relied on British markets for their goods and British suppliers for the materials of life. How to deal with this situation provoked divisions within the Washington administration and ultimately laid the groundwork for the emergence of the Democratic-Republican opposition.

Too often, this course of events is seen as a primitive way of organizing a supposedly inevitable two-party system. Politics began amid the machinations of statesmen, we are told, and around questions of foreign policy, as if these were unnatural, even infertile grounds for the development of a healthy (read mass-party) polity. Yet popular politics has begun in precisely this way in most new nations. Linda Colley and Kathleen Wilson stress the key role of foreign affairs in mobilizing ordinary people to think of themselves as Britons—and to act politically—in the mid-to-late eighteenth century.[20] This active (if often reactive) interest in national affairs joined traditional popular culture to innovative material and political conditions.

Foreign affairs mattered deeply in the lives of ordinary people in an era when trade wars, real wars, piracy, embargoes, and the like could make or ruin merchants' fortunes, alter the demands for crops, and create or eliminate work for artisans. Thus the American Revolution combined popular dissent arising from local conditions with abstract discussions of English (now British) rights. Because the nation itself emerged from such conflicts, postrevolutionary Americans had good reason to fear for the future of the Republic, given the difficulties of an American political economy in the midst of the next, Napoleonic wave of the wars for empire.

This dynamic of local, regional, and national interest in international politics seemed more rational when wars in Europe created flush times for those most tied to the mercantile economy in the 1790s. The re-export trade that allowed the seaport cities to flourish once again was a distinct product of warfare on the European continent and the high seas. It depended on recognition of American neutrality and thus was threatened by the very conditions that created its possibility. As a result, the Adams administration would find itself at the brink of war, Jefferson would create a cold war known as the embargo, and Madison would replay the War of Independence against England, with less successful results. At least until these conditions changed, Americans north and south had every reason to conflate international and domestic politics.

When we consider how much warfare and international political economy has continued to shape the structure of American politics, we probably ought to pause before calling the party system of the early Republic primitive or a "failure."[21] Such a developmental fallacy haunts even the most subtle accounts of "the transformation of political culture" in the early Republic, and it has prevented us from fully appreciating how foreign affairs helped nationalize a diverse and dispersed citizenry and created two-party politics in a particular mode. While crediting the first party system with advancing "national integration," the first wave of political development scholarship did not sufficiently account for the texture of that integration and its deeply politicized nature. The link here was not only political economy but also the issue of participation itself in the wake of a republican revolution.

The American Revolution energized a citizenry to object to its second-class status in the empire, leading to other challenges to deference and, often, to more inclusive approaches to politics in the states and towns of the new nation. Similar processes were at work elsewhere during the age of democratic revolutions. In a secondary development, failed and successful revolts in Europe and Great Britain propelled numerous exiles to America, where they further cosmopolitanized political discourse. In short, domestic issues concerning the nature and identity of virtuous leaders, the extent and styles of political participation, and, in some urban centers, the cultural politics of class dovetailed with different visions of cosmopolitanism, Enlightenment, and foreign policy vis-à-vis the contending nations of England and France.[22]

Anglophile and Francophile political styles further enabled politics to have a deep and everyday cultural dimension, as everything from dress to the songs sung in taverns came to be politicized. Recent scholarship stresses the extra-electoral nature of popular politics during the 1790s, a politics that nonvoters—including women—could participate in as easily as they could read a banner or hear an oration. As during the Revolution, the press emerged as a key link between the politics of the street and the politics of statesmen and the metropole. National politics during the 1790s consisted of a desire for unity amid periodic bursts of popular participation, bursts of interest that brought people to meetings and celebrations, produced manifestos and toasts for the newspapers, and seemed utterly appropriate to the crisis-paced nature of foreign affairs (and may even have engendered more regular and sustained participation than today's focus on biennial national elections).

The Democratic-Republican societies pushed the envelope by actually organizing in local groups while addressing the nation in print, only to be successfully attacked by the Federalists as an *imperium in imperio* that had not only illegally interfered with French ambassador Edmond-Charles Genet's mission but also seemed to inspire, interestingly, a frontier rebellion. The seeming paranoia of the Washington administration in 1795, prefiguring the national crackdown on dissent three years later, makes sense only if we can appreciate the metastasizing symbols of corruption and liberation amid mass migration, a hot-house re-export economy, and foreign revolution.

For the time being, at least, partisanship, whether in favor of the administration or against it, could be justified in the name of local and international necessities. The pattern of crisis on the frontier and the Atlantic waters, and the circulation of news through eastern seaports vitally connected to Europe, meant that internationally oriented parties made more sense than any state or national election–centered two-party system could have. Parties were not intended to have a life of their own. They were expedients to ensure that the nation would have such a life and could be seen as noble precisely insofar as, like the Revolution itself, they were demonstrably supported by the people in the present.[23]

Cultural Forms as National Celebration

The quintessential cultural form in this political universe was the partisan nationalist celebration. Occasional yet adaptable, referring to international and national events (and often explicitly to episodes of violence, such as the anniversaries of battles), the political festival with its parade, oration, and toasts allowed particular ends to be pursued in the context of calls for national unity. It allowed any number of binary oppositions to be expressed in terms of what was celebrated and associated with the glorious Revolution and what was attacked and associated with British (or racial) others. Its printed dimension enabled the celebrations to have extralocal reach, where they could be experienced vicariously and even interpreted variously as part of the process of gauging political similarity and difference across growing expanses of space.

The partisan festivity of the early Republic was a synthesis of various devices that allowed Americans to have their partisanship and their anti-partisanship, their deference and their participation at the same time. It also created a very particular space for women's participation, as ratifiers of putative consensus—or in other words, nonpartisan patriots, as opposed to politicians.[24] Anti-partyism, then, did not so much characterize the politics of the early Republic as it revealed continuities in the dialectical relationship between parties and the other entities that might or might not be identified with them: nationalism, regionalism, the federal government, foreign countries, and social movements. It helped tremendously that any party could simultaneously constitute itself in alliance with or opposition to both a state and a federal regime, while both the Federalists and the Jeffersonian opposition clearly stood for different foreign policies and a different attitude toward popular participation in politics itself.

Democratic-Republicans made spectacular gains in response to the Federalists' repressive excesses of 1798–1799, and for the first time, the different seasonalities of local, state, and presidential elections began regularly to refer to one another, making each demonstrably more partisan. In most states after 1800, parties wholeheartedly accepted the label of party as part of a process of organizing for state elections. A rhetoric of renewed peaceable "revolution" justified the regime change that brought Thomas Jefferson to the presidency, which is rightfully called the first critical election in American history. Although the moment of polarization differed from state to state, the trend for the years around 1800 was the innovative linkage of local and national elections, as Federalists and Republicans alike experimented with alliance or opposition at two levels of government.[25]

Federalists, as in so many other cases, had set the pattern by identifying their often surprisingly tight networks of influence with the government itself, actively employing the state, whether through treasury measures or the use of the army in the Old Northwest, to bind men of influence to the administration. Yet the very creativity of the ruling coalition in creating extralocal networks played into the identification of the Democratic-Republicans with the "real" people, the new men of the Enlightenment who had only their own virtues to stand on—whether an urban artisan escaping apprenticeship, a struggling farmer, or a planter desperately seeking to avoid debts to (British) merchants. The Democratic-Republican dictum that ordinary people deserved a greater and more regular role in politics could also mean different things in different places, for who counted as "the people" could only be determined locally.

The polarization of Federalist versus Republican did not always line up in the same ways when it came to state issues, though the two groups often reflected class and intrastate regional differences, with newly mobile men and workers generally favoring the "democrats" and well-connected persons continuing to make their "interest" with the Federalists. The class politics of Federalism was muted by an ability to claim the "revolutionary center" through their nationalism and pro-trade policies. Meanwhile, the venue for dissent provided by the Democratic-Republican movement sped significant democratization even in those states with the most entrenched oligarchic and deferential patterns. South Carolina enfranchised more of its frontiersmen in 1808; Connecticut, its Federalist establishment staunchly defended by an elaborate church-state alliance, finally eliminated its intimidating voting rules a decade later.[26]

The despair of Federalists who were out of power nationally after 1800, their laments for the end of their golden age, should not obscure the regularization of partisan conflict. Nor should it distract us from the real, if temporary, successes of their opposition at moments of crisis in the internationally driven political economy, such as the embargo and the War of 1812. Although some elite Federalists engaged in a creative withdrawal from politics, much of their rhetoric of decline was actually a protest, a justification for dissent and creative opposition. As much as at any subsequent time, there were two bitterly opposed, nationally oriented parties in America—if not a "system"—and every matter of national political import had partisan resonances and could be played on as part of a strategy of electoral ambition.

This is a point of no small import, because the stress on the emergence of a more fully integrated, institutionalized "system" during the 1830s has led scholars to underestimate how crucial the legacy of the Revolution had been in solidifying an Atlantic American political culture, whose dominant logic demanded both binary oppositions and a kind of anti-partisanship that justified partisan activity in the name of national survival. The dualistic or binary political vision of opposition, the "country" mentality of the old and the revolutionary Whigs, proved infinitely malleable because of the multiple ways decline could be recognized and denounced in the state, in the capital, on the frontier, and abroad. The structure of politics at the accession of Jefferson, then, relied on and promoted not just parties but also the crucial number of parties: two.

Two parties triangulated three regions, two foreign powers, and two levels of government—state and national. The flexibility required by this system made mediating and nonpartisan gestures not just an ideological preference but a practical necessity if national coalitions were to be rendered at least marginally workable. Such gestures worked best during Jefferson's first term, when the South and the West successfully isolated seaboard New England and enthusiastically embraced the Jeffersonian paradox of limited government activism except where it concerned further expansion into the interior. Yet Jefferson's attempt to limit government while trying to get out of the Atlantic conundrum polarized national politics again during his second term and put the nation on the road to another divisive war with England. Indeed, Jefferson's attempt to escape from Atlantic politics, by limiting the Atlantic commerce he had hoped to free, only ratified the primacy of foreign policy and international political economy in national politics.

Thus the "neocolonial" eastward gaze across the ocean continued to dominate during his and his successor's presidencies. The Jeffersonian legacy lies in the association of democracy and individual self-sufficiency with the escape from entanglements with Europe.[27] Seeing Europe, especially England, as the cause of corruption, weakness, and aristocracy in American politics enabled Jefferson to lead an uneasy coalition of plebeians, slaveholders, and land-hungry settlers, each of whom had some reason to deny the Atlantic connections that had brought them to be where, and who, they were.

Jefferson's successes and limitations also show us the role of a distinct and formative kind of presidency, a "first American presidency" that at once energized successive oppositional coalitions and forestalled the need for lasting political parties. The presidency in the early United States had profound differences from later models, yet it set a strong template for the future of the institution. The model, inarguably, was the British monarchy, a crucial institutional rallying point in an age of empire and a continuing focus of dissent for those who felt that a particular region or class had been systematically oppressed. George Washington set the monarchical tone by insisting that he was above party and by seeking to personify nationalist consensus and the federal government itself. Yet the presidents from Washington through Madison were hardly above party. Their actions gave parties a reason for being and for continuing to exist.

Mobilization of opposition through abuse of the chief executive led each president to identify the opposition as a national menace and encouraged each to take the country to the brink of war in part in an effort to crush that opposition. Thus was born the American pattern of presidents energetically pursuing war abroad or in frontier territories to unify the fractious polity at home. This strategy, so apparent in recent times, dates back to the early years of the Republic. Washington leading the charge against the whiskey rebels, Adams dressing up in military garb during the naval quasi-war of 1797–1799, and Madison gleefully embracing the War of 1812 demonstrate the pattern. The confusion that resulted from Adams's reversion to peacemaking in 1799 is the exception that proves the rule, for in doing so, he sought to undercut a faction within his own party that had turned out to be at least as dangerous to his administration as the Jeffersonians.[28]

Presidents, then, were the high priests of partisan anti-partisanship and of unifying, state-sponsored violence in the early Republic. A partial return to the "presidential synthesis" of American history helps illuminate important aspects of political structure in this regard. In a constitutional order predicated on ease of rotation in office, "the power to recreate order hinges on the authority to repudiate it." Thus the presidency institutionalized the logic of republican politics, in which affirmation and purgation of representatives and representative institutions continue in an endless cycle. If the presidency is at the pinnacle of such a political culture, standing for both the highest virtues and the successful cleansing of the corrupt "court," it is little wonder that, as Stephen Skowronek argues, presidents find it easier to negate than to further "articulate" the political and policy achievements of their predecessors.

Skowronek goes so far as to argue that coalitions and party systems in American politics change because of presidential change, and his case rests persuasively on the foundational power shifts of the early Republic.[29] It is a truism too often ignored by "party system" scholarship that in both the first and second party systems, truly national parties solidified only around successful presidential candidates. Jefferson ostentatiously refused to embrace the trappings of power and seemingly called for an end to party distinctions. But what he really did was to ratify the process of making partisan gestures, however subtle, a patrician, republican, nationalist, executive duty.

Some of the most successful two-term presidents find creative ways of contradicting their own negative, galvanizing, and polarizing gestures (or, in the case of Madison and Monroe, those of their sympathetic predecessors), thus saving the country from the potentially disruptive effects of putting into practice their own rhetorical revolutions. In such a light, we are in a better position to understand a key fact of early national politics: why the four Virginia presidents led more successfully than the two New Englanders, despite the brilliance and experience of John and John Quincy Adams. For the most part, Washington, Jefferson, Madison, and Monroe proved better able to negotiate the desire for expansion and empire and the threat of neighbors and Indians at the borders and of slave rebellions in the midst of the Republic.

Yet these Virginian national heroes, for all their revolutionary and constitutional credentials, also anticipated most clearly the president as party leader, far more so than the republican (nonpartisan) literalists John and John Quincy Adams. As national leaders hailing from New England, it is not surprising that the latter two presidents ran afoul of geopolitical and racial issues. But because of their own robust nationalism, both Adamses also put the skids on the convergence of partisanship and New England regional nationalisms that had roiled national politics, only to be jousted out of office when, in 1800 and 1828, national parties birthed themselves in the aura of a (southern) populist opposition candidate.

The seeming decline of coherent party identities after the War of 1812 can be traced not just to the discrediting of "disloyal" Federalism (the war and especially the Madison administration were not that popular) but also to the problem of presidential succession and the fanning of sectional politics after 1816, both of which were predictable results of successful expansion and associated frontier and Atlantic warfare. The culmination of national politics in its Atlantic vein—the conflations of party, region, and nation so evident on the home front during the multifront War of 1812—also spelled its end: perhaps not so much the failure of an Atlantic national politics as the price of its success.

Racialization: The Rise of Continental Politics

The war ratified some of the main principles of the Jeffersonian Republicans, as they moved toward acceptance of a more active role for government. It also turned westerners, who had threatened at times to perform the American Revolution all over again, into textbook partisan patriots. Their Indian hating and fighting became a mark of political virtue. Moreover, the war reinforced the embattled partisan nationalisms of both the Federalists and the Democratic-Republican minority in New England. Likewise, the discrediting of the Federalists as a disloyal fifth column was an experience that actually watered the seeds of distrust in southern- and western-led majorities on the part of New Englanders.

The neglected significance of New England Federalism, however, may lie less in its resort to states' rights or anti-government arguments, both of which were being kept alive by dissenting southern Old Republicans, than in these Federalists' persistent resort to the race issue: their insistence that Jeffersonians wanted a republic of slaves and slaveholders and their contention that Jeffersonian rule would, paradoxically but actually, strengthen both slavery and blacks themselves. This was another development from the early Republic that set the pattern for the later nineteenth century.

New England Federalists, shocked by their weakness in national councils, rightly pointed out how much power they had lost because of the three-fifths clause. This new appreciation of unequal representation dovetailed with an earlier tradition of associating the black presence in the streets with the rabble, the uninformed multitude that many Federalists still wanted to empower, but only as long as they ratified the decisions of their gentry leaders. Indeed, the Federalist pursuit of regional and class politics in racial terms shows key continuities from the revolutionary era, when Tories reviled American Whigs as a multiracial rabble. Revealingly, even New England populist patriots like Samuel Adams had blasted the king for freeing the slaves of rebels, while keeping mum about the black presence in northern street protests.

Though they hardly embraced black equality or citizenship, New England Federalists challenged the expansion of slavery and published satirical exposés of the hypocrisy of pro-slavery Jeffersonian democracy, relentlessly nationalizing an issue that might otherwise have remained local and regional. Whether blaming slave revolts in Virginia on the influence of the French Revolution or showing what appeared to southerners to be an alarming sympathy for newly independent Haiti, Federalists learned how to play the race card—to relate the question of rights for African Americans to other, primary issues of national politics.

As with the Alien and Sedition Acts, the Federalist embrace of "ascriptive Americanism" had its roots in political struggles and called for a compensatory response by their opponents.[30] And in fact, a number of southern political leaders and writers began to develop a sense of specific sectional identity and sought common cause with westward-moving settlers, in defense of white prerogatives. Spurred in large measure by partisan competition, the Jeffersonians built on the foundations laid by Jefferson himself in developing modern scientific and nationalistic varieties of racism. Meanwhile, in the states, whenever anyone brought up the possibility of free blacks' voting or of emancipation, the other party gleefully seized the opportunity to racialize their opponents as friends to blacks.

Given the emergence of the race card as a dynamic in state and federal politics, it is perhaps surprising that emancipation proceeded in the northern states, albeit gradually—a testimony to the truly unsettling results of the American Revolution, which decisively freed a substantial number of African Americans and laid the foundations for free black communities up and down the eastern seaboard.[31] It may have helped that emancipation laws were passed before partisanship became institutionalized, and the race card nationalized, in the revolution of 1800. By the 1810s, these free black communities had begun to agitate against slavery and for their rights.

Ultimately, the uses of the race card would multiply because the actions of African Americans and their allies began to shift into a new, more radical phase, even while slavery's economic power in the nation grew exponentially. It is little wonder that Virginians and other national statesmen from the upper South and the mid Atlantic took the lead in proposing the colonization of free blacks and their relocation as an American colony in Africa or on a frontier cleared of hostile natives.[32] The idea of "removal" had first emerged, and would be more successfully pursued, as a solution to the Indian problem. Nonetheless, the creation of the American Colonization Society in the wake of the War of 1812 reveals precisely how imperial, and Atlantic, American politics remained.

The final "neocolonial" struggle—the "last tournament," as Robert H. Wiebe called the War of 1812—ended, in telling fashion, with victories not on the Atlantic seaboard but in the far-away Northwest and Southwest. Yet if the quarter century that followed spelled the beginning of a newly continental political order, it was one with its roots in the past. Andrew Jackson and William Henry Harrison, the war's two most celebrated slaughterers of Britons and Indians, became the party standard-bearers who would, with victories in presidential contests, usher in each of the new so-called permanent mass parties. The decisiveness of the War of 1812, moreover, had more to do with the high-stakes game of domestic politics and events on the eastern Atlantic front than with any actual gains made in western battles.

The end of the French and the decline of the Spanish empires in North America made England less dangerous and more tractable. If, in the end, the United States still found itself constrained by British capital and by British overseas ambitions, the constraints seemed suddenly enabling and quite compatible with national honor and with at least one party's political record. In this light, the broad (to some historians, incoherent) "National Republican" coalition that moved under Monroe to develop a set of postwar policies can be seen as intending to make good on the Jeffersonian promise to take the United States out of Atlantic politics and into a new continental politics.

Some former Federalists joined less nervous Republicans such as Henry Clay and John C. Calhoun to think creatively about transportation and other ways of binding the nation together with institutions. In the short term, they were aided by a groundswell of creativity at the state level, the end result of a politics of development (the preconditions for a "market revolution") that had factionalized politics in the states for some time. For national statesmen in Congress, nationalism, in the guise of federally sponsored market development and defense, would provide the glue that would put the pieces of factionalized state politics back together. With divisiveness blamed on the Federalists, even innovative governmental programs could be cast as Jeffersonian, whatever their actual origins.

But the national politics of development proved easier in the abstract than in the concrete, for its concrete manifestations opened various cans of worms. There were controversies over banking policy, especially after the boom and bust in land speculation wrapped up in the panic of 1819. There were controversies over tariffs and taxation, as different interests would be served by different schemes of paying for internal improvements. There were, of course, controversies over the problem of slavery in the newly developed states.

The rising importance of state politics would be reflected in the reemergence of states' rights arguments in the mid-1820s and in the general debate about the meaning of federal union. The "Monrovian" interlude, as Robert P. Forbes has named the period from 1816 to 1828, might best be considered as the moment when rapid, intertwined economic and territorial development took political culture beyond the old partisan-nationalist logics, relocating the traditional nationalist commitment away from the Atlantic and along a spectrum of attitudes toward union and the risks to union. The sources of risk were changing, but their nature remained rooted in political economy. They remained structural in the sense that every solution to the problem of drift and uneven partisanship threatened to cause a structural, even constitutional, crisis.[33]

In such a context, it seems reasonable to wonder whether "incomplete" is the right way to describe a national (and nationalist) politics that quite rationally avoided, when it did not seek to transcend through new institution building, the local and sectional economic issues that did not have easy national solutions. Although the rise of Jackson may indeed be traceable to the triumph of democratic electoral procedures and of universal white male suffrage in the states, the measures he pursued to solidify a Democratic coalition under his leadership— Indian removal, anti-nullification, the bank war, the castigation of abolitionism, and "cultural" legislation generally—no longer seem inherently progressive, democratic, or modern. His administration mainly reinforced the trends associated with his election in the first place: the triumph of the presidency over the legislative branch; the southern-western alliance in favor of populist expansion; and ultimately the revival of two-party competition, as the Whigs coalesced in classic republican style against "King Andrew," his court, and his handpicked successor, Martin Van Buren.[34]

The landscape of politics did look different in 1830 (and 1836) than it had in 1816. Presidents emerged as party leaders once again instead of transcenders of party, and American politics began to take on systematic, vertically integrated attributes, with parties structuring binary opposition from top to bottom. Whigs and Democrats developed utterly different worldviews and policies, giving voters ample choice. Economic and "ethnocultural" issues then worked in tandem, except when the slavery issue occasionally—and, in the end, finally—sounded the death knell for a stable, healthy, national politics.

Or so the story is usually told. That version, however, celebrates as positive and inevitable the very outcome that party managers, particularly Democrats, advanced in justifying themselves. It ignores the continuance of anti-partisanship in new (partisan) forms. It underestimates the stresses in the system and the difficulty both parties had in continually differentiating themselves.[35] If this was a polity that lurched from ethnocultural to economic issues, it is because the opportunities of regime change and cultural politics did not offer themselves with sufficient regularity to save the parties from the complex issues of economic development.[36] Most of all, the "second party system" synthesis minimizes the increasing salience of race issues as Americans turned westward. The program of continental development, with the combined effects of the long revolutionary settlement, spelled a racialization of American politics that structured the rise of the two-party system itself. As a result, we need a more encompassing rubric for understanding the politics of the 1820s and 1830s than the second party system.

The Inexorable Spread of Racial Issues

The Missouri Compromise settled the difference between slave and nonslave states and imposed its geography of 36°30' on the incoming group of states. The controversies of 1819–1821 did even more, however, in bringing out the difference between northern and upper-southern assumptions regarding gradual if "conditional" emancipation, the possibility of free blacks' rights, and a lower-southern vision of expansion through slavery (and slavery through expansion). With the battle for middle-state votes in Congress, American national politics for the next four decades would be in danger of turning into a sectional politics, with the West as both the subject of debate and the location of the other swing votes.

It is this bogeyman, of course, that the "second party system" historians, like their Van Burenite counterparts in the 1830s and 1840s, see as the tragic consequence of a loss of coherence in the party system. Forbes takes a quantum leap in this regard by reinterpreting the Missouri Compromise and its aftermath as the seeding ground of the Democratic Party and ultimately of a new two-party system predicated on the status quo with respect to slavery: "the defense of slavery, in short, constituted the most important reason for the creation of the Second Party System." Van Buren seized on the political potential of a "solid south" that emerged from the sectional polarization, championing the idea of a negative state and opening the door for the reassertion of states' rights as a guiding principle of union.[37]

Jackson, and former National Republicans such as Clay and Daniel Webster, replied that union itself should ultimately come first. But the difference between unionist and states' rights perspectives in the budding era of "nullification" should not obscure the larger bipartisan consensus that the problem of slavery, and of free blacks' rights, should not be allowed to factionalize national politics along racial or sectional lines. The fact that these statesmen were so regularly frustrated suggests that racial politics was becoming unavoidable because of real social and political developments that the party system could not easily contain. The Missouri crisis might have been just an episode had it not been for other events of the late 1810s and 1820s: slave rebellions; controversies over the real and imagined activities of black sailors in southern ports, resulting in a Supreme

Court case over laws passed to sequester these American citizens in jail when their ships came in; and the first blowups over abolitionists such as David Walker and their printed productions.

The missing link, then, in understanding the racialization of American politics after the War of 1812 is the actions of blacks themselves, who, as Forbes insists, "could constitute a real political force." By 1827, northern free blacks had developed a stinging critique of the American political system. In the absence of the vote, free blacks engaged in pamphleteering, public celebrations, and other forms of written and oral protest to signal their community strength and their willingness to face up to white hostility on behalf of their own rights as well as those of the enslaved.[38] It is too often forgotten that the second, enabling Missouri Compromise of 1821 concerned the clauses prohibiting free black migration in the territory and guaranteeing the rights of masters to take their slaves with them into the free states. In effect, blacks were defined out of national citizenship by these provisions, a structural change (if a contested one) that "at once rendered slavery more racial and racism more national."[39] A related trend of the period explicitly denied blacks the vote in a number of new state constitutions.

Thus we can speak of the racialization of American politics in the 1820s in two senses. First, the racial proscriptions on citizenship became more formal, more official, and thus structural. Second, the subject of racial legislation, on the local and national levels, became one of the crucial substantive issues before politicians and the electorate. This political racialization set the context for the rise of scientific racism, and for the pro-slavery argument based on racial thinking, so evident during the 1820s and 1830s.[40] Racialized controversies, at least as much as other types of ethnocultural conflict, served as anvils for the reinvention of democratic politics and procedure at the grass roots.

Mary Hershberger has shown how Jackson's campaign for Indian removal spurred religiously based protests that "overwhelmed traditional forms of political participation." The national women's petition drive against removal "constituted the first time that women mobilized on a national political issue" and seems to have set the stage for the convention movements of the following decades and the nonpartisan benevolent associations women turned to as alternatives to party politics. Moreover, the possibility of mobilizing on behalf of others anticipated women's participation in the abolitionist movement, a development that falls partly outside the scope of this study but indicates the markedly politicizing possibilities of racialization. The convention movements of women and African Americans during the 1830s and 1840s constitute the best evidence that the limitations of the two-party system itself spurred the appropriation of nationalist political forms. Such appropriations, in turn, threatened to subvert the two-party system.[41]

Indeed, the manner in which the slavery and race question succeeded the Indian question in American political culture, and the ways in which both racializations of politics inspired the women's movement, demonstrates the continuing postcolonial tendency of Americans to ground so many aspects of their shared public life on what made America different from Europe. Regional conflicts over political economy—East versus West, North versus South—merged with conflicts over how to treat the natives, slaves, and free blacks in this period to such an extent that it is worth inquiring how the development of sectionalism on the anvil of race shaped actual differences in regional culture and ideology by the antebellum period. In other words, preexisting regional culture did not automatically produce the myths of sectional divergence. Rather, political battles provoked the creation of the myths at the center of sectionalism and its partisan variants, myths that had important racial and gender components.

According to the Jacksonian Democratic myth encouraged by the plantation elite and its northern allies, southern paternalist slaveholders treated their slaves better than northern manufacturers treated their workers. The corollary was that southerners made natural allies against "aristocrats," and blacks were not deserving of sympathy. Moreover, southern women, in myth if not in reality, belonged higher on the pedestal, supposedly for their own good, but also to cement an alliance of small farmers and plantation patriarchs east and west, north and south. Myths such as these became the stuff of politics in the 1830s, leaving sophisticated historians to piece out the shifting triangulations of race, class, region, and party identities that culminated in the war against the apparently mutually enslaving, terrorizing, and emasculating tendencies of the slave power and the abolitionist North.[42]

During this crucial period, when the myths of anti-capitalist, anti-aristocratic slaveholders and northern industrial "free labor" were taking shape, extrapartisan violence began to rock the nation. David Grimsted's study of antebellum rioting demonstrates a sectional pattern to violence that reveals real differences in the mores and practices of public life. Almost half the riots of 1835 were either pro-slavery or race affairs, but the southern ones revealed a pattern of complete mob control and violence against persons, which the civil authorities accepted. In that year of abolitionist mass mailings, southerners began to speak of anti-slavery activists as actual plotters of rebellion and demanded that northerners put them down. The resulting controversies over free speech and the right of assembly gave the abolitionists the issue with which they ultimately went mainstream: the problem of white rights affected by the culture and practice of slave mastery. It was the same issue that pro-slavery southerners saw as being at stake in giving the federal government the authority to legislate on questions of slavery.[43]

As Grimsted makes clear, the South was well on its way to becoming a police state, with slave patrols and an ever-growing slave code attempting to regularize, or minimize, the violence inherent in slavery. Yet the resurgence of rights issues on both sides, and the reality of violent conflicts on the streets and in the frontier, licensed a resurgence of republican nationalist gestures—including the demand that corruption and the abuse of law be cleansed from the body politic, by force if necessary. It is not that big a step from the Abraham Lincoln of the 1838 lyceum address, lambasting abolitionist and anti-abolitionist rioters and calling on his generation to preserve the founders' rule of law, to the Lincoln of 1861, calling on his fellow Americans to take up arms to preserve the republic that the slave power threatened. In the process, another onetime frontier brawler, Indian fighter, and party hack found in war a way to ennoble the party battle, unify Americans, and relive the Revolution.[44]

The period that began with debates over slavery that held up discussions of the structure of a federal government ended with the institutionalization of the gag rule. This structural prop, which tabled anti-slavery petitions whenever they were brought to Congress, denied the salience of the very race issues it forbade members of Congress to raise. But the discussion went on, thanks at least in part to the parliamentary legerdemain of the frustrated New England nationalist Representative John Quincy Adams, who insisted that the silencing of anti-slavery was the silencing of all citizens.

Adams was not so much rising above race as attempting to turn the tables back. A decade earlier, when his opponents wanted to discredit his National Republican pretensions during the election of 1828, they pointed to the satirical poems he had written about "Black Sal," Jefferson's lover, for the newspapers two decades before. Adams, as president, had tried to use gradual expansion and economic development to bind the nation together against the potentially divisive tendencies of Indian removal and slavery's extension. But his career— early, middle, and late—showed that nationalism did not save the nation from racial politics but actually provided the grounds for racism's articulation, politicization, and institutionalization.[45]

This can be seen in the seemingly least likely of places. One of the more unacknowledged aspects of the "log cabin" presidential campaign of 1840 was the prominence of the race issue. Traditionally, the campaign has been described in terms of the rise of a contentless, entertaining mass politics. More recently, historians have seen the key economic and ethnocultural issues of the second party system emerging in the election of 1840. But it is time we reassess the significance of the ways in which the Harrison campaign gave as good as it got on the race issue as well, calling Van Buren a closet abolitionist and a lover of blacks. In campaign newspapers such as the *Log Cabin Advocate,* Van Buren was portrayed as not only willing but eager to entertain a dialect-speaking black at his sumptuous table. Together they threatened to make all who did not follow them "Jump Jim Crow."[46]

Jim Crow, of course, referred to the minstrel show, that still-controversial and quintessentially American cultural form in which whites, dressed as blacks, commented on the differences made manifest by migration, travel, and the simultaneous existence of slavery and freedom for blacks in the same republic. The

Whigs who distanced themselves from Jim Crow and all it symbolized by chuck-
ling at this story conflated, in true minstrel fashion, blacks and those who
trucked with blackface. By 1840, after all, minstrelsy was associated with the
other party. At the same time, when Whigs performed black dialect to denounce
shape-shifting Democratic politicians, they ratified—by participating in—the
very racialization they attempted to blame on Van Buren.

Can it be an accident, then, that the first known blackface minstrel song,
"Backside Albany," dates from the politically transformative moment of 1815?
That it was "sung in the character of a black sailor" and took as its subject the
Battle of Plattsburgh, which it compares for its dunking of the British in Lake
Champlain to "a nudder tea party"—that moment when Atlantic rebels dressed
as Indians? Or that the original Jim Crow song, like other mainstays of the genre,
not only referenced the War of 1812 but also commented extensively on national
political events such as nullification?[47]

Sometimes the evidence for larger transformations in political culture are
right under our noses, if we refuse to be led away by the partisans who celebrated the two-party system in a desperate attempt to have a systematic national
politics devoid of race or the violence that racial domination required. It is a
mark of the racialization of American politics by the 1820s and 1830s that this
new cultural form of minstrelsy would be recognized as national, captured by
and identified with the Jacksonians, and finally stripped by the late 1830s of
much of its original anti-slavery meaning.

Nevertheless, it would still not be appreciated by southerners, who had taken
up the logics and practices of nationalization and racialization and were inventing, with them, a different political culture, one all the more dangerous for
its mimicking of the original.[48] A product of political nationalization, racialization accelerated the process of sectional divergence and party breakdown even
as it sought to mute the divisive implications of Indian removal, the extension
of slavery, and anti-slavery. In the end, both nationalization and racialization created as much conflict as they muted. So it often went in the violent, impolite, unevenly developed, but deeply meaningful world of early U.S. politics.

Notes

1. Gordon S. Wood, *The Radicalism of the American Revolution* (New York, 1991), pt.3;
   Alan Taylor, *William Cooper's Town: Power and Persuasion on the Frontier of the Early
   American Republic* (New York, 1995), 141–291; David Waldstreicher, *In the Midst of
   Perpetual Fetes: The Making of American Nationalism, 1776–1820* (Chapel Hill, N.C.,
   1997); Simon P. Newman, *Parades and the Politics of the Street: Festive Culture in the
   Early American Republic* (Philadelphia, 1997); Rosemarie Zagarri, "Festive Nation-
   alism and Antiparty Partyism," *Reviews in American History* 26 (1998): 506, 509.
2. Compare, for example, the two most recent entries in the John Harvard Library

of American classics: Joel Silbey, ed., *The American Party Battle: Election Campaign Pamphlets, 1828–1876* (Cambridge, Mass., 1999), and Michael Merrill and Sean Wilentz, *The Key of Liberty: The Life and Democratic Writings of William Manning, "A Laborer," 1747–1814* (Cambridge, Mass., 1993). For contrasting views that date democratization later, see, for example, Robert H. Wiebe, *The Opening of American Society* (New York, 1984), and *Self-Rule: A Cultural History of American Democracy* (Chicago, 1995); Joel Silbey, "The Incomplete World of American Politics, 1815–1829: Presidents, Parties, and Politics in The Era of Good Feelings," *Congress and the Presidency* 11 (1984): 1–18, and *The Partisan Imperative: The Dynamics of American Politics before the Civil War* (New York, 1985), 33–68. For mediating or gradualist views, see Ronald P. Formisano, *The Transformation of Political Culture: Massachusetts Parties, 1790s–1840s* (New York, 1983), and Michael Schudson, *The Good Citizen: A History of American Civic Life* (New York, 1998).

3. Especially telling critiques of the division between political and social history appear in James Oakes, *Slavery and Freedom: An Interpretation of the Old South* (New York, 1990), xvii–xix, 209; William W. Freehling, *The Reintegration of American History: Slavery and the Civil War* (New York, 1994), vii–xi, 253–74. See also Samuel P. Hays, "Politics and Society: Beyond the Political Party," in *The Evolution of American Electoral Systems*, ed. Paul Kleppner et al. (Greenwood, Conn., 1981), 245–50; Mark H. Leff, "Revisioning U.S. Political History," *American Historical Review* 100 (1995): 849–53.

4. Richard R. John, "Govermental Institutions as Agents of Change: Rethinking American Political Development in the Early Republic, 1787–1835," *Studies in American Political Development* 11 (1997): 347–80; Richard R. John, *Spreading the News: The Postal System from Franklin to Morse* (Cambridge, Mass., 1996). See also Martin Shefter, *Political Parties and the State: The American Historical Experience* (New York, 1994), esp. 68–74.

5. William Nisbet Chambers, "Party Development and the American Mainstream," in *The American Party Systems: Stages of Development*, ed. William Nisbet Chambers and Walter Dean Burnham (New York, 1967), 7, 11; Ronald P. Formisano, "Federalists and Republicans: Parties, Yes—System, No," in Kleppner et al., *Evolution of American Electoral Systems*, 34–76; Joel H. Silbey, *The American Political Nation, 1838–1893* (Stanford, Calif., 1991); Richard L. McCormick, *The Party Period and Public Policy: American Politics from the Age of Jackson to the Progressive Era* (New York, 1986), 29–140.

6. David R. Roediger, *The Wages of Whiteness: Race and the Making of the American Working Class* (London, 1991); Alexander Saxton, *The Rise and Fall of the White Republic* (London, 1990); Noel Ignatiev, *How the Irish Became White* (New York, 1995); Matthew Frye Jacobson, *Whiteness of a Different Color: European Immigrants and the Alchemy of Race* (Cambridge, Mass., 1998); Michael Omi and Howard Winant, *Racial Formation in the United States: From the 1960s to the 1990s*, 2d ed. (New York, 1994).

7. Saxton, *Rise and Fall of the White Republic*; William W. Freehling, *The Road to Disunion*, vol. 1, *Secessionists at Bay, 1776–1854* (New York, 1991); Freehling, *Reintegration of American History*; Eric Foner, *Reconstruction: America's Unfinished Revolution, 1863–1877* (New York, 1988); Eric Foner, *The Story of American Freedom* (New York, 1998); Robert P. Forbes, "Slavery and the Meaning of America, 1819–1833" (Ph.D. diss., Yale University, 1994); John Ashworth, *Slavery, Capitalism, and Politics in the Antebellum Republic*, vol. 1, *Conflict and Compromise,*

1820–1850 (Cambridge, 1995); Michael Goldfield, *The Color of Politics: Race and the Mainsprings of American Politics* (New York, 1997); Rogers M. Smith, *Civic Ideals: Conflicting Visions of Citizenship in U.S. History* (New Haven, Conn., 1997); Paul Frymer, *Uneasy Alliances: Race and Party Competition in America* (Princeton, N.J., 1999); Mark Brandon, *Free in the World: American Slavery and Constitutional Failure* (Princeton, N.J., 1999).

8. Freehling, *Reintegration of American History*, viii–ix, 254–56.

9. Nationalism has been a relatively neglected topic since the rise of "republican-ism" and party ideologies as central areas of inquiry since the 1970s. For earlier studies that addressed nationalism as a central problem, see, for example, George Dangerfield, *The Awakening of American Nationalism, 1815–1828* (New York, 1965); Marshall Smelser, *The Democratic Republic, 1801–1815* (New York, 1968); and Lawrence Friedman, *Inventors of the Promised Land* (New York, 1975).

10. Waldstreicher, *In the Midst of Perpetual Fetes*, chap. 5; see also Peter S. Onuf, "Feder-alism, Republicanism, and the Origins of American Sectionalism", in *All over the Map: Rethinking American Regions*, ed. Edward L. Ayers et al. (Baltimore, 1996), 11–37.

11. The most provocative and helpful recent work on the relationship of race to na-tionalism is Etienne Balibar and Immanuel Wallerstein, *Race, Nation, Class: Am-biguous Identities* (London, 1991). See also Paul Gilroy, "One Nation under a Groove: The Cultural Politics of 'Race' and Racism in Britain," in *Anatomy of Racism*, ed. David Theo Goldberg (Minneapolis, 1990), 263–82.

12. A useful examination of riot, public testimony, and other challenges to politics as usual is Kimberly K. Smith, *The Dominion of Voice: Riot, Reason, and Romance in An-tebellum Politics* (Lawrence, Kans., 1999). On the importance of considering vio-lence as part of sociopolitical structure, see Anthony Giddens, *The Nation-State and Violence* (Stanford, Calif., 1991).

13. The test of this or any new synthesis of political history should be its ability to explain nonelectoral as well as electoral events, reflecting a properly expansive— and I would say realistic—notion of the political. It should also, in my view, ac-count for what I call the "six degrees of separation" phenomenon in pre–Civil war politics: the tendency for every issue to turn out to have less than six degrees of separation from the slavery question. For recent debates on the significance and limits of parties and the nature of political culture during the mid-nineteenth cen-tury more generally, see the two roundtables in the *Journal of American History*, one focused on Glenn C. Altschuler and Stuart M. Blumin, "Limits of Political En-gagement in Antebellum America: A New Look at the Golden Age of Participa-tory Democracy," *Journal of American History* 84 (1997): 855–909, and the other on Ronald P. Formisano, "The 'Party Period' Revisited," and Mark H. Leff, "The 'Third Party Tradition' Reconsidered," *Journal of American History* 86 (1999): 93–166.

14. Wiebe (*Opening of American Society*, 18–19) calls this period "neocolonial," im-plying a kind of weakness that was admittedly present but without noticing just how much of politics all over the Western world partook of colonial dilemmas. For early national culture and identity as postcolonial, I am indebted to Kariann Yokota, who addresses the subject in her forthcoming UCLA dissertation.

15. For the imperial context, see David Armitage, "Greater Britain: A Useful Cate-gory of Historical Analysis," *American Historical Review* 104 (1999): 427–45; T. H. Breen, "Ideology and Nationalism on the Eve of the American Revolution: Re-visions Once More in Need of Revising," *Journal of American History* 84 (1997):

13–39; P. J. Marshall, ed., *The Oxford History of the British Empire*, vol. 2, *The Eighteenth Century* (Oxford, 1998); Peter S. Onuf, *Jefferson's Empire: The Language of American Nationhood* (Charlottesville, Va., 2000).

16. Fred Anderson, *Crucible of War: The Seven Years' War and the Fate of Empire in British America* (New York, 2000); Richard White, *The Middle Ground: Indians, Empires, and Republics in the Great Lakes Region, 1650–1815* (New York, 1991); Christopher L. Brown, "An Empire without Slaves: British Concepts of Emancipation on the Eve of the American Revolution," *William and Mary Quarterly* 56 (1999): 273–306; Paul Goodman, "The First American Party System," in Chambers and Burnham, *American Party Systems*, 63; James E. Lewis, Jr., *The American Union and the Problem of Neighborhood: The United States and the Collapse of the Spanish Empire, 1783–1829* (Chapel Hill, N.C., 1998).

17. Donald L. Robinson, *Slavery in the Structure of American Politics, 1765–1820* (New York, 1971); James Roger Sharp, *American Politics in the Early Republic: The New Nation in Crisis* (New Haven, Conn., 1993); Richard S. Newman, "Prelude to the Gag Rule: Southern Reaction to Antislavery Petitions in the First Federal Congress," *Journal of the Early Republic* 16 (1996): 571–600; Saul Cornell, *The Other Founders: Anti-Federalists and the Dissenting Tradition in America, 1788–1828* (Chapel Hill, N.C., 1999); Freehling, *Road to Disunion.*

18. Robert Olwell, *Masters, Slaves, and Subjects: The Culture of Power in the South Carolina Low Country, 1740–1790* (Ithaca, N.Y., 1998); Woody Holton, *Forced Founders: Indians, Debtors, Slaves, and the Making of the American Revolution in Virginia* (Chapel Hill, N.C., 1999).

19. Gregory Evans Dowd, *A Spirited Resistance: The North American Indian Struggle for Unity, 1745–1815* (Baltimore, 1992); Andrew R. L. Cayton, "'Separate Interests' and the Nation State: The Origins of Regionalism in the Trans-Appalachian West," *Journal of American History* 79 (1992): 37–64; Thomas P. Slaughter, *The Whiskey Rebellion: Frontier Epilogue to the American Revolution* (New York, 1986); Rogan Kersh, *Dreams of a More Perfect Union* (Ithaca, N.Y., forthcoming), chap. 3.

20. Formisano, *Transformation of Political Culture*, 5; Linda Colley, *Britons: Forging the Nation, 1707–1837* (New Haven, Conn., 1992); Kathleen Wilson, *The Sense of the People: Politics, Culture, and Imperialism in England, 1715–1785* (Cambridge, 1995).

21. Richard P. McCormick, "Political Development and the Second American Party System," in Chambers and Burnham, *American Party Systems*, 95; Paul A. C. Koistinen, *Beating Ploughshares into Swords: The Political Economy of American Warfare, 1606–1865* (Lawrence, Kans., 1996).

22. William Nisbet Chambers, *Political Parties in a New Nation: The American Experience, 1776–1807* (New York, 1963); Formisano, *Transformation of Political Culture*; Richard Buel, *Securing the Revolution: Ideology in American Politics, 1789–1815* (Ithaca, N.Y., 1972); Michael Durey, *Transatlantic Radicals in the Early American Republic* (Lawrence, Kans., 1998); Seth Cotlar, "In Paine's Absence: The Trans-Atlantic Dynamics of American Popular Political Thought, 1789–1804" (Ph.D. diss., Northwestern University, 2000); Newman, *Parades and Politics of the Street*; Waldstreicher, *In the Midst of Perpetual Fetes*, chap. 3.

23. David Waldstreicher, "Federalism, the Styles of Politics, and the Politics of Style," in *Federalists Reconsidered*, ed. Doron S. Ben-Atar and Barbara B. Oberg (Charlottesville, Va., 1998), 97–117; Newman, *Parades and Politics of the Street*; Susan Branson, "Politics and Gender: The Political Consciousness of Philadelphia Women in the 1790s" (Ph.D. diss., Northern Illinois University, 1992); Buel, *Securing the Revolution.*

24. See Waldstreicher, *In the Midst of Perpetual Fetes*, chaps. 3–4.

25. Donald J. Ratcliffe, *Party Spirit in a Frontier Republic: Democratic Politics in Ohio, 1793–1821* (Columbus, 1998); Daniel Sisson, *The Revolution of 1800* (New York, 1974); Noble E. Cunningham, Jr., *The Jeffersonian Republicans: The Formation of a Party Organization, 1789–1801* (Chapel Hill, N.C., 1957).

26. Formisano, *Transformation of Political Culture*, 57–83; Andrew R. L. Cayton, "Radicals in the 'Western World': The Federalist Conquest of Trans-Appalachian North America," in Ben-Atar and Oberg, *Federalists Reconsidered*, 77–96; Taylor, *William Cooper's Town*; Stephen R. Grossbart, "The Revolutionary Transformation: Politics, Economy, and Society in Connecticut, 1765–1818" (manuscript courtesy of the author); Rachel Klein, *The Unification of a Slave State: The Rise of the Planter Class in the South Carolina Back Country, 1760–1808* (Chapel Hill, N.C., 1990); Merrill and Wilentz, *Key of Liberty*, 1–86; Joyce Appleby, *Capitalism and a New Social Order: The Republican Vision of the 1790s* (New York, 1984); Sean Wilentz, *Chants Democratic: New York City and the Rise of the American Working Class* (New York, 1984), 61–103; Gary J. Kornblith, "Artisan Federalism: New England Mechanics and the Political Economy of the 1790s," in *Launching the Extended Republic: The Federalist Era*, ed. Ronald Hoffman and Peter J. Albert (New York, 1997), 249–72.

27. Drew R. McCoy, *The Elusive Republic: Political Economy in Jeffersonian America* (Chapel Hill, N.C., 1980); Onuf, *Jefferson's Empire*.

28. Ralph Ketcham, *Presidents above Party: The First American Presidency, 1788–1828* (Chapel Hill, N.C., 1984); Donald R. Hickey, *The War of 1812: A Forgotten Conflict* (Urbana, Ill., 1989); Alexander DeConde, *The Quasi-War* (New York, 1966); Stanley Elkins and Eric McKitrick, *The Age of Federalism, 1788–1800* (New York, 1993), chaps. 12–15.

29. Thomas C. Cochran, "The 'Presidential Synthesis' in American History," *American Historical Review* 53 (1948): 148–59; Stephen Skowronek, *The Politics Presidents Make: Leadership from John Adams to George Bush* (Cambridge, Mass., 1993), 27, 61–154 ; Richard P. McCormick, *The Presidential Game: The Origins of American Presidential Politics* (New York, 1982), 10.

30. Linda K. Kerber, "The Federalist Party," in *The History of U.S. Political Parties*, ed. Arthur M. Schlesinger, Jr. (New York, 1971), 22; Linda K. Kerber, *Federalists in Dissent* (Ithaca, N.Y., 1971); Douglas R. Egerton, *Gabriel's Rebellion: The Virginia Slave Conspiracies of 1800 and 1802* (Chapel Hill, N.C., 1993); Waldstreicher, *In The Midst of Perpetual Fetes*, chaps. 4–5; Patricia Bradley, *Slavery, Propaganda, and the American Revolution* (University, Miss., 1998); Michael Zuckerman, "The Color of Counterrevolution," in his *Almost Chosen People* (Berkeley, Calif., 1996); Smith, *Civic Ideals*, 140–44, 163–64.

31. Gary B. Nash, "Forging Freedom: The Emancipation Experience in the Northern Seaport Cities," in *Slavery and Freedom in the Era of the American Revolution*, ed. Ira Berlin and Ronald Hoffman (Urbana, Ill., 1983), 3–48; Sylvia Frey, *Water from the Rock: Black Resistance in a Revolutionary Age* (Princeton, N.J., 1991); Ira Berlin, *Many Thousands Gone: The First Two Centuries of Slavery in America* (Cambridge, Mass., 1998), 219–365.

32. Onuf, *Jefferson's Empire*, 147–88; Thomas N. Ingersoll, "A 'Tempestuous Sea of Liberty': The Rage for Equality in 1800" (paper presented to the McNeil Center for Early American Studies, February 2000); Gary B. Nash, *Race and Revolution* (Madison, Wis., 1991); Waldstreicher, *In the Midst of Perpetual Fetes*, chap. 6; Freehling, *Road to Disunion*.

33. Wiebe, *Opening of American Society,* 127–233, Charles G. Sellers, *The Market Revolution: Jacksonian America, 1815–1848* (New York, 1991); Major L. Wilson, *Space, Time, and Freedom: The Quest for Nationality and the Irrepressible Conflict, 1815–1861* (Westport, Conn., 1974); Richard E. Ellis, *The Union at Risk: Jacksonian Democracy, States Rights, and the Nullification Crisis* (New York, 1987); Forbes, "Slavery and the Meaning of America."

34. Silbey, "Incomplete World of American Politics"; Skowronek, *Politics Presidents Make,* 133; M. J. Heale, *The Presidential Quest: Candidates and Images in American Political Culture, 1787–1852* (London, 1982).

35. Silbey, *Partisan Imperative,* 33–84; Silbey, *American Political Nation;* Harry L. Watson, *Liberty and Power: The Politics of Jacksonian America* (New York, 1990). On the need for partisans to pose questions in terms of clear alternatives and the regular difficulties partisans faced in doing this, see Michael F. Holt, *Political Parties and American Political Development from the Age of Jackson to the Age of Lincoln* (Baton Rouge, 1992), and Michael F. Holt, *The Rise and Fall of the American Whig Party* (New York, 1999).

36. Ronald P. Formisano, "The Rise of the Ethnocultural Interpretation," *American Historical Review* 99 (1994): 453–77; Ronald P. Formisano, "The New Political History and the Election of 1840," *Journal of Interdisciplinary History* 23 (1993): 661–82. Formisano's insistence on multicausality in explaining why, for example, the Whigs won in 1840 is precisely right in terms of the long view, but like Holt, he at times underestimates the crucial rhetorical dimensions of politics, in which issues do not neatly separate into "economic," "ethnocultural," and "racial" boxes but rather seek useful combinations that speak to more than one category of concern at the same time. The issues that historians defined as "ethnocultural" were themselves syntheses of this sort. On the primacy of the symbolic in the definition of political issues and opponents, see Murray Edelman, *The Symbolic Uses of Politics* (Urbana, Ill., 1971); Murray Edelman, *Constructing the Political Spectacle* (Chicago, 1988); and Anne Norton, *Reflections on Political Identity* (Baltimore, 1991).

37. Forbes, "Slavery and the Meaning of America," 325–27, 336; Richard H. Brown, "The Missouri Compromise, Slavery, and the Jacksonians," *South Atlantic Quarterly* 65 (1966): 55–70; Frymer, *Uneasy Alliances.* For a later-dating but related argument, see William G. Shade, "'The Most Delicate and Exciting Topics': Martin Van Buren, Slavery, and the Election of 1836," *Journal of the Early Republic* 18 (1998): 459–84. Ashworth considers Indian removal and slavery politics as two of the four important factors in the emergence of the two-party system (*Slavery, Capitalism, and Politics,* 369–81).

38. James Oliver Horton and Lois Horton, *In Hope of Liberty: Culture, Community, and Protest among Northern Free Blacks, 1700–1860* (New York, 1997), 155–236; Simon P. Newman, "Black Racial Politics in Jacksonian America" (paper presented at the Society for Historians of the Early American Republic conference, Lexington, Ky., July 1999); Shane White, "'It Was a Proud Day': African Americans, Festivals, and Parades in the North, 1741–1834," *Journal of American History* 81 (1994): 13–50; Waldstreicher, *In the Midst of Perpetual Fetes,* 322–48.

39. Freehling, *Road to Disunion,* 144–286; Oakes, *Slavery and Freedom,* 154–55; William W. Wiecek, *The Sources of Antislavery Constitutionalism in America, 1760–1848* (Ithaca, N.Y., 1977), 106–50; Forbes, "Slavery and the Meaning of America," 65. Forbes's phrasing here indicates less his own incredulity than the absence of this perspective from the existing scholarship.

40. Forbes, "Slavery and the Meaning of America," 283–84, 365–415; George M. Frederickson, *The Black Image in the White Mind: The Debate over Afro-American Character and Destiny, 1817–1914* (New York, 1971), 43–70; James Brewer Stewart, "The Emergence of Racial Modernity and the Rise of the White North, 1790–1840," *Journal of the Early Republic* 18 (1998): 181–217.

41. Mary Hershberger, "Mobilizing Women, Anticipating Abolition: The Struggle against Indian Removal in the 1830s," *Journal of American History* 86 (1999): 15–40; Nancy Isenberg, *Sex and Citizenship in Antebellum America* (Chapel Hill, N.C., 1998); Lori D. Ginzburg, *Women and the Work of Benevolence* (New Haven, Conn., 1990); Julie Roy Jeffrey, *The Great Silent Army of Abolitionism: Ordinary Women in the Abolitionist Movement* (Chapel Hill, N.C., 1998); Paul Goodman, *Of One Blood: Abolitionism and the Origins of Racial Equality* (Berkeley, Calif., 1998), 174–231. For the importance of the convention movement in the revised two-party politics, see William G. Shade, "Political Pluralism and Party Development: The Creation of a Modern Party System, 1815–1852", in Kleppner et al., *Evolution of American Electoral Systems,* 77–111.

42. William Taylor, *Cavalier and Yankee: The Old South and American National Character* (New York, 1961); David Brion Davis, *The Slave Power Conspiracy and the Paranoid Style* (Baton Rouge, 1969); Eric Foner, *Free Soil, Free Labor, Free Men: The Ideology of the Republican Party in the 1850s* (New York, 1970); Ashworth, *Slavery, Capitalism, and Politics;* Stephanie McCurry, *Masters of Small Worlds: Yeoman Households, Gender Relations, and the Political Culture of the Antebellum Southern Low Country* (New York, 1995); LeAnn Whites, "The Civil War as a Crisis in Gender," in *Divided Houses: Gender and the Civil War,* ed. Catherine Clinton and Nina Silber (New York, 1992), 3–21; Amy Dru Stanley, "Home Life and the Morality of the Market," in *The Market Revolution in America: Social, Political, and Religious Expressions, 1800–1880,* ed. Melvyn Stokes and Stephen Conway (Charlottesville, Va., 1996), 74–96.

43. David Grimsted, *American Mobbing, 1828–1861: Toward Civil War* (New York, 1998); Christopher Waldrep, *Roots of Disorder: Race and Criminal Justice in the American South, 1817–1880* (Urbana, Ill., 1998), 1–58; John, *Spreading the News,* 257–80.

44. Andrew Delbanco, ed., *The Portable Abraham Lincoln* (New York, 1992), 17–26, 209–25.

45. "Song," *Philadelphia Mercury,* August 23, 1828, reprinted in Vera Brodsky Lawrence, *Music for Patriots, Politicians, and Presidents: Harmonies and Discords of the First Hundred Years* (New York, 1975), 239; Merrill D. Peterson, *The Jefferson Image in the American Mind* (New York, 1960), 22, 182, 462. On the politics of the gag rule, see Freehling, *Road to Disunion,* 287–351, and William Lee Miller, *Arguing against Slavery: The Great Debate in the United States Congress* (New York, 1996). On Adams and race, see Saxton, *Rise and Fall of the White Republic,* 23–48, 88–90.

46. "From the Log Cabin Advocate. POMPEY SMASH," *The Campaign,* Frankfort, Ky., September 3, 1840, 318–20; Grimsted, *American Mobbing,* 7. The standard history of the campaign is Robert Gunderson, *The Log Cabin Campaign* (Lexington, Ky., 1957); revisionist accounts that stress more substantive issues include William Nisbet Chambers, "The Election of 1840," in *History of American Presidential Elections, 1789–1968,* ed. Arthur M. Schlesinger, Jr. (New York, 1971), 1:643–90; William J. Cooper, *Liberty and Slavery: Southern Politics to 1860* (New York, 1983), 194–95; Ashworth, *Slavery, Capitalism, and Politics,* 394–403; Richard Carwardine,

Evangelicals and Politics in Antebellum America (New Haven, Conn., 1993), 50–70; Freehling, *Road to Disunion*, 345–49, 360–62; Holt, *Rise and Fall of the Whig Party*, 105–21; Formisano, "New Political History."

47. For "Backside Albany," see Waldstreicher, *In the Midst of Perpetual Fetes*, 326–27. For Jim Crow, see Jon W. Finson, *The Voices that Are Gone: Themes in American Popular Song* (New York, 1993), 163–65. My interpretation of minstrelsy and its political significance draws on a rich literature, including Jean Baker, *Affairs of Party: The Political Culture of the Northern Democrats in the Mid-Nineteenth Century* (Ithaca, N.Y., 1983); Saxton, *Rise and Fall of the White Republic*, 165–82; Eric Lott, *Love and Theft: Blackface Minstrelsy and the American Working Class* (New York, 1993); W. T. Lhamon, Jr., *Raising Cain: Blackface Performance from Jim Crow to Hip Hop* (Cambridge, Mass., 1998); Dale Cockrell, *Demons of Disorder: Early Blackface Minstrels and Their World* (New York, 1998), esp. 72–73. To varying extents, Lott, Lhamon, and Cockrell stress the ambivalences of the genre and see in it anti-racist as well as racist moments and possibilities, especially (for Cockrell) before minstrelsy became part of mass culture.

48. Kenneth S. Greenberg, *Masters and Statesmen: The Political Culture of American Slavery* (Baltimore, 1985); Kenneth S. Greenberg, *Honor and Slavery* (Princeton, N.J., 1996). Revealingly, southerners would not embrace the minstrel show until it could be made into the South's own national form, in a new polity that embraced slavery itself as the ultimate expression of political difference. Drew Gilpin Faust, *The Creation of Confederate Nationalism: Ideology and Identity in the Civil War South* (Baton Rouge, 1988).

3. "To One or Another of These Parties Every Man Belongs"

The American Political Experience from Andrew Jackson to the Civil War

Joel H. Silbey

Collapsing prices, contracting markets, widespread bank failures, individual bankruptcy, loss of entrepreneurial nerve, rising unemployment, and significant rural dislocation—the detritus of a faltering capitalist economy—littered the American landscape in the year following the onset of the panic of 1819, which is the starting point for this exploration of the political dynamics of what scholars once called the "middle period" of American history. Explosive political tensions—from fierce local and state-level challenges to existing institutions through the congressional outburst over the admission of Missouri—added strength to growing expressions of uncertainty, even despair, about the nation's present condition and future prospects.[1]

Still, as dark as the picture seemed to be in 1820, to focus on only the downside of the American situation at that moment distorts reality. The panic of 1819 was a single aspect of a much larger national experience as the United States broke free from geographic and economic bonds rooted in the colonial era, bonds that had affected much of American life through the second war with Great Britain. The Appalachian Mountain barrier was breached, the population spread beyond previous borders, and Indian tribes in the way were removed. The nation's economy, led by southern cotton, northern shipping and financial resources, and western wheat, plus the onset of significant manufacturing enterprise, grew exponentially. Newer areas became part of the equation as well. Texas, Oregon, and California were acquired in part to increase output, find new markets, and open up further economic opportunity. Significant transportation improvements followed, geographically linking all that was occurring into a rational national system.[2] It should not be surprising that politics, too, changed fundamentally.

Transforming the Political Realm

The years after 1820 were ones of extraordinary material growth and transformative change in both the economy and the society beyond, reshaping the United States into a geographically massive, increasingly diverse, always vibrant, and usually prosperous country. Older rural areas, whose previous connections to larger economic processes were often uneven and erratic, if they existed at all, now moved toward commercial enterprise; others became sites of nascent industrialism. Although the effect of these socioeconomic changes was felt at different rates in different parts of the nation, their overall impact was clearly established from an early date as the restless, unsettling, often destabilizing stirrings of the market revolution kept increasing in magnitude and power.[3]

As these changes took hold, as investment skyrocketed, as new enterprises were essayed and new markets developed, economic boom and bust cycles appeared. But despite another serious economic setback in 1837, the pressures of growth never settled down, and by the mid-1840s, they demonstrated even more vigor than they had earlier. The powerful changes under way in this massive industrial and commercial revolution continued apace. The American economy, throughout the rest of the century, enjoyed a period of unprecedented overall expansion.

Unsurprisingly, this transforming experience in American life had a significant political dimension. The American political world was also in profound transition after 1820, rooted in the same pressures that roiled the socioeconomic landscape. Every society contains both consensual elements defining its basic nature and significant shards of conflict. There was no single American culture in these years, but there were many assumptions shared and values held in common among those inhabiting the political landscape. Americans basked in the consensual platitudes that permeated their political discourse at the outset of this era. Calls for civic virtue, to maintain and strengthen what everyone called republican values, to protect and preserve the nation and its singular virtues from its many enemies, foreign and domestic, remained commonplace—and, I suggest, revealed deep pockets of commitments and ideals that were shared by at least a significant portion of white America.[4]

These platitudes masked, however, another, more divisive quality. There was never much, if any, agreement at that level of public consciousness where shared values become policy agendas. Amid the nation's common notions, and the rhetoric that followed, lurked issues and politically charged interests growing out of both the force of rapid change and the hangover of long-standing ideological conflicts going back to the furious political battles of the 1790s, as well as ancient memories and hatreds that still retained meaning, even in the new world of transformative restructuring.[5] Christopher Clark argued that, after 1820, "issues central to the development of markets and industrial capitalism were . . . placed largely outside the realm of politics," that is, basic stabilizing and promotional decisions occurred out of sight, in the world of the courts, legal processes, and legal culture, rather than in the more open air of election campaigns and legislative sessions. This is true enough. The judiciary played a crucial role in the "freeing" of American enterprise from restrictive rules left over from an earlier time and in promoting market-oriented practices.[6]

Beyond such judicial activity, however, there were still many matters remaining in those other, more open parts of the public sphere—enough to provoke a range of contentious confrontations and to stimulate institutional processes. The whole pattern of geographic growth, pursuit of advantage, and changes in lifestyles that were under way promoted political needs and political advocacy, not to mention sharp partisan conflict. Although political passions had cooled somewhat since 1815, all these matters sharply and relentlessly divided Americans as their world changed rapidly, giving strong impetus to an effort to find an institutional way to deal with the new realities they faced. Public action to cope with, advance, and protect the new society was considered a necessity by those caught up in the system and trying to take advantage of it, resist it, or just contend with its power.[7]

Critically, however, the long-standing political society in the United States, consisting of a range of established outlooks, well-understood approaches, and familiar institutions, quickly proved to be inadequate to deal with the forces now unleashed. At the same time, the great expansion of popular participation in the political world (though still largely restricted by gender and race) added to the tumult and the pressures on the existing system. "The science of politics," to use a term from the *Federalist Papers,* demanded something beyond what was at hand—different ways of thinking about, organizing, and directing the political arena.[8]

The political world responded. The years after 1820 were a time of remarkable political innovation and energy in the United States. The ideological and cultural assumptions undergirding politics changed; new values and outlooks came to dominate the scene. And at its center were critical new forms of political organization, activity, and engagement—specifically, the popularly driven two-party system dominated first by Democrats and Whigs, then by Republicans and Democrats—evolving into deeply embedded permanence. Political parties shaped, clarified, and gave coherence to the socioeconomic forces so vigorously in play. Through careful organization, pointed articulation, advocacy and appeal, constant electoral mobilization, and the thousands of humdrum activities they engaged in during every campaign season and legislative session, the parties absorbed, embodied, represented, and channeled much of the external world and its array of needs and demands.[9]

Their triumph was remarkable. Political parties had been seen quite negatively in American civic society in the years up to 1820, even in the days of sharp confrontation between Federalists and Republicans in the 1790s. Many aspects of that long-standing anti-partyism continued to hang over the scene into the 1820s. But much was changing in terms of the nation's political culture. The republican heritage—at least the part that feared the dangers of (and therefore sought to discourage) internal political conflict, particularly when organized by wily partisan leaders—became sorely tested ground in this new situation and ultimately fell from its preeminence in American thought.[10] John Quincy Adams, the last of the presidents of the old political style, urged Americans to "discard every element of rancor" and work together on behalf of universally held national interests. The new men emerging in national politics strongly disagreed. Whether they were fully aware of the transformation under way in the United States or not, New York's Martin Van Buren and his like-minded colleagues were acutely aware of how different some things had become since 1815, particularly the renewed potential for sharply edged political warfare.[11]

Unlike their predecessors, these men had come to believe that such political conflict was not aberrant, manufactured, or temporary but normal and unavoidable. They stressed that the United States was beset by deep ideological and political differences *and* threatened by a powerful group determined to push forward economic and political policies that were dangerous to a majority of Americans. Given those realities, wide-ranging management institutions were needed, they argued, to order and direct a fractious but purposive politics across a vast battlefield of contending groups, to organize those who were on the same side in the conflicts, and to set them against those on the other side of the policy-ideology dividing line. To these men, policy advancement, partisan organization, popular mobilization, and the art of management all went hand in hand.

The lesson of the presidential election of 1824 was particularly stark to this emerging political class, and it reinforced their determination to build a new politics. In a chaotic political situation, divisions among the majority had led to a minority victory, one that threatened many important interests as President Adams aggressively pushed for a revival of Federalism's heresies of national power. In the face of these realities, Van Buren and his followers posed the question: how could local interests be protected, the nation's liberties preserved, and the country's development accomplished in ways compatible with its Jeffersonian liberal tradition? They understood what needed to be done. Between 1825 and 1828, Van Buren energized a movement among political leaders in the states and in Washington to establish structures that would guarantee that the will of the nation's political majority would always triumph, along with its critical policy commitments.[12]

What happened was not foreordained, nor did the political development that was under way settle in all at once. The idea was there early in some state political arenas, but given the hangover of the cultural norms against political parties and the extraordinary number of cross-cutting local conflicts, sectional antagonisms, personal commitments and disagreements, group hatreds, and other potential cleavages, the four parts of the party system—leadership, organization, policies advocated, and committed supporters—matured into an all-encompassing form only at the end of the 1830s.

When the system finally settled into the soil, two-party-based political mobilization and management became a normal part of the American world and received an enormous response from those brought under its wing. Americans involved in politics took to the teachings of party leaders with mounting awareness and increasing enthusiasm; growing numbers inhabiting the political nation became convinced that the major political parties served both their immediate and their long-range purposes. As a result, the growing power of the partisan imperative, the need—and wish—to join, support, and promote one's party, affected almost everyone who was abroad and active on the landscape.[13]

Ideology, Class, Clan, or Interest: Sources of Political Commitment in the Party Period

The development of political parties, the evolution of their institutional structures, and the hardening of partisan commitments into a permanent two-party system consolidated and made coherent an otherwise chaotic political world. The politics that this particular generation constructed had, at its center, the parties' sharply different perspectives about the nation and its needs, important differences that grew out of the expectations of each party's loyal supporters. Historians have never agreed about the primary animating impulses that shaped voter choice in this era. The best reading of the evidence suggests that the American voting universe was fired by an eclectic mix of enduring confrontations rooted in past experiences, as well as by aspects of the new socioeconomic forces coming into play.

This was always a politics driven by a variety of distinct impulses and revolving around different axes. These divided people within each section of the country and within rural and urban settings and crisscrossed class lines.[14] A number of historians have stressed, in addition, the highly contextual nature of American voting behavior in this era, arguing that voters were affected by distinct local conditions that influenced how they reacted to specific stimuli when they went to the polls. Such widespread variety is not surprising, given the vastness, diversity, and uneven development of the nation, all of which provided room for different impulses to operate in different ways in different situations.[15]

It all added up to a complicated mix of voter concerns that were not always directly, or solely, driven by economic variables. The market revolution's influence, as profound as it was, was not as complete as some recent arguments claim. Its reach and influence were more like a patchwork, with room for other influences to operate as well. There may have been times when a single issue overcame these variations, localisms, and differences, such as reaction to the panic of 1837. But these were exceptions to the general rule of multiple operative sources and contextual differences from place to place and from time to time. The battles that erupted in the 1820s and 1830s over banks and tariffs, over the proper role of the national government, and over the reach and authority of the president triggered a range of popular responses, rational and otherwise, that were marvelously variegated, offering persistent grist for subsequent historiographic disagreements over these matters.[16]

It is possible, however, to narrow these varieties into a more focused construction, a task that the party leaders of the day were engaged in unstintingly. Americans drew their political consciousness after 1820, first, from their commitment to the residue of existing ideologies about the nature of a good society and the role of the state, that is, from memories of past political conflicts that had long structured political notions in the United States, especially those between the Federalists and the Jeffersonian Republicans, now infused with questions stemming from the forces unleashed by the economic revolution under way. In the many places where the market revolution was advancing rapidly, not everyone welcomed, benefited from, or adjusted readily to its vast changes and disruptions, nor did the benefits of commerce and credit appeal to all.[17]

Specifically, some of those who called themselves Jacksonian Democrats espoused a deep hostility to the emerging economy. They feared the vulnerabilities unleashed by market forces, believing that they corrupted the land and promoted greed, shady practices, and pressures on government to act narrowly and prejudicially. Speculative capitalism, in their view, made success the product of chance, ruse, or illegality, rather than the result of productive labor. Imbued with an "anti-commercial animus," in John Ashworth's words, they made their distress clear and sought to use political weapons to forestall further market penetration of their lives and livelihoods. Their nostalgia for a lost Arcadia, their hatred of what Andrew Jackson referred to as "the predatory portion of the community," with its replacement world of malicious intrigue, new inequalities shaped by the uncontrolled power of some, and the loss of individual autonomy, led them to support the like-minded Old Hickory and the political party forming around him.[18]

Many of those who became Whigs, in contrast, had an "orientation toward the commercial economy." Located in and fully caught up by the new world of extensive, deeply penetrating, and expanding commercial development, their ideology enthusiastically embraced this new world order and looked for ways, through government support and action, to promote, expand, and strengthen it—to make it the normal strain in American economic life, with all the beneficent rewards that would be reaped by individuals and by the nation as a whole. Unlike many of the Democrats, they did not look longingly back to a different world. The Arcadia that they celebrated was in the here and now, as well as stretching into the future.[19]

At the same time, however, there were some cold calculations involved in the party choices of many Americans. Lambasting capitalism had more complex meanings than simply revealing a deeply held ideological opposition to distortive market forces, and defending it often had more specific implications than a generally positive notion of the new economics of the market revolution. In the decades after 1820, the economic dimensions of American politics took on the qualities that Theodore Lowi would later refer to as interest-group liberalism—battles over how government power would or would not be used in specific cases in the interest of particular groups fully caught up in market competition and values.[20]

The pursuit of economic self-interest, new markets, and new opportunities caused people to look to the government, seeking policies useful to themselves. Their search helped to define political purposes, party stances, and specific agendas. To these people, the market revolution was not necessarily dangerous by itself, though its implementation led to activities that would have harmful consequences for some of the participants. A distributional policy state was always going to be divided over the specific details of government activities, because various groups would be convinced that one entrepreneur's attempts to foster economic development in a particular direction would be detrimental to the interests and well-being of others on the scene. One entrepreneur's vital national bank was another's obvious barrier to easy credit and initiative. Therefore, conflict over the concrete elements of the nation's political economy dominated much congressional and state legislative activity. The question always posed was: which particular interests would have priority in the political realm?[21]

Finally, the modernizing politics of economic development, with its different conceptions about the nature of the economy and different approaches to the use of state power, existed side by side and intertwined with a politics of social conflict, defined in many parts of the country by ethnic and religious differences and tensions. In an era such as the present, when identity politics has been reinvigorated and is recognized to be as American as apple pie, it may not be difficult for scholars to appreciate that ethnic and religious loyalties, differences, and prejudices, with roots deep in the primordial past of cultural confrontation, were such a large part of the American political scene and could shape voter choice—not always or exclusively, but reliably as a factor of some importance in an America seeking to determine which groups and cultural perspectives constituted the nation.[22] Every social group had its own burdens, felt needs, claims, jealousies, and prejudices. Each developed relevant political perspectives out of these elements.

These ethnoreligious partisan identifications were widespread and intense. Daniel Walker Howe's formulation with regard to political conflict in the northern states seems particularly pertinent: The "most violent conflicts" in Jacksonian politics "involved racial and religious hostilities: white against black, abolitionist against anti abolitionist, Protestant against Catholic, Mormon against Gentile. Often they pitted workers against workers. In such cases, cultural conflict cut across economic class lines rather than coinciding with them." As Richard Cawardine argued, voter choice often turned on relationships with the religious establishment in different places. "Methodists' partisan allegiances," he wrote, "were neither accidental nor incidental. They were to a considerable degree shaped by meaningful ideological conflict between competing religious groups." Other religious groups reacted similarly, all their anxieties stoked by an ongoing debate over the nature of America—the identity of its inhabitants, the elements constituting its core belief system, its heritage, and its specific values.[23]

There were, then, several different *mentalities* and issue axes defining political confrontation, voter choice, and party stance. Never entirely separate from one another, these defining influences—cultural, economic, and ideological; market driven or otherwise—often interacted and came together as people defined themselves, confronted change, or just moved through the vicissitudes of everyday life. Voters had many concerns and much on their minds as they thought about and decided to join one party or the other, in light of their particular situations. Although there was some randomness and contextualism in the way that different groups sorted themselves out between the parties, the Whigs, the Democrats, and, later, the Republicans drew sustenance from and represented interests, groups, ideas, and policies drawn from distinct parts of the political spectrum.

The Culture of Political Commitment

Each of these partisan assemblages of the like-minded had an underlying unity. Although there was always the potential for disagreement within both coalitions as different blocs maneuvered for preference or fought with their party colleagues over specific policies, once the partisan system had settled in, the parties were neither ideologically unwieldy nor confused about where they stood. American voters recognized that clarity early on, and in the years after 1820, almost all of them linked themselves with one of the dominant political parties, because they believed that their well-being depended on their party's victory in the next (and every subsequent) election.[24] Yet a crucial issue remained: ensuring that there would always be full participation by these committed voters in the electoral process.

Whatever people's commitment to the cause, no one expected that there would be automatic, spontaneous, popular surges to participate in campaign activities or even to appear at the polls. Party meetings were often far away, as were polling stations. There was always something else to do. It was therefore necessary to rouse the troops in each new election campaign and get them to the starting line. Andrew Jackson's popularity and energizing conception of office drove the system in its early days. But this political era was also dominated by numerous middle-level organizers and managers in every state. Their burdensome task was to keep all Democrats and Whigs working effectively together, understanding what was at stake, and to move them to the polling stations so that each party would maximize its vote totals by pulling in all the support available.[25]

The parties of this era were almost always led by those who had some social standing in the community, whatever the egalitarian claims of their populist rhetoric. In the years after 1820, lawyers and professional politicians took central stage in political affairs, replacing the long-dominant social and economic elites of an earlier age. Like those previous elites, the new men of politics were very conscious of the need to touch base with, and listen to, the people they were trying to mobilize. Earlier political leaders had used various means of winning the support of their flocks, from the mobilization of deference to persuasion to rum swilling and other rousing social activities. Post-1820 political leaders used various means to achieve similar results. But there was a major difference in their efforts, one emblematic of the new political system.[26]

Whig, Democratic, and, later, Republican leaders always had much decisional leeway in party conventions and everyday campaign activities. They were rarely closely supervised by their supporters in these settings. Nevertheless, the leaders felt constrained in their actions by the realization that they could not go beyond, in their choices, activities, and advocacy, what their constituents would accept. Harry Watson is clearly correct when he suggests that despite their elite positions, these political leaders "sought to persuade the voters rather than command them." They were always concerned about grassroots responses to the way they went about their business. They worked hard to dominate the political scene but never forgot that they shared it with others.[27]

The heart of these efforts to engage the voters lay in the public advocacy of each party, particularly the sharp and repetitive enunciation of the differences between them, and in the specific legislation and executive actions that were needed. The whole partisan process was glued together by a public idiom of intense combat between two warring armies. Each made its way through the political terrain by stridently producing competing images of themselves, their world, and their opponents, an endeavor that was constant, widespread, and relentlessly reinforcing. They let everyone in on the fact that each of them occupied a different part of the spectrum of ideologies, attitudes, and policy demands; that they were sharply polarized, both generally in their dream of the good society and in the specific legislation and executive actions that were needed to achieve each party's notion of what was best for America both domestically and abroad.[28]

The earsplitting partisan noises they raised were never only sound and fury. The parties were deeply divided over both domestic matters and foreign policy, although the latter no longer commanded as much sustained attention as it had a generation before in the Federalist-Republican confrontation. Both Democrats and Whigs offered consistent lines of argument, anchored directly in the outlooks of each component group of supporters. Party leaders did this by reducing the many substantial issues into a number of generalized themes to which people would rally, perceiving in party rhetoric the way to achieve their more individual goals.

Both parties always enunciated their loyalty to the republican values of the founders, for example. Each made it clear that it "contend[ed] for our Constitution and our country." The particular arguments that followed revolved around general themes of liberty and power, freedom and equality, openness and elitism, linked together into general perspectives that sharply differentiated the parties from each other.[29] Democratic and Whig publicists each told a story of liberty, the quest for freedom, and their desire to protect and advance such cherished values within a prosperous nation. They began their tales in the past, with each emphasizing a distinct history of the nation and the lessons to be drawn from that history. These explorations culminated by turning from what had once been and toward the present and the future, with each party staking out its version of the particular highway that would lead to ever-greater national achievement.[30]

Democrats, without stint or letup, expressed a fervent anti-statism in domestic affairs. They believed themselves to be the real nation: agricultural freeholders and village and town artisans—the producer classes, sturdy and independent, the backbone of the American experiment in liberty. They felt themselves at risk, however, due to the pressures of rapid change, capitalist power, and the prejudices of the host culture using the hand of government to misshape society and the economy on behalf of certain favored groups, applying its overweening strength to limit the rights of those outside the majority culture, thereby ignoring the pluralism inherent in the American landscape.

To Democrats, the central issue confronting Americans was the fragility of liberty if the federal government, in particular, intervened either in economic affairs or in the lives of adult white males. To them, a "splendid" government was always "built on the ruins of popular rights." The grand coalition of Democratic-Republicans of Jackson's time had originated, they reminded their audiences, in the fiery resistance of Jefferson and Madison to the liberty-threatening consolidationism and power surge of Federalism in the 1790s. That battle was not dead. All the parties that opposed Jeffersonian Republicanism were cut from the same cloth, and each one succeeded an earlier one with the same base intentions: each willing to destroy American liberty in pursuit of other purposes.[31]

"What else is Whigism," Democrats asked, "than the degenerate offspring of Federalism?" Their principles were the same, always consisting of "an unhallowed thirst for power arrayed against popular rights." They remained predators against the freedom and interests of the nation's producing classes and of its outsider religious and ethnic groups. Whigs would use the power of banks and the credit system to undermine those producers and force people into different relations with the economy. A national bank or a protective tariff was parochial and prejudicial and created hierarchies of power over popular rights. Similarly, social legislation about schools, alcohol consumption, or other social practices was limiting and threatening. Under the Whigs, many Americans would be exploited and denied what was theirs: equal treatment under the law, equal treatment within the society, and equal opportunity in the economic realm.[32]

The clamor that rose out of the Democrats' concerns was strongly populist in tone. Whatever the elite nature of their leadership, there was much rhetorical allegiance to an egalitarian dynamic that proclaimed that everything should reflect the popular will more closely than earlier generations had allowed. They exhibited enormous ideological hostility toward policies and institutions that they perceived to be promoting aristocracy or privilege. As part of their hostility, they equated bigness with such privilege. The anti-market elements among them resisted that kind of institution and its malevolent practices—from the Bank of the United States to the growth of corporations—in alliance with, and made possible by, the surge of illegitimate government power.[33]

To forestall this, they believed that the producer and outsider classes, the country's majority, had to be organized into a permanent political army fighting on behalf of basic American economic and social institutions and ideals and against parochial privilege, inequality of treatment, and destructive federalist notions of national authority. As the *Democratic Review* put it, their party wanted to restore "the government of the country to its primitive simplicity." In addition, they proclaimed the democratic qualities of their own tribune of the people—Jackson and his successors—and their determination to resist the encroachments on American liberty that were under way from their opponents. The Democrats' tale was drawn directly from the glorious year 1776, with appropriate embellishments and revisions.[34]

The Whigs inhabited a different world. While they ultimately learned to rabble-rouse in election campaigns as effectively as did their opponents, the arguments they offered were always on behalf of a different conception of government, one that stressed its benignity and necessity. As well as railing against the excessiveness and manipulative boisterousness of the Democrats, with their threat to societal stability and well-considered policies, the Whigs wanted to focus primary attention on the needs of a growing nation and the dangers posed by the Jacksonians' reactionary localism, which went far beyond any rational reason for forestalling the useful role of the national government in economic and social affairs. Whigs clearly attracted groups who believed that they personified the values that had produced the United States, those associated with the initiative and drive of Anglo-Saxon Protestantism and all that that implied—initiative, imagination, and personal discipline, the elements that had established a prosperous Arcadia in the New World.[35]

They sought, therefore, the fullest possible promotion of the market revolution in all its many industrial and commercial dimensions. At the same time, they went beyond the economic, calling on Americans to build a harmonious and united society using schools, the church, and the power of government to frame a direction for the United States that would ensure its moral health and the correct behavior of its citizens; they wanted to maintain that moral health, along with the constant infusion of appropriate ideals for the same purpose, in generations to come.[36] These things could be achieved, they reiterated, only by the effective mobilization of both state and national authority. To the Whigs, governments were not automatically evil and oppressive and should not be seen that way. Liberty and power were intertwined, not opposites. "The hand of governance," one of their pamphlets argued, "never touches us, but to promote the general good." In the party's canon, there was nothing to fear from the more extensive use of government power that its members wished to deploy—quite the contrary, in fact.[37]

Finally, the desirable ends they sought could be accomplished, the Whigs argued, only through a government run by tried and efficient managers, not by raw and untrained individuals unversed in the arts of civic leadership and finance, no matter how personally popular. Many Whigs were initially hesitant about the demands of a popular politics expressed through organized parties, along with the messiness, unpredictability, and emotion that such political organizations personified and promoted. These hesitations had to be overcome for the party's own electoral good, and for the most part, they were in time. Still, the Whigs never wavered in their view that leadership based on rabble-rousing and corrupt patronage was the road to national disaster. The United States needed the equivalent of a George Washington in every generation, not what the Democrats treasured instead: uncouth, undisciplined, and overly rash Indian fighters or manipulative partisan lawyers, skilled only in the backroom political arts. To the Whigs, unlike their opponents, civil experience counted.[38]

A Government After All

These contrasting notions were expressed in the mountains of pamphlets issued, editorials written, fliers distributed, and speeches made, all constituting the basic coin of the realm of campaign activity—an exhausting and repetitive enterprise. The expansion of the post office in these years provided an important asset for the distribution of the growing number of party newspapers, franked legislative documents, and partisan tracts. The politics of mobilization expressed in these numerous publications was constant; the language in which it was framed was always extreme, often hair-raising, designed to paint pictures of the depravity of the other side and containing dire warnings of the collapse of the Republic if their opponents won. Negative campaigning was a standard of political discourse from the 1820s onward, involving personal, group, and party slanders as the norm. The Whigs, for example, as Harry Watson described their rhetoric, "linked Democrats to every variety of subversive doctrine in religion, family life, and class relations." The Democrats responded in kind. The ghosts of royal oppression, aristocratic depravity, and Hamiltonian greed filled their discourse. No holds were barred in this intense political warfare.[39]

Civic ceremonies reinforced these political truths. Americans were accustomed to communal gatherings of various kinds—market days, religious meetings, militia musters, mass demonstrations on behalf of some cause—where the verities of the national culture were transmitted and reinforced. The two parties now infused these gatherings with a regularity and a systematic quality previously unknown. Elaborate partisan spectacles during campaigns became a normal aspect of political life and were used effectively to transmit the relevant partisan messages. Every campaign season was overrun with parades, "grand rallies of the faithful," barbecues, and similar community events, drawing people at all social levels into the battle for America. All the gatherings were filled, as well, with oratory, appeals to each party's foot soldiers, and all the other elements of public discourse. In these events, both parties pulled out all the stops to awaken and draw in the faithful in time for the next election, and the one after that.[40]

This energetic activity paid large dividends. The leaders of both parties were quite successful in their efforts to unite their people behind an ideological, cultural, and self-interested perspective that they could all share. The constituent groups of both parties had been inculcated quite early, in their family and community settings, with the basic truths that they should hold. They now found something in a public argument, repeatedly offered, that they believed was relevant to them in such terms, and they responded as party leaders hoped they would. Given the high popular turnout at the polls and for other campaign activities and the strong, persistent support given to the two main parties, the partisan appeals and their singular idiom accomplished their purpose of knitting together the party system into its distinctive shape and turning its members into committed, even rabid, partisans who were mobilized, armed, and ready for civic war.[41]

The purpose of all this partisan combat was to push for, or energetically resist, the enactment of particular public policies, especially those revolving around what the government should do to preserve and protect the American people from forces in the environment beyond their individual control— largely domestic, but occasionally stemming from foreign sources as well. But because this era was largely Democratic before 1860, the resulting public policy dimension was unprepossessing, despite the extraordinary clamor about what was at stake on each election day. Historians have been struck by how much this system utilized its vast energies in the expressive politics of electoral mobilization and how little payoff there was in the governmental realm.[42] Both the states and the national government engaged in some legislative and bureaucratic policy initiatives. State governments enacted a range of distributive initiatives from the 1820s onward—the granting of corporate charters, for example—and they financed transportation and other improvements in support of private as well as public efforts. At the national level, Congress passed a certain amount of legislation in the forty years before the Civil War.

Yet land distribution, Indian removal, tariff laws, and other desiderata of the distributive state joined with foreign policy to take up relatively little of the federal government's time. Moreover, there was not much administrative heft in the American system. Tocqueville's description remains accurate. "There are so few matters with which the [national] government is concerned," he wrote. "Its acts are important but rare." Or, as Heather Cox Richardson put it, "before the Civil War, the American national government's economic activities were as limited as one would expect from a country capital mired in a swamp." Americans, goes a familiar refrain, were largely ungoverned. Their politics saw to that.[43]

Some recent research suggests that the nation's policy dimension may not have been as bare-bones as the conventional wisdom suggests, that there were more administrative and regulative activities by government at all levels than we usually credit. The Whigs sometimes had their day. Communications and tax policies by Congress, state legislatures, and local governments directed people into certain channels and shaped what they could do there, limiting their opportunities rather than simply allowing a mad rush of uncontrolled development. Beyond that, William Novak's description of the amount and breadth of local and state regulative activities goes far to challenge what he calls "the myth of [American] statelessness" in the first half of the nineteenth century. Such activities extended to the national government as well.[44]

Such evidence of governmental vigor may constitute only a few fragments on the landscape and not add up to as much as some now claim. Nevertheless, however overexcited they may have been, the Democrats were not entirely wrong in their perception of what their opponents were up to. The Whigs did not always come away empty-handed when they pushed for a more energetic use of government power. The lineaments of a nascent American state were becoming somewhat more visible in this era than they had been at any time since the Federalist era.[45]

At Odds

The founders of the partisan political nation wanted it to be all-embracing in its reach and all-powerful in its command of public affairs. They believed that their hopes had been realized. Not only had the size of the active and involved voter pool grown steadily, but in addition, the system often reached beyond the voters and pulled others into it at some level of engagement. Nevertheless, despite the reach of the partisan system, there were always contrary impulses in the nation that were never fully contained under the aegis of the two main parties.

Not everyone was part of, or accepted, their ways and definitions. Some Americans remained uninvolved in, unimpressed by, or hostile to the partisan culture. A range of voices articulated instead their commitment to older political values and vented their continuing hostility to the new impulses. To be sure, some of this anti-party expression was brought forward for partisan purposes. Major Wilson has referred, for example, to "the antiparty pieties of the furiously partisan Whigs" during the Van Buren administration. Other such expressions were probably not partisan in intent but reflective of a persistent ideological resistance, in different places, to the emergent political assumptions of this era.[46]

Beyond the skeptics about the party system as a whole, others tried to improve on the existing structure. Much about the political world remained exclusionary, for example, despite the triumph of all-but-universal white male suffrage by the 1830s. American society contained important areas of gender and racially defined restrictions and limits that were never faced in any sustained way by those engaged in political activity.[47] The formal political realm breathed both a strong exclusionary masculinity and a persistent commitment to whiteness. As Mary Ryan wrote, "by statute and pervasive prejudice, the majority of Americans were kept out of electoral procedures and representative government, the most important areas of civic engagement."[48]

These restrictions created their own political dynamics in this era, much of it outside the two-party system and often outside formal politics entirely. There were many politically conscious Americans ready and eager to critique, with fiery intensity, the system's shortcomings in the areas of race, class, and gender, its exploitiveness, insensitivity, and failure to live up to its egalitarian claims. Middle-class women's groups, humanitarian critics, abolitionists, Anti-Masons, and nativists were all eager to expunge the evils rampant in American society. Similarly, craftsmen, displaced workers, and other members of the producer classes, under severe pressure from the capitalist intrusion into their lives, often fiercely resisted and sought political remedies for their plight: ten-hour workdays, the revival of anti-monopolistic commercial practices, and various kinds of guarantees for their security and their worth as productive members of the nation.[49]

These movements enjoyed a rich historiography that emphasized the complexity of the roots of their protest, the complicated character of their political thought, and the problematic nature of their commitment to existing political notions and institutions. In particular, many of them saw the need for a political mentality that went beyond the pragmatic and electoral concerns of the Whigs and Democrats. To them, the Democrats—and even most Republicans, when they came onto the scene—were designed primarily to manage affairs as they were, not to change things for the better. Wrapped in their own parochial concerns, the major parties did nothing to correct and improve society.[50]

Those at odds with the prevailing system proselytized incessantly—their clamor could be as harsh and as persistent as that of the main parties—and vigorously cut out their own political channels to achieve their ends. These took several forms. Some functioned as pressure groups on the major parties. Movements on behalf of women's political rights were an imposing feature of alternative politics; some women, however, managed to operate within the formal political world despite their legal exclusion—as petitioners and pamphleteers, agenda setters, and participants in partisan campaign activities. Some efforts were also made, through advocacy and pressure, to end racial definitions of citizenship and political participation.[51]

Some of the constituent elements of these outsiders followed traditional patterns drawn from the majority's example. They organized numerous third parties. Between Jackson's original victory and the wartime race of 1864, no presidential election was limited to the two major parties. Dissatisfied with the thrust and nature of the main parties, Anti-Masons, American Republicans, Liberty men, Free-Soilers, the Workingman's Party, and the Know-Nothings, among similar efforts, fought to win office. Although these groups never garnered large numbers of votes, Whig and Democratic party managers, busily seeking to scrape together popular majorities in the many closely contested elections that occurred, had to think about the minor parties all the time and deal with them as best they could.[52]

At the same time, this politics of impatience and challenge operated beyond the boundaries of the formal channels of elections, parties, legislatures, and government agencies, although its activities sought to influence those channels. Collective actions embodying public expression of discontent—street demonstrations, riots, and similar actions against perceived evils—were commonplace in American life (extending, it should be noted, to campaigns and even election days, as partisan mobs often engaged in brawls at rallies and near polling stations). Protest demonstrations by workingmen against their condition were widespread; several American cities saw repeated expressions of this tactic throughout the 1830s and 1840s. In rural areas, there were similar moments of collective action with a political purpose, protests against the inequitable conditions imposed on those living in the countryside. New York's anti-rent war of the mid-1840s, for one, underlined a stark and desperate challenge to the existing society, one that demanded political remedies before it was too late.[53]

All this added another dimension to America's political life. There was impressive variety among the challengers at odds with the party system, different groups and individuals with different notions, strategies, and responses to the world around them. Some of those espousing alternative political impulses were middle or upper class; some were not. Some were part of the dominant American ethnoreligious culture; others were not. Some lived in fear, others in hope. Some of their demands were mildly reformist in tone and purpose, and some exuded a more radical perspective about society than that evidenced in conventional politics, one that constantly pushed against the system's boundaries.[54] Those at odds with the dominant partisan regime occupied their share of the public space of the time and considered themselves anything but peripheral to the political nation. Their expressions of discontent, demands for social and economic change, constant mobilization efforts, impatience with and hostility toward the realm of ordinary politics as it had evolved, and expressions of political attitudes and aspirations outside the two-party system were certainly energetic and noticeable.

Some made occasional headway, and all were stimulants threatening the complacent attitudes of the majority about their society.[55] But did they significantly nuance the dominant force of the political world of that time or suggest to us, more than a century later, that some important revisions to the partisan-imperative narrative are in order because of their presence? Ronald Formisano argued that these exceptions to the majority mentality—the resisters to it, and those not incorporated in it—were numerous enough, the energy they expended important enough, and the directions they took askew enough to create serious questions about how far-reaching and dominant the partisan system really was in those years.[56]

I am not so sure. Reformers spoke loudly and sometimes had influence. But whatever their "acute dissent from the political status quo," the results they attained were disappointing.[57] Most of the time, adherents of alternative political mentalities were unable to strip away the basic structure of the dominant system or change its direction—with one gigantic exception: the sectional alternative to Van Buren's political way. For the rest, their active numbers were small, and the number who supported them on election day was even smaller. Most voters showed their interest and their involvement by coming to the polls in record numbers and indicating their essential Whig or Democratic commitment on their ballots. As a result, the challengers to the system rarely achieved the kinds of policy victories they sought. Their efforts remained well bounded by the powerful political institutions on the scene that drew so many white male Americans into their embrace, dividing them, as voters, across class and sectional lines and making most of them indifferent to external challenges. The partisan center largely held against the various torments that beset it to continue its impressive sway over the American political nation.[58]

Civil War in the Making

Sectional tensions were palpable and persistent in the United States after 1820. Frequent spasms of sectionally driven unrest and concern—in 1819–1820, again in 1831–1832, in the patterns of electoral support for Jackson, in the southern difficulties of Van Buren in 1836, in the growth of abolitionism, in the congressional petition controversy of the late 1830s, and in John C. Calhoun's long campaign to arouse and unify the political South—attested to the presence of sensitivities of a high order rooted in the realities of important social, economic, and ideological differences between North and South.[59]

Despite the fact that there were always those in both sections who believed (and acted on the notion) that sectional differences and tensions were not only inevitable but also central to public affairs, these advocates had to cope with the powerful inter-sectional forces shaping American society, including the partisan framework of national politics. The United States may have been half slave and half free, but politics within both North and South usually echoed the larger political trends of the nation as a whole. The party system developed in the slave South in the 1820s and 1830s. Both Whigs and Democrats attracted significant support throughout the region, albeit with patchiness and incompleteness in some places, especially in South Carolina—always the great exception in any exposition of the nature of American politics in this era.[60]

Party builders were acutely sensitive to the sectional anxieties (and anger) present in their society. But to most of them, such impulses were largely diversionary of their main concerns. The inter-sectional political alliances that characterized both the Whig and the Democratic Parties were so potent not only because many feared the danger posed by the divisiveness of slavery and sought ways to dampen the issue but also because they believed that there were more compelling issues on the political agenda, issues that united people across sectional lines. To the Democrats, for example, resurgent Federalism was always the primary issue, everything else a diversion.[61]

Therefore, national party leaders responded to the alternative sectional perspectives as their culture, commitments, and self-interest dictated. They resisted strongly and acted within the formulation offered by John Ashworth: Whigs and Democrats subscribed "to different and opposing ideologies or world views, and the antagonism that this difference generated was sufficient to unite northerners and southerners within the same parties." In short, "northerners and southerners divided over some fundamental questions that did not directly relate to slavery." The result was that through the 1840s, whatever the difficult moments, there was a sense of being able to manage sectional confrontation and keep it within bounds. Whatever its occasional impact, it proved to have little staying power in the formal political world. Despite the intense commitment of some individuals on these matters, others were not caught up in them. To many Americans, sectional pressures remained another variable to be considered, not one that readily overwhelmed their political consciousness.[62]

In the mid and late 1840s, the territorial issue disrupted the political landscape with unusual ferocity; sectional discord threatened to become more sustained than it had ever been. But the forces of partisan containment, marked by the compromise measures of 1850 and the parties' finality resolutions in 1852, took hold. They did so because of the determination of party leaders and the response of their followers. The sectionalized, hothouse atmosphere of the national capital did not penetrate into voter consciousness outside of Washington. At the electoral level, party commitment largely held and remained rooted in the same matters that had always defined it. Once again, the existing inter-sectional political institutions effectively restrained the disruptive possibilities of the onrushing sectional tension.[63]

To be sure, the situation was never as stable as it appeared to be. William Freehling convincingly demonstrated that the aggressive demands of southern rights leaders within the Democratic Party successfully pushed the party toward a stronger pro-southern stance as time passed. There was a continuing ideological impulse underlying this, however. With their fervent, all but religious, faith in local authority triumphing over all else, most Democrats had to agree that the role of the national government in limiting slave extension was, at best, problematic. As a re-sult, they found themselves defending domestic slavery and its expansion. And that, when combined with other factors, ultimately brought them great trouble.[64]

Nevertheless, whatever the partisan power displayed, things did change. The well-working system began to unravel and become dysfunctional in 1854, be-ginning with an explosive electoral disruption in a series of off-year contests for state and congressional offices. For the only time in our political experience, a voter realignment led to one major party replacing another—with far-reaching consequences for the nation. At its end, a sectional dynamic at last took hold in American politics. The sectionally exclusive Republicans replaced the inter-sectional Whigs, incorporating many of that party's previous commitments in their appeal but, critically, mixing them with other brews on the scene, to bite deeply into northern consciousness.[65]

At the same time, one of the striking things about the wrenching political shift of the 1850s was how much it occurred within the existing institutional system of persistent partisan conflict. At first, the anti-immigrant Know-Nothing Party had the upper hand in the realignment that was under way, being seen for a time as the Democrats' major national competitor, in place of the fading Whigs. But the Know-Nothings slipped badly, and their rivals for anti-Democratic votes, the Republicans, were able to pick up the pieces as events unfolded to the latter's advantage. The violent battle for control of the Kansas territory, both on the scene and in the halls of Congress, demonstrated to many northern voters the truth of what the Republicans were claiming about the predatory, domineering nature of southern politicians. They had to be stopped.[66]

That realization provoked an intense reaction that drew more voters into the Re-publican fold at the expense of both the Whigs and the stumbling Know-Nothings. The latter were not forgotten, however. In the best tradition of partisan coalition-ism, Republican leaders moved to expand their support by incorporating as many Know-Nothings into the Republican complex as they could, integrating their anti-immigrant strain with the other elements in play in the mid-1850s. They estab-lished, as the bedrock of their appeal, that it was the surge of a ravening southern power that accounted for the nation's discontents, which could be confronted only by a northern crusade to defeat the southern-dominated Democratic Party, always aided in its premodern wrongheadedness by the votes of too many recently arrived Irish Catholics. In their appeal, the Republicans fully endorsed the society's modernizing impulses, most importantly, free labor capitalism, the Americanization of outsiders, and hostility to those in the system who were not part of the modernizing equation: certain immigrants, Democrats, and southerners.[67]

The ideological, rhetorical, and behavioral framework in which Republicans cast these remarks was familiar, albeit overlaid now with the interpenetration of partisan and sectional impulses. The Democrats resisted in their traditional fashion, as their political understanding continued to dictate. They did not see themselves as too pro-southern or too pro-slavery. To them, those were not the issues of this (or any) moment in the partisan world they inhabited. The Republicans were, in their view, the latest reincarnation of the Federalists. Like their predecessors, they too would use the power of government to redo the nation in unacceptable ways. They had to be resisted, as they always had been, by the followers and successors of Thomas Jefferson.[68]

Despite this resistance by the Democrats, the surge of popular support for the Republicans was impressive. As northerners began to take notice of the aggressive slavocracy, and as events unfolded that indicated the extent of southern aggression and power—all giving unredeemed force to the Republican perspective—the balance between the sectional argument and the substantive forces that had so long underpinned American political conflict shifted. Old sources of division remained and continued to stimulate confrontation. But they were increasingly embedded in the sectional construct that the Republicans so persuasively articulated and that brought them victory in 1860.[69]

Southerners were horrified by the direction that northern politics was taking. Like their enemies, many of them relied at first on the party system to protect them, using the Democratic Party as their champion, insisting throughout the late 1850s on its full commitment to protecting slavery—a position that some northern Democrats accepted to the end and that others rejected, ultimately splitting the party. At the same time, internal partisan conflict continued in the South in the 1850s. There were always those—sometimes called Whigs; at other times, Americans, opposition, or Unionists—who fought hard against the increasingly dominant Democrats in the region. Infused as it was with sectional fears and distress, this intense combat echoed earlier themes and ways, even as it adopted the new perspectives present.[70]

By 1860, the sectional and the partisan were fully intertwined in American political life. Martin Van Buren's plan for the permanent dominance of intersectional political dynamics had faltered in a manner that he had feared and that the system he had helped construct had forestalled for so long. Still, and ironically, the realigning experience of 1854–1860 also reinforced most of the tendencies already present in the American political nation. Conflict was, if anything, reinvigorated, and politics in all its dimensions flourished within the

structure of a party system bent out of shape but not broken—still the basic re-
ceptacle within which confrontation over the society's essential nature, and its
growing pains, was organized and carried on.

Coda: The Civil War as a Confirming and Reinforcing Political Experience

Finally, there was an extraordinary unleashing of political energy after 1861, as a
result of war-induced pressures that led to a critical redefinition of national authority, a change in the arc of government power, and a major transformation in
economic life and in race, class, and gender relations, all of which had an impact
far beyond the war that motivated them. In the name of defending the Union,
northern Republican leaders undertook a policy offensive whose component legislative elements went well beyond what the Democrats would accept. The
Democrats resisted in the long-established style of their political generation, because they took seriously the threat underscored in a Republican campaign pam-
phlet in 1864 that "the war has taught us some valuable lessons of constitutional
law, which plain men who are not lawyers can understand. It has taught us that
the government must have power to save the nation; that whatever is necessary
to that end is constitutional . . . that the Constitution exists for the people . . . and
we have a right to modify it to suit our needs according to our will."[71]

The Lincoln administration's policies certainly seemed to demonstrate the
pertinence of that bravura statement. Both the legislative and the executive
branches exercised power to the fullest extent of their abilities. Every policy
realm, from economics to civil liberties, underscored the government's full
commitment to the most nationalist perspective present in American political
discourse—a protective tariff, a national banking system, conscription, and restrictions on civil liberties, all in the name of saving the nation. Never had the
energies of national power been so fully stretched.[72]

To the horrified Democrats, it was 1791—and 1825—all over again. The Federalists were on the prowl and had to be smashed once more. They tried mightily
to do so throughout the war and beyond, engaging in all the traditional actions
of a political party determined to challenge and overthrow the government in
power. As they did, political passions were inflamed to unprecedented levels;
policy arguments erupted, accompanied as always by extraordinary de-
monology between the two contending parties. Campaigns and elections were
tense affairs, as they had always been. The howls on both sides were memo-
rable—and familiar. Even as Americans engaged in bloody internecine warfare,
little seemed to have changed in the nation's public arena.[73]

The Confederacy did not show the same continuation of two well-organized
parties locked in mortal conflict. Some Southerners expressed a great deal of

hostility toward ordinary political confrontation and the seeking of particular-
ist advantage in the crisis situation in which they were caught. As these people
saw it, politics should be adjourned until the war ended. Nevertheless, there was
an intense and sustained political dialogue there throughout the war, as there
had always been, between those espousing different notions of the nature and
reach of government power. Political echoes of past battles were as prominent
in the Southern air as they were in the Northern states, and, at the state level,
there were occasional flurries of partisan activities and organization. Given their
history, the possibility of national political organizations reviving in order to contest a presidential election, for example, was not unthinkable.[74]

None of this was surprising, given the region's history in the partisan era. All
of it, in both nations, was a fitting coda to an era of partisan inflammation rooted
in the diversity, sprawl, and multidirections of a rapidly changing American society and economy, along with the very different fears, desires, hopes, and persistent conflicts spawned by the transformation under way—all expressed in a
political arena dominated, as it had been for many years, by a conception of politics rooted in constant conflict between distinct perspectives, interests, and cultures and over the power, reach, and legitimacy of national political parties.
Whatever its bending and recasting, the party period had not ended. Its essential
dictates remained alive even in wartime, and in the North, at least, its institutional
structure was as powerful as it had ever been. Americans remained unable and
unwilling, as they had been for so long, to follow the advice of John Quincy
Adams and "discard every element of rancor" in their politics, even amidst civil
war, and certainly not in the vigorous confrontations that followed during Reconstruction and beyond. Martin Van Buren's template remained in place.

Acknowledgment

The quotation in the chapter title is from the *Nashville Union*, November 9, 1838.

Notes

1. On the panic of 1819, see Murray Rothbard, *The Panic of 1819: Reactions and Policies* (New York, 1962).
2. Douglas North, *Economic Growth of the United States, 1790–1860* (New York, 1961);
   Peter Temin, *The Jacksonian Economy* (New York, 1969).
3. Charles Grier Sellers, Jr., *The Market Revolution: Jacksonian America, 1815–1846*
   (New York, 1991).
4. There have been many attempts to describe an American ideological-values consensus. See, for example, Louis Hartz, *The Liberal Tradition in America: An Interpretation of American Thought since the Revolution* (New York, 1955); Eric Foner, *The*

Story of American Freedom (New York, 1998); and, relevant to the early nineteenth century, Steven Watts, *The Republic Reborn: War and the Making of Liberal America, 1790–1820* (Baltimore, 1987).

5. A good introduction to this is Lee Benson, *The Concept of Jacksonian Democracy: New York as a Test Case* (Princeton, N.J., 1961).

6. Christopher Clark, "The Consequences of the Market Revolution in the American North," in *The Market Revolution in America: Social, Political, and Religious Expressions, 1800–1880,* ed. Melvyn Stokes and Stephen Conway (Charlottesville, Va., 1996), 37. See also J. Willard Hurst, *Law and the Conditions of Freedom in the Nineteenth Century United States* (Madison, Wis., 1956); Harry Scheiber, *The Ohio Canal Era: A Case Study of Government and the Economy, 1820–1861* (Athens, Ohio, 1968).

7. Joel H. Silbey, *The American Political Nation, 1838–1893* (Stanford, Calif., 1991).

8. As in Federalist No. 9.

9. Silbey, *American Political Nation.* The current scholarly mood insists on broadening politics to include a wide range of activities, impulses, and power relationships, many of them outside the formal political arena, in family settings and in the workplace. Politics, of course, exists everywhere; there are power dynamics in every relationship. The politics of individual gender situations is real and plays an important role in American life, as do other such power realities embedded within workplace and other socioeconomic settings. These matters, it seems to me, are important areas of study and perhaps the rightful domain of social rather than political historians, except when they impinge on the formal political world and its realities. See my comments on these matters in "The State and Practice of American Political History: The Nineteenth Century as a Test Case," *Journal of Policy History* 11 (1999): 1–29.

10. Richard Hofstadter, *The Idea of a Party System: The Rise of Legitimate Opposition in the United States, 1780–1840* (Berkeley, Calif., 1969); Michael Wallace, "Changing Concepts of Party in the United States: New York, 1815–1828," *American Historical Review* 74 (December 1968): 453–91. For its continuation, see Richard L. McCormick, *The Party Period and Public Policy: American Politics from the Age of Jackson to the Progressive Era* (New York, 1986).

11. Adams is quoted in Harry L. Watson, *Liberty and Power: The Politics of Jacksonian America* (New York, 1990), 86. Van Buren's reactions and activities can be traced in Robert V. Remini, *Martin Van Buren and the Making of the Democratic Party* (New York, 1959), among other places.

12. On 1824, see James F. Hopkins, "Election of 1824," in *The History of American Presidential Elections,* ed. Arthur M. Schlesinger, Jr., and Fred I. Israel (New York, 1974), 1:349–409; Remini, *Van Buren and the Democratic Party.*

13. Richard P. McCormick, *The Second American Party System: Party Formation in the Jacksonian Era* (Chapel Hill, N.C., 1966); Benson, *Concept of Jacksonian Democracy;* Silbey, *American Political Nation.*

14. Ronald P. Formisano, "The New Political History and the Election of 1840," *Journal of Interdisciplinary History* 23 (spring 1993): 661–82; Ronald P. Formisano, "The Invention of the Ethnocultural Interpretation," *American Historical Review* 99 (April 1994): 453–77.

15. Formisano, "New Political History"; Paul Bourke and Donald DeBats, *Washington County: Politics and Community in Antebellum America* (Baltimore, 1995); Donald J. Ratcliffe, "The Crisis of Commercialization: National Party Alignments and

the Market Revolution, 1819–1844," in Stokes and Conway, *Market Revolution in America*, 177–201.

16. Michael F. Holt, "The Election of 1840, Voter Mobilization, and the Emergence of the Second American Party System: A Reappraisal of Jacksonian Voting Behavior," in Holt, *Political Parties and American Political Development from the Age of Jackson to the Age of Lincoln* (Baton Rouge, 1992), 151–91; Formisano, "New Political History"; Watson, *Liberty and Power*.

17. There were many elements of what Sellers referred to as "democratic resistance to a stressful market revolution." Charles G. Sellers, Jr., "Capitalism and Democracy in American Historical Mythology," in Stokes and Conway, *Market Revolution in America*, 311.

18. John Ashworth, *Slavery, Capitalism, and Politics in the Antebellum Republic* (Cambridge, 1995), 1, 494. The Jackson quotation is in Watson, *Liberty and Power*, 173; Sellers, *Market Revolution*.

19. The quotation is from William Shade, "Society and Politics in Antebellum Virginia's Southside," *Journal of Southern History* 43 (May 1987): 178. The values and outlook of the Whig Party have received a great deal of attention from historians. See, for example, Daniel Walker Howe, *The Political Culture of the American Whigs* (Chicago, 1979); Michael F. Holt, *The Rise and Fall of the American Whig Party: Jacksonian Politics and the Onset of the Civil War* (New York, 1999); Gabor Boritt, *Lincoln and the Economics of the American Dream* (Memphis, 1977).

20. Theodore J. Lowi, *The End of Liberalism: Ideology, Policy, and the Crisis of Public Authority* (New York, 1969); Bray Hammond, *Banks and Politics in America from the Revolution to the Civil War* (Princeton, N.J., 1957).

21. Joel H. Silbey, *The Shrine of Party: Congressional Voting Behavior, 1841–1852* (Pittsburgh, 1967); Herbert Ershkowitz and William Shade, "Consensus or Conflict? Political Behavior in State Legislatures during the Jacksonian Era," *Journal of American History* 58 (December 1971): 591–622; Holt, *Rise and Fall of American Whig Party*.

22. Robert Kelley, *The Cultural Pattern in American Politics: The First Century* (New York, 1979); Robert P. Swierenga, "Ethnoreligious Political Behavior in the Mid-Nineteenth Century: Voting, Values, Cultures," in *Religion and American Politics, from the Colonial Period to the 1980s*, ed. Mark A. Noll (New York, 1990), 146–71.

23. Daniel Walker Howe, "The Market Revolution and the Shaping of Identity in Whig-Jacksonian America," in Stokes and Conway, *Market Revolution in America*, 266; Richard Cawardine, "'Antinomians' and 'Arminians': Methodists and the Market Revolution," in ibid., 301. A number of scholars have suggested that with regard to ethnic antagonisms demonstrated in election campaigns and class-based and economically rooted confrontations, "ethnicity and class cannot be divorced." I am not so sure. Obviously, some of these conflicts had roots in differential economic situations and opportunities and, to that degree, certainly reflected aspects of America's political economy. But many of them lay outside the kind of economic interest-group politics and ideological confrontations over the nature of the nation's economic core that structured so much of politics after 1820. The particular form they took suggests how deeply rooted they were. Why would some political perspectives take the particular shape of ethnoreligious identities and commitments unless they had meaning and power in people's lives, a meaning and power that had some independence from economic forces and that remained rooted in historical memories and a group's specific experience? See Sellers, "Capitalism and Democracy," 320; Kelley, *Cultural Pattern*.

24. Jean Baker, *Affairs of Party: The Political Culture of Northern Democrats in the Mid-Nineteenth Century* (Ithaca, N.Y., 1983), introduces the theme of the political socialization of Americans in this era.

25. This process is described in Silbey, *American Political Nation.*

26. Benson, *Concept of Jacksonian Democracy;* Edward Pessen, *Riches, Class, and Power before the Civil War* (Lexington, Mass., 1973); Whitman Ridgeway, *Community Leadership in Maryland, 1790–1840: A Comparative Analysis of Power in Society* (Chapel Hill, N.C., 1979); Ralph Wooster, *The People in Power: Courthouse and Statehouse in the Lower South, 1850–1860* (Knoxville, Tenn., 1969); and Charles Sydnor, *Gentlemen Freeholders: Political Practices in Washington's Virginia* (Chapel Hill, N.C., 1952), are a few of the studies that deal with the nature of political leadership and the way its members operated in the system.

27. Watson, *Liberty and Power,* 90. In these remarks about the constant need to mobilize voters to do their duty and about how party leaders operated in caucuses and conventions, I am responding to a recent challenge to the partisan-dominant narrative of these years, offered by Glenn C. Altschuler and Stuart M. Blumin in several articles and a new book. See "'Where Is the Real America?' Politics and Popular Consciousness in the Antebellum Era," *American Quarterly* 49 (June 1997): 225–67; "Limits of Political Engagement in Antebellum America: A New Look at the Golden Age of Participatory Democracy," *Journal of American History* 84 (December 1997): 855–85; *Rude Republic: Americans and Their Politics, 1820–1890* (Princeton, N.J., 2000).

28. Joel H. Silbey, *The American Party Battle: Election Campaign Pamphlets, 1828–1876,* 2 vols. (Cambridge, 1999).

29. Ibid., xvii, quoting "Speech of Mr. Bartlett at a meeting of citizens Opposed to the Re-Election of Andrew Jackson" (Portsmouth, N.H., 1832).

30. "Every election," Watson argues, "became an urgent referendum on the character of the future" (*Liberty and Power,* 15).

31. Silbey, *American Party Battle,* 1:16.

32. Ibid., 7 et seq.

33. Ibid., 154, lays out the ideological constructs of each party.

34. *United States Democratic Review* 40 (December 1857): 517.

35. Howe, *Political Culture of American Whigs;* Holt, *Rise and Fall of American Whig Party.*

36. Ibid.

37. "Proceedings and Address of the Convention of Delegates . . . to Nominate . . . John Quincy Adams" (Columbus, Ohio, 1827), 7, quoted in Silbey, *American Party Battle,* 1:14.

38. See the discussions in Howe, *Political Culture of American Whigs,* and Holt, *Rise and Fall of American Whig Party.*

39. On the post office expansion, see Richard R. John, *Spreading the News: The American Postal System from Franklin to Morse* (Cambridge, 1995). The idiom of party warfare is discussed in Silbey, *American Party Battle;* Watson, *Liberty and Power,* 223.

40. William Gienapp, "'Politics Seems to Enter into Everything': Political Culture in the North, 1840–1860," in *Essays on American Antebellum Politics, 1840–1860,* ed. Stephen E. Maizlish and John Kushma (College Station, Tex., 1982), 14–69; Baker, *Affairs of Party.*

41. See the discussion of party loyalty, voter turnout, and persistent partisanship in voting behavior in, among other places, Silbey, *American Political Nation.*

42. See McCormick, *Party Period and Public Policy,* and Ballard Campbell, *The Growth of American Government: Governance from the Cleveland Era to the Present* (Bloomington, Ind., 1995).

43. Tocqueville is quoted by Michael Kammen in his *Alexis de Tocqueville and Democracy in America* (Washington, D.C., 1998), 47; Heather Cox Richardson, *The Greatest Nation of the Earth: Republican Economic Policies during the Civil War* (Cambridge, 1997), 27.

44. William Novak, *The People's Welfare: Law and Regulation in the Nineteenth Century United States* (Chapel Hill, N.C., 1996), 3; see also Richard R. John's useful review article "Governmental Institutions as Agents of Change: Rethinking American Political Development in the Early Republic, 1787–1835," *Studies in American Political Development* 11 (fall 1997): 347–80.

45. Theda Skocpol, *Protecting Soldiers and Mothers: The Political Origins of Social Policy in the United States* (Cambridge, 1992); Stephen Skowronek, *Building a New American State: The Expansion of National Administrative Capacity, 1877–1920* (Cambridge, 1982); Richard Bensel, *Yankee Leviathan: The Origins of Central State Authority in America, 1859–1877* (Cambridge, 1990).

46. Major L. Wilson, *The Presidency of Martin Van Buren* (Lawrence, Kans., 1984), 132.

47. On the expansion of the electorate, Chilton Williamson, *American Suffrage, from Property to Democracy* (Princeton, N.J., 1960), remains the essential introduction.

48. Mary P. Ryan, "Civil Society as Democratic Practice: North American Cities during the Nineteenth Century," *Journal of Interdisciplinary History* 29 (spring 1999): 575. See also David Roediger, *The Wages of Whiteness: Race and the Making of the American Working Class* (London, 1991). Some historians have stressed the many gendered qualities present in this political system as it evolved. In their robust determination to confront domestic enemies and pick at least rhetorical fights with foreign countries threatening the nation, the Democrats exuded what Watson refers to as "the raw masculine appeal of Jackson and his movement" (Harry Watson, *Andrew Jackson versus Henry Clay: Democracy and Development in Antebellum America* [Boston, 1998], 38), underscoring the pugnacious articulation of male values in much of that movement's rhetoric and understanding of the world they inhabited. At the same time, we appreciate from the work of Varon how much women were involved in Whig Party activities and in helping to shape that party's outlook and approach in certain matters. Elizabeth Varon, *We Mean to Be Counted: White Women and Politics in Antebellum Virginia* (Chapel Hill, N.C., 1998). See also Mary P. Ryan, *Women in Public: Between Banners and Ballots, 1825–1880* (Baltimore, 1990).

49. Ronald G. Walters, *American Reformers, 1815–1860* (New York, 1978); Ellen DuBois, *Feminism and Suffrage: The Emergence of an Independent Women's Movement in America, 1848–1869* (New York, 1978); Sean Wilentz, *Chants Democratic: New York City and the Rise of the American Working Class, 1788–1850* (New York, 1984).

50. The pamphlets, speeches, and platforms of these movements are filled with such denunciations of major-party culture and behavior. See, as one example, "Address of the Liberty Party of Pennsylvania to the People of the State" (Philadelphia, 1844), included in Silbey, *American Party Battle,* 1:178–207.

51. Varon, *We Mean to Be Counted.*

52. Mark Voss-Hubbard, "The 'Third Party Tradition' Reconsidered: Third Parties and American Public Life, 1830–1900," *Journal of American History* 86 (June 1999): 121–50. There are numerous studies of the individual third parties on the scene, many of which are included in preceding notes.

53. David Grimsted, *American Mobbing, 1828–1861: Toward Civil War* (New York, 1998); Reeve Huston, "Land and Freedom: The New York Anti-Rent Wars and the Construction of Free Labor in the Antebellum North," in *Labor Histories: Class, Politics, and the Working Class Experience*, ed. Erie Arnesan et al. (Urbana, Ill., 1998), 1944.

54. A useful study of a range of these parties is Richard H. Sewell, *Ballots for Freedom: Antislavery Politics in the United States, 1837–1860* (New York,1976).

55. Voss-Hubbard, "'Third Party Tradition."

56. Ronald P. Formisano, "The 'Party Period' Revisited," *Journal of American History* 86 (June 1999): 93–120.

57. Voss-Hubbard, "Third Party Tradition," 150.

58. Silbey, *American Political Nation*. There are useful comments on this in Richard Oestreicher, "Urban Working Class Political Behavior and Theories of American Electoral Politics, 1870–1940," *Journal of American History* 74 (March 1988): 1257–86.

59. There is no shortage of intelligent historiography recounting the sectional story. Among the most recent, see William Freehling, *The Road to Disunion: Secessionists at Bay, 1776–1854* (New York, 1990); John Ashworth, *Slavery, Capitalism, and Politics in the Antebellum Republic*, vol. 1, *Commerce and Compromise, 1820–1850* (Cambridge, 1995); Bruce Levine, *Half Slave and Half Free: The Roots of Civil War* (New York, 1992).

60. There are studies of the development of the party system in the individual southern states. See, among many, Marc Kruman, *Parties and Politics in North Carolina, 1836–1845* (Baton Rouge, 1983); M. Philip Lucas, "The Development of the Second Party System in Mississippi, 1817–1846" (Ph.D. diss., Cornell University, 1984); J. Mills Thornton, *Politics and Power in a Slave Society: Alabama, 1800–1860* (Baton Rouge, 1978); William Shade, *Democratizing the Old Dominion: Virginia and the Second Party System, 1824–1861* (Charlottesville, Va., 1996).

61. This certainly was true of Martin Van Buren, whose fear of the return of Federalism shaped his attitudes toward sectional rumblings for much of his career.

62. Ashworth, *Slavery, Capitalism, and Politics*, 368.

63. Michael F. Holt, *Political Crisis of the 1850s* (New York, 1983); Silbey, *Shrine of Party*; Michael Morrison, *Slavery and the American West: The Eclipse of Manifest Destiny and the Coming of the Civil War* (Chapel Hill, N.C., 1997).

64. Freehling, *Road to Disunion*.

65. The best introductions to the voter realignment of the 1850s are William E. Gienapp, *The Origins of the Republican Party, 1852–1856* (New York, 1987), and Holt, *Political Crisis of the 1850s*.

66. Ibid.

67. Gienapp, *Origins of the Republican Party*; Joel H. Silbey, *The Partisan Imperative: The Dynamics of American Politics before the Civil War* (New York, 1985), 127–65.

68. The best introductions to the condition of the Democrats and Republicans in the late 1850s include Holt, *Political Crisis of the 1850s*; David Potter, *The Impending Crisis* (New York, 1976); and Robert Johannsen, *Stephen A. Douglas* (New York, 1973).

69. Potter, *Impending Crisis*; Holt, *Political Crisis of the 1850s*.

70. See, for example, Kruman, *Parties and Politics in North Carolina*; Daniel Crofts, *Reluctant Confederates: Upper South Unionists in the Secession Crisis* (Chapel Hill, N.C., 1989).

71. Philip Paludan, *The Presidency of Abraham Lincoln* (Lawrence, Kans., 1994); "Address of the Union League Club of Philadelphia" (Philadelphia, 1864), 25.

72. Paludan, *Presidency of Lincoln*; Richardson, *Greatest Nation*.

73. On the northern Democrats, one can usefully begin with Joel H. Silbey, *A Re-*

spectable Minority: The Democratic Party in the Civil War Era, 1860–1868 (New York, 1977).

74. Although he and I disagree about its meaning, there is a wealth of useful information about politics in the Confederacy in George Rable, *The Confederate Republic: A Revolt against Politics* (Chapel Hill, N.C., 1994). See also Thomas B. Alexander and Richard Beringer, *The Anatomy of the Confederate Congress: A Study of the Influences of Member Characteristics on Legislative Voting Behavior, 1861–1865* (Nashville, 1972).

4. Change and Continuity in the Party Period

The Substance and Structure of American Politics,
1835–1885

Michael F. Holt

When examining the substance and structure of American politics between the mid-1830s and mid-1880s, it is useful to address one of the most venerable interpretive problems confronted by historians: disentangling and weighing the relative importance of change and continuity, of flux and stasis, over time. Until twenty years ago, many historians would have found this suggestion dumbfounding, since the predominance of change in political life during this period seemed apparent. Except for the 1840s, foreign policy exerted less influence on domestic politics than at earlier or later times. But these were years of almost ceaseless internal demographic, social, economic, inter-sectional, political, and constitutional transformations.

Almost all historians believed that those changes, plus the dislocations they caused, provided both the structural framework and the substantive basis for politics by creating class, ethnic, religious, racial, sectional, and ideological cleavages in the population. Those societal cleavages generated the issues that government had to address and the distinctive electoral coalitions that rival political parties sought to mobilize in order to win control of government. From this perspective, in short, the only thing that was constant about politics in that half century was change itself.

Until twenty years ago, most political historians would also have found it odd, if not positively bizarre, to analyze the half century from the mid-1830s to the mid-1880s as a single, coherent political unit. After all, this period encompassed all of one and parts of two other distinct political eras in which historians were traditionally trained as specialists. And those specialists rarely trespassed on each other's chronological turf.

The first of these eras was the Jacksonian period, 1824 to 1848, during which the nation's first mass-based two-party system emerged and the population moved westward, expanding the nation's boundaries to the Pacific Ocean. The focus of partisan combat was primarily, though never exclusively, the ideological dimensions and practical consequences of economic policy and of government's role in promoting economic development, a process some historians have recently referred to as the "market revolution."

Second was the era of the Civil War and Reconstruction, usually dated from the introduction of the Wilmot Proviso in 1846 to the withdrawal of federal troops from the South in 1877. According to conventional wisdom, during these years, American politics (certainly national politics) was shaped primarily by sectional conflict between the North and South, first over questions involving slavery and its westward expansion, then over issues connected with the conduct of the Civil War and the abolition of slavery, and finally over the terms for reintegrating the former Confederate states back into the Union and for defining and protecting the civil and political rights of former slaves.

The years after 1877, in turn, were traditionally the bailiwick of a different group of specialists. They studied the Gilded Age, the origins of the so-called New South, or the social and economic background to Populism and Progressivism. Here, especially for those who did not focus on the South, where racial cleavages continued to structure political life, the stress was on the disruptive impact of railroad expansion and consolidation, industrialization, urbanization, and immigration. In these post-Reconstruction years, economic issues returned to the center stage of politics, whether in the guise of battles over currency, squabbles over tariff rates, or demands for reform of government and regulation of business enterprise.

In other words, the defining societal cleavage that structured and provided the substantive basis for partisan and policy conflict changed at least twice in this half century. From the mid-1830s to the late 1840s, it pitted those who benefited from a cash-based market economy, accepted its value system, and wanted to expand the geographic area and number of people it encompassed against those who feared, resented, or had been victimized by the market economy and who accordingly rejected its value system and resisted its expansion. Between 1846 and 1877, the defining societal cleavage aligned white northerners against white southerners, although each group had partisan allies in the other section. And from 1877 until the end of the century, the most important fault line was between an industrial and financial metropole stretching from New England to Chicago and a southern and western periphery whose heavily agrarian and extractive economy bore an almost colonial relationship to that of the metropole and whose residents evinced the kind of resentments such subordinate status often engendered.

Alternatives to the Conventional Periodization

Some historians, of course, never accepted this conventional periodization or the idea of a chronological transition in the issues that formed the substance of political combat. Almost fifty years ago, Frederick Merk and Lee Benson argued that there were eastern antecedents in the 1840s and 1850s for the railroad rate regulation that we associate with the midwestern Grange movement of the 1870s.[1] Others have insisted—correctly, in my opinion—that a recurring determination to strip private banks of their control over the nation's currency engendered Jacksonian calls for hard money in the 1840s, Greenbackism in the 1860s and early 1870s, and demands for the free coinage of silver in the late 1870s and 1880s.

The so-called new political historians of the 1960s and 1970s—now a decidedly aged and largely ignored cohort—offered a more formidable and temporarily influential challenge to the conventional wisdom. On the one hand, they adopted the voter-based paradigm of realignment and party systems first advanced by Walter Dean Burnham and others and thus rejected the issue-based periodization that posited an evolution over time of distinctively different Jacksonian, Civil War, and post-Reconstruction political eras. On the other hand, they argued that ethnoreligious values were the primary shapers of the electorate's partisan choices throughout the nineteenth century and thus posited a striking continuity in the variables, if not in their specific configurations during different party systems, that structured electoral cleavages from 1835 to 1885 and beyond.

Yet even these new political historians might find it odd to treat those years as a single unit, certainly as a single static unit. According to their framework, those years encompassed the stable phase of the second party system; the electoral realignment or fluctuating phase, in which that system was replaced by a third or Civil War party system; and the first years of the stable phase of that new system. That historians who have adopted this framework disagree about the chronological boundaries of these various phases and about the factors that engendered the transitions between them further suggests that change, not continuity, was the dominant characteristic of these years.

Nor do claims about the persistent centrality of ethnoreligious voting cleavages hold much water on close inspection. For one thing, with the exception of William G. Shade's examination of antebellum Virginia,[2] the proponents of this argument never studied the South, where ethnic and religious identities were patently not the engine that drove popular voting behavior, let alone governance. Paul Kleppner, the crown prince of the ethnoculturalists, admits as much by excluding the South altogether from his book *The Third Electoral System, 1853–1892*.[3] To his credit, Kleppner also admits that ethnoreligious divisions between Democrats and Republicans crystallized only during the stable phase of the third party system, which began in 1876. The years between 1853 and that election, in contrast, constituted a prolonged fluctuating or realigning stage in which other factors alternated in sporadic fashion with ethnoreligious disputes to shape governance and voting behavior.

One can demonstrate with relative ease that primarily nonethnocultural variables accounted for fluctuations in voter turnout and election results in most contests between 1836 and 1852 as well. Arguably, it is precisely the temporal fluctuation in the salience and impact of ethnocultural issues, not their constancy over time, that makes them interesting. The instances in which political parties tried to exploit them tell us much about chronological variations in the importance, or at least the partisan usefulness, of other kinds of substantive issues in mobilizing the electorate in this period. On balance, both the party system–realignment periodization of politics and the emphasis on ethnocultural issues advanced by the new political historians reinforce the conclusion that change was far more important than continuity in American politics between the mid-1830s and the mid-1880s.

Yet that ranking of the two variables was decisively reversed some twenty years ago in an exciting and imaginative attempt to reframe and reconceptualize our understanding of nineteenth-century politics. The major architects of this reinterpretation were Richard L. McCormick, then a historian at Rutgers University and now president of the University of Washington, and Joel R. Silbey of Cornell University, a contributor to this collection of essays and one of the founding fathers of the new political history. Silbey hinted at this reconceptualization in some earlier papers, but McCormick first presented it to a wider audience with a seminal article published in September 1979 titled "The Party Period and Public Policy: An Exploratory Hypothesis."[4] An essay collection with the same main title followed in 1986.[5] Meanwhile, Silbey elaborated the interpretation in two important books: *The Partisan Imperative* (1985) and, especially, *The American Political Nation, 1838–1893*, which appeared in 1991.[6]

Both men sought to replace the realignment–party system framework of political periodization by arguing that the years from the late 1830s to almost 1900—that is, the entire period under consideration here—should be understood as a single, distinctive whole whose politics differed markedly from both earlier and later periods. What defined this period and provided its internal unity was the importance of major political parties in dominating political life, in shaping the behavior of both voters and officeholders, in arousing previously unprecedented and thereafter unequaled levels of partisan commitment and political engagement in the populace at large, and in eclipsing alternative methods or routes by which citizens and interest groups sought to shape what government did. The issue concerns and demands of citizens might have fluctuated over time. But what was most striking and important about political life during the last six decades of the nineteenth century was the continuity, the constancy, the fixedness of the intermediary political institutions that structured politics and governance and thereby channeled society's interaction with the state—the major political parties.

Although agreeing on much, McCormick and Silbey present slightly different versions of the "party period" paradigm. Silbey, for example, still embraces the ethnocultural interpretation he helped formulate, and he argues that along with economic and sectional issues, ethnic and religious variables constantly influenced voting behavior during the life of the "American political nation." Yet what matters most to Silbey is not the exogenous socioeconomic environment in which politics was situated or the particular issues that environment generated.

Rather, it is the centrality of major political parties and the intense partisan commitment they generated in determining how the public and government interacted from the 1830s to the 1890s.

Despite the realignment of the 1850s and the cataclysmic impact of the Civil War and Reconstruction, he contends, "The rituals of politics, its rhetoric, its institutions, and most of all its commitments, were all partisan. Partisanship was the glue that held the political nation together, provided its understanding of what was at stake, and established the structures, rules, and sanctions through which all else ran." Or again, "unrelieved, unstinting partisan devotion . . . characterized a population that took its politics, and especially its parties, more than seriously. . . . It created an unprecedented static element in American political life, one that dictated that all matters had to begin with the fact of intense party loyalty driving the political world."[7]

McCormick agrees with Silbey that political parties were "the objects of vital attachments" and that the years between 1840 and the late 1890s constituted "the period when parties dominated political participation and channeled the flow of governmental policies."[8] Whereas Silbey stresses the intermediary role of parties between state and society as the key to the period's uniqueness and internal coherence, McCormick insists "that the world of politics and government was decisively influenced by the socioeconomic environment." Though underdeveloped from a modern perspective, the American economy between the late 1830s and 1900 possessed enormous potential for growth. Thus it allowed "entrepreneurial-minded Americans" who wanted "governmental policies promoting capitalist development" to place "their demands at the head of the governmental agenda and [keep] them there for the rest of the century."[9]

Earlier historians, McCormick contends, failed to appreciate "the role of distributive issues in calling forth and fueling party competition." Some Americans, he admits, always objected to these promotional or "distributive" governmental economic policies, but to no avail. Despite "the intrusion of sectional differences that party politics could not resolve, entrepreneurial elites and their political allies kept distributional issues at the fore" between 1840 and 1900. "Not until the early 1900s, when social and economic changes necessitated the adoption of a new structure of governmental policies did the basic patterns of American politics change."[10]

Despite minor differences, McCormick and Silbey are in accord about the fundamental continuity, sameness, and stasis of American politics from the mid-1830s to the mid-1880s. "Once the party period's unique patterns of politics and policy came into being," summarizes McCormick, "political leaders, party organizations, and government officials worked diligently and successfully to maintain them, despite the countervailing pressures emanating from the sectional controversy and, later, from demands for policies of economic regulation."[11]

* * *

Reconstituting the Party Period

Silbey and McCormick were hardly the only scholars to stress the importance of political parties and the uniquely high levels of public participation in partisan life and electoral politics in these years. In 1982, for example, William E. Gienapp published an influential essay on the intensity and pervasiveness of popular engagement in partisan political life during the antebellum period, one that, in effect, rang changes on the theme Burnham had advanced seventeen years earlier in his pathbreaking article "The Changing Shape of the American Political Universe."[12] Although it was hardly their major purpose, historically oriented political scientists and sociologists such as Stephen Skowronek, Richard Bensel, and Theda Skocpol also contributed to the credibility and dominance of this new conceptual paradigm.[13]

Interested primarily in charting the emergence of an autonomous and bureaucratic national administrative state, one that was insulated from partisan control and thus provided an alternative to political parties, along with monopolization of the channels linking the state with society, they demonstrated that in contrast to the twentieth century, no such nonpartisan state emerged in the nineteenth. Thus, Skowronek characterized the late-nineteenth-century political regime as one of "courts and parties, not an administrative state." Bensel admits in his *Yankee Leviathan* that the surge in the power and reach of the national government in Washington during and after the Civil War was inextricably dependent on Republican Party control of that government and that by the mid-1870s, Republicans had joined Democrats in abandoning the activist state. Skocpol recognizes that the seeds of a modern welfare state lay in the program of pensions for Civil War veterans and their dependents, which Republican politicians supported for nakedly partisan reasons.

As the shrinking fraction of historians of the United States who remain interested in politics is well aware, the "party period" paradigm has recently come under assault in a series of articles in the *Journal of American History*. In an intentionally provocative, methodologically questionable, and ultimately unpersuasive analysis, two of Silbey's colleagues at Cornell, Glenn Altschuler and Stuart Blumin, attempted to debunk the idea that antebellum Americans were intensely engaged by or interested in partisan political life.[14] Ronald Formisano, yet another participant in this collective examination of American politics from the Constitution to the present, insists that Silbey and McCormick exaggerate the dominance of the major political parties over public life and governance, especially at the state and local levels.[15] And Mark Voss-Hubbard argues that the frequent appearance of third parties in the nineteenth century is evidence of a sharp disjunction in citizens' attitudes toward electoral politics, which they expected to be partisan, and toward policy making or governance, which, he asserts, they insisted should be nonpartisan.[16]

In my opinion, some of the criticisms advanced by Formisano and Voss-Hubbard go too far in dismissing the central role of major parties during the party period.[17] Nonetheless, one can still view that paradigm from a perspective that is different from that of its leading proponents. Those proponents tend to ignore or at least downplay political change over time *within* the years between the mid-1830s and 1890s, in order to stress the constancy of the partisan framework and the socioeconomic environment that structured and froze electoral politics and governance into predictable and unchanging patterns during those years. Silbey's contention about "an unprecedented static element in American political life" emphasizes stasis at the expense of flux in those years.[18] Simultaneously, McCormick's contention about the unshakable dominance of distributive policy making obfuscates important changes in the nature of governance and its relationship to partisan conflict during the party period.

If political life was so fixed between 1835 and 1885, for example, one must wonder why economic issues were more central to interparty conflict during the second party system than during the third; why the depression from 1837 to 1843 had a demonstrably different impact on the major parties at both the policy-making and the electoral levels from the depression of the 1870s; and why the orientation of dissident third parties was toward noneconomic questions before the Civil War but primarily on economic issues after it.[19] These changes across time raise serious questions about how "static" public life was and whether mantras about the centrality of "distributive" policy making and governance are useful in explaining or even describing the impact of economic issues and conditions on politics. To phrase the matter differently, even if the structural framework and substantive basis of politics were similar before and after the Civil War with regard to economic questions, the politics itself was not. It changed in intriguing ways.

But in fact, the structural framework shaping economic policy making was *not* the same before and after the Civil War. With regard to economic policies and much else, there was a significant change between the 1830s and 1880s in the allocation between the national and state governments of jurisdictional authority over different policy areas of public life. One of the most striking omissions from the literature on the party period, and from the recent debates about it, for that matter, is any serious consideration of federalism and its evolution in the nineteenth century. Among other things, looking at federalism allows one to appreciate the role of courts in shaping the framework that structured politics and governance in the period under consideration here.

For example, suppose one punctuated the beginning and end of this period with Supreme Court decisions—the *Charles River Bridge Case* and *New York City v. Miln* in 1837 and the *Wabash* decision of 1886. The two early decisions defended and expanded the regulatory and police powers of state governments, in apparent open violation of the Constitution's supremacy and interstate commerce clauses in the case of *Miln*.[20] And *Charles River Bridge* opened the way for the apparently infinite distributive policies by state governments that McCormick finds so characteristic of the party period. *Wabash*, in contrast, restricted the regulatory power of state governments over railroads and invited Congress to move, however hesitantly, into that breach the following year with the Interstate Commerce Act of 1887, thus marking a shift from state to national regulation of economic life.[21]

Within the period under consideration, state governments, not Washington, exercised the primary regulatory powers over the nonmonetary sectors of the economy and society. That fact helps explain why third parties seeking, for example, railroad regulation, the dissolution of monopolies, or even Prohibition focused primarily on the capture of state governments in this period. (In contrast, the later Populists sought the nationalization of railroad firms rather than state regulation of them.) Yet the sharp lines dividing the jurisdiction of state and national governments could also work in the other way. Because before the Civil War only the national government could decide whether slavery would be permitted in federal territories, the Free-Soil Party, when arranging coalitions with Whigs or Democrats between 1848 and 1853, always demanded control over U.S. House and Senate seats in return for helping the major party win control of state governments.

When considering changes in the federal system between the 1830s and the 1880s, most historians probably think first of the increase in the federal government's responsibility for the civil and political rights of blacks during the Civil War and Reconstruction. Once it was fashionable to speak of the Civil War as a watershed that permanently shifted power and authority away from the states to the national government. Years ago, however, historians such as Harold Hyman and Morton Keller taught us that government at all levels of the federal system, not just the national government, increased its activity and intrusion into society during the Civil War era and, during the 1870s, retreated from that unprecedented surge of activism.[22]

Specifically with respect to the new federal role in securing and protecting black rights, careful historians such as Michael Les Benedict and Herman Belz reminded us that even most Republicans—let alone Democrats, who remained intransigently committed to states' rights and anti-statist dogma—were determined to preserve state-centered federalism and to avoid a concentration of all effective power in Washington.[23] And it has long been known that whatever new rights Congress granted blacks in the Fourteenth and Fifteenth Amendments, the Enforcement Acts of 1870 and 1871, and the Civil Rights Act of 1875, those rights and especially the ability of the federal government to secure them were quickly and severely limited in a series of Supreme Court decisions between 1873 and 1883.

Federalism, Policy Making, and the Rules of the Game

Other important changes in the federal system occurred within this period that affected both the structure and the substance of political life. One can begin with federal regulation of electoral politics itself. Prior to 1840, state governments had virtually complete control over suffrage rights in state and federal elections, over the scheduling and conduct of congressional elections, and, to a more limited extent, even over the scheduling of popular balloting for president, which was not held on the same day in November until 1848. This control had a marked impact on partisan competitiveness, on differentials among states in turnout rates, on the agendas of both major and minor parties, and ultimately on the policy outputs of state legislatures and Congress, since all these factors influenced who won control of those bodies.

With regard to these "rules of the game," most historians have focused on suffrage rights and especially the changes wrought, particularly in the South, by the federal government's enfranchisement of blacks during Reconstruction. That achievement did help restore two-party competition to former Confederate states and was absolutely essential to the temporary dominance the Republican Party exercised in them. It also made race itself a far more open issue in southern politics than it had been before the Civil War.

But blacks were not the only demographic group whose suffrage rights became an issue in this period largely because state governments retained control over them. Immigrant voting, for example, became a partisan football because states could—and some of those controlled by Democrats did—allow unnaturalized aliens to vote years before they became U.S. citizens. State authority over suffrage also helps explain why state judges, and not just federal courts, had jurisdiction over naturalization itself. Almost everyone correctly expected most immigrants to vote Democratic, which accounts for the failure of the pro-Catholic, pro-immigrant strategy the Whig Party pursued in the presidential election of 1852.

State control of suffrage rights with regard to immigrants also explains why the nativist backlashes of the 1840s and 1850s concentrated first on capturing control of state governments, as well as why congressional Republicans attempted to neutralize the immigrant vote, at least in congressional elections, through federal enforcement legislation in 1870 and 1871 that allowed Republican-appointed federal judges and marshals to monitor the polls in urban areas. In short, only by asserting a national regulatory power over congressional elections could Republicans offset the control the Democrats had achieved over state and local governments by 1870 in New York, New Jersey, Maryland, Missouri, and elsewhere.

Though much less examined, congressional attempts to reshape the conduct and calendar of congressional elections were in fact of far greater consequence.

During the 1840 election cycle, six of twenty-six states chose congressmen on statewide at-large tickets rather than in individual districts, and both New York and Pennsylvania had multimember local districts in their largest cities. This practice obviously made it easier for one party or another to sweep all the seats in those elections than would single-member districts. In 1842, Congress passed a law to stop this practice by requiring all states to use single-member districts, although even in the 1842–1843 contests, four states continued to use at-large tickets.

Conversion to the single-member district suddenly made control of state legislatures and governorships all-important, since the majority party could draw—that is, gerrymander—district lines and thus rig the partisan balance of congressional delegations. Two examples must suffice to demonstrate the impact. In 1840, Whigs carried all six House seats on New Jersey's at-large ticket. In the next election, after Democrats designed individual districts, Whigs carried only one of five seats, even though their average percentage of the popular vote actually increased in four of five districts.[24] Conversely, in Georgia, Whigs won none of the eight seats on the at-large ticket in 1842, even though they garnered 48.5 percent of the statewide vote. Two years later, after a Whig legislature apportioned the districts, they won four of eight, with exactly the same percentage of the popular vote.[25]

Changes in the calendar of congressional elections were even more decisive in determining who controlled the House of Representatives and thus what kinds of policies Congress could and could not enact. As the result of a law Congress passed in 1872, voters in November 1874 chose every member of the House of Representatives on the same day. From that time until today, the economic, political, and issue context in which congressional races occurred was similar, though never identical, across all districts. In part as a result of this change, Democrats in 1874 enjoyed one of the most sweeping comebacks in American history, as voters everywhere sought to punish incumbent Republicans for failing to do anything meaningful to end the depression. The simultaneity of congressional elections, I suspect, also helps explain the stunning surge of the Greenback-Labor vote in the 1878 elections.

Prior to 1874, each state scheduled congressional elections to suit itself, and very few were held on the same day. As a result, elections to select the members of any new House ranged over an eighteen-month period, starting in August of even-numbered years and extending through November of odd-numbered years. Because the economic conditions, salient issues, and partisan context of those elections could and often did vary sharply over time, and because the influence of presidential coattails was minimal even during presidential election years, it was highly unusual for any party to enjoy the kind of sweep the Democrats achieved in 1874. One wonders, indeed, whether the Republican rout would have been so extensive had the old system continued to prevail in the 1870s, for by the time of the elections traditionally held in odd years (1875, in this case), Republicans already would have passed the Specie Resumption Act and reinstigated anti-Catholic sentiment to mobilize traditional Republican voters.

One need not rely on speculation, however, to demonstrate how decisive the peculiar election calendar was in shaping control of Congress and the partisan balance of power prior to 1874. In 1848, the Whigs won 57 percent of the House seats filled that year. In 1849, they won only 30 percent of the ninety seats contested, most of which were in the South. Consequently, Democrats won control of the next House of Representatives. The 1849 results, in turn, were caused largely by an intensification of sectional antagonism between November 1848 and the spring of 1849 and by a pronounced drop-off in Whig turnout that reflected disillusionment with the new Taylor administration. Had all seats been determined in November 1848 on the same day as the presidential election, Whigs would have undoubtedly won over 60 percent of the House seats. In particular, they would have won far more southern seats, since the unpopularity of Lewis Cass in Dixie would have depressed Democratic turnout in congressional contests just as it did in the presidential race.

What might have happened if the Whigs had controlled the House in the Thirty-first Congress? Equally important, what would have been the result of the absence of southern Democratic victories in the 1849 congressional elections, which would not have taken place? Obviously, it is impossible to say. But it is certainly arguable, given what did happen, that there would have been no Compromise of 1850. Instead, well before Zachary Taylor died, California would probably have been admitted as a free state without the accompanying measures and the damaging maneuvers that actual events inflicted on the Whig Party.

Yet control over suffrage and congressional elections was not the only area in which changes in federalism during the party period transformed the structural framework in which politics took place. Those changes also influenced which level of the federal system had jurisdiction over particular policy areas, and thus the mix and resonance of issues that parties used to compete for office at the state and national levels. Let me illustrate this impact by contrasting the continuity or stability of disputes over ethnocultural questions from the mid-1830s to the mid-1880s with the marked reconfiguration of battles over monetary and banking policy during those same years.

One reason why banking and money questions sparked intense interparty combat from the panic of 1837 until the early 1850s is that both state and national governments had a voice in regulating such matters. Thus the stands parties took on state banking policy could reinforce the stands Whigs and Democrats took in Congress on, say, the independent treasury system and its hard-money requirements for the national government. Since the credibility of state banknotes, the amount of them in circulation, and the interest rates on bank credit ultimately depended on the size of the nation's specie reserves and thus on international specie flows, both parties saw tariff policy as integrally linked to banking and monetary policy. Thus, both parties could provide the electorate with coherent and distinctive platforms on two of the most important aspects of economic policy.

Actions by Congress during the Civil War dramatically changed these patterns of partisan conflict. The National Banking Acts, the corollary effort to tax state banks out of business, and the Legal Tender Act effectively ended the role of state governments in banking and monetary policy. It was no longer grist for partisan combat at the state level; only Congress was now a player. In turn, the issues were now the expansion or abolition of the national banking system, the method for paying off the national debt, the expansion or contraction of the amount of greenbacks in circulation, and, after passage of the Specie Resumption Act in January 1875, whether gold or silver should be the coin in which greenbacks, bonds, and national banknotes were eventually redeemed. And on those questions, the fault line was not so much Republicans versus Democrats as eastern and western blocs of both parties against each other.

In contrast, although ethnic and religious charges and countercharges occasionally characterized partisan appeals in congressional and presidential elections during these years—1844, 1854–1860, and 1884, to name some obvious examples—they were hardly a continuous or pervasive presence in elections for national office. The reason is that except for its ability to establish the length of the naturalization period for immigrant aliens, the national government simply lacked jurisdiction over the specific public policies that fueled ethnocultural conflict. Prohibition, for example, fell under the aegis of state police powers, whose scope and immunity from federal oversight had been celebrated by Justice P. P. Barbour in the Supreme Court's *New York v. Miln* decision of 1837. Thus, when Prohibitionism influenced congressional elections during the party period, it was almost always because those elections coincided with contests for state legislatures, which could actually do something about regulating liquor. An exhaustive survey of all 234 congressional races in 1854 and 1855, during the height of the Maine Law and Know-Nothing mania, found only three men who ran on explicit and exclusive Maine Law tickets.[26]   ·

An even better example concerns the specific policy issue that fueled intense if episodic outbursts of anti-Catholic sentiment from the 1830s to the 1880s and beyond. This was the effort of the Roman Catholic Church to secure municipal or state legislation that banned reading of the King James version of the Bible in public schools and that provided public (tax) funding for Catholic parochial schools. This remained a live and bitter issue in ways that it cannot be today, in large part because of a dispositive Supreme Court decision in 1833, *Baron v. Baltimore*, which ruled that the first ten amendments of the U.S. Constitution, including the First Amendment ban on governmental establishment of religion, applied only to the national government, not the states. In short, the school issue and its capacity to provoke politically salient religious conflict remained the exclusive preserve of state and local governments because of a court ruling on federalism.

This fact became clear when Republicans consciously tried to resurrect and nationalize the school issue in 1875, to divert voter attention from the economic grievances that had produced their rout in 1873 and 1874 and to remobilize their Protestant supporters in time for the 1876 congressional and presidential elections. The leader of this effort was President Ulysses S. Grant, who announced at a Union army reunion in September 1875 that the greatest threat now facing the country was the Catholic menace to the integrity and financial support of the public school system. Protestant anger at supposed Catholic assaults on the public schools proved crucial in Rutherford B. Hayes's victory in the pivotal gubernatorial campaign in Ohio that fall, and Grant then moved to inject the issue into the 1876 races.[27]

In December 1875, Grant asked Congress to pass a constitutional amendment forbidding state governments to fund Catholic schools. Since Republicans lacked the votes in either the House or the Senate to enact such an amendment, this was clearly an electioneering gambit. James G. Blaine introduced the requested amendment in the House; in the Senate, every Republican voted for it; and the Republican national platform of 1876 endorsed it. Paul Kleppner suggests that this conscious if cynical resurrection of anti-Catholic sentiment crystallized the ethnoreligious cleavage of the electorate in 1876 and brought enough Republican voters back to the fold to help Republicans win the presidential election and sharply reduce the Democratic majority in the House.

Quite unlike the state and local elections of 1875, however, Republicans devoted their 1876 campaigns for national offices to "bloody shirt" cries that a Democratic victory would restore Confederates to power in Washington. Sectional (not religious) prejudices produced their comeback from the rout of 1874, because in national (unlike state and local) elections, the threat that southerners might resume control of the national government through the agency of the Democratic Party remained powerfully salient. Nor is it clear that religious cleavages determined voting behavior in subsequent national or even state elections. The surge of the Greenback-Labor vote in 1877 and 1878 suggests that common economic grievances could unite workers and farmers across religious lines. Even in local contests, Protestant and Catholic workers often combined behind labor candidates when labor organizations ran such men.[28]

The Plasticity of the Political System

The desperate attempt of Republicans to fan anti-Catholic sentiment in 1875 points to an even more important flaw in the party period paradigm, one that Formisano and Voss-Hubbard also allude to in their recent articles. McCormick,

Silbey, and others are undoubtedly correct that political parties channeled the political behavior of most people during the last six decades of the nineteenth century. But they are wrong to suggest that either the supposed dominance of distributive public policies or the intense party loyalty that allegedly drove political life in these years gave politics a static or predictable dimension. Instead, one of the most important things structuring politics in these years was a widespread perception among political actors that was almost exactly the opposite of what McCormick and Silbey assert.

This was the belief that partisan loyalties among voters and leaders were not fixed in concrete, that the political parties that existed at any point in time during the period were not necessarily permanent and might imminently be displaced, and that the political system as a whole was therefore malleable, mutable, and open to change and reorganization. This perception of the real possibility of effecting partisan reorganization and voter realignments was arguably every bit as important as the central role of political parties in distinguishing the so-called party period from twentieth-century political life. Ironically, it was this very sense of instability and impermanence that produced a continuity of sorts from the mid-1830s to the mid-1880s. There was a constant tension between political actors who sought to start new or newly configured parties and major party politicians whose careers depended on perpetuating the existing organizations. That dynamic shaped much that happened in these years.

To a large extent, the ease of starting new parties—because parties themselves rather than state governments printed and distributed ballots—generated this sense of plasticity. This fact obviously helps explain why so many more third parties mushroomed in the nineteenth century than in the twentieth. In this respect, the adoption in the 1890s of state-printed ballots, which limited the access of new and third parties to the electorate, marks a fundamental watershed in American political history. What has been less emphasized is the fear that many of these insurgencies provoked among major party leaders. This fear hardly bespeaks a faith in the constancy of partisan loyalty among the electorate. It reflected instead a belief that third parties could, as they sometimes did, make crippling incursions into the rank and file of the major parties. That belief, in turn, often forced shifts in major-party strategies and provoked important policy outputs, such as the Specie Resumption Act, in an attempt to prevent or limit those incursions.

But it was not just third parties, even those that represented genuine grassroots insurgencies, that provide evidence for this sense of plasticity. After 1840, a stunning number of important national officeholders believed that they could reorganize partisan political life from the top down through the creation of new issues, the manipulation of previously existing issues, or the strategic allocation of federal patronage. Isolated from both the Democrats and the Whigs, President John Tyler hoped to build a new party on the Texas annexation question. After

Henry Clay's narrow but shocking defeat in 1844, several Whig leaders (though not Clay himself) urged that the Whig Party be disbanded and that Whigs mount a crusade against immigrants behind the banner of the nativist American Republican Party. To neutralize that challenge, some Whigs insisted that naturalization reform was a Whig issue; others reemphasized the need to perpetuate the Whig Party to oppose the new Polk administration.

Zachary Taylor ran as a "no party" or "people's" candidate for president in 1848, and even many of the Whigs who supported him hoped that he would not be saddled with a regular Whig nomination. Once Taylor was elected, his administration, led by Secretary of State John M. Clayton, tried to displace the Whig Party with a differently configured Taylor Republican Party. That attempt influenced almost everything Taylor's administration did with respect to policy and patronage during 1849, and resentment by regular Whig congressmen explains much that happened in Congress during 1850. Taylor's successor, Millard Fillmore, was a loyal Whig who wanted no part of a new party movement—at least as long as he was president. But his secretary of state, Daniel Webster, from the moment of his appointment until his death in 1852, repeatedly tried to organize a new Union Party that combined pro-compromise Whigs and Democrats. And once Fillmore left office, he and his closest advisers also attempted to replace the Whig Party with a new Union Party.

There is no need to rehearse the details of the system-changing realignment of the 1850s and the displacement of the Whig Party by the differently configured and oriented Know-Nothing and Republican Parties. What requires emphasis is the enduring impact those events had in creating the impression that the now exclusively northern and explicitly anti-southern Republican Party would and should be a temporary, ephemeral, and quickly replaceable organization. That belief, that specter of partisan realignment and reorganization, shaped Republicans' actions and their internal disputes almost continuously from 1856 until at least the Hayes administration in the late 1870s. As soon as Abraham Lincoln was elected in November 1860 and Deep South states began to secede, for example, foes of secession in the Upper South called on Lincoln and other Republicans to abandon the Republican Party's anti-slavery, anti-southern stance and to combine with them in a new bisectional Union Party that encompassed some northern Democrats as well.

Important Republicans such as William H. Seward and Thurlow Weed were quite receptive to these pleas, and Lincoln's initial cabinet selections as well as his later military appointments convinced some angry Republicans that this was indeed Lincoln's goal. "Is there not a movement . . . to build a 'union' party in the north," asked one dismayed Indiana Republican in early 1861, "done for the purpose of killing what they term the Abolition element of the Republican party, aimed at men of our Stamp? The movement cannot amount to anything unless it should be the disruption of the Republican party."[29] "The Republican organization was voluntarily abandoned by the president and his leading followers and a no-party Union was formed," fumed Senator John Sherman, an Ohio Republican, when explaining Democratic gains in the 1862 elections. Only if Republicans had "the wisdom to throw overboard the old debris that joined them in the Union movement" could they succeed.[30]

As I have argued elsewhere, Lincoln did in fact desire to replace the exclusively northern and overtly anti-southern Republican Party of 1860 with a differently configured and oriented Union Party during the Civil War.[31] Resentment of that effort by congressional Republicans helped fuel many of the policy disputes between them and the president during the war. In 1864, the Republican National Convention adopted the Union Party label, and the delegates placed Andrew Johnson of Tennessee on the Union ticket with Lincoln to indicate their desire to extend the party's base beyond the original northern strongholds of the Republicans. That apparent consensus, however, was belied by disputes between Lincoln and congressional Republicans over Reconstruction policy and even over the rapidity with which Confederate states should be readmitted to Congress.

As many historians have demonstrated, after Lincoln's assassination, Andrew Johnson sought to perpetuate and broaden the new Union Party in order to permanently supplant the Republican Party.[32] That effort influenced Johnson's Reconstruction policies, as well as how congressional Republicans, who openly turned against the Union Party by the fall elections of 1866, reacted to his policies. Yet Johnson's Union Party effort also reflected widespread commentary after the Civil War that both the Republican and the Democratic Parties had outlived their usefulness now that the war was won and slavery abolished. Both major parties, rumor had it, would be displaced by different organizations with different agendas.

Predictions of impending partisan reorganization and realignment emerged as soon as the Civil War ended. "Since the slavery question is all over," wrote one Republican congressman within days of Lee's surrender in April 1865, "new parties must arise." In December of that year, a New York newspaper commented that throughout the preceding year the belief had spread that "the old parties must soon give way to new combinations." In May 1866, Virginia's *Richmond Times* echoed that "the welfare of the South can only be secured by the erection of a new conservative party, upon the ruins of the old parties which agitated the slavery question for forty years."[33]

Nor did such predictions stop with the collapse of Johnson's Union Party scheme and the smashing Republican victory in the elections of 1866 and 1868. As Michael Perman told us, southern ex-Whigs who had come to power in Dixie after the war as supporters of Johnson's Union Party movement hoped to build a new centrist conservative party behind President-elect Grant himself. Grant's cooperation during 1869 with Virginia's True Republican leaders against that state's regular Republican Party only fanned those hopes. One way to conceptualize the maneuvering in southern politics from 1869 to 1873 between the centrist ex-Whigs who led both the Republican and the Democratic Parties is as a conscious attempt to bring about a realignment that benefited former Whig politicians and programs and prevented a polarization of politics along racial lines.[34]

Although these ex-Whigs failed and politics did become racially polarized (for reasons that Perman fully explains in his wonderful *Road to Redemption*), the perception that southern politics remained malleable and open to change stayed alive, at least in some quarters. From his nomination in 1876 until almost the end of his second year in office, yet another ex-Whig, the new Republican president Rutherford B. Hayes, sought to bring about realignment in the South by using presidential rhetoric and patronage to recruit the South's educated white elite and drive blacks and carpetbaggers from control of the Republican Party. Doing that, argued his Ohio advisers, would focus partisan conflict "on the great commercial and industrial questions rather than on the questions of race and color." It would also allow Hayes to build "a conservative Republican party in the South that shall effectively destroy the color line and save the colored people." To that end, Hayes set out in his inaugural address in March 1877 to "assure [his] countrymen of the Southern States" of his "earnest desire" to adopt "a civil policy which will forever wipe out in our political affairs the color line and the distinction of North and South."[35]

Realignment from the Top Down?

Northern politics also experienced almost constant predictions of (and attempts at) voter realignment, partisan reorganization, and a reorientation of the governmental agenda after Grant's election. For example, the Liberal Republican movement that emerged in the border states as early as 1869 and attempted to combine anti-Grant Republicans, Democrats, and anti-party, good-government reformers aimed at far more than defeating Grant's reelection in 1872. The new party sought "the break-up of the old parties," boasted E. L. Godkin on the eve of its 1872 national convention. "Reconstruction and slavery we have done with; for administrative and revenue reform we are eager."[36]

The crusade of Liberal Republicans to displace the existing parties obviously failed, just as the Union Party effort of Andrew Johnson had failed earlier. Yet within months of Grant's reelection, the outbreak of a severe economic depression, coupled with widespread and intense taxpayer anger at governmental corruption and extravagance, led to the mushrooming in 1873 and 1874 of an extraordinary number of Greenback, Independent, Anti-Monopoly, Granger, Labor Reform, and low-tax, clean-government splinter parties that challenged both major parties. As Burnham has demonstrated statistically, voter volatility in the northern elections of 1874 was higher than in that section's realigning elections exactly twenty years earlier. For good reason, therefore, calls for (and predictions of) the demise and displacement of the existing major parties reemerged. "Party disintegration appears to be inevitable," editorialized the *New York Herald* in 1874, because, as another paper put it that year, major "party lines no longer signify anything but past prejudices." Even a leader of the Mississippi Democratic Party admitted in 1874 that in the face of new economic conditions, "old issues have become extinct, and party names have lost their prestige."[37]

Silbey would undoubtedly say that the bottom line is that with the exception of the 1850s, no such partisan reorganization and realignment ever occurred; that the major parties remained in control of political life; and that third parties proved to be minor, if annoyingly frequent, threats to that control. As he correctly emphasizes, however, inertia alone hardly explains the continued dominance of the major parties. Both before and after the Civil War, major-party leaders worked hard to justify the perpetuation of their parties and to retain their hold on most voters. They did so in part by restressing the continued importance of the old issues that divided the existing major parties, issues that new challengers repeatedly denigrated as being obsolete. They also attempted to co-opt or at least neutralize the issues on which third-party or elite-led challenges to the existing two-party system were mounted.

Demonstrating how Whig and Democratic leaders did this with regard to the Liberty Party, John Tyler, the American Republican and Native American Parties, and the Free-Soil Party between 1840 and 1852 constitutes one theme of my new book on the Whig Party. After Henry Clay's shocking defeat in the presidential election of 1844, for example, Whigs responded to the nettlesome antislavery Liberty and nativist American Republican Parties, which many Whigs blamed for their loss, with both tactics. On the one hand, they instantly predicted that Democrats would ruin the economy by lowering the tariff and enacting the independent treasury system. To stop that calamity, they repeatedly asserted "that whatever good can be hoped for the country must be accomplished through the agency of the Whig party, in its present form and constitution." On the other hand, they tried to lure nativist and Liberty voters by introducing a bill to reform the naturalization process in the Senate (which they still controlled); by orchestrating northern opposition to Texas annexation even after Congress had authorized it; and, in New York, by pushing for enfranchisement of black adult male residents.[38]

Again in 1848, when the creation of the Free-Soil Party threatened to attract far more northern Whig defectors than previous minor parties had, Whigs responded with a two-pronged strategy. They insisted that the only realistic way to stop slavery expansion was to elect northern Whig congressmen who would pass the Wilmot Proviso, along with Whig presidential candidate Zachary Taylor, who was pledged not to veto it. Simultaneously, they declared that the tra-ditional economic policies that had separated Whigs and Democrats—protec-tive tariffs, abolition of the independent treasury system and the expansion of bank credit, and federal subsidies for internal improvements—were still very much at stake in the election and that the one-idea Free-Soil Party, now headed by ex-Democrat Martin Van Buren, could never be trusted to advance the Whig position.

In short, the sharp contrast between Whig belief in activist government and Democratic adherence to negative state doctrines, Whigs cried, remained of vital importance, regardless of the slavery-extension issue. "To present a firm and un-broken front to the enemy," Whig leaders asserted, they must "press home upon the public mind the great principles by which and for which we exist as a party." Whigs, they iterated and reiterated, "constantly endeavor to identify the inter-ests of the people with those of the government"; Democrats, in contrast, "op-posed every national measure which should call the creative and protective func-tions of government into action."[39]

Republicans reacted to threats of new parties in similar fashion after the Civil War. The genuine need for new federal legislation to protect the rights of blacks after Appomattox is undeniable. So is the egalitarian commitment of many Re-publican policy makers who voted for the civil rights and Freedmen's Bureau bills and the Fourteenth Amendment in 1866. Nonetheless, Republican Recon-struction policies in 1866 also represented the party's attempt to quiet the wide-spread talk in 1865 of an imminent partisan reorganization. One thing that fueled such talk was the bipartisan acclaim for Andrew Johnson and his policies throughout 1865, a consensus that caused Connecticut's pro-Johnson Republi-can senator James Dixon to exclaim that it seemed to be a restoration of the Era of Good Feelings.

To end such talk and remind voters that the Republican Party remained nec-essary precisely because it differed sharply with Democrats on Reconstruction policy, congressional Republicans attempted to put a distinctive Republican spin on Johnson's Reconstruction program in 1866 in order to turn Democrats against it. They knew from wartime voting records in Congress that nothing could pro-voke Democratic opposition more quickly than policies that expanded black rights. What they did not expect, of course, was that Johnson would side with the Democrats against their modifications of his program. But they quickly discovered that opposing Johnson himself provided as equally successful a rationale for continuing the Republican Party as did their Reconstruction program.[40]

From 1866 until 1884, Republicans went out of their way to justify the per-petuation of their party and of its control of the federal government by arguing that the fruits of northern victory in the war would be lost if Republicans ever lost power. Again, there is no need to accuse the Republicans of blatant cynicism, for they were both sincere and accurate in this assertion. But the fact that they felt the need to iterate it continually reflects how seriously they took the talk that their party deserved to be replaced. As even the Republican *New York Times* admitted in early 1870, "There is no doubt that a feeling prevails that the work of the Republican party . . . ends with the adoption of the Fifteenth Amendment."[41] To counteract that feeling, Republicans in effect asserted again and again that the party's mission was not yet completed, that its work was not yet done.

Take, for example, the response of regular Republicans to the combined Liberal Republican–Democratic challenge they faced in 1872. Liberal Republicans vowed to break up the old parties and shift the agenda from race and Reconstruction to fiscal and administrative reform. Meanwhile, Democrats, in adopting the so-called New Departure that year, explicitly insisted that questions involving black rights and Reconstruction were "no longer issues before the country," since Democrats were now prepared to acquiesce in the statutes and constitutional amendments the Republicans had previously passed.[42] Republicans responded in part by advocating civil service reform, passing the sweeping Amnesty Act of 1872, repealing all Civil War federal taxes except the excise tax on tobacco and alcohol, and reducing tariff rates by 10 percent in order to co-opt and neutralize the Liberal platform.

Simultaneously, however, their own national platform congratulated the party for accepting "with grand courage the solemn duties of the time" during its years in power, boasted that "this glorious record of the past is the party's best pledge for the future," and contended that federal enforcement of the Reconstruction amendments "can safely be entrusted only to the party that secured those amendments."[43] In 1876, when warning of the disaster that would ensue should ex-Confederates regain control of the national government, the Republican national platform explicitly announced that "the work of the Republican party is unfinished.[44] In 1880 and 1884, their platforms rang changes on the same themes. Such rhetoric was obviously aimed at contrasting the Republican Party favorably with the Democrats, but it was also prompted by Republicans' sense of their vulnerability to potential obsolescence and displacement.

During the years from the mid-1830s to the mid-1880s, in sum, major parties did structure much that happened in politics and governance. But so did a perception among political actors both within and outside those major parties that those organizations could be displaced. Along with the vitality of federalism, which allotted certain politically salient functions exclusively to state and local governments and others to Washington, this sense of the likely evanescence of existing major parties, of the openness of the system to partisan realignment and reorganization, sharply distinguished those years from what would follow in the twentieth century.

People's awareness from personal experience of the ease with which new parties could be created in part fostered this sense of uncertainty and precariousness. But it sprang as well from social, economic, inter-sectional, constitutional, and political changes during those years that generated demands among some groups for a shift in the substantive issue agenda on which politics and governance focused. Those changes and the concern they caused political leaders rendered the politics of the party period anything but static.

Notes

1. Frederick Merk, "Eastern Antecedents of the Grangers," *Agricultural History* 23 (1949): 1–8; Lee Benson, *Merchants, Farmers, and Railroads: Railroad Regulation and New York Politics, 1850–1887* (Ithaca, N.Y., 1955).
2. William G. Shade, *Democratizing the Old Dominion: Virginia and the Second Party System, 1824–1861* (Charlottesville, Va., 1996).
3. Paul Kleppner, *The Third Electoral System, 1853–1892: Parties, Voters, and Political Cultures* (Chapel Hill, N.C., 1979).
4. Richard L. McCormick, "The Party Period and Public Policy: An Exploratory Hypothesis," *Journal of American History* 66 (September 1979): 279–98.
5. Richard L. McCormick, *The Party Period and Public Policy: American Politics from the Age of Jackson to the Progressive Era* (New York, 1986).
6. Joel H. Silbey, *The Partisan Imperative: The Dynamics of American Politics before the Civil War* (New York, 1985); Joel H. Silbey, *The American Political Nation, 1838–1893* (Stanford, Calif., 1991).
7. Silbey, *American Political Nation*, 126, 130.
8. McCormick, *Party Period*, 200–1.
9. Ibid., 19.
10. Ibid.
11. Ibid., 20.
12. William E. Gienapp, "'Politics Seems to Enter into Everything': Political Culture in the North," in *Essays on American Antebellum Politics, 1840–1860*, ed. Stephen E. Maizlish and John J. Kushma (College Station, Tex., 1982), 14–69; Walter Dean Burnham, "The Changing Shape of the American Political Universe," *American Political Science Review* 59 (1965): 7–28.
13. Stephen Skowronek, *Building a New American State: The Expansion of National Administrative Capacities, 1877–1920* (Cambridge, 1982); Richard Bensel, *Yankee Leviathan: The Origins of Central State Authority in America, 1859–1877* (Cambridge, 1990); Theda Skocpol, *Protecting Soldiers and Mothers: The Political Origins of Social Policy in the United States* (Cambridge, Mass., 1992).
14. Glenn C. Altschuler and Stuart M. Blumin, "Limits of Political Engagement in Antebellum America: A New Look at the Golden Age of Participatory Democracy," *Journal of American History* 84 (December 1997): 855–85. For a fuller and more temperate version of this argument, see Glenn C. Altschuler and Stuart M. Blumin, *Rude Republic: Americans and Their Politics in the Nineteenth Century* (Princeton, N.J., 2000).
15. Ronald P. Formisano, "The Party Period Revisited," *Journal of American History* 86 (June 1999): 93–120.
16. Mark Voss-Hubbard, "The 'Third Party Tradition' Reconsidered: Third Parties and American Public Life, 1830–1900," *Journal of American History* 86 (June 1999): 121–50.

17. I raised these concerns in a brief response published with the Formisano and Voss-Hubbard articles. See Michael F. Holt, "The Primacy of Party Reasserted," *Journal of American History* 86 (June 1999): 151–57.

18. Silbey, *American Political Nation*, 130.

19. I attempt to answer these questions in Michael F. Holt, "From Center to Periphery: The Market Revolution and Major-Party Conflict, 1835–1880," in *The Market Revolution in America: Social, Political, and Religious Expressions, 1800–1880,* ed. Melvyn Stokes and Stephen Conway (Charlottesville, Va., 1996), 224–56.

20. Harold M. Hyman and William M. Wiecek, *Equal Justice under Law: Constitutional Development, 1835–1875* (New York, 1982), 78–80.

21. The Interstate Commerce Act was not the first national attempt to regulate even the transportation sector of the economy, let alone economic life as a whole. In response to a series of exceedingly gory steamboat explosions in the 1830s and 1840s, Congress in 1851 passed a law establishing federal standards for the quality of iron used in making the steam used on such ships, as well as the pressure capacity of the boilers that generated that steam. It also created a cohort of federal inspectors to make sure that those standards were adhered to. Nor did the *Wabash* decision or subsequent Interstate Commerce Act end state regulation of other areas of economic and social life.

22. Harold M. Hyman, *A More Perfect Union: The Impact of the Civil War and Reconstruction on the Constitution* (Boston, 1975); Morton Keller, *Affairs of State: Public Life in Late Nineteenth Century America* (Cambridge, Mass., 1977).

23. Michael Les Benedict, "Preserving the Constitution: The Conservative Basis of Radical Reconstruction," *Journal of American History* 61 (June 1974): 65–90; Herman Belz, *Emancipation and Equal Rights: Politics and Constitutionalism in the Civil War Era* (New York, 1978).

24. The Democrats' gerrymander was so successful that in the fifth district the Democratic winner was unopposed.

25. Michael F. Holt, *The Rise and Fall of the American Whig Party: Jacksonian Politics and the Onset of the Civil War* (New York, 1999), 153, 159.

26. Robert Scott Burnet, "Creating the 34th Congress: House and Senate Elections, 1854–1855" (Ph.D. diss., University of Virginia, 1997).

27. For the importance of the school issue in state elections in Ohio and elsewhere in the 1870s, see Kleppner, *The Third Electoral System*, 214–35; Samuel T. McSeveney, "Religious Conflict, Party Politics, and Public Policy in New Jersey, 1874–75," *New Jersey History* 110 (spring–summer 1992): 18–44; and Ward M. McAfee, *Religion, Race, and Reconstruction: The Public School in the Politics of the 1870s* (Albany, N.Y., 1998).

28. Richard Oestriecher, "Urban Working-Class Political Behavior and Theories of American Electoral Politics, 1870–1940," *Journal of American History* 74 (March, 1988): 1257–86.

29. B. F. Diggs to George W. Julian, January 16, 1861, quoted in T. Harry Williams, *Lincoln and the Radicals* (Madison, Wis., 1941), 15.

30. John Sherman to William T. Sherman, November 16, 1862, quoted in ibid.

31. "Abraham Lincoln and the Politics of Union," in Michael F. Holt, *Political Parties and American Political Development from the Age of Jackson to the Age of Lincoln* (Baton Rouge, 1992), 323–53.

32. Pride of place here belongs to John H. Cox and LaWanda Cox, *Politics, Principle, and Prejudice, 1865–1866: Dilemma of Reconstruction America* (Glencoe, Ill., 1963),

but see also Michael Perman, *Reunion without Compromise: The South and Recon-struction, 1865–1868* (Cambridge, 1973).

33. Eric Foner, *Reconstruction: America's Unfinished Revolution, 1863–1877* (New York, 1988), 216, 219; Perman, *Reunion without Compromise*, 197.

34. On these developments, see Michael Perman, *The Road to Redemption: Southern Politics, 1869–1879* (Chapel Hill, N.C., 1979).

35. Allen Peskin, "Was There a Compromise of 1877?" *Journal of American History* 60 (June 1973): 70; Keith Ian Polakoff, *The Politics of Inertia: The Election of 1876 and the End of Reconstruction* (Baton Rouge, 1973), 250; Brooks D. Simpson, *The Re-construction Presidents* (Lawrence, Kans., 1998), 205; James D. Richardson, ed., *The Messages and Papers of the Presidents* (Washington, D.C., 1903), 7:458–60.

36. Foner, *Reconstruction*, 500.

37. Perman, *Road to Redemption*, 152–53, 155.

38. I develop these themes in some detail in Holt, *Rise and Fall of American Whig Party*, chap. 8; quotation, 213.

39. I develop these themes in considerable detail in ibid., chap. 11; quotations, 350.

40. I spell out these arguments at greater length in chapters on Reconstruction I wrote for a third edition of the textbook *The Civil War and Reconstruction* (New York, 2001), coauthored with Jean H. Baker and David Herbert Donald.

41. Quoted in Simpson, *Reconstruction Presidents*, 148.

42. Arthur M. Schlesinger, ed., *History of U.S. Political Parties*, 4 vols. (New York, 1973), 2:936.

43. Ibid., 1355.

44. Ibid., 1371.

5. The Transformation of American Politics
Political Institutions and Public Policy, 1865–1910

Peter H. Argersinger

Lord Bryce, in his classic 1889 study *The American Commonwealth*, declared, "that which Europeans call the machinery of government is in America conspicuous chiefly by its absence." But as Bryce himself realized, although the structures of government in the United States were less obtrusive, they were more complex. And Bryce was writing precisely as America was sliding into a political crisis that would recast governmental machinery, political behavior, public opinion, and public policy.

A description of the American polity and its transformation during this important era, while necessarily sketchy, can suggest some of the key linkages in American politics, particularly relationships between its structure and its substance. Indeed, the machinery of government powerfully shaped both political conduct and public policy. But if constitutions, legislative and executive institutions, and electoral rules shaped politics, they were themselves the legacies of past political actions, products of what one scholar aptly described as the continuing "dialectical interplay of meaningful decisions and structural constraints."[1]

Legislatures, for example, were not merely fixed and neutral arenas within which political actors responded to external factors in shaping public policy. Their changing rules and procedures, committee structures and leadership roles, norms of behavior and other organizational characteristics channeled, restrained, impeded, and facilitated legislative activity. Similarly, the electoral structure was not an impartial given, simply a formal framework for politics itself. Instead, systems of representation and apportionment, voting rules and ballot formats, and the conduct of elections were all derived from previous political decisions; they determined who participated in the political process, with what power, and with what success; and they were subject to subsequent changes for just such reasons.

In short, the structure and substance of American politics interacted, and neither can be fruitfully considered except in the context of the other. Political development during this period occurred through political struggles based in and influenced by existing institutional arrangements.

*   *   *

The Place of Inherited Structures

Many of the most important structural influences on politics had their origins in the Constitution, which in turn reflected both the institutional precedents of the late eighteenth century and its ideological suspicions of centralized power. Accordingly, the Constitution fragmented the institutions and authority of government, both through a system of dual federalism, which divided power between national and state governments, and through a federal government composed of three separate branches whose powers checked and balanced one another. The Constitution ensured the political power of the states with specific grants of authority and few restrictions, leaving state governments to be guided primarily by their own constitutions.

State governments were by far the most active part of the polity, with an "immense compass" of functions compared with the limited reach of the federal government. Even so, Bryce found that state constitutions reflected "a singular distrust by the people of its own agents and officers." Indeed, they emphasized both procedural and substantive restrictions on government action. Uniformly, they also dispersed authority among legislative, executive, and judicial branches. The Civil War and Reconstruction curtailed the extreme assertions of states' rights but, ironically, prompted state governments to expand their authority and activities. Shifts in electoral politics, however, brought a wave of state constitutional revisions in the 1870s that indicated, in one observer's words, "a grand design to reduce the field of state law and withhold from it every subject which it is not necessary to concede."[2]

Other factors further limited state governments in the Gilded Age. Legislatures were the most important branch, but they met infrequently and briefly, usually once every two years for sixty days. Legislators were amateurs, generally serving only one term and lacking permanent staff. Even the Speaker was often a first-termer, sometimes unaware of parliamentary rules or his own prerogatives. Legislative procedures often frustrated rather than facilitated public business; they were vague, inconsistent, and haphazardly followed. In one session in North Dakota, thirteen bills simply disappeared after their passage, prompting one newspaper to add a new category to its daily summary of legislative activity: "Lost, Stolen, or Strayed."[3]

Numerous constraints also hampered state executives. None had an executive budget. Some lacked the veto. Others lacked the authority to dismiss their own appointees. Their staffs were small, sometimes only a single secretary. Department heads were often elected independently of the governor and were not subject to his control. One Ohio governor described his position as "Not too much hard work, plenty of time to read, good society, etc." The "small questions" of public policy he had to deal with, however, were not worth "the worry and anxiety" experienced in politics.[4]

Still more restricted was the federal government. The Constitution narrowly enumerated its powers and fragmented its authority through a tripartite system of checks and balances. A bicameral legislature in which each house reflected different constituencies and constituted a check on the power of the other was further balanced by an independent executive branch, chosen through an electoral college rather than by popular vote, and by an independent judiciary.

Congress was the foremost branch of the national government. It exercised authority over the federal budget, oversaw the cabinet, debated public issues, and controlled legislation. Woodrow Wilson concluded in the 1880s that Congress "has virtually taken into its own hands all the substantial powers of government." Its leaders, as one senator conceded, "tolerated no intrusion from the President or from anybody else."[5] Yet Congress was scarcely efficient. Its chambers were noisy and chaotic. Few members were committed to a congressional career, and frequently a majority of House members were inexperienced first-termers. High turnover stemmed not simply from electoral defeat but also from party norms such as rotation and from partisan reapportionments of congressional districts by state legislatures. From 1876 through 1886, Ohio conducted six consecutive elections with six different districting plans, indicating how representational systems and state politicking helped shape national politics.[6]

Outmoded norms and complex rules limited the House's capacity to respond to economic and social changes. Some rules restricted the introduction of legislation; others prevented its passage. The "disappearing quorum" referred to the rule requiring that a quorum not only be present but also vote, often enabling the minority to block all business simply by refusing to answer the roll. "The power of obstruction was without limit," one member noted. The Speaker had some ability to direct business, but authority was dispersed, and each committee, as one member said, "comes to regard itself as a little legislature, and contends with great jealousy against encroachments on its own authority."[7]

Despite institutional differences in both representation and rules, the Senate resembled the House in its limited capacity to address issues of public concern. Its presiding officer exercised less authority than the Speaker; its rules were fewer and less restrictive than those of the House. As a result, no one provided much direction, and each senator "kept in his own orbit and shone in his own sphere." "What ultimately may seem most remarkable about early Gilded Age Congressional Government," Margaret Thompson observed, "is that it managed to function at all."[8]

The presidency was a weak and restrained institution following the assassination of Abraham Lincoln. Reconstruction legislation impaired presidential authority and autonomy, and the impeachment of President Andrew Johnson undermined the office. President Ulysses S. Grant then clearly subordinated it to Congress by deferring on appointments and legislation and promising to be "a purely administrative officer." Succeeding presidents between 1877 and 1897 were all conservatives with a narrow view of the office. They made little effort to reach out to the public or to exert legislative leadership and proposed few initiatives.[9] The presidency was further hampered by the absence of any overall executive budget and by its limited control over departments and bureaus, which submitted their own budgetary estimates to Congress and responded more directly to that institution than to the chief executive.

Inadequate staff resources also hindered the president. Congress first appropriated funds for a single clerk in 1857. President Grant had a White House staff of three. Such aides were essentially clerical rather than participants in substantive policy decisions. President Rutherford B. Hayes's choice for secretary not only declined the position but even felt "hurt that I suggested it to him." A decade later, Grover Cleveland complained, "If the President has any great policy in mind or on hand he has no one to help him work it out." For that matter, Cleveland himself answered the White House doorbell, recorded household expenses, and wrote checks to pay the White House bills. It is small wonder that a recent scholar described the era as one "of diminished presidential prestige and authority and of severely limited institutional capacity."[10]

Indeed, the entire federal bureaucracy was small and inefficient. There were only 50,000 government employees in 1871. Moreover, the political patronage system produced a civil service, in the words of one historian, "largely composed of misfits employed on a temporary basis." This often meant more than corruption or incompetence; departments were disrupted as officials fulfilled conflicting administrative and political roles. Even after the passage of the Pendleton Act in 1883, the merit system scarcely penetrated the civil service.[11]

The Institutional Role of Party

Despite these difficulties, the same Constitution that fragmented governance also provided, unintentionally and indirectly, the institutional means for its integration and its linkage with a decentralized electoral politics of mass participation. The electoral college virtually created the political parties its devisers had hoped to discourage.[12] By the 1840s, the major parties had developed institutional features and modes of operation that persisted through the political disruptions of the 1850s and the Civil War and much of the Gilded Age. During this "party period," parties dominated the political system, establishing many of its structures and rules, organizing and mobilizing its electorate, and guiding its legislative and administrative activities.[13]

Even so, parties themselves, like the federal system, were decentralized. The national parties had no continuous or powerful institutions but consisted merely of coalitions of largely autonomous state and local organizations. Parties had no legal status, no official list of members. They were simply, as Bryce observed, "extralegal groupings of men." The party organization consisted of pyramidal networks of elected committees and conventions at the local, county, district, state, and national levels, paralleling the system of representative government. Such a system made possible a popular institution that was responsive to rank-and-file sentiment, but in practice, party leaders generally dominated party processes, and a persistent theme in all parties was the demand for the Crawford system, or nomination by primary rather than convention. More work analyzing the internal dynamics of parties is needed to determine the degree to which parties were democratic vehicles of the popular will.[14]

Regardless, parties functioned best as electoral machines. With legal regulations and public machinery for elections negligible, parties controlled the electoral process. They nominated and financed candidates and organized rallies, partisan clubs, and parades. To mobilize their supporters, they kept detailed records of voters, transported them to the polls, saw that they were registered where necessary, and sometimes paid their poll taxes or naturalization fees. With voting open, not secret, parties controlled balloting by printing and distributing party tickets and by ruling the polls with partisan clerks, judges, and challengers and with bummers and hawkers, party workers who sought to enforce party voting. Fighting and intimidation were so common at the polls that one state supreme court ruled in 1887 that they were "acceptable" features of elections. These open and partisan aspects of the electoral process required men to demonstrate publicly their commitment to their party and its values, thereby reinforcing their partisan loyalties. High turnout characterized the party period.[15]

After Reconstruction, a remarkably competitive electoral balance prevailed between the two major parties, which was one reason they worked so hard to get out the vote. Rarely did either party control both Congress and the presidency at once, further constraining policy initiatives. Victories were the outcome of carefully organized parties fully mobilizing their supporters. Interrelated regional, ethnic, religious, and local factors determined the party affiliations of most Americans, but for some, they overlapped with or were mediated by economic variables. Like religious belief and ethnic identity, partisan loyalty was largely a cultural trait passed from father to son; women, of course, were excluded from the suffrage.

Most social groups found party identification a means of declaring and defending their cultural values. Those values acquired partisan salience as groups tried to implement their beliefs through public policy and perceived support in party actions and rhetoric. Originally, group conflicts had focused on specific issues: Civil War and civil rights divided southern voters primarily along racial lines. In the North, Prohibition laws, Sabbatarian legislation, or efforts to regulate parochial schools divided voters along ethnocultural lines. Continuing conflict over such issues strengthened party loyalties and the social-group basis of partisanship.[16]

Republicans were strongest in the North and Midwest, where they benefited from their party's role as the defender of the Union. But not all northerners voted for the Grand Old Party. It appealed to particular social groups, primarily old-stock Americans and other Protestants whose pietistic perspective led them to demand state action to promote a moral society. African Americans, loyal to the party that had emancipated and enfranchised them, also supported the GOP where they could vote. Democrats were strongest in the South, where they stood as the defender of the traditions of the region's white population. But Democrats also drew support in the urban Northeast, especially from Catholics and recent immigrants, and from related groups in the Midwest and the West.

Each major party thus consisted of a complex coalition of groups with different traditions and interests. One observer described the Democratic Party in California as "a sort of Democratic happy family, like we see in the prairie-dog villages, where owls, rattlesnakes, prairie dogs, and lizards all live in the same hole."[17] This internal diversity often threatened party stability. To hold its coalition together, each party identified itself with an imagery that appealed broadly to all its constituents while suggesting that it was menaced by the members and objectives of the opposing party.

Republicans identified their party with patriotism, morality, and national authority and attacked the Democrats as an "alliance between the embittered South and the slums of the Northern cities." They combined a "bloody shirt" appeal to the memories of the Civil War with positive government efforts to regulate social behavior and promote economic development.[18] Democrats portrayed themselves as the party of "personal liberties," a theme that appealed to both the racism of white southerners and the resentment of Catholics and immigrants toward the nativist meddling of Republicans. The Democrats' commitment to personal liberties had limits. They supported the disfranchisement of African Americans, the exclusion of Chinese immigrants, the subordination of women, and the dispossession of American Indians. With more consistency, they upheld their other major conviction: that the role of the government should be minimal. This opposition to "paternal and bureaucratic government" and support for traditional individualism and localism proved popular.[19]

Despite their attraction for most Americans, however, the major parties faced dissenters. The party period concept, it is increasingly clear, does not effectively account for a variety of other activities in the public sphere. A persistent antipartyism, rooted in classic republican suspicions of power and in a crusading evangelical Protestantism, was a significant part of the nation's political culture. Some Americans regarded party loyalty as a threat to individual conscience. Said one Kansan, "It is better to be right than to belong to a party." Others objected to parties because of their allegedly baneful effects on public policy or because of their success in mobilizing a mass electorate.[20]

The constant presence of third parties also weakens the party period concept. It casts doubt on the pervasiveness of partisanship and the responsiveness of the major parties and reveals serious frustration with their style or substance of governance. A series of farmer and labor third parties countered the ethnocultural focus of the major parties. Other third parties organized around specific issues such as Prohibition. But most third parties stemmed less from economic or social stress than from political factors—particular dissatisfactions with parties and their apparent indifference to or inability to resolve those stresses. Structurally, it was easy to form third parties and nominate candidates, and the discontented did so regularly, especially at the state and local levels. The frequent occurrence of third parties also points up the anti-partyism within the political culture, for they often appealed to that attitude. The Populist leader Annie Diggs described her party's origins as "a protest against the dangers and tyranny of permanent party organization."[21]

Diggs's political role suggests more challenges to the party period concept. Historians have long emphasized the masculine nature of the era's politics: the military-style campaigning, the combative nature of partisan rhetoric, the absence of women's suffrage, and the rough balloting that was used to justify it. In fact, however, politics hardly excluded women. Some, like Diggs, were active partisans and party strategists, organizing, campaigning, and holding party and public positions. More commonly, women used voluntary associations rather than parties to participate in politics. The Women's Christian Temperance Union (WCTU), organized in 1874, was but the largest and most active of such associations. Under the slogan "Do Everything," the WCTU launched political campaigns for social and economic reforms far beyond temperance. In such nonpartisan institutions, women developed a distinctive political culture, with defined programs focused on the needs of women and children and with a preference for an interventionist state responsive to the public rather than to parties.[22]

Others also developed nonpartisan organizations to gain political influence and achieve public policies beneficial to their members, laying the basis for interest-group politics. Farmers organized many such groups. The Grange, established in 1867, with both women and men eligible for membership, had 22,000 local lodges and nearly a million members by 1875. Its campaign for public regulation of railroads and grain elevators helped persuade midwestern states to enact the so-called Granger laws.[23] Industrialists too formed pressure groups. The American Iron and Steel Association lobbied Congress for high tariff laws and made campaign contributions to friendly politicians from both parties. Other pressure groups focused on cultural politics. The American Protective Association, rabidly anti-Catholic, agitated for laws restricting immigration and taxing and regulating Catholic institutions. All such interest groups constituted important intermediary organizations for politics; like parties, they linked social groups to government institutions.[24]

Electoral Rules, Partisan Attitudes, and Political Dynamics

Despite widespread anti-party beliefs, the significance of third parties, and the gradual emergence of self-conscious interest groups, the two major parties generally dominated politics in the Gilded Age. A major reason for that dominance lay in America's system of representation, a crucial aspect of political structure. There were actually numerous systems for both national and state governments, but nearly all included the single-member district and the plurality vote. Since only one candidate could win in each district, such an electoral system encouraged coalitions and discouraged multiple parties.

These institutional arrangements thus underpinned the two-party system, one of the most important and enduring features of American politics. This system also favored the dominant party by exaggerating its representation relative to its popular vote. These two factors often prompted third parties and the lesser of the major parties in any district to engage in fusion, in the hope of sharing political influence that would otherwise be denied to both when acting separately. Although a difficult tactic, fusion enabled third parties to survive and influence politics in a two-party system.

Parties had other reasons to focus on representational systems. The latter helped determine—sometimes quite independently of changes in popular voting behavior—the possession, distribution, and exercise of political power. For partisan advantage, each major party engaged in a disruptive state politics of constant gerrymandering of districts. Such actions constituted, as one legislator explained, "usurpation under the forms of law." But they also indicated that parties recognized the political origins as well as the consequences of the electoral structure and constantly strove to reshape it.

The election of minority presidents in the Gilded Age illustrates the partisan implications of representational systems. It derived from the common decision by state legislatures that electors should be elected on a general ticket. By producing a winner-take-all result, the general ticket transformed a state into the functional equivalent of a single-member district within the electoral college, maximizing the influence of the dominant party in each state and effectively disfranchising voters in the minority. Given the geographic distribution of party voters, the general ticket biased the electoral college in favor of the Republicans, even though the Democrats polled more popular votes.[25]

Despite their minority status, Republicans also usually held the Senate, ensuring their institutional control by manipulating the state admission process. With each state having equal representation in the Senate regardless of its population, the selective admission of sparsely populated western states extended the Republican advantage first gained by the secession of southern Democrats. By the time the South returned to Congress, Republicans had a large bloc of senators from states admitted during the Civil War and Reconstruction. Additional new states admitted thereafter enabled Republicans to control the Senate even when they suffered major losses in the House. Divided government in the Gilded Age was not merely a function of a closely balanced electorate but a consequence of partisan manipulation of representational systems.[26]

Representation particularly affected parties in their role as potential instruments of government, the final purpose of party organization. Scholars disagree over the extent to which parties managed government and made policy, and indeed, it seemed to vary by issue, time, institution, and region. Certainly, however, the spoils system of patronage enabled parties to staff government offices and shape governmental administrations according to party interests. Parties also provided the internal organization of legislative bodies. Moreover, studies of Congress demonstrate that party structured congressional voting more in the late nineteenth century than at any other time and over a wider range of issues. A high and stable level of partisanship, reflecting strong party cohesion, characterized roll-call voting.[27]

More studies of state legislative behavior are needed, but at this level, too, party was the primary determinant in voting, even though much legislation did not evoke partisan discord. Parties had particularly high unity on issues affecting them as institutions, such as election laws, apportionment bills, or contested seats. Otherwise, the range of issues that produced party voting varied considerably by state—predominantly ethnocultural in some, economic in others. Reconstruction legislatures, North as well as South, witnessed sharp party divisions across a wide variety of issues. Where third parties had significant representation in Gilded Age legislatures, partisan voting was especially intense.[28]

Party caucuses directed the state legislative process. Party officials who were not even legislators sometimes presided over caucuses that decided the party agenda, and they prowled the legislative floor to give advice or fortify resolve. The "party whip" was often employed against reluctant legislators, and those who voted against the caucus decision were summoned home by local party meetings to defend their apostasy, indicating the linkage between electorate, organization, and governance.[29]

Partisan goals also brought important institutional changes to Congress, finally breaking the deadlock that had limited its activity. The conventional view of congressional development in the Gilded Age stresses that the increasing workload imposed by economic and social change prompted a gradual reform of procedures and the centralization of power in order to improve the institution's productive capacities. Such reform typically limited the rights of individuals and minorities to delay or obstruct the legislative process and thereby contributed to institutional efficiency and responsibility. This view links procedural change within the institution to changing external pressures.[30]

But new studies indicate that such change derived instead from interaction between party goals and the institutional context within the House.[31] Most members of both parties believed in party government. Elected less on their own merits than on the basis of the party's organization, platform, and appeal, they felt obligated to support party leaders and programs. By determining possible behavior, rules distributed power and had partisan implications. Thus partisanship shaped decisions on procedure as well as on policy. Roll calls over procedural changes brought near-total party disagreement.

The small majorities Republicans sometimes held in the House during this period increased the rules' effect on their ability to enact their party agenda. Democrats consistently used the delaying procedures allowed by House rules to block action on Republican proposals. Even the small Democratic minority during Reconstruction often succeeded in thwarting Republican action. Dilatory motions to adjourn, for example, consumed as much as 23 percent of roll-call votes in some Congresses. Thus it was not increased workload but Democratic obstructionism that drove Republican procedural reform efforts to limit minority rights to challenge majority decisions, offer amendments, demand a quorum, or have committee representation.[32]

Democrats, even when in the majority, were less interested in changing the rules to curb obstructionist tactics, regardless of external pressures, for they believed in negative government. As one Democrat said during a rules debate, "the curse of our age is too much legislation, not too little." "The Democratic party wants no legislation," fumed Republican Thomas B. Reed. "All their plans, whether in power or out of power, are centered in obstruction."[33] In 1890, Reed earned the name "Czar" when as Speaker he led the Republicans in abolishing the obstructionist rules.

Party government served as the justification for revolutionizing House procedure. The changes institutionalized the role of party in House rules; official prerogatives and party discipline put the Speaker firmly in control. Thus, although House rules shaped political behavior, they were not immutable. They could, at times, be shaped by ambitious individuals to accomplish political goals. One member of Congress clearly linked political structure and substance by explaining that "changes in the mode of procedure and of policy must inevitably follow" the Republicans' 1888 electoral victory.[34]

Public Policies Constrained

Although party was often determinative in Gilded Age governance, the actual formation of public policy labored under many practical constraints. Structural obstacles such as divided government and procedural restraints, electoral factors such as close party competition and shifting control of Congress, and cultural beliefs in limited government and a reserved presidency often led to governmental deadlock. Moreover, the major parties had to construct broad appeals to hold their coalitions together, and regional, economic, or other divisions at times prevented parties from adopting clear or contrasting positions on important issues. Rather than separating the major parties, these issues divided each party into factions, often played only a small role in deciding elections, and were seldom resolved by governmental action.

Several major economic issues dominated politics during the Gilded Age. The first involved a set of interlocking fiscal and monetary policies collectively termed the "money question." Financial conservatives favored gold monometallism, minimal financial regulation, and the role of the national bank system in managing credit and currency distributions. They insisted that this "sound money" policy would ensure economic stability, maintain property values, and retain investor confidence. Financial reformers attacked both the gold standard and the national bank system as biasing economic opportunities to the advantage of creditors, industry, and the Northeast. They supported currency expansion, increased financial regulation, and the abolition of national banks to both stimulate and democratize the economy.[35]

Despite its importance, however, the money question was not a partisan issue. The structuring of partisan cleavages along lines of ethnocultural and sectional conflict prevented the party system from expressing economic interests. Although the leaders of both major parties favored sound money, their rank and file, especially in the West and the South, included many inflationists. The federal system, moreover, enabled each party to adopt different positions in different states, obstructing any attempt to forge a common position at the national level. Kansas Republicans and Democrats endorsed, while Connecticut Republicans and Democrats condemned, inflationary policies in their respective state platforms. To hold their diverse coalitions together, the national parties avoided the divisive issue. Accordingly, monetary policy usually consisted of bipartisan, compromise legislation, pleasing no one.[36]

It was this political failure that prompted the formation of a series of third parties, each condemning both Republicans and Democrats for failing to respond to economic problems or, worse, for deliberately promoting powerful business interests at the expense of ordinary Americans. The Greenback Party, for instance, charged that the major parties had "failed to take the side of the people" and instead supported the "great moneyed institutions."[37]

The sectional division over the money question expressed itself through the equal representation the states received in the Senate. The new Republicans from the western states, admitted to bolster their narrow control of the Senate, each provided two more votes for silver inflation, and in 1890, the Republican Senate passed silver legislation, which the Republican House then blocked. "We are punished," said one unhappy gold Republican, "for making too easy the pathway of rotten boroughs into the Union." The ability of western senators to sustain the silver issue in congressional and national politics despite the opposition of senators representing a large majority of the national population illustrates the political and policy effects of the institutional inequities in the representation of population.[38]

The money question was resolved only when a terrible depression and an inept Democratic president effectively nationalized the issue and made it partisan in the 1890s. Democrats repudiated their unpopular president by endorsing silver, thereby ironically allowing Republicans to exploit popular discontent while linking a return to prosperity with financial conservatism. The Republicans' triumph in the electoral realignment of the 1890s enabled them to end the money question by enacting the Gold Standard Act of 1900. Congressional voting on that measure was along party lines, unlike that on previous financial legislation.[39]

The tariff was a second major economic issue in the Gilded Age, one that historians have argued was a "defining point of distinction between Republicans and Democrats." Certainly, Republicans strongly endorsed the protective tariff and used it not only to rally supporters but also to suggest the party's broader commitment to an activist government to promote economic growth. Republican leaders insisted that a protective tariff not only fostered American industries but also benefited farmers by expanding the home market and workers by protecting their wage rates. Any surplus revenue generated by high tariffs could fund internal improvements and promote other economic interests.[40]

By contrast, Democrats were somewhat divided. Their commitment to a limited government certainly implied opposition to a protective tariff and its subsidies for special interests; and lower rates, by reducing the treasury surplus, would limit the government's ability to pursue activist policies. But not all Democrats accepted the formal party position, and in Congress, they voted for tariffs that would benefit their districts. "Reform is beautiful upon the mountain top," conceded one Democrat, but "very unwelcome as it approaches our own threshold." Party leaders tried to blur the issue in campaigns, and when Democrats briefly controlled all three branches of the government, they sidestepped their pledge of tariff reform to concoct a hash of a bill denounced as "party perfidy and party dishonor."[41]

Despite its identification with Republicans, then, the tariff had a broader appeal. It represented a distributive policy, one that enabled parties to allocate direct aid to a wide variety of groups while dispersing the costs less obviously and more indirectly. Party leaders preferred distributive to regulatory policies, which were far more divisive.[42]

Government land policy was another important distributive mechanism. Republicans had long been committed to transferring public land for productive use. The Homestead Act of 1862, providing free land to western settlers, was an original party principle, and Republicans thereafter enacted land grants for railroad development and agricultural education and a series of laws providing land for cattle, mining, and timber interests. Democrats did not generally dispute this distributive policy itself, but they did oppose specific land grants to "corporations and syndicates" and urged that the public domain "be sacredly held as homesteads for our citizens."[43]

By 1880, Congress had enacted more than 3,000 land laws; fully one-quarter of all legislation was related to the public domain and its settlement. But rather than formulating any long-range policies, Congress simply responded to a variety of special-interest groups. It made no attempt at systematic resource management and never established a bureaucratic system capable of withstanding the demands of aggressive private interests. Administratively underdeveloped, the federal government could subsidize development and distribute resources but remained incapable of effectively regulating for the long-term public good.[44]

Pensions for Union army veterans, another distributive policy, constituted the largest category of federal expenditures, and although there were clear partisan differences on the subject, they were largely suppressed for political reasons. The pension system began as a program to care for veterans disabled by military service, but partisan forces rapidly expanded coverage until it consumed 42 percent of the federal budget by 1893. Republicans actively supported the expansion, and northern (not southern) Democrats generally felt obliged to do so to prove their patriotism and to compete for the large veteran vote. The Pension Bureau became "the largest executive bureau in the world," and when it did not approve pensions under established rules, Congress regularly passed private pension bills. In the mid-1880s, special pension acts constituted nearly half of all legislation.

The Pension Bureau also became part of the Republican electoral machine. Party officials took pension examiners into doubtful states during election campaigns, worked with veterans' groups to find potential applicants, helped them apply for pensions, and told them to vote Republican to ensure approval of their claims. Democrats denounced the Pension Bureau as "corrupt, disgraceful, and dishonest" but felt that it was politically necessary to endorse liberal pensions, and the Pension Act of 1890 extended benefits to virtually every veteran and his dependents. This sudden expansion of pensions, accompanied by obvious fraud and corruption, provoked further criticism, but Republicans loosened their partisan grip only when the old soldiers' vote was no longer crucial to electoral success.

At its peak, the pension system aided 60 percent of the dependent elderly, all in the North, and pensions eventually became essentially old-age and survivors' benefits for Union soldiers. This experiment in patriotic and partisan social welfare confirmed southern hostility to the nationalization of relief, and it established a precedent that women's groups would soon use to argue for "mother's pensions" for worthy widows with dependent children.[45]

State governments too assumed greater responsibility for social welfare, traditionally overseen by private charities and local government. Beginning in 1863, northern states under Republican control established state boards of charities. As industrialization led to increasing social problems, states slowly began to create other boards, such as boards of health.[46] The stresses produced by rapid industrialization also led state governments to expand their role in regulating economic conditions. State governments, relying on their police power, had a long tradition of establishing economic regulations to secure public rights and welfare, and although changing attitudes and judicial decisions challenged that tradition in the Gilded Age, aspects of it persisted.[47]

By the turn of the century, most states had created commissions to investigate and regulate various aspects of the industrial economy. One observer noted in 1887 that state governments enacted laws in "utter disregard of the laissez-faire principle." In Minnesota, for example, state inspectors examined steam boilers, oil production, sawmills, and sanitary conditions. Other laws regulated railroads, telegraphs, and dangerous occupations and otherwise protected the public welfare.[48] Not all such laws were effective, nor were all state governments as diligent as Minnesota's. Southern states especially lagged, preferring to promote rather than to regulate corporate interests. And efforts to regulate the workplace were generally defeated, diluted, or invalidated by conservative courts. Still, state power expanded in nearly every field.

The growth of great new industrial corporations, disrupting traditional practices and values, profoundly alarmed the public and opened the way to a more powerful national government. States led in regulating both railroad policies and the anti-competitive practices of the trusts, but the Supreme Court soon ruled that only the federal government could regulate interstate commerce. Congress promptly approved the Interstate Commerce Act of 1887 with the support of both major parties. This law not only asserted national authority but, in establishing the Interstate Commerce Commission (ICC) with important discretionary powers, also initiated the administrative agency as the fourth branch of government.

Although a bipartisan law, it was not without controversy or weaknesses. The Interstate Commerce Act was the product of political pressure from many groups: farmers and merchants wanting to abolish discriminatory rates; even railroad officials seeking to curtail disruptive competition. Regulation thus involved attempts to reconcile conflicting economic interests, and the creation of the ICC prefigured developments in the Progressive Era. But this early effort at administrative regulation stalled. The ICC vainly asked Congress for amendments "to make the substance of the law mean what it was supposed to mean"; its attempt to institutionalize a cooperative regulatory process foundered on railroad recalcitrance, and the Supreme Court soon stripped it of any real power.[49]

The Sherman Antitrust Act of 1890 was no more successful in expanding federal authority. Despite the near unanimity of its passage, the law's imprecise language and dependence on the judiciary rather than an administrative agency for enforcement limited its ability to prevent abuses and indicated the incomplete commitment to federal regulation. Moreover, Congress appropriated no funds to enforce the act, presidents of both parties took little interest in it, and the Supreme Court gutted it by ruling that it did not apply to industrial combinations.[50] The failure of the ICC and the Sherman Act reflected many of the political constraints on the development of effective public policy and symbolized the incapacity of the federal government to respond to popular concerns. Even the first chairman of the ICC warned against expanding the power of "the political machine called the United States Government."[51] Such attitudes, together with the checks and balances of a hesitant system and the requirements of political parties, defined and prolonged the political impasse of the Gilded Age.

Changing Electoral Structures and Party Roles

This stalemated Gilded Age polity began nevertheless to collapse at the end of the 1880s. Not all attitudes, institutions, participants, and policies changed at the same time, at the same pace, in the same place, or in the same direction. Yet many factors began to reshape politics, often interacting in fascinating ways, and they were more commonly structural than substantive in nature. The power of party organizations reached a peak, and anti-party sentiment swelled in reaction. In rapid order, there were first advances for and then restraints on parties and their control over voters and government.

The political deadlock seemed broken when the Republicans swept the presidency, the House, and the Senate in 1888. But Benjamin Harrison received a minority of the popular vote and became president only because of the electoral college. The Republicans also captured the House despite being outpolled nationally by the Democrats, and they controlled the Senate through their rotten boroughs in the West and gerrymandered legislatures elsewhere. In short, their sweeping national victory was less a popular endorsement than a reflection of their success in manipulating representational systems and of their organizational ability to mobilize voters at the right places. The first seemed unfair; the second seemed the product of electoral fraud, provoking a vociferous reaction from a variety of groups demanding ballot and other electoral reforms.

The suddenly dominant Republicans moved aggressively to enact their party agenda. In Congress, Czar Reed overrode, ignored, and eliminated the procedural restraints on majority action, thereby imposing party control on a more powerful and activist institution. The Republican Congress enacted the McKinley Tariff Act, the Dependent Pension Act, the Land Revision Act, and other major laws; admitted two more western states; and threatened to enact a "force bill" authorizing federal supervision of elections, a prospect that alarmed Democrats everywhere, but especially in the South. At the same time, Republican-controlled state legislatures in the Midwest enacted strong ethnocultural laws.[52]

Such partisan actions provoked an immediate backlash in the 1890 elections, and Republicans suffered the greatest congressional defeat to that time, a defeat that both reflected and promoted important changes in the structures of politics.

Beginning in 1889, in the wake of the alleged fraud of the 1888 elections, public opinion endorsed a movement for ballot reform, long pushed by three groups standing outside the normal two-party political system. Labor organizations, patrician mugwumps, and radical third parties, each with quite different motivations, demanded the adoption of the Australian ballot to weaken the control of the major parties over the electoral process.

The new system provided for an official, blanket, and secret ballot under state control, stripping parties of one of their most influential organizational functions and theoretically eliminating electoral corruption while facilitating more independent parties, candidates, and voting than had been possible under the party-ticket system. Some major-party leaders acceded to popular demand, foreseeing that the new ballot system might still serve party purposes. In any case, ten states passed Australian ballot laws in 1889, and the rest followed quickly. Democrats were convinced that ballot reform facilitated their landslide victory in 1890 and national sweep in 1892. Republicans held on in some states only because of desperate and alarming tactics. Some defeated incumbents refused to give up their offices; others precipitated "legislative wars." Public anxiety mounted over such dangerous partisanship.[53]

At the same time, discontented Americans launched the period's greatest third party, the People's Party, challenging the two-party system that had ignored their interests in currency, banking, and regulatory issues and in representative government. Populists demanded governmental action on behalf of farmers and workers, along with increased popular control of government. Elected to western state legislatures, they pushed an extensive reform agenda. In Congress, they publicized new ideas and attitudes about government, even as institutional procedures were used to stifle their activity.[54]

Now in power, Democrats pursued their own partisan objectives. On the state level, they enacted flagrant gerrymanders, limited only by the unprecedented involvement of partisan courts, whose decisions plunged several states into a frightening chaos that brought further popular condemnation of partisanship. In the South, Democrats began to disfranchise not only blacks who voted Republican but also poor whites seeking political influence through the Populist Party.[55] At the national level, the Democrats—taking control just as a terrible depression intensified the sense of crisis and spread unemployment, suffering, and discontent—stubbornly pressed their vision of negative government, repealing silver legislation, repealing federal election laws, rejecting demands for public works for the unemployed, and denying the federal government's responsibility for resolving social distress.

This inept and insensitive leadership splintered the party and alienated the electorate. In reaction, Democrats were crushed in the 1894 state and congressional elections, suffering a greater defeat than the Republicans had experienced in 1890. This staggering reversal of the recent landslide indicated the straying of voters from party lines, as did a 50 percent increase in Populist voting. Most Democrats themselves now broke from their party leadership. In 1896, they reorganized under William Jennings Bryan and repudiated many of their own party's traditional positions. It was not enough. Even a fusion with the Populists did not prevent the Democrats from another crushing defeat as voters turned to the Republicans and their program of governmental action to promote economic growth.[56]

The elections of 1894 and 1896 ended the years of political equilibrium by bringing about a voter realignment behind the Republicans, who would rule for a generation. The highly competitive party system was replaced by a regionally based system with only scattered areas of real competition. Democrats retained strength only in the South, where they continued to ensure their power through further disfranchisement legislation. Populists gradually faded, but only after contributing to the realignment of political parties and to expanded popular expectations for government. Government would soon change, but so would the role of parties and the nation's political style.

In the North and West, Republican legislatures exploited the opportunities under the Australian system to establish state control over electoral procedures previously left to party organizations. Almost everywhere, Republicans enacted anti-fusion ballot laws, fragmenting the potential opposition and undermining the viability of third parties. The final collapse of the Populist Party owed much to these laws. Other laws regulated nominations, restricted independent voting, and transformed the Australian system, as one critic recognized, into "a means for the repression instead of the expression of the will of the people." Such laws defined and protected the major-party organizations, granting them privileged access to the ballot and making them part of the official election machinery of the state itself.[57]

But the new laws could not suppress the growing dissatisfaction with party politics, which soon produced other electoral laws that reduced the electorate and the party's ability to mobilize it. States abolished alien suffrage and adopted procedural barriers to voting, including educational and duration-of-residency requirements and stringent registration laws. These laws particularly reduced voting among the working class and ethnic groups. Anti-party reformers wanted to "refine" the electorate so that voting reflected good citizenship, not blind partisanship. Rather than a right, suffrage became a privilege, and northern restrictions resembled those in the South directed at allegedly ignorant blacks and poor whites.[58]

But most important in reducing turnout and transforming politics was the electoral realignment of the 1890s. The successive electoral changes of those years had loosened partisan loyalties. Perhaps most voters in the North now considered themselves Republican, but party commitments were felt less intensely than before. With all social groups having shifted toward the GOP, ethnocultural divisions no longer overlapped and reinforced party divisions. Moreover, by eliminating party competition within most regions, the realignment reduced popular interest in politics and the incentive to vote. Turnout naturally declined as well.[59]

Laws manipulating political representation further decreased party competition. In many formerly competitive states, Republican legislatures enacted new apportionments. Some of these persisted for decades, broadly freezing party divisions and ironically reducing the previously intense interest in representation. Several states in the East and Midwest revised their constitutions to ensure less democratic but more Republican representation.[60] Parties found it harder to mobilize less committed voters for less competitive contests. Laws restricting campaign contributions added to the problem. And as civil service reform spread, parties had fewer rewards to attract workers to organize campaigns and crowds. The adoption of the direct primary, beginning in 1902, also weakened parties by stripping them of their control of nominations and encouraging factionalism centered around individuals who built their own personal organizations.

All these electoral changes after 1888, political and legal, brought to an end the party period of American history. They undermined the role and influence of parties, weakened partisan loyalties, redefined the electorate, and curtailed the traditional third parties. The major parties that had once regulated the political order were now regulated themselves. Such changes would inevitably affect the nature and scope of government as well.

The New Governance

As partisanship and mass voting declined, and as party organizations followed more gradually, nonpartisan interest groups became increasingly numerous, active, and influential. Unlike the party coalitions that had tried to subsume different interests in a partisan conception of the common good, these groups had more narrowly based memberships and more narrowly focused interests. Although much historiography emphasizes the importance of business groups seeking governmental assistance of various kinds, other groups more marginal to the direction of the party system also developed new organizational models for political participation.

Besides farmers and workers, women in particular formed nonpartisan associations that plunged into nonelectoral politics, both to secure social and economic reforms and to develop organizations that exercised dominion over child welfare policy or protective labor legislation for women. Other Americans, outraged by corporate abuses and party complicity exposed in the 1890s depression, organized as consumers and pressed for government regulation.[61] Such organized groups became permanent features of the polity in the early twentieth century. Their often conflicting goals pointed to increased regulatory activity by governments at all levels.

Whereas a key theme of the Gilded Age was that parties and the machinery of government had shaped or constrained public policies, in the Progressive Era the new regulatory policies and the demand for them shaped the institutions of government and parties. First, they called forth administrative agencies that assumed control over much of governmental decision making. The Bureau of Corporations, created in 1903, asserted administrative oversight of trusts. The Interstate Commerce Commission had its regulatory authority greatly expanded by the Hepburn Act (1906) and the Mann-Elkins Act (1910). Other popular laws in 1906 established the Food and Drug Administration to regulate drugs and empowered the Department of Agriculture to administer a federal program of meat inspection.

The creation of nonpartisan commissions and regulatory agencies, staffed by experts committed to an overarching public interest, would presumably resolve social and economic conflicts more satisfactorily than legislatures composed of partisan representatives of localistic interests. Legislation creating and expanding regulatory and administrative powers, in turn, reflected a variety of political and economic interests, including those of the regulated industries, and scarcely guaranteed regulation in the public interest. But the creation of new governmental agencies as a consequence of new policies added important features to the structure of government. Seeing Congress and the state governments lose authority, one observer noted the trend "to concentrate all power in Washington and to govern the people by commissions and bureaus."[62]

But the trend was at all levels of government. Expert commissions to regulate railroads, banks, insurance, and social welfare soon became characteristic of state governments, gradually gaining authority at the expense of elected local officials. A Virginian noted that the emphasis on efficiency and expertise caused the government to "delegate all new functions, and some old ones, to state departments or commissions instead of to county officers." In the nation's cities, municipal reformers were devising administrative offices to manage sanitation, utilities, land use, and construction.[63]

The new policy perspective also contributed to an expansion of the executive branch and its authority. Of course, more than most political institutions, the presidency reflects not simply its formal structural features but also the personality of its incumbent, and Theodore Roosevelt took a far more expansive view of presidential authority than had his predecessors, regarding it as limited only by explicit constitutional prohibitions. Thus individuals made a difference, but the government's new regulatory role also affected the executive. In a society of conflicting interests, only the president had the information, perspective, and ability to represent the people as a whole, to resolve, not suppress, conflict through impartial regulation.

Congress, declared Roosevelt, was "a helpless body when efficient work for good is to be done." He therefore provided legislative leadership, spelling out policy goals, submitting draft bills for regulatory legislation, and pressing for their passage. To popular approval, he expanded the president's role in the economy in the Northern Securities case and the anthracite coal strike. He also sought to institutionalize efficiency and expertise in special commissions and administrative procedures and by sharply expanding the classified civil service. Some members of Congress complained of his "executive arrogance" and "dictatorship," but his activities helped shift the balance of power within the national government.[64]

Roosevelt's view of the presidency as a steward of the public also led him to use his office as a "bully pulpit" to organize and rally public opinion behind his goals. Previous presidents had rarely addressed the public, their reticence being not merely a matter of style or custom but indicative of a fundamentally different view of the office: the president as a formal executive, not a popular leader. Roosevelt, however, linked his office directly to a "rhetorical presidency." One opponent complained that Roosevelt so "roused the people that it was impossible for the Senate to stand against the popular demand."[65]

Responding to the growing pressures on government, both Roosevelt and his successor, William Howard Taft, moved to establish executive control over administration, an authority previously claimed exclusively by Congress. Both presidents appointed commissions to consider executive reorganization, the first assertions that the president held primary responsibility for the conduct of government operations. Both commissions sought not the traditional congressional concern for economy but organizational rationalization and the expansion of the executive's capacity for management. Congress denounced these commissions as executive encroachment on the sphere of congressional action and rejected their recommendations. Both presidents attempted to implement some proposals through "executive regulation" rather than legislation, and both defended an expanded presidential authority over policy making and public management as an executive responsibility, too complex for Congress. Despite Taft's judicial background, his commission justified its proposals for expanding executive authority on functional, not constitutional, grounds: to perform the functions required of it by changing popular expectations, the presidency must have the necessary powers.

Congress resisted, fearing that it was becoming a victim of "bureaucratic advance to power." But these presidential efforts at executive reorganization provided what scholars have called both "the origins of the managerial presidency" and "the roots of the institutionalized presidency." Those roots soon bore fruit, most notably in the Budget and Accounting Act of 1921. Observed one magazine in 1910: "Mr. Taft's conception of the government is of a gigantic machine, its many parts so regulated as to move from a single source of energy." This centralization of executive powers in the administrative state was a long way, if a short time, removed from Bryce's inability to perceive the machinery of government in a fragmented polity.[66]

One clear example of the changing governmental focus was the shift in policy orientation on natural resources from promoting exploitation under congressional direction to promoting conservation under executive control. Whereas land policy had involved a distributive approach responsive to the most interested groups, the management of natural resources would require administrative agencies, mediating among (and regulating) competing interests seeking access to land, timber, and water. Conflict would also arise between the executive branch, asserting its claim to represent the larger public good, and Congress, responding variably to particular pressures.

The General Revision Act of 1891 and the Forest Management Act of 1897 ended a century of unlimited distribution of the public domain by repealing or amending most land laws, authorizing the president to withdraw timberlands from development, and providing for federal regulation of grazing, lumbering, and hydroelectric sites. New agencies such as the Reclamation Service (1902) and the National Forest Service (1905) brought rational management and regulation to resource development. Conservation was often controversial; essentially, the argument was over the proper mix of distributive and regulatory policies, but opponents especially objected to decisions being made by "some bureau in Washington."[67]

Another major source of the expanded presidency lay in foreign and military affairs, where the Constitution grants most authority to the president. Most Gilded Age presidents took little interest in foreign affairs, and those who did often found themselves thwarted by congressional opposition. The Grant administration's plans to obtain Caribbean possessions were blocked by Congress, including the Senate's defeat of a treaty annexing the Dominican Republic. In any event, the military was weak, and a professional foreign service was lacking. Diplomatic posts were routinely awarded for political service, not diplomatic ability, and an 1872 investigation found officials characterized by "incompetency, low habits, and vulgarity." Grant's minister to Ecuador was an unstable drunk who tried to assassinate the British minister before dying in an alcoholic delirium.[68]

But as economic, strategic, and ideological pressures built in the late nineteenth century for expansionism, presidents periodically if haphazardly asserted themselves in foreign policy. The growth of organized interest groups such as the Committee on American Interests in China pressed for activism too. The Spanish-American and Filipino-American Wars at the turn of the century spurred the expansion of presidential authority. McKinley made all the crucial decisions for war and territorial acquisition and masterfully directed a fractious Congress and an excited public to endorse his goals.

Roosevelt went further and insisted on presidential primacy even in the absence of congressional approval. Convinced that Congress was ill informed about international affairs, he repeatedly ignored or circumvented congressional wishes, particularly by means of executive agreements. McKinley, Roosevelt, and Taft all sent troops abroad without congressional consent. They thus strengthened the institutional status of the president in foreign affairs by staking out a role bounded by neither specific constitutional provisions nor explicit congressional approval. Contemporary critics, not merely subsequent historians, referred to the imperial presidency.[69]

A Progressive Era

As Congress lost its former primacy to a newly activist presidency that was capable of developing programs, mobilizing public opinion, and directing legislation, the institution also underwent significant internal change. The regional stabilization of the party system after the realignment of the 1890s, the increasing commitment to careerism, and a declining reliance on the party organization for nomination and reelection produced a growing number of Republicans who were less committed to traditional norms of party loyalty and less willing to yield their own views to the conservative vision held by the powerful Speaker, Joe Cannon.

The tariff issue, which had formerly served to unite the party, was now a source of division, as midwestern Republicans could no longer see how high tariffs, which Cannon continued to support, would benefit their constituents. Attempting to enforce party government, Cannon removed such insurgents from key committee positions. But the declining hold of party led the insurgent Republicans to cooperate with Democrats in a bipartisan coalition that, in 1910, revised House rules to strip the Speaker of much of his power and thereby change the House as a political institution.[70]

Indeed, the revolt against Cannon marked 1910, in the words of David Brady, as the end of the nineteenth-century House. The loss of the Speaker's authority led to a gradual disintegration of party control mechanisms such as steering committees, a decline in party cohesion, and a decentralization of power in the House. Seniority became the only acceptable principle for assigning key committee positions without provoking further disputes and weakening the party. These developments increased the power and independence of individual members, especially the committee chairs. Deprived of formal authority, party leaders would "function less as the commanders of a stable party majority and more as brokers trying to assemble particular majorities behind particular bills." Changes in substantive policy objectives had again brought about changes in institutional structure.[71]

By 1910, the Senate too was on the verge of significant change, also involving the interaction of rules and policy. From the 1890s, there had been increasing demands for popular, rather than legislative, election of senators. Senate seats often went unfilled because of partisan impasses in state legislatures, fueling a growing conviction that Senate elections were corrupted by party machines and corporate influence. Populists and Democrats led the attack on indirect elections, the first on ideological grounds and the second on partisan grounds. Indirect elections by malapportioned legislatures and by the rotten boroughs of the West worked to the disadvantage of both. In contrast, disfranchisement made the South a giant rotten borough, which the Democrats tried to protect by coupling all proposals for popular election with prohibitions against federal control of Senate elections. This caused some Republicans who were otherwise supportive to oppose popular election and led to another impasse, with designing parties, biased electoral rules, and possible policy consequences completely intertwined.[72]

By 1910, however, thirty state legislatures had adopted resolutions demanding direct election of Senators, and in 1911, the Senate finally approved a constitutional amendment, which went into effect in 1913. Direct election, like other electoral changes, weakened organizational and partisan linkages and enhanced the independence of senators. And, as in the House, party leaders lost some of their control over proceedings, and power devolved to committee chairs. To some extent, Americans again looked to the presidency for strong leadership.

One final change in these years involved suffrage, both a key part of the structure of politics and one of its most basic substantive concerns, carrying considerable cultural weight as well. Changes in suffrage rights derive from contingent politics, not linear development, as suggested by the reverse trajectories of black suffrage and women's suffrage. African Americans gained their rights during Reconstruction, primarily for partisan reasons. Most Republicans saw black suffrage as the only way to ensure a loyal South, to obviate the need for prolonged federal intervention in the region, and to build a truly national Republican Party. Women were simultaneously and deliberately excluded from the Fifteenth Amendment, not simply because Republicans declared it the "Negro's hour," but because there were no pragmatic political reasons for enfranchising women, no obvious partisan advantage to be gained from risking male backlash.

African Americans used the ballot to exercise genuine political power to shape a more democratic society in the South during Reconstruction, but thereafter, they gradually lost their rights, as changing electoral conditions reduced their value to northern Republicans and allowed southern Democrats progressively to suppress, segregate, and disfranchise them by the turn of the century.[73] At the same time, conversely, women gradually gained rights, first in such matters as property, and then, more slowly, suffrage, made possible by other political changes.

The Australian ballot and the educational campaign eliminated voting as a masculine ritual, and suffrage became less a male right than a privilege for the intelligent citizen. Government functions expanded to incorporate the social welfare objectives of organized women, and parties declined, to be supplemented if not replaced by special-interest lobbying of the kind women had long employed to influence government, an action especially appropriate for the new agencies buffered from direct voter control. The argument that women received the vote only when it no longer mattered may be hyperbolic, but certainly political rights, partisan practices, governmental institutions, and public policies are linked in some fashion. The precise connections still wait to be fully explored.[74]

The dialectical nature of political change, of course, made the transformation of American politics during this period an incomplete process rather than a final product. Accounts of the decline of parties, for example, like reports of Mark Twain's death, are often exaggerated. Party organizations retained strength in public affairs, often proving more flexible and responsive than expected, more sophisticated in choosing and using public issues, and capable of turning nearly every electoral reform to their advantage, at least for a time. Most importantly, parties monopolized access to most ballots and offices. Partisanship came to be identified less with party organizations and hoopla than with particular leaders and policy issues. New party leaders, as James Wright wrote, were often "less political strategists than they were issue-oriented political activists. Their approach to politics held that issues made coalitions; the older political practice tended toward the opposite approach."[75]

Similarly, we should not too readily assume that interest groups and administrative agencies better aggregated, articulated, and represented the interests of most Americans than did political parties. Only some groups organized, if more than formerly thought. Many Americans, abandoned by parties or excluded by electoral reforms, never organized for interest-group politics, and powerful interests often dominated administrative agencies, whose impartial experts were sometimes neither. The evolution of Wisconsin's Railroad Commission from an idea promising to reduce railroad rates for consumers and small producers to an agency that cooperated with railroads to reduce competition and even forestall further regulation exposes the limits of administrative reform.[76]

All these subjects require much more attention. The examination of the actual membership and operations of administrative agencies has barely begun. The analysis of representational systems has been woefully neglected. Legislative policy making, especially at the state level, women's suffrage campaigns, political and organizational cultures, and many other issues all await serious investigation. Such work must be done before we can fully understand American politics and the complex interactions among the machinery of government, political parties, public policies, and the American people.

Notes

1. James Bryce, *The American Commonwealth* (Chicago, 1891), 1, 15. For useful discussions of this analytical approach, see Rogers M. Smith, "Political Jurisprudence, the 'New Institutionalism,' and the Future of Public Law," *American Political Science Review* 82 (1988): 89–108; James March and Johan Olsen, "The New Institutionalism: Organizational Factors in Political Life," *American Political Science Review* 78 (1984): 734–49; Ronald Hedlund, "Organizational Attributes of Legislatures: Structure, Rules, Norms, Resources," *Legislative Studies Quarterly* 9 (1984): 51–121; David Brian Robertson, "The Return to History and the New Institutionalism in American Political Science," *Social Science History* 17 (1993): 1–36.

2. Bryce, *American Commonwealth*, 1, 412, 442; James C. Mohr, ed., *Radical Republicans in the North: State Politics during Reconstruction* (Baltimore, 1976); Eric Foner, *Reconstruction: America's Unfinished Revolution, 1863–1877* (New York, 1988), 346–79; Morton Keller, *Affairs of State: Public Life in Late Nineteenth Century America* (Cambridge, Mass., 1977), 110–14.

3. *Fargo Forum*, March 6, 1893; Peter H. Argersinger, "Ideology and Behavior: Legislative Politics and Western Populism," *Agricultural History* 58 (1984): 43–58; Robert Cherny, *Populism, Progressivism, and the Transformation of Nebraska Politics* (Lincoln, Nebr., 1981), 37; Philip VanderMeer, *The Hoosier Politician: Office Holding and Political Culture in Indiana* (Urbana, Ill., 1985), 146–98; Ballard C. Campbell, *The Growth of American Government* (Bloomington, Ind., 1995), 20.

4. Loren Beth, *The Development of the American Constitution, 1877–1917* (New York, 1971), 73–74; Cherny, *Transformation of Nebraska Politics*, 72–73; Ari Hoogenboom, *Rutherford B. Hayes: Warrior and President* (Lawrence, Kans., 1995), 215, 233.

5. Leonard D. White, *The Republican Era* (New York, 1958), 20–92; Justus Doenecke, *The Presidencies of James A. Garfield and Chester A. Arthur* (Lawrence, Kans., 1981), 12; George F. Hoar, *Autobiography of Seventy Years* (New York, 1903), 11, 46.

6. W. R. Brock, *An American Crisis: Congress and Reconstruction, 1865–1867* (New York, 1963), 50–60; Morris P. Fiorina et al., "Historic Change in House Turnover," in *Congress in Change*, ed. Norman Ornstein (New York, 1975), 24–57; Peter H. Argersinger, "The Value of the Vote: Political Representation in the Gilded Age," *Journal of American History* 76 (1989): 71.

7. Allan G. Bogue, "Legislative Government in the United States Congress, 1800–1900," in *Parties and Politics in American History*, ed. L. Sandy Maisel and William G. Shade (New York, 1994), 119–25; William Robinson, *Thomas B. Reed, Parliamentarian* (New York, 1930), 222; Margaret Susan Thompson, *The "Spider Web": Congress and Lobbying in the Age of Grant* (Ithaca, N.Y., 1985), 71–115; W. Thomas Wander, "Patterns of Change in the Congressional Budget Process, 1865–1974," *Congress and the Presidency* 9 (1982): 23–31.

8. David Rothman, *Politics and Power: The United States Senate* (New York, 1969); Hoar, *Autobiography*, 11, 46; Bogue, "Legislative Government," 126–27; Thompson, *The "Spider Web,"* 114.

9. Brooks Simpson, *The Reconstruction Presidents* (Lawrence, Kans., 1998); Doenecke, *Presidencies of Garfield and Arthur*, 15–16, 38, 76–80, 183; White, *Republican Era*, 4, 20–25.

10. John P. Burke, *The Institutional Presidency* (Baltimore, 1992), 3–5; Richard Welch, *The Presidencies of Grover Cleveland* (Lawrence, Kans., 1988), 48–56; White, *Republican Era*, 97–103; Ezra Paul, "Congressional Relations and 'Public Relations' in

the Administration of Rutherford B. Hayes," *Presidential Studies Quarterly* 28 (1998): 68–87.

11. White, *Republican Era*, 278–302; Ari Hoogenboom, "The Pendleton Act and the Civil Service," *American Historical Review* 64 (1959): 302; Robert Goldman, "The 'Weakened Spring of Government' and the Executive Branch: The Department of Justice in the Late 19th Century," *Congress and the Presidency* 11 (1984): 165–77; Stephen Skowronek, *Building a New American State: The Expansion of National Administrative Capacities* (New York, 1982), 47–84.

12. Richard P. McCormick, *The Presidential Game: The Origins of American Presidential Politics* (New York, 1982).

13. Richard L. McCormick, "The Party Period and Public Policy: An Exploratory Hypothesis," *Journal of American History* 66 (1979): 279–98; Joel H. Silbey, *The American Political Nation, 1838–1893* (Stanford, Calif., 1991); Skowronek, *Building a New American State*, 24–26.

14. Bryce, *American Commonwealth*, 11, 3; Robert Marcus, *Grand Old Party: Political Structure in the Gilded Age, 1880–1896* (New York, 1971); Silbey, *American Political Nation*, 45–71.

15. Peter H. Argersinger, *Structure, Process, and Party: Essays in American Political History* (Armonk, N.Y., 1992), 47–50, 122–49; *Tarbox v. Sughrue*, 12 Pac. Rep. 935 (1887).

16. Paul Kleppner, "Partisanship and Ethnoreligious Conflict: The Third Electoral System," in *The Evolution of American Electoral Systems*, ed. Paul Kleppner et al. (Westport, Conn., 1981), 113–46; Paul Kleppner, *The Third Electoral System, 1853–1892: Parties, Voters, and Political Cultures* (Chapel Hill, N.C., 1979), 143–97.

17. R. Hal Williams, *The Democratic Party and California Politics, 1880–1896* (Stanford, Calif., 1973), 60.

18. Lewis L. Gould, "Party Conflict: Republicans versus Democrats, 1877–1901," in *The Gilded Age: Essays on the Origins of Modern America*, ed. Charles W. Calhoun (Wilmington, Del., 1996), 215–34; Keller, *Affairs of State*, 559; Robert Salisbury, "The Republican Party and Positive Government: 1860–1890," *Mid-America* 68 (1986): 15–34.

19. *Appletons' Annual Cyclopedia, 1880* (New York, 1883), 498; R. Hal Williams, "'Dry Bones and Dead Language': The Democratic Party," in *The Gilded Age*, ed. H. Wayne Morgan (Syracuse, N.Y., 1970), 129–48; Robert W. Cherny, *American Politics in the Gilded Age, 1868–1900* (Wheeling, Ill., 1997), 22–31.

20. Ronald P. Formisano, "The 'Party Period' Revisited," *Journal of American History* 86 (1999): 93–120; Richard L. McCormick, *The Party Period and Public Policy: American Politics from the Age of Jackson to the Progressive Era* (New York, 1986), 228–59; Peter H. Argersinger, *The Limits of Agrarian Radicalism: Western Populism and American Politics* (Lawrence, Kans., 1995), 64–79; *Kansas Farmer* (Topeka), January 1, 1890; Michael McGerr, *The Decline of Popular Politics* (New York, 1986), 42–68.

21. Peter H. Argersinger, *Populism and Politics* (Lexington, Ky., 1974), 20–21, 307, passim; Richard Oestreicher, "Urban Working-Class Political Behavior and Theories of American Electoral Politics, 1870–1940," *Journal of American History* 74 (1988): 1276–77; Argersinger, *Limits of Agrarian Radicalism*, 7; Mark Voss-Hubbard, "The 'Third Party Tradition' Reconsidered: Third Parties and American Public Life," *Journal of American History* 86 (1999): 121–50; Leon Fink, *Workingmen's Democracy: The Knights of Labor and American Politics* (Urbana, Ill., 1983); Michael Hyman, *The Anti-Redeemers: Hill Country Political Dissenters in the Lower South from Redemption to Populism* (Baton Rouge, 1990); Jeffrey Ostler, *Prairie Populism* (Lawrence, Kans., 1993).

22. Paula Baker, "The Domestication of Politics: Women and American Political Society," *American Historical Review* 89 (1984): 620–47; Michael McGerr, "Political Style and Women's Power, 1830–1930," *Journal of American History* 77 (1990): 864–85; Michael Lewis Goldberg, *An Army of Women: Gender and Politics in Gilded Age Kansas* (Baltimore, 1997); Rebecca Edwards, *Angels in the Machinery: Gender in American Party Politics from the Civil War to the Progressive Era* (New York, 1997); Melanie Gustafson, Kristie Miller, and Elisabeth Israels Perry, eds., *We Have Come to Stay: American Women and Political Parties, 1880–1960* (Albuquerque, 1999); Ruth Bordin, *Woman and Temperance: The Quest for Power and Liberty* (Philadelphia, 1981).

23. George H. Miller, *Railroads and the Granger Laws* (Madison, Wis., 1971).

24. Joanne Reitano, *The Tariff Question in the Gilded Age* (University Park, Pa., 1994), 115–17; Donald Kinzer, *An Episode in Anticatholicism: The American Protective Association* (Seattle, 1964).

25. Argersinger, "Value of the Vote," 59–90.

26. Charles Stewart III and Barry Weingast, "Stacking the Senate, Changing the Nation: Republican Rotten Boroughs, Statehood Politics, and American Political Development," *Studies in American Political Development* 6 (1992): 223–71.

27. David Brady, "The Party System in the United States House of Representatives," in Maisel and Shade, *Parties and Politics*, 185; William G. Shade et al., "Partisanship in the United States Senate: 1869–1901," *Journal of Interdisciplinary History* 4 (1973): 185–206; Jerome Clubb and Santa Traugott, "Partisan Cleavage and Cohesion in the House of Representatives, 1861–1974," *Journal of Interdisciplinary History* 7 (1977): 375–401; David Brady, *Congressional Voting in a Partisan Era* (Lawrence, Kans., 1973).

28. Ballard Campbell, *Representative Democracy: Public Policy and Midwestern Legislatures in the Late Nineteenth Century* (Cambridge, Mass., 1980), esp. 97, 199; Allen Trelease, "Republican Reconstruction in North Carolina: A Roll-Call Analysis of the State House of Representatives, 1868–1870," *Journal of Southern History* 42 (1976): 319–44; Mohr, *Radical Republicans*; Argersinger, *Limits of Agrarian Radicalism*, 176–212; James E. Wright, *The Politics of Populism: Dissent in Colorado* (New Haven, Conn., 1974), 94, 164, 178.

29. *Wisconsin State Journal* (Madison), February 18, 27, 1896; Argersinger, *Limits of Agrarian Radicalism*, 80–101, 190.

30. See Joseph Cooper, "Congress in Organizational Perspective," in *Congress Reconsidered*, ed. Lawrence Dodd and Bruce Oppenheimer (New York, 1977); Nelson Polsby, "The Institutionalization of the U.S. House of Representatives," *American Political Science Review* 62 (1968): 144–68; Joseph Cooper and Cheryl Young, "Bill Introduction in the Nineteenth Century: A Study of Institutional Change," *Legislative Studies Quarterly* 14 (1989): 67–105; Keller, *Affairs of State*, 299–307.

31. Peter H. Argersinger, "No Rights on This Floor: Third Parties and the Institutionalization of Congress," *Journal of Interdisciplinary History* 22 (1992): 655–90; Sarah A. Binder, *Minority Rights, Majority Rule: Partisanship and the Development of Congress* (Cambridge, 1997); Douglas Dion, *Turning the Legislative Thumbscrew: Minority Rights and Procedural Change in Legislative Politics* (Ann Arbor, Mich., 1997).

32. Michael Abram and Joseph Cooper, "The Rise of Seniority in the House of Representatives," *Polity* 1 (1968): 78–80; Joseph Cooper and David Brady, "Institutional Context and Leadership Style: The House from Cannon to Rayburn,"

American Political Science Review 75 (1981): 413; Dion, *Turning the Legislative Thumbscrew,* 717; Binder, *Minority Rights,* 110–25.

33. Robinson, *Reed,* 222; Dion, *Turning the Legislative Thumbscrew,* 133–34; Bogue, "Legislative Government," 121.

34. *Congressional Record,* 51st Cong., 1st sess., 1236; Dion, *Turning the Legislative Thumbscrew,* 125–38; Binder, *Minority Rights,* 125–31. For changes in the Senate, see Bogue, "Legislative Government," 125–27; Rothman, *Politics and Power.*

35. Gretchen Ritter, *Goldbugs and Greenbacks: The Antimonopoly Tradition and the Politics of Finance in America, 1865–1896* (New York, 1997); Walter Nugent, *Money and American Society* (New York, 1968); Irwin Unger, *The Greenback Era* (Princeton, N.J., 1962)

36. *Appletons' Annual Cyclopedia, 1878* (New York, 1883), 221, 467–68.

37. Peter H. Argersinger, "The Greenback Party, 1873–1886," in *The Encyclopaedia of Third Parties in America,* ed. Immanuel Ness and James Ciment (Armonk, N.Y., 2000), 11:271–75; Fred E. Haynes, *Third Party Movements since the Civil War* (Iowa City, 1916), 155, 173.

38. John Spooner to Jeremiah Rusk, January 27, 1891, John C. Spooner Papers, Library of Congress; Argersinger, "Value of the Vote," 87.

39. Cherny, *American Politics in the Gilded Age,* 128.

40. Charles W. Calhoun, "Political Economy in the Gilded Age: The Republican Party's Industrial Policy," *Journal of Policy History* 8 (1996): 291–309; Lewis L. Gould, "The Republican Search for a National Majority," in Morgan, *The Gilded Age,* 171–87.

41. Reitano, *The Tariff Question;* Festus P. Summers, *William L. Wilson and Tariff Reform* (New Brunswick, N.J., 1953), 163–205.

42. McCormick, *Party Period,* 197–227. As Cherny has pointed out, "State and local governments also practiced a form of distribution when they scattered new state institutions to various parts of the state, subsidized railroad construction, and improved the infrastructure by building roads and bridges" (*American Politics in the Gilded Age,* 19).

43. W. U. Hensel, *Life and Public Services of Grover Cleveland . . . and Allen Thurman* (Philadelphia, 1888), 481; Welch, *Presidencies of Cleveland,* 74–76.

44. Paul Wallace Gates, *History of Public Land Law Development* (Washington, D.C., 1968); Harold Dunham, "Some Crucial Years of the General Land Office, 1875–1890," *Agricultural History* (1937): 117–41; Harry N. Scheiber, "Legislatures and American Economic Development," in *Encyclopedia of the American Legislative System,* ed. Joel H. Silbey (New York, 1994), 111, 1206; White, *Republican Era,* 196–208.

45. Theda Skocpol, *Protecting Soldiers and Mothers: The Political Origins of Social Policy in the United States* (Cambridge, Mass., 1992), 102–51; Heywood T. Sanders, "Paying for the 'Bloody Shirt': The Politics of Civil War Pensions," in *Political Benefits: Empirical Studies of American Public Programs,* ed. Barry Rundquist (Lexington, Mass., 1980), 137–59; Mary Dearing, *Veterans in Politics: The Story of the G.A.R.* (Baton Rouge, 1952); Donald McMurry, "The Political Significance of the Pension Question, 1885–1897," *Mississippi Valley Historical Review* 9 (1922): 19–36.

46. William R. Brock, *Investigation and Responsibility* (Cambridge, 1984), 93–147.

47. William J. Novak, *The People's Welfare: Law and Regulation in Nineteenth-Century America* (Chapel Hill, N.C., 1996).

48. Brock, *Investigation and Responsibility,* 2–3.

49. Cherny, *American Politics in the Gilded Age*, 78–81; Ari Hoogenboom and Olive Hoogenboom, *A History of the ICC: From Panacea to Palliative* (New York, 1976), 8–38; Gerald Berk, "Adversaries by Design: Railroads and the American State, 1887–1916," *Journal of Policy History* 5 (1993): 338–45.

50. Keller, *Affairs of* State, 436–38; William Letwin, *Law and Economic Policy in America: The Evolution of the Sherman Antitrust Act* (New York, 1965), 53–181. These court decisions point to another major structural feature of American politics that cannot be addressed here: the judiciary, federal and state. For a useful introduction to some of the issues in a contentious and expanding field, see Daniel R. Ernst, "Law and American Political Development, 1877–1938," *Reviews in American History* 26 (1998): 205–19. For critics of the judiciary and the political and institutional factors that limited their success, see William Ross, *A Muted Fury: Populists, Progressives, and Labor Unions Confront the Courts, 1890–1937* (Princeton, N.J., 1994).

51. Keller, *Affairs of State*, 430.

52. R. Hal Williams, *Years of Decision: American Politics in the 1890s* (New York, 1978), 24–47.

53. Argersinger, *Structure, Process, and Party*, 53–54, 84–86, 109–10; John F. Reynolds and Richard L. McCormick, "Outlawing 'Treachery': Split Tickets and Ballot Laws in New York and New Jersey, 1880–1910," *Journal of American History* 72 (1986): 835–58.

54. Robert C. McMath, Jr., *American Populism* (New York, 1993); Argersinger, "No Rights on This Floor."

55. Peter H. Argersinger, "Chaos and Anarchy: The Politics of Apportionment" (forthcoming); J. Morgan Kousser, *The Shaping of Southern Politics: Suffrage Restriction and the Establishment of the One-Party South, 1880–1910* (New Haven, Conn., 1974).

56. Cherny, *American Politics in the Gilded Age*, 110–26.

57. Peter H. Argersinger, "'A Place on the Ballot': Fusion Politics and Antifusion Laws," *American Historical Review* 85 (1980): 287–306; *Baltimore Critic*, March 12, 1896.

58. John F. Reynolds, *Testing Democracy: Electoral Behavior and Progressive Reform in New Jersey* (Chapel Hill, N.C., 1988); Samuel T. McSeveney, "The Fourth Party System and Progressive Politics," in Maisel and Shade, *Parties and Politics*, 157–60.

59. Paul Kleppner, *Who Voted? The Dynamics of Electoral Turnout* (New York, 1982), 55–82; Cherny, *American Politics in the Gilded Age* , 130–32.

60. Argersinger, "Chaos and Anarchy."

61. Elisabeth Clemens, *The People's Lobby: Organizational Innovation and the Rise of Interest Group Politics in the United States, 1890–1925* (Chicago, 1997); Elizabeth Sanders, *Roots of Reform: Farmers, Workers, and the American State* (Chicago, 1999); Robyn Muncy, *Creating a Female Dominion in American Reform, 1890–1935* (New York, 1991); David P. Thelen, *The New Citizenship: Origins of Progressivism in Wisconsin* (Columbia, Mo., 1972).

62. John Morton Blum, *The Republican Roosevelt* (Cambridge, Mass., 1954), 87–105; John Milton Cooper, *Pivotal Decades* (New York, 1990), 94–99; Arthur Link and Richard L. McCormick, *Progressivism* (Arlington Heights, Ill., 1983), 36–38, 61–66; Lewis Gould, *Reform and Regulation*, 2d ed. (New York, 1986), 88–90, 100.

63. Dewey Grantham, *Southern Progressivism: The Reconciliation of Progress and Tradition* (Knoxville, Tenn., 1983), 301–2; Richard L. McCormick, *From Realignment to Reform: Political Change in New York State* (Ithaca, N.Y., 1981), 255–56, 266–69;

Cherny, *Transformation of Nebraska Politics*, 161–66; Martin Schiesl, *The Politics of Efficiency: Municipal Administration and Reform in America* (Berkeley, Calif., 1977).

64. Lewis L. Gould, *Presidency of Theodore Roosevelt* (Lawrence, Kans., 1991), 149–52, 197–99; Martin Shefter, *Political Parties and the State* (Princeton, N.J., 1994), 75–81; George Mowry, *The Era of Theodore Roosevelt* (New York, 1958), 215. At the state level as well, the executive expanded its authority and activity in the early twentieth century, often at the expense of legislatures. See, for example, David P. Thelen, *Robert M. La Follette and the Insurgent Spirit* (Boston, 1976), 32–51.

65. Jeffrey Tulis, *The Rhetorical Presidency* (Princeton, N.J., 1987), 97–116; Elmer Cornwell, *Presidential Leadership of Public Opinion* (Bloomington, Ind., 1965); Stephen Ponder, "Executive Publicity and Congressional Resistance, 1905–1913," *Congress and the Presidency* 13 (1986): 177–86; Robert Hilderbrand, *Power and the People: Executive Management of Public Opinion in Foreign Affairs, 1897–1921* (Chapel Hill, N.C., 1981). For a less dichotomous view of the presidency, but one that holds that the decline of parties in the 1890s contributed to the rise of the rhetorical presidency, see Michael J. Korzi, "The Seat of Popular Leadership: Parties, Elections, and the Nineteenth-Century Presidency," *Presidential Studies Quarterly* 29 (1999): 351–69.

66. Oscar Kraines, "The President versus Congress: The Keep Commission, 1905–1909," *Western Political Quarterly* 23 (1970): 554; Peri E. Arnold, "Executive Reorganization and the Origins of the Managerial Presidency," *Polity* 13 (1981): 568–99.

67. Elmo Richardson, *The Politics of Conservation: Crusades and Controversies, 1897–1913* (Berkeley, Calif., 1962); Samuel P. Hays, *Conservation and the Gospel of Efficiency* (Cambridge, Mass., 1959) ; G. Michael McCarthy, *Hour of Trial: The Conservation Conflict in Colorado and the West* (Norman, Okla., 1977).

68. Robert L. Beisner, *From the Old Diplomacy to the New, 1865–1900* (Arlington Heights, Ill., 1986), 28–29.

69. Lewis L. Gould, *The Presidency of William McKinley* (Lawrence, Kans., 1980); Lewis L. Gould, "Theodore Roosevelt, Woodrow Wilson, and the Emergence of the Modern Presidency," *Presidential Studies Quarterly* 19 (1989): 41–50; Sidney Milkis and Michael Nelson, *The American Presidency* (Washington, D.C., 1999), 206–12; *Weekly Capital* (Olympia, Wash.), April 12, 1901.

70. Peter Swenson, "The Influence of Recruitment on the Structure of Power in the U.S. House, 1870–1940," *Legislative Studies Quarterly* 7 (1982): 7–37; John D. Baker, "The Character of the Congressional Revolution of 1910," *Journal of American History* 60 (1973): 679–91.

71. David Brady and John Ettling, "The Party System in the United States House of Representatives," in Maisel and Shade, *Parties and Politics*, 180–81; Cooper and Brady, "Institutional Context and Leadership Style," 411–17. For the revolt in Congress against the regular party leadership, see Lawrence Dodd and Richard Schott, *Congress and the Administrative State* (New York, 1979), 58–100. For the continuing emphasis on party government by now-conservative Republicans such as Cannon and Taft, see Donald Anderson, "The Legacy of William Howard Taft," *Presidential Studies Quarterly* 12 (1982): 27–30.

72. Daniel Wirls, "Regionalism, Rotten Boroughs, Race, and Realignment: The Seventeenth Amendment and the Politics of Representation," *Studies in American Political Development* 13 (1999): 1–30.

73. Michael Les Benedict, "The Politics of Reconstruction," in *American Political His-*

tory: Essays on the State of the Discipline, ed. John Marszalek and Wilson Miscamble (Notre Dame, Ind., 1997), 54–107.

74. Baker, "Domestication of Politics," 639–47; Suzanne Lebsock, "Women and American Politics, 1880–1920," in *Women, Politics, and Change*, ed. Louise Tilly and Patricia Gurin (New York, 1990), 36–37, 57–59; Suzanne Marilley, *Woman Suffrage and the Origins of Liberal Feminism in the United* States (Cambridge, Mass., 1996).

75. James Wright, *The Progressive Yankees: Republican Reformers in New Hampshire, 1906–1916* (Hanover, N.H., 1987), 169; Thomas R. Pegram, *Partisans and Progressives: Private Interest and Public Policy in Illinois, 1870–1922* (Urbana, Ill., 1992), 213–23. Jerome Clubb and Howard W. Allen note the continuing importance of party in the voting behavior of senators in "Party Loyalty in the Progressive Years: The Senate, 1909–1915," *Journal of Politics* 29 (1967): 567–84.

76. Stanley P. Caine, *The Myth of a Progressive Reform: Railroad Regulation in Wisconsin, 1903–1910* (Madison, Wis., 1970).

6. Democracy, Republicanism, and Efficiency
The Values of American Politics, 1885–1930

Richard Jensen

A small set of core ideas and values structured political options and decisions between 1885 and 1930, such that the manner of their unfolding (and interaction) shaped the politics of that era. Republicanism, purification, modernization, and efficiency became central themes of the era. As a result, most major political conflicts either pitted them against their nemesis—"corruption," in its many forms—or reflected differing interpretations of the same core values. The concern here, however, is not so much the internal history of these ideas but rather their political history: how they shaped political discourse, created issues, and changed form as the American polity, society, and economy evolved.

The context of 1885 to 1930 encompasses the end of the third, or Civil War, party system, which gave way during the depression of the mid-1890s to the fourth, or Progressive, system. Along the way, the partisan competition and sociocultural divisions of the Gilded Age gave way to an extended era of one-party dominance in which the main conflicts were about how to realize progressive values appropriately, and in which the struggle for the soul of the Republican Party became the key political division. The crisis of the Great Depression ended that era and brought on the fifth, or New Deal, system.[1]

The centrality of ideas helps explain why social, demographic, and economic correlates of voting behavior were much weaker in the Progressive Era than in the Gilded Age. Intellectuals of the time insisted on observable, materialistic, "hard" explanatory factors, but these do not seem to work in terms of explaining progressivism. Modern historians looking both at popular voting patterns and at the collective biography of leaders have reported weak or zero correlations between progressivism and various background indicators. And indeed, only a handful of small ethnocultural differences can be discerned. Scandinavian Lutherans, for example, were more supportive of Robert La Follette and Theodore Roosevelt; Catholics were more Democratic.

In one line of argument, if powerful socioeconomic factors cannot be identified, then the very existence of "progressivism" should be called into question. But the simple statistical problem is lack of variation: practically all political leaders between 1900 and 1930 considered themselves to be progressive, in terms of a commitment to republicanism, efficiency, and democracy. If everyone was progressive, correlations would necessarily be low—precisely because the importance of the phenomenon was so correspondingly high.[2]

Since 1776, America has been dedicated to the core values of "republicanism." At its most basic, republicanism means civic virtue, with the loyal citizen dedicated to supporting and improving the polity. In the late nineteenth century, there was no question of the strong commitment to republicanism among Republicans and Democrats, as well as independents, mugwumps, Prohibitionists, Populists, and the capital-*P* Progressives associated with Roosevelt's Bull Moose Party. For a rejection of republicanism, historians must thus look to the far left wing of the Socialist Party, and especially to the Industrial Workers of the World, anarchists, and Communists, who insisted that class was the basic unit of the polity, not the civic-minded citizen, and that civic duty was a fraudulent cover for class warfare against the workers.

Republicanism demands that the good citizen become politically aroused to stop violations of the code.[3] The main violation is "corruption," the perverse use of government power for illegitimate goals. Thus, fervent republicans recoiled in horror at treason, such as secession in 1861 or loyalty to Germany in 1917; at rejection of the principle of civic virtue, for example, by proponents of class warfare; at Caesarism, alleged against presidents Andrew Jackson, Ulysses Grant, and eventually Franklin Roosevelt; at "yielding power to foreigners," such as the pope, carpetbaggers, or the colored races; or at the creation of private domains outside the reach of state power, such as Mormon cities or the corporate domains of "robber barons," with the term *baron* more fearful than *robber.*

The private use of violence was also an unacceptable corruption of democratic procedures, as in lynchings, assassinations, mob actions, or attacks on strikers or strike breakers. In more routine politics, corruption meant use of government power for private financial gain, either by greedy individuals or by insidious "special interests." This notion also extended to illegitimate control of government itself, by "bosses" who frustrated the civic virtue of honest men. Finally, corruption meant being a slave to ignorance or, in the eyes of the more extreme republicans, being too timid or too traditional to support thoroughgoing reform.[4]

The End of the Civil War Party System

A party system dies when its core issues are resolved and new issues surge to the fore. This happened to the third, or Civil War, party system in the late 1880s. The Civil War itself had been a purification process. The nation was committed to "equal rights" for all good and true republicans—but just who was good and true, and who was not, was the contested terrain. The United States fought the war to restore the Union, abolish slavery, and make permanent a modern nation-state that would never again be threatened by secession. By mid-1865, President Andrew Johnson (supported by Democrats and ex-

Confederates) already argued that war goals had been achieved and Reconstruction should end immediately.

Radical Republicans thought otherwise. The nation had a duty to guarantee a "republican form" of government to the South, and they questioned whether the ex-rebels were truly loyal to American republicanism or were secretly devoted to rebellion. The freedmen appeared more trustworthy in this regard. To secure final victory in the war, they were given the vote by Reconstruction legislation, with the hope that the school of practical politics would transform them from downtrodden, ignorant slaves into independent citizens and intelligent voters. It was assumed, in passing, that they would always vote for their liberators, the party of Lincoln and Grant.

By 1872, however, nearly everyone, including half of the most radical antislavery and reform leaders, concluded that war goals had been achieved. They rejected President Grant as corrupt and formed a new Liberal Republican Party. In 1874–1875, the Democrats recaptured Congress, while the "Redeemers" split off and defeated the Radical Republican coalition in all but three southern states. As the implicit understanding for his election, President Rutherford Hayes withdrew federal troops from those three states in 1877. Reconstruction was over; the war had been won.

The Redeemers, being republicans, found repugnant the use of violence and bribery to suppress or control the black vote. Nevertheless, the conclusion was general nationwide—that black voting led to such massive corruption and violations of the norms of republicanism that it made fair elections impossible and incited populistic demagogues such as Ben Tillman and Tom Watson, who challenged paternalism in the name of white supremacy. The Redeemers, therefore, began in the late 1880s to revise state constitutions to add hurdles that effectively eliminated black voting power and simultaneously weakened the power of populistic demagogues appealing to poor whites in the name of herrenvolk democracy. The poll tax was the central device here—a one- or two-dollar tax, the equivalent of several days' pay.

By 1910, all the southern states had adopted the poll tax. Turnout of poorer, less educated men plunged dramatically, and in most areas, only the all-white Democratic primary still mattered. Disfranchisement was presented as a purification of the ballot, a rejection of fraud and violence, and a return to true republicanism. Instead of inciting fresh Yankee criticism, southern policies were actually adopted as model national policies with respect to Hawaii, Puerto Rico, and the Philippines. After 1900, leading northern states imposed literacy tests and registration requirements to purify and uplift their own electorate and reduce the "ignorant" or boss-controlled votes in the larger cities.[5]

In 1890, the GOP waved the bloody shirt one last time, with a force bill to protect southern black Republicans, inhibit illegal voting in northern cities controlled by Democratic bosses, and woo back the reformist mugwumps who had supported Grover Cleveland. Only a few die-hard radicals, however, remained to argue that neoconfederacy or neoslavery still threatened America's security. Senators from new western states with little memory of the war were more interested in trading their votes to get silver coinage. "I shall vote against the Federal Election bill," announced Senator Don Cameron, Republican of Pennsylvania. "The South is now resuming a quiet condition. Northern capital has been flowing into the South in great quantities, manufacturing establishments have been created and are now in full operation, and a community of commercial interests is fast obliterating sectional lines, and will result, in the not far distant future, in forming one homogeneous mass of people, whether living in the North, South, East, or West."[6]

In other words, sectionalism was dying, and the economic and social forces of modernization could be relied on to resolve any remaining problems. As the Civil War was finally ending, the party system based on Civil War issues was itself near death. Southern enthusiasm for war with Spain then silenced any lingering doubts about the region's patriotism. William McKinley appointed former Confederate general Joseph Wheeler to a senior command. As his white and black troops pushed the Spaniards off San Juan Hill, "Fighting Joe" excitedly yelled out, "We've got the damn yankees on the run!" Be that as it may, there was zero support for Spain from southern whites, blacks, or Hispanics.[7]

Most other purification efforts were minimally controversial. Laws against polygamy, prostitution, and obscenity, for example, won widespread support. The political conflict came when a targeted group reacted in outrage, claiming that the morality being imposed was foreign to it and demanding its republican right to "personal liberty." The Prohibition issue was just such a mainstay of state and local politics during the third and fourth party systems, until final repeal in 1933. The pietistic drys, led by Methodists and other low-church denominations, sought to purify society and individuals through the abolition of beer and whiskey; the wets were annoyed to be subject to purification by these Puritans.

Thus, ethnocultural politics helped structure voting alignments primarily by injecting religious and ethnic definitions of purity into the quest to end corruption. Liturgical ethnoreligious groups (Catholics, German Lutherans, and high-church Episcopalians) rejected the notion that the state should overrule their church and set their personal standards of morality. They argued that this was an unrepublican violation of personal liberty. The GOP needed the support of 30 to 40 percent of liturgicals to win elections in critical states of the Midwest and Northeast, but whenever it supported Prohibition or attacked German-language parochial schools, the backlash cost it the election. The massive defeats of 1890 and 1892 forced the Republican leadership to call a halt. Thereafter, they blocked pietistic amateurs who had been using the democratic local convention system to impose Prohibition platforms.[8]

The final element of the GOP Civil War agenda involved modernization of the economy and federalization of the judicial system to support a strong nation-state. The Republican Party operationalized this agenda through high tariffs, generous railroad land grants, a banking revolution, massive national debt, and strong judicial appointments. The centerpiece was the Fourteenth Amendment, interpreted to protect corporations (as "persons") in their ability to make contracts free from excessive state regulation. This was not laissez-faire at all, but rather an aggressive program to modernize the economy and provide judicial protection.

There is no question that the modernization program was remarkably successful and that the federal courts vigorously protected liberty of contract. The program aligned the GOP with the rapidly emerging industrial and financial elite of the nation. Modernity equaled industry, industry equaled efficiency, and that equation was destined to last.[9] Its enduring character was helped by the fact that the Democratic Party split over modernization. Strong support came from powerful northeastern leaders, especially Samuel Tilden and Grover Cleveland. Agrarian critics of modernization had much diffuse support in the West and South, but before William Jennings Bryan's crusade in 1896, they were unable to control the party.[10]

The Coming of a Progressive Party System

With the fourth, or Progressive, party system, economic issues came to the fore. Cleveland accomplished this, almost at a stroke, in 1887 with his stunning attack on the tariff. He managed to escalate a technical tax issue into a question of fundamental American values by charging that the tariff was unnecessary to the modernization of America, was inherently corrupt, was opposed to true republicanism, and was inefficient to boot:

> The theory of our institutions guarantees to every citizen the full enjoyment of all the fruits of his industry and enterprise, with only such deduction as may be his share toward the careful and economical maintenance of the Government which protects him . . . the exaction of more than this is indefensible extortion and a culpable betrayal of American fairness and justice. This wrong inflicted upon those who bear the burden of national taxation, like other wrongs, multiplies a brood of evil consequences. The public Treasury . . . becomes a hoarding place for money needlessly withdrawn from trade and the people's use, thus crippling our national energies, suspending our country's development, preventing investment in productive enterprise, threatening financial disturbance, and inviting schemes of public plunder.[11]

The Republicans took up Cleveland's challenge, defeated him for reelection in 1888, and in 1890 used the McKinley bill to raise the tariff. Foreigners (not

Americans) paid the tax, they claimed, while American manufacturers and factory workers reaped higher profits and higher wages. Praising tariffs as a positive good that would speed up industrialization and urbanization, Republicans envisioned a golden future of high wages, high profits, and a rich "home market" for farmers and manufacturers. The problem was that long-run gains came after the election, and short-run costs could sting at the polls.

The favorite Democratic argument was that the tariff was a tax on the consumer for the benefit of rich industrialists. To drive home the point, the Democrats sent young partisans disguised as door-to-door peddlers to McKinley's Ohio congressional district. They offered to sell tinware to housewives at double the usual price, and when the women complained, they were told that the new McKinley tariff was to blame. McKinley was defeated for reelection in 1890 as the GOP suffered its worst defeat in history, opening the way for Cleveland's return in 1892.[12]

In control of both Congress and the White House for the first time since 1858, the Democrats were obliged to lower the tariff. The unexpected consequence of winning so many marginal districts and enemy strongholds in 1890 and 1892, however, was that for the first time, the Democratic caucus was overflowing with representatives of manufacturing and mining districts that demanded high tariffs. In the event, enough Democratic senators from industrial areas cooperated with the GOP to moderate the Wilson-Gorman Tariff Act of 1894. Instead of slashing rates, it trimmed the 49 percent rate of the McKinley tariff to 41 percent. Cleveland, humiliated at this "party perfidy and party dishonor," allowed it to become law without his signature. When the Republicans returned to power, they raised the rates back to 49 percent with the Dingley tariff of 1897, which stood for a dozen years.[13]

Actually, the tariff made little economic difference. Both sides of the tariff debate assumed that Europe was poised to flood American markets with cheap manufactured goods. Yet by 1885, Europe could no longer hope to compete with the American advantages of large and efficient factories, huge capital investment, innovative entrepreneurs, vast internal markets, cheap internal transportation, ample raw materials, sophisticated advertising, and highly competitive retail distribution systems, not to mention 100 million more affluent and cost-conscious consumers.[14] America had become the low-cost, high-volume producer of manufactured goods, with large and aggressive corporations capable of moving their products.

The Republicans, using a complex calculus of costs and benefits to constituents helped or hurt by specific rates, had created a net positive benefit for nearly all their districts and feared losing this wonderful party glue. The rhetoric that the tariff guaranteed prosperity, as Republicans asserted, or that it constituted "the mother of trusts," as Democrats alleged, was so convincing to politicians and voters alike that it remained a central theme throughout the fourth party system.

Economic power could still potentially destroy republicanism, a fear that dated back to Jefferson's and Jackson's attacks on the First and Second National Banks. In the 1880s, consolidation was indeed producing ever-larger corporations. The railroads likewise were being consolidated into vast regional systems, culminating with the Northern Securities Company of 1901. At the same time, big industrial corporations were buying up smaller competitors and attempting to form trusts or monopolies, culminating with U.S. Steel in 1901.

Would unscrupulous robber barons use these behemoths to undermine equal rights and democracy? California took the lead in identifying railroads as the enemy of republicanism. Other states were less frantic but no less puzzled over how the danger could be confronted.[15] Supreme Court Justice John Marshall Harlan, a conservative Republican, later recalled the "deep feeling of unrest" in the late 1880s:

> The conviction was universal that the country was in real danger from another kind of slavery . . . that would result from the aggregation of capital in the hands of a few individuals controlling, for their own profit and advantage exclusively, the entire business of the country. . . . All felt that it must be met firmly and by such statutory regulations as would adequately protect the people against oppression and wrong.[16]

The Interstate Commerce Act of 1887 and the Sherman Antitrust Act of 1890 reflected the national consensus that monopoly threatened republicanism. Furthermore, it was inefficient because competition was the "natural" order. The "free labor" credo of republicanism was expanded to encompass free enterprise—specifically, the right of the businessman to operate without unfair competition or being forced to sell out. As Ohio Senator John Sherman put it, "If we will not endure a king as a political power, we should not endure a king over the production, transportation, and sale of any of the necessaries of life."[17]

The national banking system set up during the Civil War gave the nation a solid institutional base for industrial growth, but fear never went away, culminating in Bryan's 1896 crusade against corrupt instruments of fraud and political repression. Bryan promised that free coinage of silver would break the power of the bankers, put money in the pockets of miners and farmers (and eventually wage earners), and relieve the terrible depression. Yet his "silverites" were out of touch with economic reality. Their central argument was that the supply of gold grew too slowly, making the bankers who controlled the gold more powerful every year. In fact, by 1890, a new "currency" had largely displaced gold: bank checks. Although small transactions still took place using paper money and gold coins, the vast bulk of the nation's business was transacted through checking accounts. Checking was a hocus-pocus that further alarmed the silverites, who denied its importance and promised to abolish paper money issued by banks.

The Republicans met the silverite challenge head-on in 1896. They refuted the silverites' monetary ideas, demonstrating that free silver would bankrupt the railroad system (which had to pay its bonds and mortgages in gold) and would be of no benefit to workers. Worst of all, free silver was a repudiation of honesty, they argued, a bald-faced raid on private wealth that violated the commandment "thou shalt not steal." Taking a positive approach, McKinley argued that real economic recovery meant reopening the factories, getting the industrial economy moving again, and restoring the rich home market for farm products.

To answer the silverite charge that gold was inherently corrupt because it gave the rich bankers too much political power, the Republicans discovered a powerful reply: prosperity was the true test of national policy, not inequality. Cleveland had failed the prosperity test, and Bryan would make it even worse. Sound money and high tariffs, the GOP argued, would make everyone more prosperous. They did not deny that the rich would indeed become richer. Instead, the Republicans warned voters that with free silver they would be poor and—pointing to the silver-based economies of Mexico, China, and Japan—their children would become paupers. Bryan was whipped on the silver issue. By the latter part of the campaign, he had retreated to the argument that McKinley and his campaign manager Mark Hanna would bring about an oligarchy that would destroy republicanism.[18]

In 1896, McKinley was in an advantageous position to promote ethnocultural pluralism and lay the ethnocultural wars of the old system to rest. The status of the most controversial groups—Chinese, African Americans, and Mormons—had recently been "settled" by exclusion, segregation, and integration, respectively. Prohibition had been shelved for the time being.[19] That left the liturgicals, who constituted about 35 percent of the northern electorate (compared with 40 percent pietists and 25 percent unaffiliated).[20] Liturgicals had been harassed by anti-Catholicism and language wars, angered by attempts at Prohibition, impoverished by the depression, frightened by free silver, and disquieted by the explicitly religious moralism of the Bryanites. They could be moved.

McKinley made a systematic appeal to these liturgicals, and his army of campaigners made sure that they all heard his message: jobs, sound money, no more Prohibition, no more letting one ethnic group use the government to insult another. McKinley broadened the republican concept of equal rights for individuals to mean equal rights and fair play for all ethnoreligious groups. All groups would share in the national prosperity, and the government would not target any of them for punishment, nor mobilize group hatred in a political cause.

The strategy of pluralism worked brilliantly, as the Republicans strengthened their appeal to Germans in particular and liturgicals generally. In 1894–1896, the Republicans made major gains in all the nation's cities, and especially among Germans, who accounted for 15 to 50 percent of the urban vote.[21] McKinley's pluralistic solution to ethnocultural conflict worked and ended the threat of a Kulturkampf of the sort that had ripped apart other countries. But it came at the cost of weakening democracy inside the Republican Party and opening up charges of bossism.

The realignment of the 1890s cleared the stage for the Progressive Era by resolving the main issues of the Civil War era and by installing in power for four decades a party committed to continuing modernization. The depression during Cleveland's second term destroyed the Democratic Party's claim that it was the best manager of an industrial economy, just as it validated McKinley's argument that unless the GOP controlled economic policy, America would suffer poverty, economic backwardness, and a general failure to attain the opportunities that lay within the grasp of an enterprising people.

Bryan succeeded in redefining the corruption issue in a lasting way. Whereas the third party system had defined corruption in terms of slavery, secession, and personal greed, attention now turned to the political party and the business corporation as vehicles of corruption. Because the realignment of 1896 seemed to guarantee the continuation of government in the hands of the GOP, reformers inside the party, such as Governors Hazen Pingree of Michigan, Robert La Follette of Wisconsin, Albert Cummings of Iowa, Hiram Johnson of California, and Theodore Roosevelt and Charles Evans Hughes of New York, now had more maneuvering room to focus on the new forms of corruption.

The Populists had come close to a direct challenge of the modern economy, but Bryan drew back, arguing that he wanted only to remove corruptions and distortions and enable the true wealth creators—farmers, laborers, and small businessmen—to get on with their work unmolested by predators.[22] After 1896, the economy revived, and with the fulfillment of McKinley's promise of a full dinner pail, industrial America now voted Republican, including most workers in factories, mines, mills, and railroads, together with the engineers, foremen, superintendents, and financiers of industry.[23]

Structure and Substance for a Progressive Era

Realignment helped redefine who could vote. The strong trend was toward purification of the electorate, to protect republicanism and to weaken the power of the ignorant or purchased vote. Millions of pure women were enfranchised, and (with less controversy) millions of ignorant voters were eliminated. Blacks were disfranchised in most of the Deep South (though not in the border states or the North), along with some poor southern whites. The Australian secret ballot (around 1890) and registration laws in large cities (after 1900) made voting more difficult for machine politicians to control, as well as more difficult to navigate for people who could not read English.

The dominant style of campaigning switched away from the "army" mode, which assumed that nearly every man was a committed partisan, so that the function of the campaign was to rally supporters and guarantee a high turnout. By 1892, the predominant campaign style was the "advertising" approach, which assumed that voters were not precommitted to one party or the other but could be convinced through (advertising) campaigns that this party or that candidate was the one to support.[24] Simultaneously, the rise of independent newspapers and muckraking magazines around the turn of the century changed the media rules of the game of politics by weakening parties and giving crusaders direct access to the public, unmediated by politicians.

Publishers discovered that they could build their fortunes (and enhance their power) by achieving high circulations—the key to attracting revenue from advertisements. During the heady days of the war with Spain, William Randolph Hearst's *New York Journal* and Joseph Pulitzer's *New York World* sold upward of a million copies a day on the streets of the metropolis. Previously, over 90 percent of the nation's newspapers had been party organs, devoted to providing useful information to leaders and the rank and file. Editors and publishers were typically party leaders themselves; they were often rewarded with lucrative postmasterships and occasionally won nomination to national office. Yet being tied to one party meant relinquishing half their potential audience, so the move was on toward political independence. Whereas a party newspaper could be counted on to expose the enemy's corrupt practices and defend its own people, an independent would profit by exposing—and wounding—both sides and by endorsing candidates from both parties.

The rise of high-circulation, high-budget national magazines early in the new century created for the first time a national market for the exposure of corruption. Celebrity journalists promptly supplied copy for a middle-class readership that was strongly committed to modernity and loathed corruption and waste. Bryan, La Follette, and Roosevelt edited national magazines to open a direct line of contact with their supporters. Thus, by 1900–1904, a media revolution had set the stage for nationalizing the purification of politics in a nonpartisan fashion. By the end of the fourth party system, national and regional newspaper chains centralized editorial policies in the hands of sixty or so publishers, who reached over a third of the nation's readers.[25]

The combination of new restrictions and a decreased emphasis on mobilization had the effect of sharply lowering average turnout rates. In New York State, for example, turnout had averaged 88 percent of eligible voters in presidential elections from 1840 through 1900. It slipped to 72 percent in 1912, bottoming out after women's suffrage at 56 percent in 1920 and 1924.[26] In contrast, women's suffrage, after decades in the doldrums, gained new life after 1900. Opponents argued that suffrage would defeminize women and violate the norms of republican motherhood; that wives and daughters would be controlled by their menfolk and not be independent citizens; and that because women could not fight in the army, they should not become full citizens.

In response, a younger generation downplayed the "equal rights" rhetoric of 1848 and instead emphasized the efficiency of having mothers-as-experts and housewives-as-experts help decide questions of municipal housekeeping, schooling, and child welfare. The women's club movement was central to fostering the sense of efficiency at social engineering, as were the many muckraking articles in the "big six" women's magazines. The success of suffrage in the more progressive western states, coupled with the strikingly enthusiastic service of women during the First World War, refuted the antis and boosted the suffragists over the top.[27]

More generally, "modernization" after 1885 came to mean a search for efficiency—the elimination of waste, the discovery of the one best way to solve problems. Ignorance was the ultimate problem, and education became the favorite cure-all. Progressives dramatically expanded the educational system at all levels, expecting to make the next generation more efficient and more republican. Education was counted on to cure all problems, even racism. Booker T. Washington became the dominant black leader in the nation by promoting broad-based industrial education that would eventually elevate the entire race. Opposition came from W. E. B. DuBois, who despaired of the lowly condition of most African Americans and put his hopes on a small elite—the "talented tenth"—who would receive a classical education that was not efficient for businessmen but was suitable for political agitators. Most friends of blacks supported Washington, agreeing with him that eradication of ignorance was the only way to achieve full citizenship. Andrew Carnegie argued, "I say to our colored friends, seek ye first education and all rights will soon be added to you in this country."[28]

Modernization was the systematic transformation of old into new. Progressives assumed that if a practice was old, it must therefore be encrusted with layers of waste and inefficiency that had to be stripped off. The remarkable success of economic modernization in the last years of the nineteenth century, together with its political reaffirmation in 1896, encouraged America to broaden the concept to cover all forms of social and political modernization and to sharpen it to attribute all success to efficiency and education.

The efficient engineer as exemplar of modernity seized the public imagination—none more so than Henry Ford in industry, Thomas Edison in invention, Frederick Winslow Taylor in engineering, and Herbert Hoover in public service. Social movements flourished as they followed the suffragists and downplayed moralistic attacks on corruption in favor of an emphasis on efficiency instead. They included world peace, where arbitration conducted by experts would replace warfare; philanthropy, where John D. Rockefeller demonstrated the value of specialized welfare experts; medicine, revolutionized by the Flexner Report of 1910; and civil service reform at the state and local levels. The drys even started promoting Prohibition as a way to sober up more efficient workers.[29]

What the progressives lacked was a sense of limits. They assumed that every problem had a solution—indeed, one best solution. They believed that disinterested experts could research and solve any problem if they were protected from the forces of ignorance, partisan politics, or old-fashioned selfishness. They could not conceive of the possibility that their ideal solutions might contain hidden complications that could frustrate reform or create even worse problems.

Progressives favored a direct attack on ignorance; they demanded compulsory school attendance laws. Together with new restrictions on child labor, this forced schooling on students regardless of individual aptitude for scholarship or preference for immediate cash income. The resistance to compulsory education was only passive, a matter of dodging truant officers and neglecting school assignments. Child labor, however, was a contested area, with intense emotional interests at stake. Woodrow Wilson's Congress eventually managed to prohibit child labor, but the law was overturned by the Supreme Court. Advocates of the law stressed the greater efficiency that could be achieved through human capital, as well as the republican need for an educated citizenry, and warned against the ignorance of parents and traditional communities.

Opponents, led by the Catholics, insisted that the republican ideal included a sanctuary for family rights, on which the state must not intrude (a principle that eventually led to the Supreme Court's recognition of the right of privacy in *Griswold* in 1965). Efforts in the 1920s to pass a constitutional amendment prohibiting child labor failed because of Catholic opposition. In real life, children were inefficient workers, and economic reality proved decisive. After 1920, children were rarely employed outside of farming. Compulsory education laws, in contrast, probably did have a direct impact on improving the cognitive and social skills of many reluctant students.[30]

The progressives were always at risk of a taxpayer revolt, like the one that defeated the movement in Wisconsin in 1914. Therefore, they paid special attention to eliminating waste and mismanagement in local government, for municipal taxes were much higher than rural, state, or federal taxes, and efficiency meant lower taxes.[31] In the early 1890s, private reform organizations also emerged in major cities to improve government efficiency and fight bosses, who were attacked as both corrupt and inefficient.

In Chicago, the spectacular revelations of corruption by William Stead led to the founding of the Civic Federation of Chicago, with strong backing from leading newspapers and bankers. The chief organizer, Ralph Easley, moved to the national stage in 1900 with his National Civic Federation. Its main objective—in large part, successful—was to bridge the gap between capital and labor. By 1916, it had helped arbitrate or settle 500 labor disputes and had pioneered techniques of industrial arbitration and welfare capitalism. The goal was labor peace through mutually satisfactory agreements that would generate high wages, high profits, and few strikes.[32]

The 1890s was a decade of business depression, but it also brought a remarkable technical revolution in every large city as motorized electric streetcars replaced the much slower, less efficient horse-drawn or cable-drawn systems. New technology made the streetcar systems natural monopolies. They were controlled by national syndicates that collected a nickel every morning and evening from millions of clerks and office workers. The straphangers paid the dividends—that is, the companies made the most money when service was the worst. Charles Yerkes, the "titan" of Chicago, was representative of the energetic entrepreneurs who pioneered this new technology.

The streetcar companies needed votes in the city councils to obtain and renew their monopolistic franchises. But city after city—led by Detroit, where Hazen Pingree built a career as mayor and governor fighting the traction companies—became alarmed at the bribery and manipulation typified by Yerkes. The streetcar workers were easy to unionize, but strikes were countered by hiring strikebreakers. At first, the public sympathized with the unions, until they had to walk a few miles to work or until they had to dodge bricks aimed at scab conductors. Using violence to settle disputes was an ugly violation of republicanism; anyone who advocated it was even worse. The public inevitably turned against violent strikers. In a few cities, the unions won big. In most, the strikers lost, but fare gouging by the companies also displeased the public. The stage was set for the sudden realization that both unions and corporations could be dangerous violators of republican norms.[33]

In the fourth party system, corruption became a sin. In political discourse, it displaced the personal sins of intemperance and secessionism that had bedeviled the third party system. Theologically, the idea was reinforced by the Social Gospelers, "the praying wing of Progressivism," who preached the replacement of personal sin with public sin. The point was explicit in *Sin and Society,* a popular 1907 book by sociologist E. A. Ross, with a preface by Roosevelt. The new morality committed the progressives to active intervention in social and economic realms. Social control in the name of progress seemed an efficient way to apply the social gospel and justified interventions along many different fronts.[34]

The introspection and yearning for self-expression characteristic of nineteenth-century romantic idealism gave way to the materialism and community solidarity of twentieth-century pragmatism. Bertrand Russell grumbled that the philosophy of John Dewey and William James—so materialistic, so confident of progress, yet oblivious to unintended consequences, and so much in need of personal reassurances—perfectly fit the "obnoxious aspects of American industrialism."[35] The progressives did focus on materialistic factors, and the worst kind of corruption was indeed financial. "Tainted money" was a favorite bogey. Even when money was decades old, if it had been acquired by dubious means, it was still tainted and must be refused.[36]

Reformers favored the self-image of David battling Goliath, even through direct democracy was not necessarily controversial. The secret (Australian) ballot swept the nation after 1890; the direct primary encountered little opposition in its spread from Wisconsin in 1903 to thirty-nine states by 1913. Indeed, much major substantive legislation was uncontroversial and passed Congress almost unanimously, including the Sherman Antitrust Act of 1890 and the income tax amendment of 1909. Once the one best solution had been found, Americans rallied behind it.[37]

Looking for corruption under every desk, muckrakers turned to Congress. A series of exposés, "The Treason of the Senate" by David Graham Phillips, appeared in *Cosmopolitan* magazine in 1906; the "treason" consisted of voting in favor of parochial state interests, especially higher tariffs for local products. Phillips assumed unself-consciously that there was such a thing as "the national interest" and that senators who failed to vote for it were therefore corrupt. Real-life newspaper correspondents, with a much closer view of congressmen, observed little practical corruption. Nevertheless, editors complained to Lincoln Steffens when his reports on Congress failed to uncover sin. The editors wanted only the sensational, he grumbled, "That was their criterion: dishonesty, stealing, graft."[38]

The Battle for the Soul of the Republican Party

Were trusts good or bad? Did big business represent efficiency and modernity, or did it threaten to strip power from the citizenry? The crisis came to a head in 1905–1906, under the influence of spectacular investigations and intense muckraking coverage—not to mention Democratic partisanship. Explicit exposés of political corruption by giant corporations in numerous industries, especially railroads, oil, and insurance, shifted the burden of proof: indisputably, there were bad trusts out there, and bigness itself became evidence of perfidy. Hearst, Louis Brandeis, and Woodrow Wilson proclaimed that bigness was inherently bad. Somebody had to stop the evil trusts.

That was Bryan's copyright issue, but Theodore Roosevelt stepped in and promised to rein in the bad trusts and not hurt the good ones. That is, Roosevelt had an efficiency solution and could be counted on to discriminate between the trusts that were good and fostered national efficiency and those that were bad and threatened republican virtues.[39] The left-wing progressives argued that monopolies were both inherently sinful and inherently inefficient. More conservative progressives, led by William Howard Taft and his Justice Department, focused primarily on inefficiency, arguing that monopolistic trusts made the rest of the economy inefficient by distorting prices and natural economic flows. Thus Taft took pride in breaking up more trusts than anyone else, including the most famous of them all, Standard Oil.[40]

The panic of 1907 then had major reverberations for economic and political history. In the summer and fall of that year, a loss of confidence hit depositors, who began demanding cash for their deposits. Although the crisis was worldwide, one of the hardest hit centers was New York City, where trust companies proved especially vulnerable. J. P. Morgan, in semiretirement, rallied the leading banks to assemble funds to prop up first one trust company then another, and then the entire New York Stock Exchange and the city of New York itself. The final critical episode was the rescue of a brokerage whose debt was backed by stock of Tennessee Coal and Iron (TCI), the largest steel company in the South. The only solution, Morgan felt, was to sell TCI to U.S. Steel. President Roosevelt personally approved the takeover, even though it strengthened U.S. Steel's monopoly hold on its market.

The most decisive legislation of the Progressive Era was the creation of a powerful and efficient central bank, the Federal Reserve System. Only bankers seemed to appreciate the real problem: the United States was the last major country without a central bank that could provide stability and emergency credit in times of financial crisis, not to mention support for expanded foreign trade in good times. The threat perceived by the financial community was not so much excessive power around Morgan but the frailty of a vast, decentralized banking system that could not regulate itself without the extraordinary interventions of one old man.

Nelson Aldrich, the well-connected Republican leader of the Senate (his son-in-law was John D. Rockefeller, Jr.), created and ran the National Monetary Commission personally, with the aid of a team of brilliant economists. They toured Europe and were astonished at how successful central banks in London and Berlin were in stabilizing their economies and promoting international trade. Despite the vast size of the American economy, the dollar was an also-ran currency in world trade compared with the pound or even the mark. Aldrich's impartial investigation was the high-water point of progressive fact-finding and led in 1912 to his detailed plan to reform banking, with promises of financial stability, expanded international roles, control by impartial experts, and no political meddling in finance.

Aldrich realized correctly that a central bank had to be decentralized somehow, or it would be ganged up on by local politicians and bankers, as had the First and Second Banks of the United States. His solution was a regional system, which was quickly adopted by a key Democratic leader, Virginia congressman Carter Glass. Bryan, by now secretary of state, had not forgotten the menace of Wall Street and threatened to destroy the bill. President Wilson masterfully bargained, negotiated, and cajoled, coming up with a deal that bought off the agrarians by making Federal Reserve currency into a liability of the government rather than of private banks—a symbolic change—and by including provisions for vast new federal loans to farmers.

Something for everybody was the final result. The bankers got their central bank; their opponents got to boast that they had stripped the titans of Wall Street of their monopolistic powers and returned to the people control of their economy and their polity. The Federal Reserve System itself rarely came in for criticism, even when its policies seriously damaged the economy, as they would in the 1929–1932 crisis. Amazingly, the money issue now disappeared from political discourse, replaced eventually by a renewed emphasis on class conflict.[41]

The political reverberations of the panic of 1907 echoed for years. La Follette charged that the bankers had engineered the whole panic to reap a big profit.[42] Roosevelt deliberately escalated the political tension, blaming the crisis primarily on Europe but then lambasting the rich: "It may well be that the determination of the government . . . to punish certain malefactors of great wealth, has been responsible for something of the trouble; at least to the extent of having caused these men to combine to bring about as much financial stress as possible, in order to discredit the policy of the government and thereby secure a reversal of that policy, so that they may enjoy unmolested the fruits of their own evil-doing."[43]

Willing to attack unpopular trusts, Roosevelt was clever enough to avoid taking on the tariff issue while in office. It came due on Taft's watch. The 1908 Republican platform promised tariff "reform," which everyone assumed meant a lower tariff. In the House, the Payne bill did lower rates. In the Senate, however, Aldrich, a master of the complexities of the issue, used the tariff to humiliate his enemies. The insurgents were midwestern politicians who apparently believed the theory, propounded by Democrats and muckrakers, that the tariff was the mother of trusts, that it was responsible for the high cost of living, that it was sheer robbery for the benefit of rich monopolists, and that, anyway, the seat of republican virtue was the family farm, not the countinghouse.[44] Aldrich baited them. Did the insurgents want lower tariffs? Aldrich lowered the protection on their farm products.

Taft called it the best tariff ever. The new tariff actually changed little and had little economic impact one way or the other, but the insurgents felt tricked and defeated and swore vengeance against Wall Street and its minions Taft and Aldrich. Taft thus gained a sack of failures, a retinue of new enemies, and no rewards for his remaining political friends.[45] The GOP was ready to explode. Under heavy attack from inside and outside his party, Taft shook off his lethargy and counterattacked. In the summer of 1910, well before Roosevelt, La Follette, or anyone else, he began to control the 1912 convention.

Buoyed by outrage, La Follette began organizing the insurgents in early 1911, but just as he gained momentum, he went into seclusion to write his autobiography. The baffled insurgents shifted their hopes to Roosevelt, who proved uncharacteristically paralyzed. By the fall of 1911, Taft had locked up alliances with party leaders in most major states, including Roosevelt's own New York. In February 1912, La Follette's emotional hysteria during a major speech raised the insurmountable charge that the crusader was mentally unstable. Roosevelt now announced his candidacy, sweeping up most of La Follette's backers. The Wisconsinite turned away from Taft to refocus his crusade as an all-out attack on Roosevelt's betrayal. Meanwhile, Taft's men rolled up state after state.

Roosevelt's war against Taft for control of the GOP was largely personal, but the public focused on Roosevelt's crusade in the name of popular sovereignty against the corruption of politics by the bosses, by corporate interests, and by judges unresponsive to the will of the people. The Democrats had been sounding such themes since Jackson's day, but they were new for the Republicans. In thirteen states, the progressive forces had succeeded in setting up primaries, expecting that the voice of the people would be calling them. In these primaries, Roosevelt won 50 percent of the popular vote against the divided (Taft–La Follette) opposition, though he gained 77 percent of the contested delegates. Direct democracy was thus working for Roosevelt, but it fell far short of a majority of delegates.

Despite Roosevelt's rhetoric, the Taft conservatives were not defending corporate interests. In 1908, financiers had been chilly to candidate Taft, who did indeed have an anti-business streak and a strong taste for anti-trust. "Wall Street, as an aggregation," Taft told his brother, "is the biggest ass I have ever run across." Roosevelt had advised Taft that anti-business rhetoric "helps you in the West. It hurts you among all the reactionary crowd, both the honest reactionaries and the corrupt financiers and politicians in the East." In 1912, contributions to the Taft campaign tallied barely a third of the total raised in 1908. Taft and his allies instead saw themselves as defending a cornerstone of republicanism, the rule of law as interpreted by the judiciary.[46]

The fundamental issue was who would have final interpretation of the laws and the Constitution. Attacks on the Supreme Court had antecedents back to Thomas Jefferson and to the Republican Party assault on the *Dred Scott* decision. Conversely, the strengthened role of the federal judiciary had been a powerful achievement of the Civil War. In 1896, it was the Bryan Democrats who vehemently attacked the Supreme Court for striking down the income tax and breaking the Pullman strike two years earlier. The devastating counterattack to Bryan's legal views was that he condoned anarchism, a reference to Governor John Altgeld's pardoning of the Haymarket anarchists. After 1900, federal courts frequently issued injunctions against labor unions and, on several occasions, struck down protective labor laws.

The climax came in 1905, when in *Lochner v. New York* the Supreme Court declared unconstitutional a maximum-hours law for bakers, announcing that the Fourteenth Amendment guarantee of liberty of contracts trumped the police powers of the state to eliminate work practices that were both inefficient and deleterious to workers' health.[47] Stimulated by the dissent from Oliver Wendell Holmes, the radical progressives denounced the decision as a surrender to property interests—that is, the Supreme Court itself was corrupt.[48] Roosevelt, who never trusted lawyers, judges, or "the law," took up the banner and went after the state courts as undemocratic and unrepublican. "The courts [are] the ultimate irresponsible interpreters of the Constitution, and therefore . . . represent a system as emphatically undemocratic as government by a hereditary aristocracy." He announced in late 1907 that federal court injunctions were sometimes "used heedlessly and unjustly."[49]

In terms of legislation, the great showdown over the role of the courts came in 1906, as Roosevelt attempted to put independent experts, rather than profit-seeking railroad executives or federal judges, in control of railroad rates. The Hepburn bill passed the House overwhelmingly but stalled in the Senate, where most Republicans demanded explicit provisions for court review of rate decisions handed down by the Interstate Commerce Commission (ICC). The issue was not whether railroad rates should be regulated; everyone agreed on that. The issue was whether the determination of "fair" rates should be made by economists on the ICC or judges on the federal bench.

Aldrich led those who favored letting the judiciary have the final say about fairness. He artfully put the bill in the hands of "Pitchfork" Ben Tillman, a vulgar demagogue from South Carolina who was the senior Democrat on the committee. Tillman was unable to secure enough Democratic votes, so Roosevelt was forced to accept the Aldrich version that gave control over rates to bureaucratic experts but allowed for appeals to the courts. The final synthetic bill passed with only three dissenting votes.[50]

As early as 1908, Roosevelt was demanding reforms to make the judiciary more responsive to democratic forces. In 1912, he crossed the Rubicon, calling for state constitutional amendments that would create referenda whereby citizens could overrule state judges. Like most left-wing progressives, Roosevelt paid little attention to "constitutional rights" claimed by individuals, lest they be used by corporations to have reforms declared unconstitutional. Roosevelt's challenge to judicial finality dismayed his closest supporters, who saw judges as professional experts in fairness and the rule of law as a core republican value. They rejected Roosevelt's plan to bring in academically trained scientific experts as the final arbiters of the economy, society, and polity and insisted on the superiority of judge-made law to legislative enactments.

Roosevelt had attended law school (while busy writing his first book) but never fell in love with the law. His closest political advisers, including Henry Cabot Lodge, Elihu Root, Henry Stimson, and his son-in-law Congressman Nicholas Longworth, all tried to reason with him, to no avail. They were more in love with the law than with Roosevelt, and reluctantly, they each announced for Taft.[51] Root, a leading corporate lawyer, apostle of efficiency and modernization, and Roosevelt's secretary of war and state, made the best case for the conservative progressive claim that only the judiciary could transcend frivolous democracy to express republican values. For Root, a judgeship was almost sacred:

Profoundly devoted to the reign of law, with its prescribed universal rules as distinguished from the reign of men with their changing opinions, desires and impulses, our people have always ascribed a certain sanctity to the judicial office, have invested its holders with special dignity, and have regarded them in the exercise of their office with a respect amounting to almost reverence, as above all conflicts of party, and of faction, because these officers are the guardians of the law as it is.[52]

Root presided over the GOP National Convention. Regardless of his Nobel Peace Prize, he was a fighter and ruled in favor of Taft at every point. By Root's official count, Taft held a slim but unshakable majority. Roosevelt, alleging that Taft had purchased black delegates from the South to put himself over, cried theft, walked out, and formed a new "Bull Moose" Progressive Party. Very few officeholders followed Roosevelt, except in California, where Hiram Johnson's Progressives controlled the GOP and kept Taft entirely off the ballot in November. The Bull Moosers were otherwise political outsiders, utopians, and former insiders who had fallen on hard times.

The Progressives had become a one-man show. By dividing the GOP, they guaranteed an electoral majority for the Democrats, as well as control of Congress, while relinquishing their own standing in their party.[53] When the Democrats nominated New Jersey Governor Woodrow Wilson, the Bull Moosers realized that they could never achieve a cross-party alliance. Wilson was a conservative progressive on economic matters and did not attack trusts, bankers, or railroads. Rather, he exemplified expertise in higher education. His successful crusades against corrupt political bosses in New Jersey validated his republican credentials.

Taft hardly campaigned. It hardly mattered, for he had already achieved a major and lasting impact. The GOP was purged of its radicals; never again would they regain power. During Taft's presidency, he had quietly seized control of the Supreme Court, with five conservative appointments. His own 1921 appointment as chief justice would guarantee conservative control of the third branch of government, leaving the insurgents in the cold for another two decades.[54]

Consolidation and Consensus

Wilson and the Democrats truly believed that high tariffs begat monopolies; after they sharply lowered the tariff in 1913, they were confident that no more ugly devils would be born. They then supplemented the guillotine of the Sherman Act with two scalpels that could be used by expert surgeons: the Federal Trade Commission (FTC) and the Clayton Antitrust Act. The anti-trust movement had climaxed. Its moralistic and democratic mission had been achieved, leaving only efficiency.

For a decade, business had been on the defensive. Now, in the war years, it managed to seize leadership of efficiency and modernization once more and redeem its claim to an honored place in the republican order. By contrast, the agrarians made little progress, because the mood was changing. The grudge so many still harbored toward Rockefeller paled before the national celebration of Henry Ford. He was as much a monopolist as the oil magnate, but he built 15 million cheap Model Ts that put America on wheels and at the same time lowered prices, raised wages, invented the superefficient assembly line, and created "Fordism," the promise that high wages would cause prosperity. Ford became the greatest hero of the day because he empowered the consumer. Americans (who never developed brand loyalties for gasoline) loved their Tin Lizzies.

The government never dared attempt to break up Ford's company; talk of trust-busting faded away as America accepted bigness. Wilson promised that the FTC would become an ally of legitimate business, and his Republican successors restructured it to promote efficiency through cooperation, with scant attention to trust-busting. The FTC did promote purification, however, by eliminating misleading advertising and the shady practices of marginal and fly-by-night businesses, which threatened established firms more than anyone else. The pleasant discovery that some government regulation would help big business guaranteed its support for the securities regulations of the 1930s.[55]

Ethnocultural pluralism collapsed temporarily during the war, as debates on national security policy turned into debates about whether "hyphenated" ethnics were truly devoted to American republicanism. The German-American and Irish-American communities, hostile to Britain, came out strongly in favor of neutrality, condemning the massive sales and loans to the Allies as a violation of that policy. They recalled that an ironclad component of republicanism since the days of Washington and Jefferson had been "no entangling alliances." Conversely, Roosevelt identified German militarism as the supreme threat to American republicanism, and he loudly raised the issue whether the German Americans and Irish Americans were more loyal to their mother countries or to America: "Those hyphenated Americans who terrorize American politicians by threats of the foreign vote are engaged in treason to the American Republic."[56]

Once war was declared, Americanization programs targeted recent arrivals to assimilate them more quickly to republican ideals. Anti-German activity escalated informal policies of destroying all forms of Germanic civic culture. Foreign-language newspapers were suspect, and many were shut down by their owners or by the Post Office. Public schools ended courses dealing with the German language. German-American behavior was scrutinized, especially their purchase of war bonds. The drys stressed the association of Germanism with beer and saloons—that is, with sin, corruption, and inefficiency.[57]

With McKinleyite pluralism cracked by the war, ethnocultural conflicts thereafter found outlets for debate over Prohibition, Americanization, immigration restriction, and the Ku Klux Klan (KKK). Some historians have argued that powerful nativist forces sought the purification of American society, implying that their goals were an illegitimate denial of equal rights. Although this was true enough regarding the Chinese and Japanese, thoroughgoing nativism was articulated by only a handful of publicists who do not seem to have garnered much popular or elite support.

As for restrictions on immigration, the main goal was efficiency. Throughout the 1900–1930 period, the movement for immigration restriction was dominated by American Federation of Labor unions, which were often led by immigrants themselves, such as Samuel Gompers. The issue was not purification of American ethnicity; it was competition from cheap labor. American labor could never be fully efficient and well paid, the unions argued, if unskilled workers flooded and cheapened the labor pool. If they stopped coming, industry would concentrate on upgrading skills.

Before 1914, some industries, along with steamship companies and railroads, had promoted immigration and financed anti-restriction organizations that ostensibly represented the voice of the ethnics.[58] Yet the war proved that the economy could do very well without immigrants. The unions won their point; opposition to restriction withered. Moreover, the new immigrants matured rapidly during the war. They enthusiastically served in the U.S. military; they bought war bonds; they voluntarily "Americanized" themselves. With the successful establishment after Versailles of new nation-states, interest in European political aspirations largely faded away. With the exception of some Jewish groups that identified with the fate of Jews in Eastern Europe or were committed to Zionism, most American ethnics simply lost interest in Europe.[59] Conversely, with both "push" and "pull" factors weakened, fewer Europeans showed interest in going to the United States.[60]

Women's suffrage became a reality in 1920. Simultaneous success in other major countries strongly suggests that the most important reason for this timing was women's contribution to the war effort. In terms of republicanism, women had decisively answered the question of what service contribution they could make to a nation's war effort. Feminists looking back to the 1920s have often underestimated the impact of the new vote on politics. Although few women were elected to office, male officeholders certainly paid them attention. Many of the highly salient issues of the 1920s were distinctly "women's issues," especially pacifism and Prohibition at the national level and consumerism, anti–child labor, welfare, medical care, anti–obscenity, sanitation, and education at the state level.

Women's suffrage can be seen as the final triumph of the purification of democracy. Masculinity was to return with a vengeance in the 1930s, discarding both pacifism and Prohibition and minimizing women's voice in politics.[61] Although the women's suffrage movement was a success, however, Prohibition was a failure as a social movement. Drys assumed that a utopia would automatically result: corruption would dry up, machines would wither, and the naturally angelic impulses of civic virtue would come to the fore. Hence they did not create a body of precedent, an administrative apparatus, a support mechanism, or a system of alliances with other reforms. Once the government started to enforce the Volstead Act, its flaws became glaringly apparent, and the initiative switched to the wets.[62]

The KKK could have played a major role in the enforcement of Prohibition. Instead, it preempted the field of moralistic movements, weakening its rivals such as the Anti-Saloon League. Yet as a secret society, it was unable to forge serious links with other groups. Indeed, the KKK restructured mainly to achieve one goal: to acquire new members. It developed a pyramid scheme that made growth lucrative for the organizers; grassroots recruiters collected $10 dues and were allowed to keep $4, forwarding the remainder upward to the next level of leadership. But concentration on sheer growth meant that in 1924, for example, Klan leaders were not players at the national convention of either party. Moreover, once they had fleeced most of the eligible membership pool, the functioning of the group itself nearly stopped. There was no longer a reason to be a Klan leader, and the fragile organization imploded after 1925, even faster than it had grown.[63]

Meanwhile, the KKK's message that ethnics were unrepublican and immoral stimulated the countercrusading organization of its enemies, as various Catholic ethnics managed to join together—often coordinating their work with the Jewish community and Protestant newspaper editors. Under the First Amendment banner of religious freedom and "personal liberty," the new coalition claimed that it, rather than the KKK, best represented republican virtue. Further energized by the Al Smith candidacy, a "new ethnic" coalition emerged for the first time. It played a major role in the 1928 election and the subsequent campaign for repeal of Prohibition; it became a permanent and major component of the New Deal coalition.[64] Immigration laws set the flow of future immigrants into the United States in exact proportion to the actual distribution of ethnicity, so that new arrivals would not upset the balance in any way. Thus by 1930 there had emerged a new consensus that accepted the republicanism of all the white ethnic groups.

Critical to republicanism was the notion of the independent citizen who pursued civic virtue by attending to speeches, evaluating the candidates, and voicing his opinions at the polls. Yet the rules of this game were changing fast. The success of massive advertising campaigns for war bonds, and of "four-minute men" who rallied theater audiences during the war, proved that organized publicity could be decisive. Chicago's leading advertising genius, Albert Lasker, lent his skills to the Harding campaign in 1920. By the late 1920s, Washington had become the "happy home of propaganda," thanks to some 2,000 press agents. Add another 5,000 public-relations men in the media capital of New York City, and it was no wonder that over half the stories that appeared in newspapers had been planted there by paid press agents more attuned to Sigmund Freud than to Thomas Jefferson.[65]

Intellectuals recoiled at the provincialism of Main Street. Some fled to cosmopolitan Paris; H. L. Mencken remained in Baltimore to orchestrate the ridicule of government led by ignorant fools and controlled by demagogues and advertising agencies. Political scientists called for a government run by experts (themselves). Bryan, himself the embodiment of government by the people, was made the fool in the Scopes trial of 1925 when he insisted that the democratic majority should control what science was taught. Walter Lippmann, who had served as a propagandist during the war, decided that the truly independent civic citizen was all too rare; most people's ideas were controlled by stereotypes rather than rational argument.

From this perspective, it was just as well that the very act of voting had fallen out of favor. The turnout rate of eligible citizens plunged to 53 percent outside the South in 1924, contrasted with 85 percent in 1896. Big-city machines discovered that small turnouts were easier to control and discouraged voting themselves; in New York City in 1924, only 40 percent of 6 million adults (including noncitizens) voted for president. By 1926, Lippmann was forced to conclude, "The democratic phase which began in the eighteenth century has about run its course."[66]

The Coming of the New Deal Party System

One by one, the major issues of the Gilded Age and Progressive Era had dissolved or been resolved.[67] Only the efficiency-oriented plans of Herbert Hoover were left to achieve the ultimate modernization of the nation. Hoover, a hyperactive progressive with a strong commitment to republicanism, had an unquestioning belief that there existed one best solution to the depression and that his expertise could discover it.[68] Rejecting the advice of Treasury Secretary Andrew Mellon to liquidate the downturn quickly, Hoover took a series of steps that slowed the rate of descent but at the same time prolonged the process and set the stage for a massive system collapse in 1931–1932. Each measure brought surprises that were incomprehensible (or at least unpredictable) to the progressive mentality. A few economic examples show how the law of unintended consequences worked so inexorably to destroy the last remnants of Progressivism.[69]

The Republicans evidently continued to believe their half-century sloganeering about the miraculous curative powers of the tariff. The Smoot-Hawley tariff, signed by Hoover in 1930, raised rates but incited Britain, Canada, France, Germany, and other trading partners to retaliate, thus further reducing American trade opportunities while producing the sort of economic autarchy and hostility that undercut trade partnerships and bilateral friendships. Second, Hoover succeeded in stimulating state and local government, as well as Washington, to increase public works spending sharply. The long-term effect was to exhaust credit resources and financial reserves, forcing state and local governments to slash unemployment relief programs and to turn to sales taxes to cover their deficits.[70]

Hoover appealed to industry in the name of Fordism to keep wage rates high. They did so, at least into 1931, despite falling consumer prices. Yet this necessitated cutting hours and, much more seriously, installing rigid hiring practices that turned away underqualified "B" workers at the personnel office. The result was youth who would never get decent first jobs, laid-off workers over age forty-five who would never be hired again, and less-educated "B" workers who would never become "As." For the first time ever, the cities started filling with millions of long-term unemployed, able-bodied workers.[71] Compounding the misery caused by all these mistakes, the Federal Reserve was systematically cutting the money supply. The concept of gross national product (GNP) was just being invented and had not been measured, so perhaps the Federal Reserve did not see that its actions were cutting back credits and business loans, slashing consumers' discretionary spending power, weakening banks, and reducing the GNP by a third.[72]

All along, Hoover tried to boost business confidence by optimistic projections—which always turned out wrong—and eventually the voters booted him out of office. Under the genius of Democratic National Chairman John Raskob, the Democrats systematically ridiculed Hoover-as-engineer, and Hoover-as-politician had no resources left to fight back. The depression thus destroyed not only Hoover's career but also his progressive politics. It was time for a realignment and a new party system. The goals of efficiency, modernization, democracy, and republicanism were not dead, of course, but now they would assume new forms, with new rules and a new cast of leaders to shape a New Deal in politics.[73]

Notes

1. On different possible approaches, see Richard Jensen, "Historiography of Political History," in *Encyclopedia of American Political History*, vol. 1, ed. Jack Greene (New York, 1984), 1–25.
2. See James Wright, *The Progressive Yankees: Republican Reformers in New Hampshire, 1906–1916* (Hanover, N.H., 1987); David P. Thelen, "Social Tensions and the Origins of Progressivism," *Journal of American History* 56 (1969): 323–41; Mark Elton Carlile, "The Trials of Progressivism: Iowa Voting Behavior in the Progressive Era, 1901–1916" (Ph.D. diss., University of Iowa, 1995); Roger E. Wyman, "Middle-Class Voters and Progressive Reform: The Conflict of Class and Culture," *American Political Science Review* 68 (1974): 488–504.
3. Some historians have assumed that social Darwinism was also anti-republican and that this was the ideology that dominated late-nineteenth-century politics.

The problem is that it is difficult to find any evidence of social Darwinism among political, legal, or business leaders. Rather, they thought in the language of republicanism and of classical laissez-faire of the Adam Smith liberal variety. As Thomas Cochran discovered after reading thousands of letters, businessmen almost used the language of social Darwinism (*Railroad Leaders: 1845–1890* [New York, 1965]). See especially Robert C. Bannister, *Social Darwinism: Science and Myth in Anglo-American Social Thought,* 2d ed. (Philadelphia, 1988); Irwin G. Wylie, "Social Darwinism and the Businessmen," *Proceedings of the American Philosophical Society* 103 (1959): 629–35; Paul Crook, "Social Darwinism in European and American Thought, 1860–1945," *Australian Journal of Politics and History* 45 (1999): 110–20.

4. The best overview of corruption in the third party system is Mark Wahlgren Summers, *The Era of Good Stealings* (New York, 1993), which ends in 1877. The best study of voting corruption is John F. Reynolds, *Testing Democracy: Electoral Behavior and Progressive Reform in New Jersey, 1880–1920* (Chapel Hill, N.C., 1988). On the political history down to 1901, see Mark Wahlgren Summers, *The Gilded Age: Or the Hazard of New Fortunes* (Upper Saddle River, N.J., 1997).

5. As Hackney demonstrated, many insurgents hated blacks with a passion that alarmed the paternalistic planters and middle classes. The paternalists thought that African Americans could eventually be educated and uplifted to become good republicans. The insurgents insisted that they could never be political equals. Lynch mobs, which had targeted mostly whites in the 1880s, focused on blacks after 1890, in defiance of the paternalists, who sought law and order. Sheldon Hackney, *Populism to Progressivism in Alabama* (Princeton, N.J., 1969); see also Stephen Kantrowitz, *Ben Tillman and the Reconstruction of White Supremacy* (Chapel Hill, N.C., 2000), and Russell Korobkin, "The Politics of Disfranchisement in Georgia," *Georgia Historical Quarterly* 74 (1990): 20–58. Richard Nelson, "The Cultural Contradictions of Populism: Tom Watson's Tragic Vision of Power, Politics, and History," *Georgia Historical Quarterly* 72 (1988): 1–29, stresses Watson's lifetime opposition to enemies of republicanism. See C. Vann Woodward, *The Origins of the New South* (Baton Rouge, 1951), chap. 12; for a black perspective on loss of power, see Glenda Elizabeth Gilmore, *Gender and Jim Crow: Women and the Politics of White Supremacy in North Carolina, 1896–1920* (Chapel Hill, N.C., 1996), chaps. 4–5.

In the 1960s, race would become a central issue of the sixth party system. As the Civil Rights Act of 1965 reversed the disfranchisement laws, revisionist historians would reverse the moral polarities of the 1890s, arguing that disfranchisement was a far worse violation of the republican principle of equal rights than any corruptions or shortcomings on the part of the victimized minority. J. Morgan Kousser, *The Shaping of Southern Politics: Suffrage Restriction and the Establishment of the One-Party South, 1880–1910* (New Haven, Conn., 1975). More generally, the new interpretation of republicanism was that it was egregiously corrupt to limit the voting rights of "discrete and insular minorities," that is, relatively weak and powerless groups.

6. Stanley P. Hirshson, *Farewell to the Bloody Shirt: Northern Republicans and the Southern Negro, 1877–1893* (Bloomington, Ind., 1962); James M. McPherson, *The Abolitionist Legacy: From Reconstruction to the NAACP* (Princeton, N.J., 1975). On the utility of "bloody shirt" oratory, see Mark Wahlgren Summers, *Rum, Romanism, and Rebellion: The Making of a President* (Chapel Hill, N.C., 2000), chap. 3. Cameron

quoted in James Ford Rhodes, *History of the United States*, vol. 8 (New York, 1920), 361, from *Public Opinion*, ix, 428.

7. Walter Mills, *The Martial Spirit* (New York, 1931), 274; Paul H. Buck, *The Road to Reunion, 1854–1900* (Boston, 1937). Likewise, the eagerness to enlist on the part of ethnics strongly validated their claims to republican citizenship. Matthew Frye Jacobson, *Special Sorrows: The Diasporic Imagination of Irish, Polish, and Jewish Immigrants in the United States* (Cambridge, Mass., 1995), chap. 4.

8. Richard Jensen, *The Winning of the Midwest* (Chicago, 1971), chap. 7. The Comstock law of 1873, making it a felony to send obscene material through the mail, is still on the books; in the late 1990s, it was extended to the Internet. On the uneasy alliance between Irish Catholics and anti-Catholic Protestants of the Watch and Ward Society to purify the stage, screen, and bookstore in Boston, see Paula Kane, *Separatism and Subculture: Boston Catholicism, 1900–1920* (Chapel Hill, N.C., 1994), 298–313. For a sharp criticism, see David Langum, *Crossing over the Line: Legislating Morality and the Mann Act* (Chicago, 1994).

9. On judicial commitment to liberty of contract, see Owen M. Fiss, *Troubled Beginnings of the Modern State, 1888–1910* (New York, 1993).

10. Robert Kelley, *Transatlantic Persuasion* (New York, 1969), chaps. 7–8; Irwin Unger, *The Greenback Era: A Social and Political History of American Finance, 1865–1879* (Princeton, N.J., 1964); Robert P. Sharkey, *Money, Class, and Party: An Economic Study of Civil War and Reconstruction* (Baltimore, Md., 1959).

11. James D. Richardson, *A Compilation of the Messages and Papers of the Presidents: Grover Cleveland*, vol. 7 (Washington, D.C., 1910), 5166.

12. On 1888–1890, see Jensen, *Winning of the Midwest*; Hirshson, *Farewell to the Bloody Shirt*, chap. 7; Rebecca Edwards, *Angels in the Machinery: Gender and American Party Politics* (New York, 1997).

13. John R. Lambert, Jr., *Arthur Pue Gorman* (Baton Rouge, 1953), 231; Allan Nevins, *Grover Cleveland* (New York, 1932); James A. Barnes, *John C. Carlisle: Financial Statesman* (New York, 1931). For rates, see U.S. Bureau of the Census, *Historical Statistics of the United States* (Washington, D.C., 1976), series U212.

14. It was the British who watched in stunned horror as cheaper American products flooded their home islands. Wailed the *London Daily Mail* in 1900, "We have lost to the American manufacturer electrical machinery, locomotives, steel rails, sugar-producing and agricultural machinery, and latterly even stationary engines, the pride and backbone of the British engineering industry." By 1900, German businessmen faced the "horrid apparition" of American competition in steel. The quotes are from consular reports in U.S. Department of State, *Commercial Relations . . . 1900*, vol. 2 (Washington, D.C., 1901), 325, 974. See also Karen Schnietz, "Democrats' 1916 Tariff Commission: Responding to Dumping Fears and Illustrating the Consumer Costs of Protectionism," *Business History Review* 72 (1998): 1–45.

15. William Deverell, *Railroad Crossing: Californians and the Railroad, 1850–1910* (Berkeley, Calif., 1994); David P. Thelen, *The New Citizenship: Origins of Progressivism in Wisconsin, 1885–1910* (Columbia, Mo., 1972); Elizabeth Sanders, *Roots of Reform: Farmers, Workers, and the American State, 1877–1917* (Chicago, 1999), chap. 6; Gerald Berk, "Adversaries by Design: Railroads and the American State, 1887–1916," *Journal of Policy History* 5 (1993): 335–54.

16. From Harlan's opinion in the Standard Oil case of 1911 (221 US 83), in which Standard Oil was broken up largely on the basis of its scandalous activities in the 1880s.

17. Christopher Grandy, "Original Intent and the Sherman Antitrust Act: A Re-examination of the Consumer-Welfare Hypothesis," *Journal of Economic History* 53 (1993): 359–76; Thomas W. Hazlett, "The Legislative History of the Sherman Act Re-examined," *Economic Inquiry* 30 (1992): 263–76; Sanders, *Roots of Reform,* chap. 8. The intellectual mood of the 1880s is well covered in Hans B. Thorelli, *The Federal Antitrust Policy* (Baltimore, 1954); Sherman quote, xx.

18. Jensen, *Winning of the Midwest,* chap. 10; Stanley L. Jones, *The Presidential Election of 1896* (Madison, Wis., 1964); Gretchen Ritter, *Goldbugs and Greenbacks: The Antimonopoly Tradition and the Politics of Finance, 1865–1896* (New York, 1997). On the actual money supply, see *Historical Statistics,* series X415. In 1896, the stock of money was $4.35 billion, nearly triple the $1.58 billion in 1878.

19. The Mormons were systematically persecuted by the federal government and received almost no outside sympathy because their system violated republican norms. They reversed course in 1890, rejected polygamy and theocracy, and were welcomed into the world of republicanism. Edward Leo Lyman, "Mormon Leaders in Politics: The Transition to Statehood in 1896," *Journal of Mormon History* 24 (1998): 30–54.

20. Paul Kleppner, *Third Electoral System, 1853–1892* (Chapel Hill, N.C., 1979), 205.

21. Jensen, *Winning of the Midwest,* chap. 6.

22. Although only a small minority, Populists have fascinated historians because they combined intense republicanism with a whiff of radicalism and enthusiastic rejection of pro-business modernization. Thomas Goebel, "The Political Economy of American Populism from Jackson to the New Deal," *Studies in American Political Development* 11 (1997): 9–148.

23. For voting patterns, see Dale Baum, *The Civil War Party System: The Case of Massachusetts, 1848–1876* (Chapel Hill, N.C., 1984); Wright, *Progressive Yankees;* Samuel T. McSeveney, *The Politics of Depression: Political Behavior in the Northeast, 1893–1896* (New York, 1972); Jensen, *Winning of the Midwest;* Kleppner, *Third Electoral System.*

24. Michael McGerr, *The Decline of Popular Politics: The American North, 1865–1928* (New York, 1986).

25. Hearst was the most flamboyant and the most powerful. A left-wing Democrat, he helped nominate Franklin Roosevelt in 1932; feeling betrayed by 1935, he instructed his editorial writers to attack the "Raw Deal" every day. David Nasaw, *The Chief: The Life of William Randolph Hearst* (Boston, 2000); Ben Proctor, *William Randolph Hearst: The Early Years, 1863–1910* (New York, 1998). More representative of progressive journalism was William Allen White of Emporia, Kansas, who boosted small-town virtues and led purification crusades. Sally Foreman Griffith, *Home Town News: William Allen White and the Emporia Gazette* (New York, 1988).

26. Paul Kleppner, *Who Voted? The Dynamics of Election Turnout, 1870–1980* (New York, 1982).

27. Aileen Kraditor, *Ideas of the Woman Suffrage Movement, 1890–1920* (New York, 1965); Gayle Gullett, *Becoming Citizens: The Emergence and Development of the California Women's Movement, 1880–1911* (Urbana, Ill., 2000); Kathleen L. Endres, "Women and the 'Larger Household': The 'Big Six' and Muckraking," *American Journalism* 14 (1997): 262–82; R. Claire Snyder, *Citizen-Soldiers and Manly Warriors: Military Service and Gender in the Civic Republican Tradition* (Lanham, Md., 1999); John Whiteclay Chambers II, *To Raise an Army: The Draft Comes to Modern America*

(New York, 1987). For the antis, see Manuela Thurner, "'Better Citizens without the Ballot': American Antisuffrage Women and Their Rationale during the Progressive Era," *Journal of Women's History* 5 (1993): 33–60.

28. Carnegie's April 5, 1906, address is quoted in Louis R. Harlan, *Booker T. Washington: Wizard of Tuskegee, 1901–1915*, vol. 2 (New York, 1983), 139. Washington was the outstanding exemplar of how to rise "up from slavery" through a work ethic, self-help, a stress on education and self-improvement, and much less talk of rights, demonstrations, or protest. That made him a hero for the Progressive Era and a villain during the sixth party system, when the central evil of the 1890s was discovered to be the racism that Washington seemed too willing to tolerate (ibid., 2:142). David Levering Lewis, *W. E. B. DuBois: A Biography of a Race, 1868–1919* (New York, 1993), chap. 10.

29. K. Austin Kerr, *Organized for Prohibition: A New History of the Anti-Saloon League* (New Haven, Conn., 1985).

30. Jensen, *Winning of the Midwest*, 14.

31. The Wisconsin progressive movement originated in grassroots tax revolts of the 1890s (Thelen, *New Citizenship*). It crashed after rising taxes provoked a taxpayer backlash. With the state's progressives locked in internecine warfare, the conservatives won in 1914 by demanding retrenchment. John Buenker, *The History of Wisconsin*, vol. 4, *The Progressive Era, 1893–1914* (Madison, Wis., 1998), 659–61; Brett Flehinger, "'Public Interest': Robert M. La Follette and the Economics of Democratic Progressivism" (Ph.D. diss, Harvard University, 1997).

32. Martin J. Schiesl, *The Politics of Efficiency: Municipal Administration and Reform in America, 1880–1920* (Berkeley, Calif., 1977); Melvin G. Holli, "Urban Reform in the Progressive Era," in *The Progressive Era*, ed. Lewis Gould (Syracuse, N.Y., 1974), 133–52. David Paul Nord, "The Paradox of Municipal Reform in the Nineteenth Century," *Wisconsin Magazine of History* 66 (1982–83): 128–42.

33. We lack a national history of streetcar strikes and politics, but there are many good local studies; for example, Melvin G. Holli, *Reform in Detroit: Hazen S. Pingree and Urban Politics* (New York, 1969); Arthur E. Dematteo, "The Downfall of a Progressive: Mayor Tom L. Johnson and the Cleveland Streetcar Strike of 1908," *Ohio History* 104 (1995): 24–41; Sarah M. Henry, "The Strikers and Their Sympathizers: Brooklyn in the Trolley Strike of 1895," *Labor History* 32 (1991): 329–53; Robert Forrey, "Charles Tyson Yerkes: Philadelphia-Born Robber Baron," *Pennsylvania Magazine of History and Biography* 99 (1975): 226–41.

34. The Social Gospel was a driving force in most of Protestant America. The Presbyterians said it best in 1910: "The great ends of the church are the proclamation of the gospel for the salvation of humankind; the shelter, nurture, and spiritual fellowship of the children of God; the maintenance of divine worship; the preservation of truth; the promotion of social righteousness; and the exhibition of the Kingdom of Heaven to the world." See Jack B. Rogers and Robert E. Blade, "The Great Ends of the Church: Two Perspectives," *Journal of Presbyterian History* 76 (1998): 181–86. Susan Curtis, *A Consuming Faith: The Social Gospel and Modern American Culture* (Baltimore, 1991), points out the strain of efficiency.

35. Robert B. Westbrook, *John Dewey and American Democracy* (Ithaca, N.Y., 1991), 136, 148; James Livingston, *Pragmatism and the Political Economy of Cultural Revolution, 1850–1940* (Chapel Hill, N.C., 1994).

36. Philanthropy represented efficiency and redemption but could not be stretched to include perpetuating the original injustice. In 1903, the Congregationalists

fought over accepting a $100,000 gift by Rockefeller. Carnegie, promoting a Gospel of Wealth that would dedicate industrial fortunes to modernize all of society, was not amused. "Money may be the root of all evil in some sense," he snapped, "but it is also the root of all Universities, Colleges, Churches and libraries scattered through the land." Allan Nevins, *Study in Power: John D. Rockefeller,* vol. 2 (New York, 1953), 328–55; Carnegie's April 5, 1906, address at Tuskegee quoted in Harlan, *Booker T. Washington,* 139.

37. Charles Merriam in *Cyclopedia of American Government,* vol. 3 (New York, 1914), 51–55.

38. Louis Filler, *Voice of the Democracy: A Critical Biography of David Graham Phillips: Journalist, Novelist, Progressive* (University Park, Pa., 1978); Donald A. Ritchie, "'The Loyalty of the Senate': Washington Correspondents in the Progressive Era," *Historian* 51 (1989): 574–91; Lincoln Steffens, *The Autobiography of Lincoln Steffens,* vol. 2 (New York, 1931), 576–81.

39. Richard L. McCormick, "The Discovery that Business Corrupts Politics: A Reappraisal of the Origins of Progressivism," *American Historical Review* 86 (1981): 247–274; Sanders, *Roots of Reform.*

40. W. Lawrence Neuman, "Negotiated Meanings and State Transformation: The Trust Issue in the Progressive Era," *Social Problems* 45 (1998): 315–35; James C. German, Jr., "The Taft Administration and the Sherman Antitrust Act," *Mid-America* 54 (1972): 172–86.

41. Robert Craig West, *Banking Reform and the Federal Reserve, 1863–1923* (Ithaca, N.Y., 1977); Arthur S. Link, *Wilson: The New Freedom,* vol. 2 (Princeton, N.J., 1956), chap. 7.

42. Ron Chernow, *The House of Morgan: An American Banking Dynasty and the Rise of Modern Finance* (New York, 1990), chap. 7; Lester V. Chandler, *Benjamin Strong, Central Banker* (Washington, D.C., 1958); John A. Garraty, *Right-Hand Man: The Life of George W. Perkins* (New York, 1960), chap. 11; Jean Strouse, *Morgan, American Financier* (New York, 2000); William Harbaugh, *The Life and Times of Theodore Roosevelt* (New York, 1963), 296–301; Theodore Roosevelt, *Letters* (Cambridge, Mass., 1951), 5:830–31; Jon Moen and Ellis W. Tallman, "The Bank Panic of 1907: The Role of Trust Companies," *Journal of Economic History* 52 (1992): 611–30. In October 1911, Taft's Justice Department charged U.S. Steel with anti-trust violations in the TCI deal—leaving Roosevelt's integrity under a cloud. That was the last straw for Roosevelt, who decided to challenge Taft for the Republican nomination for president.

43. Speech of August 20, 1907, in Theodore Roosevelt, *The Works of Theodore Roosevelt,* vol. 16 (New York, 1926), 84. Regarding the very wealthy, Roosevelt privately scorned "their entire unfitness to govern the country, and . . . the lasting damage they do by much of what they think are the legitimate big business operations of the day" (September 21, 1907, in *Letters,* 5:802).

44. George Norris concluded in 1922, "In the country, in the agricultural communities and in the small villages, we find a stronger and more patriotic citizenship" (Richard Lowett, *George W. Norris: The Persistence of a Progressive, 1913–1933* [Urbana, Ill., 1971], 187). In contrast, William Allen White insisted that virtue was inherent in the small cities, such as his own Emporia, Kansas (Griffith, *Home Town News,* 151–55).

45. Paolo E. Coletta, *The Presidency of William Howard Taft* (Lawrence, Kans., 1973), 133, 138–52. After 1911, American business responded by investing in Canada and building branch plants. The goal was never annexation, but rather leverage in

world markets. Ronald Radosh, "American Manufacturers, Canadian Reciprocity, and the Origins of the Branch Factory System," *CAAS Bulletin* 3 (1967): 19–54.

46. Henry F. Pringle, *The Life and Times of William Howard Taft*, vol. 2 (New York, 1939), 655, quote, 829–32; Roosevelt, *Letters*, 5:781.

47. Alexander M. Bickel and Benno C. Schmidt, Jr., *The Judiciary and Responsible Government, 1910–21* (New York, 1984), chap. 3.

48. Historian Charles Beard stunned academe by arguing in 1913 that the founding fathers had acted in tune with their economic self-interest when ratifying the original Constitution. President Taft, like many readers, decided that Beard was denying the legitimacy of the Constitution itself, which Beard denied. Pringle, *Taft*, 2:860.

49. Roosevelt, *Works*, 12:234; Henry F. Pringle, *Theodore Roosevelt: A Biography* (New York, 1932), 478–82. When the court of appeals reversed a huge fine against Standard Oil in 1908, Roosevelt told his attorney general that the chief judge was "a scoundrel" and the other two were guilty of "improper subserviency to corporations" (*Letters*, 6:1142).

50. John Morton Blum, *The Republican Roosevelt* (Cambridge, Mass., 1954), 87–105. Business interests were split on the proposal, with most shippers favoring lower rates and hence a stronger ICC, and railroads demanding legal protections. Richard K. Vietor, "Businessmen and the Political Economy: The Railroad Rate Controversy of 1905," *Journal of American History* 64 (1977): 47–66. In the Midwest, cattlemen strongly resented high freight rates and organized to support more regulation. Keach Johnson, "The Corn Belt Meat Producers' Association of Iowa: Origins of a Progressive Pressure Group," *Annals of Iowa* 43 (1976): 242–60. Many reformers, especially La Follette and Wilson, believed there was one "true" price and one "fair" profit that could be discovered by experts, especially after a cost accounting of how much it cost to build and operate a railroad. This was an echo of the old "just price" doctrine and was wholly out of step with the new theory then being developed by economist Irving Fisher, that the profit of a business enterprise depends not on the sunk costs of the past but on the future flow of profits. Businessmen intuitively saw that if regulators systematically depressed profits, the value of a property would plunge.

51. George Mowry, *Theodore Roosevelt and the Progressive Movement* (Madison, Wis., 1946), 216–19. On the efforts by jurists to reassert final authority above administrative agencies and politicians, see Michael Les Benedict, "Law and Regulation in the Gilded Age and Progressive Era" (1998 SHGAPE Presidential Address); Daniel R. Ernst, "Law and American Political Development, 1877–1938," *Reviews in American History* 26 (1998): 205–19. In law and politics, the progressives replaced "rights," especially "property rights," with "duty" to the community. Morton J. Horwitz, *The Transformation of American Law, 1870–1960* (New York, 1992), 155–56.

52. "Judicial Decisions and Public Feeling," in Elihu Root, *Addresses on Government and Citizenship* (Cambridge, Mass., 1916), 446.

53. The best history remains Mowry, *Roosevelt and the Progressive Movement*; also see Norman M. Wilensky, *Conservatives in the Progressive Era: The Taft Republicans of 1912* (Gainesville, Fla., 1965). Most Bull Moosers followed Roosevelt back into the GOP in 1916; a minority went over to Wilson, especially in the mountain states.

54. Bickel and Schmidt, *Judiciary and Responsible Government*, chap. 1.

55. David L. Lewis, *The Public Image of Henry Ford: An American Folk Hero and His Company* (Detroit, 1976); James Warren Prothro, *The Dollar Decade: Business Ideas*

in the 1920s (Baton Rouge, 1954); G. Cullom Davis, "The Transformation of the Federal Trade Commission, 1914–1929," *Mississippi Valley Historical Review* 49 (1962): 437–55.

56. Roosevelt, *Works,* 18:394, from an October 12, 1912, address to the Knights of Columbus, the largest Catholic fraternal society. While many prominent Americans supported Britain, or condemned Germany for its militarism and atrocities in Belgium, British Americans operated more as individuals than as a collectivity in supporting Britain. Assimilation of the Protestant British had been virtually complete, and they were scarcely organized. See, however, Forrest McDonald, *Insull* (Chicago, 1962).

57. Nancy Derr, "Lowden: A Study of Intolerance in an Iowa Community during the Era of the First World War, " *Annals of Iowa* 50 (1989): 5–22. See also Leslie V. Tischauser, *The Burden of Ethnicity: The German Question in Chicago, 1914–1941* (New York, 1990); Melvin G. Holli, "Teuton vs. Slav: The Great War Sinks Chicago's German Kultur," *Ethnicity* 8 (1981): 406–51; David W. Detjen, *The Germans in Missouri, 1900–1918: Prohibition, Neutrality, and Assimilation* (Columbia, Mo., 1985).

58. Gwendolyn Mink, *Old Labor and New Immigrants in American Political Development: Union, Party and State, 1875–1920* (Ithaca, N.Y., 1986); Rivka Shpak Lissak, "The National Liberal Immigration League and Immigration Restriction, 1906–1917," *American Jewish Archives* 46 (1994): 197–246.

59. On Americanization, see Gary Gerstle, "Liberty, Coercion, and the Making of Americans," *Journal of American History* 84 (1997): 548–57; James R. Barrett and David Roediger, "In-between Peoples: Race, Nationality, and the 'New Immigrant' Working Class," *Journal of American Ethnic History* 16 (1997): 3–44; Russell A. Kazal, "Revisiting Assimilation: The Rise, Fall, and Reappraisal of a Concept in American Ethnic History," *American Historical Review* 100 (1995): 437–71; Ewa Morawska, "In Defense of the Assimilation Model," *Journal of American Ethnic History* 13 (1994): 76–97; James R. Barrett, "Americanization from the Bottom Up: Immigration and the Remaking of the Working Class in the United States, 1880–1930," *Journal of American History* 79 (1992): 996–1020.

60. Ashley S. Timmer and Jeffrey G. Williamson, "Immigration Policy Prior to the 1930s: Labor Markets, Policy Interactions, and Globalization Backlash," *Population and Development Review* 24 (1998): 739–60; James Foreman-Peck, "A Political Economy Model of International Migration, 1815–1914," *Manchester School* 60 (1992): 359–76.

61. Lynn Dumenil, *Modern Temper: American Culture and Society in the 1920s* (New York, 1995); Anna L. Harvey, *Votes without Leverage: Women in American Electoral Politics, 1920–1970* (New York, 1998); Kristi Anderson, *After Suffrage: Women in Partisan and Electoral Politics before the New Deal* (Chicago, 1996); Sara Hunter Graham, *Woman Suffrage and the New Democracy* (New Haven, Conn., 1996).

62. Lewis L. Gould, *Progressives and Prohibitionists: Texas Democrats in the Wilson Era* (Austin, Tex., 1973), 290; Ann-Marie Elaine Szymanski, "'Think Locally, Act Gradually': Political Strategy and the American Prohibition Movement during the Nineteenth and Twentieth Centuries" (Ph.D. diss, Cornell University, 1998); Kerr, *Organized for Prohibition.*

63. Historians once considered the KKK a group of marginal misfits, rural traditionalists baffled by the coming of modern urban society. Recent historiography shows them to be mainstream, urban, and modern. They represented a wide cross section of native Protestants, truncating both the top and the bottom of the social structure.

They were thoroughly committed to the notion of republican virtue and, contrary to myth, rarely used violence. See Stanley Coben, "Ordinary White Protestants: The KKK of the 1920s," *Journal of Social History* 28 (1994): 155–65; David O. Goldberg, *Discontented America* (Baltimore, 1999), chap. 6; Leonard J. Moore, *Citizen Klansman: The Ku Klux Klan in Indiana, 1921–1928* (Chapel Hill, N.C., 1991); Leonard J. Moore, "Historical Interpretations of the 1920s Klan: The Traditional View and the Populist Revision," *Journal of Social History* 24 (1990): 341–57.

64. David J. Goldberg, "Unmasking the Ku Klux Klan: The Northern Movement against the KKK, 1920–1925," *Journal of American Ethnic History* 15 (1996): 32–48; David E. Kyvig, *Repealing National Prohibition* (Chicago, 1979); Allan J. Lichtman, *Prejudice and the Old Politics* (Chapel Hill, N.C., 1979); Jerome M. Clubb and Howard W. Allen, "The Cities and the Election of 1928: Partisan Realignment?" *American Historical Review* 74 (1969): 1205–20.

65. Stephen Vaughn, *Holding Fast the Inner Lines* (Chapel Hill, N.C., 1980), chaps. 8–9; John Anthony Morello, "Candidates, Consumers, and Closers: Albert Lasker, Advertising, and Politics, 1900–1926" (Ph.D. diss., University of Illinois at Chicago, 1998); Michael Schudson, *The Good Citizen: A History of American Civic Life* (New York, 1998), chap. 5.

66. Walter Lippmann, *Public Opinion* (New York, 1922); Walter Lippmann, "H. L. Mencken," *Saturday Review of Literature,* December 11, 1926; for quote; Westbrook, *John Dewey,* chap. 9; David M. Ricci, *Tragedy of Political Science: Politics, Scholarship, and Democracy* (New Haven, Conn., 1984); Christopher Lasch, *The True and Only Heaven: Progress and Its Critics* (New York, 1991), 360–68.

67. Henry F. May, "Shifting Perspectives on the 1920s," *Mississippi Valley Historical Review* 43 (1956): 405–27, remains the most insightful essay on how intellectuals thought the old world had culminated, for better or worse, in the 1920s. See also Dumenil, *Modern Temper.*

68. Ellis W. Hawley, "Herbert Hoover, the Commerce Secretariat, and the Vision of an 'Associative State,' 1921–1928," *Journal of American History* 61 (1974): 116–40; Marc Allen Eisner, *From Warfare State to Welfare State: World War I, Compensatory State-Building, and the Limits of the Modern Order* (University Park, Pa., 2000), chap. 8; Stephen Skowronek, *The Politics Presidents Make: Leadership from John Adams to George Bush* (Cambridge, Mass., 1993), 260–85; Kendrick A. Clements, *Hoover, Conservation, and Consumerism: Engineering the Good Life* (Lawrence, Kans., 2000).

69. David Kennedy, *Freedom from Fear: The American People in Depression and War, 1929–1945* (New York, 1999); Albert U. Romasco, *The Poverty of Abundance: Hoover, the Nation, the Depression* (New York, 1965).

70. Ballard Campbell, *The Growth of American Government: Governance from the Cleveland Era to the Present* (Bloomington, Ind., 1995); David T. Beito, *Taxpayers in Revolt: Tax Resistance during the Great Depression* (Chapel Hill, N.C., 1989).

71. Richard Jensen, "The Causes and Cures of Unemployment in the Great Depression," *Journal of Interdisciplinary History* 19 (1989): 553–83.

72. Milton Friedman and Anna J. Schwartz, *A Monetary History of the United States, 1857–1960* (Princeton, N.J., 1963); this classic finds fresh support in Michael D. Bordo, Ehsan U. Choudhri, and Anna J. Schwartz, "Could Stable Money Have Averted the Great Contraction?" *Economic Inquiry* 33 (1995): 484–505.

73. Douglas B. Craig, *After Wilson* (Chapel Hill, N.C., 1992), chap. 9; the best depiction of the utter, total collapse of the old regime remains Arthur M. Schlesinger, Jr., *The Crisis of the Old Order: 1919–1933* (Boston, 1957).

7. The Limits of Federal Power and Social Politics, 1910–1955

Anthony J. Badger

At face value, it is a simple story. The central episode of this period is the third great critical realignment in American political history. After the realignment of the 1850s and 1890s came the New Deal realignment of the 1930s.

The party system shaped in the 1890s had cast the Republicans as the national majority party, one that drew on the support of businessmen, commercial farmers, and skilled workers in the northern states. Sectional loyalty and traditions played a large part in this northern support for the Republican Party. Equally, sectional loyalties shaped southern support for the Democrats. Old-stock, ethnocultural loyalties then cemented this Republican hegemony.

By contrast, the depression of the 1930s created a new national majority party, the Democrats. Their southern base remained intact and was now supplemented by the switch of lower-income voters, new immigrants, and African Americans in the northern cities. Class thus replaced ethnocultural loyalty as the determinant of party allegiance, just as bread-and-butter issues of economics and social welfare replaced cultural issues as the substance of politics.

The political scientists who delineated this realignment have been criticized for being excessively impressed by the one realignment they had personally experienced, that of the 1930s. Equally, New Deal historians in the United States have found it hard to escape their own personal experience of (and support for) New Deal liberalism. As someone who has written on the New Deal, I too have a professional vested interest in the long-term importance of the political transformations of the 1930s.[1] And the intellectual synthesis resulting from them has proved remarkably robust.

Yet there is another narrative of this period. In this version, the New Deal is merely a blip on the steady erosion of party loyalty and political participation in the twentieth century. The political system introduced by Joel Silbey, refined by Michael Holt, and then extended by Peter Argersinger was based on remarkably high levels of political participation and party loyalty. Elections were won by parties mobilizing core voters who plumped for a straight party ticket. From the anti-party measures of the Progressive Era onward, voter turnout has steadily and dramatically declined, party identification has weakened, voters have split their tickets, and the key to winning elections has been not the mobilizing of a declining number of core voters but the winning over of crucial independents.

In this narrative, parties have been replaced by interest groups and volunteer activists as the main mobilizers in the political system. The New Deal may have stimulated voter turnout. The Democrats may have mobilized new voters and recruited loyal followers. There may have been a radical, class-based cutting edge to the competitive politics of the 1930s at all levels. But the impact was temporary: the long-term trends that minimized the importance of party and turned voters away from the polls, introduced by Peter Argersinger at the end of his chapter, were only briefly interrupted by events of the 1930s.[2] That trend is very much with us today.

To try to find my way through these contrasting narratives, I first use the party platforms for the 1912 and 1952 presidential elections as a way of grasping in stark terms some of the basic parameters of substance and structure in politics of this period, along with the way these changed over time. I then examine three broad developments: the impact of women's suffrage, the circumscribed nature of the realignment of the 1930s, and the reinforcement and extension of a powerful anti-statist coalition in the politics of the nation. What emerges is both more stasis and more contingency than the two leading alternatives usually provide.

Scope of the Change: Before and After the Main Event

In 1912, as Richard Jensen affirms, the Democratic and Republican Party platforms concentrated on the tariff, the regulation of trusts, and control of banking and the currency. The Democrats blamed Republican tariffs for high prices, condemned Republican extravagance with taxpayers' money, called for strict anti-trust enforcement, vigorously asserted states' rights, and called for a system of rural credits to remedy deficiencies in the banking system. Republicans defended tariffs, which guaranteed high wages and the American standard of living, and championed the rule of law and the courts as far as regulation of both trusts and labor was concerned. The Republicans were suspicious of administrative rather than judicial regulation, and suspicious of any attempt to subject judges to popular political pressure. There was almost no discussion of foreign policy and no discussion of civil rights. Proposals for federal intervention in social welfare and social insurance could be found only in the Progressive Party platform.

In 1952, the first and foremost concern of both major party platforms was foreign policy and the efficacy, or otherwise, of the policy of containment. The Republicans not only denounced the ineffectiveness of the anti-Soviet foreign policy of the Truman administration but also attacked its softness on domestic communists. Both platforms next addressed the question of economic management. The Democrats claimed credit for fiscal policies that maintained high employment, for price supports that maintained farm income, and for social security to cushion retirement. The Republicans blamed government spending for inflation, lamented excessive government regulation of business, and defended the Taft-Hartley Act, which the Democrats sought to repeal. Both parties had a civil rights plank, however bland.[3]

In terms of the substance of politics, the American political world had obviously changed dramatically. In terms of the rules of the political game, perhaps less had changed. Women had the vote, effectively doubling the electorate—or, rather, the potential electorate, given the fall in turnout. And senators were directly elected, courtesy of the Seventeenth Amendment, which decreed that senators would be elected popularly rather than by state legislatures.[4] Yet African Americans in the South were still effectively disfranchised. Despite the Smith-Allwright decision outlawing the white primary in 1944, only 20 percent of southern blacks were registered to vote by 1952.

Moreover, apportionment, a burning issue in the late nineteenth century, was now largely ignored. Little was done to challenge the overrepresentation of rural areas, particularly in the South, until the *Baker v. Carr* decision of 1962. Democratic proposals in 1912 for a presidential primary and a single presidential term had disappeared. The Republicans had, however, ensured with the Twenty-second Amendment that no president would emulate Franklin Roosevelt and break the anti-third-term tradition.

Intermediary groups had changed notably. In 1912, the effective organized interests in politics were business groups, the Anti-Saloon League, and women's groups, the last lobbying for suffrage, Prohibition, and reform of working conditions. This concern for social justice found its most vocal expression in the Progressive Party, however. Farmers had abandoned third-party activity and found an effective voice in both parties, one that enabled them to enact many of the credit and educational goals of the Populists. By 1952, the Anti-Saloon League had been consigned to oblivion. Women were not an identifiable voting bloc. And business as an effective interest group had been joined by the Farm Bureau, by labor unions, and by civil rights groups.

In 1952, the United States was a superpower that had fought in two world wars, had checked Soviet expansion after 1945 in a cold war, and was currently fighting in Korea. To historians of political realignment, foreign policy is viewed largely as a marginal issue that affects the votes of particular ethnic groups, such as the Irish in the late 1930s or Jews and eastern Europeans in the 1940s. In fact, participation in the League of Nations, and later the World Court, had split the Democratic Party in the 1920s and 1930s, and neutrality legislation had been unstoppable in the 1930s.

The construction of a bipartisan internationalist consensus after World War II should not obscure the important strand of Republicanism that combined virulent anti-communism, support for a strong defense, and commitment to a balanced budget and anti-statism. Anti-communism had been a recurrent theme in American political culture from 1917 onward, from the Overman Committee after the Red scare to the Fish Committee in 1930 to the House Un-American Affairs Committee in 1937. Anti-communism was also a powerful weapon to attack the extension of federal government power, social reform, and labor unions, long before Soviet espionage was a problem. At the state level, Michael Heale showed how anti-communism had a political rhythm all its own, linked, for example, to polarized class politics in Michigan, Catholic anti-elitism in Massachusetts, and massive resistance in Georgia.[5]

But the experience of war had other important political consequences. Both world wars brought economic opportunities and rising expectations for women and African Americans. World War I also helped bring the vote for women. Both wars made possible the migration of African Americans to the northern cities, where they could vote and exercise the leverage to make civil rights a national political issue in the 1940s. World War II consolidated the power of farm pressure groups and reestablished the legitimacy of organized business. World War I saw only temporary membership gains for organized labor, while World War II made meaningful collective bargaining a reality for many trade unions.

War also made a significant contribution to the shifting of the location of the nation's political center of gravity to the Sun Belt. Defense expenditure and infrastructure investment quickened the economic development of the West and speeded up the existing population drift to the Pacific coast. In the South, war and cold war expenditures kick-started the region's economy into self-sustaining economic growth, paving the way for the in-migration of white middle- to upper-income Republican voters.[6]

The Rise of Federal Power

Beyond that, for historians like Robert Higgs, the emergency of war and the economic emergency of 1933, which was equated to war by Roosevelt and others, were the devices by which politicians remorselessly expanded the power of the federal government, in defiance of both market forces and traditional American individualism. In 1906, H. G. Wells commented that the national government in Washington "lies marooned, twisted up into knots, bound with safeguards, and altogether impotently stranded." Despite World War I, the federal government of the 1920s was still very different from the federal government after the New Deal and World War II. As William Leuchtenburg noted, "the United States in the 1920s had almost no institutional structure to which Europeans would accord the term 'the State.'" Numerous others reached the same conclusion.[7]

By the end of World War II, the federal government was a very different institution. Seventy-five percent of Americans paid federal income tax. The government told farmers what they could and could not plant, told employers what they could and could not do to inhibit trade unions, laid down minimum wages for many workers, regulated the marketing of securities, provided insurance against old age and unemployment, guaranteed bank deposits, and loaned money to bankers, farmers, and home owners. As the federal government and the importance of foreign policy expanded, so the power of the executive increased. The roots of the institutionalized presidency, which Argersinger identified with Theodore Roosevelt in the 1900s, were nurtured and developed. From Woodrow Wilson onward, presidents were active in campaigning on a platform and pushing for a specific legislative agenda. Calvin Coolidge, with his deliberate policy of self-restraint, was an exception.

Both voters and politicians by 1952 assumed that the federal government was responsible for the economic well-being of the country and had the tools to macromanage the economy. In 1912, the tariff and currency were the two areas of economic regulation over which the Constitution gave the federal government explicit authority. The impact of anti-trust legislation was severely restricted by judicial interpretation. A generation later, Roosevelt's decision to take America off the gold standard in 1933 and then the agreement at Bretton Woods took the monetary question off the political agenda. Reciprocal trade agreements and the postwar liberal trade order largely did the same for tariff protection. Anti-trust agitation had mainly died down as a political issue, although anti-trust enforcement continued a bureaucratic life of its own. When anti-trust concerns did surface, they served to protect consumers from administered prices, not to protect producers and small businessmen.[8]

If anti-trust activity had been reduced by 1952 to the status of a way to help maintain mass purchasing power, the government had by that time other solid means to macromanage the economy. The Federal Reserve Board, appointed by the president from 1935, gave the government control of interest rates and credit. The New Deal regulated both banks and the stock exchanges. Control of the level of government spending was seen as a major tool with which to secure full employment, a goal espoused, though not mandated, in 1946 legislation.[9] Yet by 1952, the substance of politics was not simply to secure the overall success of the economy but also to protect disadvantaged groups within that economy.

Daniel Rodgers noted that since the great eighteenth-century revolutions, the core "project" of radicals and reformers on both sides of the Atlantic had been "not to restrain the processes of commodification, but the concentrated powers of the monarchical state." In the United States from 1865, the political reconstitution of the nation, the civil rights of newly freed slaves, and the issues of tariffs and currency were the staples of party politics and political culture. Rapid industrialization, exploding urban populations and visible poverty, and unprecedented industrial conflict between employers and workers created a new agenda of politics: the control of new industrial giants, the delivery of public municipal services, and the protection of workers' collective action, plus protection against the vicissitudes of unemployment, industrial accidents, and simple old age. This was, in Rodgers's formulation, a "new social politics."[10]

In 1912, that social agenda had surfaced nationally only in the platform of the Progressive Party. The battleground for this "social democratic project" had instead been the cities in the 1890s and 1900s and, increasingly, the states. The alliance of academics, women reformers, and labor leaders would be able to shift the focus decisively to Washington only in the 1930s, after the worst depression in the country's history. But, as Rodgers concluded, from 1900 onward, "For the rest of the twentieth century, although parties split and polarized over the new issues, no politics could be divorced from social politics."[11]

This transformation of federal power, of notions of the legitimate functions of government, and of the substance of national politics was eventually accepted by the federal courts. The exact timing of the constitutional revolution of the 1930s, and the motivation of the judges who appeared to switch sides, remains open to dispute. But the constitutional consequences were clear. The restrictions on what the federal government could regulate under the commerce clause were largely removed. In 1942, the Supreme Court ruled that an Ohio chicken farmer growing twenty-three acres of wheat, all of which would be fed to his chickens and consumed in his own backyard, so affected interstate commerce that the secretary of agriculture could impose marketing penalties on him. Before 1937, the Court savaged economic and social legislation. Since 1937, it has never overturned legislation involving economic regulation. Between 1937 and 1946, it actually reversed thirty-two of its earlier decisions.

But if the Court exercised judicial self-restraint rather than judicial supremacy after 1937 in economic and social welfare legislation, it was not prepared to defer to the legislative branch on civil rights and civil liberties. Thus, minorities denied redress for their grievances by the legislative branch could turn to the courts. African Americans, denied anti-lynching and anti–poll tax legislation by the power of the southern Democrats in Congress, successfully turned to the courts from the 1930s to 1954 to secure voting rights, the equalization of teachers' salaries, and the desegregation of higher education and public schools. The NAACP Legal Division pioneered the campaign for public-interest litigation of a type that would become commonplace a generation later in the "rights revolution."[12]

Three other social changes not unrelated to wartime America need mention. The First World War and the legislation of 1921 and 1924 choked off new immigration, especially from southern and eastern Europe. Immigration would not resume in significant numbers until the unintended consequence of immigration reform in 1965. After Al Smith's campaign for the presidency in 1928, the depression, and the repeal of Prohibition, ethnocultural issues largely disappeared from national politics, with the exception of federal aid to education, where aid to Catholic schools divided reform supporters.

In 1930, one-third of the workforce was still in agriculture. Mechanization and wartime prosperity sparked a flight from the land, although numerical decline did not lead automatically to an equivalent loss of influence. Much of the flight was still by nonvoters, black and white. Failure to reapportion then sustained rural overrepresentation. The alliance of corn-belt Republicans and cotton southern Democrats, commodity pressure groups and sympathetic bureaucrats, ensured generous price-support legislation, notwithstanding urban liberal and ideological conservative opposition.

Finally, post-1945 prosperity, cheaper mortgages prompted by New Deal lending agencies, and the benefits of the GI bill massively expanded the percentage of home owners in the United States to the highest figure in the Western world, at the expense of the legitimacy of public housing. This suburban shift changed the class attitudes of American workers, reshaped the patterns of local and neighborhood politics, and paved the way for a new generation of volunteer political activists. A nation that had long been rural, then grudgingly urban, was to become clearly suburban in the postwar years.[13]

Women's Suffrage: A Different Electorate?

The Nineteenth Amendment dramatically expanded the electorate. The campaign for women's suffrage was ultimately successful when it eschewed a challenge to traditional gender roles in favor of a campaign that stressed difference and the reform aspirations of the networks of middle-class women concerned about social welfare legislation and municipal housekeeping. The women's groups that had campaigned so effectively for suffrage confidently expected women's vote to change the nature of politics.[14] Moreover, the efforts of the National League of Women Voters between 1921 and 1925 appeared to justify that optimism. They succeeded in securing from Congress passage of the Sheppard-Towner bill for maternal and infant health, increased appropriations for the Women's Bureau and the Children's Bureau, regulation of milk and meat processing, separate institutions for federal female prisoners, and passage of the child labor amendment.

A study of the tariff from 1890 to 1934 indicates that female enfranchisement had a statistically significant effect even on lowering the tariff. Women were recognized in both state and national party organizations. They made appointive gains from 18 percent of postmasterships in 1930 to the first female cabinet member, Frances Perkins, in 1933, followed by Republican Oveta Culp Hobby in 1953. The male partisan political world of torchlight parades, mass rallies, and campaign clubs and marching companies disappeared. Balloting in barbershops and saloons was replaced by voting in schools and churches. Kristi Anderson, a child of Republican parents in Omaha in the 1950s, recalled that both women and men handed out election literature, stuffed envelopes, served as election judges and poll watchers, and drank coffee and ate sandwiches.[15]

But the dramatic electoral influence of women was short-lived. The Sheppard-Towner Act was not renewed in 1929, appropriations for the Women's and Children's Bureaus were cut, and the child labor amendment was not ratified. Women in state and national party organizations received rebuff after rebuff. In 1952, the Women's Division of the Democratic National Committee was abolished. No longer was there an automatic national committeewoman from each state in both parties. Elected women officeholders were few and far between. In 1950, there were only eleven women in the House and the Senate. In 1952, there were only ten women mayors. Only in 1964 did women voters finally outnumber men. Overt women's political influence did not significantly increase until the late 1960s.[16]

Paul Kleppner has acquitted women of the charge that they did not vote and that they were responsible for the national fall in turnout in the 1920s. Women's participation rates, like men's, appear to be related mainly to economic and educational background. Strong party organizations could counteract some of this, but where they survived, they turned out women as well as men; many lower-income women in Boston were mobilized as voters in the late 1930s. Politicians did not perceive, however, that women voted as a bloc, and the empirical data tend to support that perception. Isolated successes, such as contributing to the defeat of Theodore "The Man" Bilbo in 1923 in Mississippi, were not often replicated. A gender gap in voter preference was not clearly established until 1952, when women were six percentage points higher than men in their support for Dwight Eisenhower.

Conservative women could also mobilize *against* social reforms sponsored by women, just as conservative elite women in both the North and the South had opposed women's suffrage. In Massachusetts, the Woman Patriot joined forces with the Catholic Church (successfully) to prevent ratification of the child labor amendment, citing the evidence of free love and prostitution in Russia, revealed by the Overman Committee, as confirmation that the regulation of child labor was an attempt by federal bureaucrats to nationalize or sovietize family life.[17] Anna Harvey argued that the impact of women's suffrage was limited because women's post-suffrage organizations abandoned electoral mobilization to the parties. As a result, their lobbying activities were handicapped by the fact that they could not threaten politicians with electoral retribution. Only when the influence of party declined in the 1960s did women's lobbying once more enjoy success.[18]

The influential role of women in the policy circles of the New Deal confirms rather than refutes Harvey's argument. Women achieved high-level jobs and wielded influence in government circles in the 1930s that would not be matched until the 1970s. They did not achieve this because of the tireless efforts of Molly

Dewson for the Women's Division of the Democratic National Committee to educate women voters. They did so because they had access and influence, not electoral leverage. A remarkable network of college-educated women of a generation that had worked in settlement houses in the Progressive Era, suffrage organizations in the 1910s, and reform groups in the 1920s not only had access to Roosevelt and James Farley, through Molly Dewson and Eleanor Roosevelt, but also had social welfare expertise that was desperately needed as the New Deal struggled to implement relief programs and social security.

Blanche Cook and Doris Kearns Goodwin portrayed the struggle between the conservative, business-oriented, isolationist wing of the New Deal and a radical, social justice, internationalist wing as largely a battle between a male New Deal mainstream and a parallel administration of women headed by Mrs. Roosevelt. But it has to be remembered that the women in the long run were not successful. They were sidelined during the war when their social welfare expertise was considered irrelevant to the needs of wartime mobilization and production. Despite the economic gains of the war, women's organizations were in no position to stave off the anti-feminist backlash after the war.[19]

Partisan Realignment: Different Political Parties?

The story of the New Deal realignment seems simple enough. Lower-income (new) immigrant voters had already tended to be Democratic in the Progressive Era. Their affiliation was in part a reaction to attempts by old-stock, rural, small-town Republicans to use the power of the state to impose moral conformity on them. But they were also responding, as John Buenker pointed out, to a new trend of urban liberalism among machine politicians. Whereas city machines had traditionally provided informal services for their constituents, relying heavily on corruption and patronage, younger politicians such as Robert Wagner and Al Smith abandoned these informal, costly devices in favor of rational, government-provided social welfare.

New immigrant voters were then mobilized for the Democrats in the 1920s by the Catholic Tammany politician Al Smith. Despite his defeat in 1928, the leading cities were delivered to the Democrats. The Smith revolution was solidified by the depression and the policies of the New Deal. Machine politicians welcomed the wealth of patronage in the New Deal. Contrary to the traditional view that such politics was rendered obsolete by the new welfare state, these politicians benefited from the New Deal because they controlled the local distribution of federal largesse. Remaining Republican organizations in urban areas were simultaneously swept aside.

Part of the mobilization and shift of lower-income voters was, especially, the dramatic shift of African Americans in the North. In 1934 and 1936, they left the party of Lincoln and joined the party of white supremacy, responding to the relative nondiscrimination by Democrats in the distribution of relief and welfare. In the long run, mayors and machine politicians looked to the federal government as the solution to their problems, bypassing unsympathetic state governments.[20]

Conversely, there was only partial realignment. The New Deal did not secure a full-scale realignment of the parties on nonsectional, ideological lines, and Roosevelt was widely criticized for failing systematically to build up liberal forces within the Democratic Party. His effort in the purge of 1938, especially in the South, was then defeated, as James Patterson and I have shown, by the forces of localism and by failure to extend the electorate itself in the South. FDR had had to work with established southern politicians in 1933 and thereby inevitably bolstered their position. He could do little to unseat them, given the restricted size of the electorate, when they tired of the nonemergency nature of the New Deal. And southerners did weary of the New Deal's pro-labor, pro-city orientation, along with its threat to local patterns of worker and racial dependency and deference.[21]

The legacy was a schizophrenic Democratic Party in which, as Patterson showed more than thirty years ago, southern Democrats would be key figures in the bipartisan conservative coalition in Congress that would stifle reform for a quarter of a century after 1938.[22] Much of the extensive literature on this realignment is devoted to debates over whether the new Democratic voters were converted from existing Republican allegiances or were mobilized, particularly women and new immigrants, for the first time. Linked to this question is the debate over which election was "critical": 1928, 1932, or 1936. However, both detailed analyses of voting data on the realignment and various attempts to pinpoint the precise turning point seem to me of limited utility. Instead, there remains a wider context in which the New Deal years are clearly important.[23]

First, whatever the composition of the electorate that voted Democratic, it elected a very different type of Democrat in the 1930s. The conservative, northern, business-oriented, urban Democrat committed to limited government virtually disappeared. As Douglas Craig showed, it was these Democrats that Al Smith courted and whose cause his Democratic National Committee chairman, John Raskob, championed. Raskob and Jouett Shouse, head of the party's Publicity Bureau, not only aimed to "stop Roosevelt" in 1932. They planned to develop a coalition of northern Democrats and sympathetic southern Democrats, such as Governor Albert Ritchie of Maryland and Harry Byrd of Virginia, who were committed to laissez-faire and limited government. The New Deal, which drove so many of these conservatives into opposition and won over the city machine politicians, ended those hopes.[24]

Second, as Gerald Gamm showed for Boston, the mobilization of new voters did not occur until 1936 and 1938 in many cases. The Democrats had already made an initial breakthrough, but new voters were thereafter responding to the new social politics of the New Deal. It is difficult not to sympathize with Bernard Sternsher's argument that you cannot have a New Deal realignment until you have had a New Deal.[25]

Third, the argument that the New Deal elections of 1934–1938 are crucial is an argument that ties in with the work of Lizabeth Cohen on blue-collar workers in Chicago. Cohen stresses the agency of industrial workers themselves in forging a new class-based loyalty to both the Democratic Party and their new industrial unions. Their activity complemented the work of the politicians and "state actors" who had delivered the Wagner Act in 1935.

What linked both these voters and the policy makers was the importance of mass purchasing power—a strategy that called for high wages and low prices, a strategy that linked them to middle-class consumers. One of the distinctive features of political discourse in the 1930s was, as Meg Jacobs emphasized, that labor and the middle class were not seen to be at odds. It was this common cause between workers and consumers that gave the new Democratic Party its reforming thrust and dynamism, not the Al Smith revolution.[26]

If the New Deal realignment was only a partial realignment, it was not, according to interpretations of the later New Deal, for want of trying. Increasingly, scholars have identified a "third New Deal" in the late 1930s. Barry Karl argued that after 1937, "Roosevelt had tried to bring off a genuine revolution and failed to do so." The elements of this revolution were executive reorganization, the Court-packing plan of 1937, and the attempt to purge the Democratic Party of conservatives in the primaries of 1938. According to this argument, these attempted reforms represented a drive to "strengthen the administrative and executive power and capacity of the president" and introduce a "politics of administration, which entailed a shift of more and more government action from the regular political process to the executive department."[27]

These executive reorganization proposals would indeed have abolished independent regulatory agencies, placing them instead in twelve executive departments and establishing an Executive Office of the President with a powerful budget bureau and planning board. The Supreme Court that would have been appointed when the Court was "packed" or enlarged would have ensured that rule-making authority could be delegated to the executive. The purge thus aimed to nationalize party politics and overcome localism and inertia. The policy complement to this administrative thrust was the National Resources Planning Board's report of 1943, *Security, Work, and Relief,* which called for guaranteed minima for all American citizens, for health care, and for low-cost housing.

The substantive policy consequence of this failure to secure a full-scale re-alignment was, according to Alan Brinkley, a very different and restricted type of liberalism. New Dealers gave up on expansive notions of an interventionist state committed to social justice. Buoyed by the creation of 17 million new jobs during World War II, they felt that they had the fiscal tools to create continued economic growth, which, in itself, would solve many of the social ills of America. They thus advocated a "commercial" rather than a "social" Keynesianism. There was no need to redistribute income or reshape capitalist institutions.

Keynesianism in this formulation "provided a way to manage the economy without challenging the prerogatives of capitalists. Growth did not necessarily require constant involvement in the affairs of public institutions . . . it did not require a drastic expansion of the regulatory functions of the state." Liberals concluded "that economic growth was the surest route to social progress and that consumption, more than production, was the surest route to economic growth. . . . They had redefined citizenship to de-emphasize the role of men and women as producers and to elevate their roles as consumers." Numan Bartley argued that for the South, economically radical "popular front liberalism" be-came civil rights–oriented "Cold War liberalism," or, as Arthur Schlesinger cele-brated in the 1950s, liberalism became qualitative rather than quantitative.[28]

This growth-focused, limited-state, consumer-oriented vision was not, in fact, uncontested. Jacobs demonstrated the persistence of redistributive, interven-tionist efforts into the 1950s, a social democratic vision of Keynesianism more akin to western European welfare and taxation policies. She stressed the legacy of the efforts of the Office of Price Administration to mobilize consumers, as well as the efforts of labor leaders such as Walter Reuther to sustain a high-wage, low-price strategy in the postwar world. In 1945 and 1946, unions sought to open the books of corporations to demonstrate that they could afford generous pay settle-ments without raising prices. There were continued policy efforts in the Demo-cratic Party of the 1950s, led by politicians such as Paul Douglas and economists such as John Kenneth Galbraith, to champion the cause of targeted investment and to tackle the problem of administered prices.[29]

Jonathan Bell argued that even in the 1946 elections and in the Eightieth Congress, "opportunities for state-centered policies seemed promising." He noted the success of Republicans Henry Cabot Lodge and Irving Ives and the acceptance by politicians as varied and apparently conservative as Robert Taft and George Malone of government solutions to social problems. I argued that in the South there was a new generation of younger politicians who not only looked to the federal government for investment in the region's infrastructure but also looked to federal and state intervention to sustain mass purchasing power through more generous and inclusive welfare measures and the pro-tection of trade unions. Indeed, in the South, as in the Democratic Parties in Wisconsin and Minnesota in the late 1940s, there was a time-lagged element of the New Deal realignment, the eventual replacement of patronage-oriented conservatives by issue-oriented liberals.[30]

Welfare Statism: A New Governing Philosophy?

Both views—of a conventional realignment and of a missed opportunity—are ultimately too simple, for the full-scale New Deal realignment was ultimately checked by a powerful anti-statist coalition, one that developed right from the start. The link between the Association against the Prohibition Amendment and the (anti–New Deal) Liberty League is well known. The usual explanation is that wealthy businessmen who feared increased taxation favored the repeal of Prohibition in order to free up an alternative source of government revenue. In fact, the leaders of the anti-Prohibition campaign, such as John Raskob and Jouett Shouse, objected to the Prohibition amendment because of its unacceptable degree of federal control and interference in individual rights. Here, a billion-dollar industry had been destroyed and assets confiscated without compensation.

Raskob and Shouse viewed the New Deal's exercise of power in the same light: a massive infringement on property rights and freedom of contract. They soon sought like-minded businessmen to join them in outright rejection of the New Deal.[31] In turn, businessmen, who were on the defensive in the 1930s, regrouped to redress the political balance that had produced the Wagner Act of 1935. Whatever adjustments they had to make to the realities of collective bargaining, they also tapped into a long-term hostility to trade unions—first in the aftermath of the sit-down strikes in the late 1930s; then during the war, when strikes threatened to disrupt wartime production; then during the strikes of 1945–1946, which accompanied rampant inflation.

The key to conservative success was the way in which business managed to drive a wedge between working- and middle-class Americans. In the political discourse of the 1930s, they had been united as consumers and producers, both concerned with protecting their incomes against monopolistic and privileged corporations. After World War II, business mounted a carefully orchestrated and successful propaganda campaign to link inflation to unions and unreasonable wage demands. The consumers' coalition of the lower and middle classes was never restored. The immediate impact was seen in the 1948 elections, in which the polarization of working- and middle-class Americans was, according to Jensen, of almost European dimensions.[32]

Old Guard Republicans, who had once sustained an expansive notion of national government powers, had made the defense of the Constitution and the independence of the judiciary a central issue ever since the 1908 national convention. Men like Nicholas Murray, Elihu Root, Henry Cabot Lodge, and William Howard Taft had been alarmed at the willingness of Theodore Roosevelt to envisage restrictions on judges' power to issue pro-employer injunctions in labor disputes, as well as his later support for the recall of judges and of judicial decisions.

New Deal legislation, plus the constitutional changes the New Dealers sought, rang those old alarm bells. As Clyde Weed argued, the logic of Republican defeat in 1932 should have been to moderate the party stance, to move it into the center to compete effectively with the Roosevelt Democrats. But hard-line conservatives continued to control the party machinery, dictated the shape of the 1936 election campaign, and were rewarded by the conservative, small-town Republicans elected in 1938. Rural and small-town conservatives continued to dominate Republican representation in the House in the 1940s.[33]

It is important to remember that western progressives in the Republican Party who deserted Hoover in 1932 and rejoiced in Roosevelt's bold leadership in the emergency of 1933 were nevertheless opposed to the direction of the nonemergency New Deal. Ronald Feinman showed how powerful anti-statist sentiments shaped their reactions to the expansion of federal power in the late 1930s. In the 1940s, western Republicans became conservatives, while previously conservative eastern Republicans, particularly in the Senate, became a liberal nucleus sensitive to urban concerns. Bell showed how conservatives used images of totalitarianism abroad, particularly of socialistic regimentation in Britain, to force many Republicans to abandon any sympathy for statist welfare and economic measures, particularly after 1948.[34]

American farmers were capable of significant dissonance reduction between their dependence on government support and their distaste for statism. Catherine McNicol Stock pointed out that New Deal relief and farm programs "were so pervasive in the reconstruction of the economy that not a single man, woman, or child who survived the drought did so without the government's intervention. . . . Altogether, by 1939 the Roosevelt administration had spent more money in North and South Dakota than had all the preceding administrations combined: $185 million in the North, $172 million in the South. Indeed, the federal government spent more money per capita in the Dakotas than in all but six states."

Yet Stock found that despite the financial support that continues today to underpin the agricultural economy, many Dakotans remembered only the disadvantages of federal intervention during the crisis of the 1930s, and some refused to recall the period at all. According to sociologist Inda Avery, many Dakotans are "reluctant to admit that they themselves received assistance." This rural espousal of self-help, in the face of the reality of government assistance, was as powerful in the West as it was in the South. This tradition of supposed individualism lay behind the refusal of organized farmers to support the Brannan Plan, which, with its combination of guaranteed farm incomes and low food prices, seemed to offer the opportunity for an all-powerful coalition among farmers, consumers, and labor. Instead, the farmers' hostility to statism led them to be a prominent part of the anti-labor coalition.[35]

The power of the anti-statist coalition was cemented by the presence of the southern Democrats. Some, notably Harry Byrd, Carter Glass, and Josiah Bailey, had opposed the New Deal as unconstitutional from the start of the 100 Days. Others who tolerated, even welcomed, New Deal measures in the economic emergency cooled over the nonemergency direction of the New Deal. Others, identified by Ira Katznelson and others, who more positively welcomed New Deal liberalism in the South in fiscal, business regulation, farm, and welfare areas did not extend that welcome to federal intervention in labor or race relations. But the original conservatives, Glass and Bailey, saw an even greater danger in Roosevelt's Supreme Court reform. They predicted that newly appointed judges would interfere in the South's traditional patterns of race relations. It seemed a far-fetched fear in 1937, given the New Deal's caution on racial issues, but, of course, they proved prescient.[36]

As a radical, participatory decade, the 1930s seems increasingly to represent just a blip in the steady erosion of popular participation and faith in politics during the twentieth century. Yet the New Deal revolutionized the agenda of American politics. Together with World War II and the national security state, it dramatically expanded the function and size of the federal government. But that expansion needs to be set in context. As former Democratic candidate James Cox said when he turned down an invitation to join the Liberty League, "We hear a good deal about regimentation. If the control of products and of acreage is regimentation, then we have had a very mild dose of it as compared to England."[37]

Nevertheless, there were permanent new roles for the federal government. Social security through contributory taxes would be impossible, just as Roosevelt intended, for future Congresses to cut. Farm price supports would prove almost as difficult to dislodge, given the strategic position occupied by organized farmers in both the legislature and the executive. Congressmen, up for reelection every two years, soon learned that service provision and infrastructure projects would bring far more lasting political rewards for incumbents than the appointment of postmasters and the delivery of Civil War pensions had brought.

But the more systematic and social-democratic expansion of the state envisaged by New Dealers between 1937 and 1945 was held in check by a powerful anti-statist coalition. One way of describing the political system that produced this stalemate is the "deadlock of democracy"— liberal, nationally oriented politics, especially in the executive, up against a sectional coalition in Congress. Another way to describe it is as a sort of dialectical consensus around internationalism and fiscal management of economic growth, rather than redistribution of that growth.

Such a consensus was consistent with the political science literature that emphasized partisan identification rather than issues as the key determinant of voting behavior in the 1950s. Such a consensus was also compatible with the fact— one that may seem at odds with the emphasis on the power of the anti-statist coalition—that in 1963, 75 percent of Americans (in contrast to less than 33 percent thirty years later) had faith in the federal government to do the right thing. What the federal government did—social security, farm price supports, infrastructure investment in interstate highways and medical research—seemed acceptable, especially during the cold war, to most Americans. What it might do in the future was a different question.

First, what would be the political effect if economic growth could not be consistently delivered, as it could not be after 1968? What would be the reaction of the taxpaying consumer in circumstances very different from those of the 1930s?

Second, what would be the political effect of the race issue? The response of the national Democratic Party to the electoral and interest-group pressure of African Americans had already disrupted the South in 1948, when the Dixiecrats bolted in the presidential election. Just at the moment V. O. Key expressed optimism about a two-party South, about desegregation, and about black votes and the strengthening of southern liberalism, there was already evidence that such hope might be groundless.

As for the North, civil rights was a cost-free reform as long as it concerned segregation in the South. If civil rights meant the invasion of the private sphere (housing and schools) of northern whites, competition for (white) jobs, or the redistribution (as well as the increase) of tax revenues to eliminate African American economic disadvantage, the reaction of the northern white taxpayer was likely to be less benign. These dilemmas of race and economic growth would decisively shape the politics of the years after 1955.

Notes

1. Byron E. Shafer, ed., *The End of Realignment: Interpreting American Electoral Eras* (Madison, Wis., 1991), 31.
2. The classic statement of the declension thesis was Walter Dean Burnham, "The Changing Shape of the American Political Universe," *American Political Science Review* 59 (March 1965): 7–28. See also Michael McGerr, *The Decline of Popular Politics: The American North, 1865–1928* (Oxford, 1986). For a rather different formulation, see Robert H. Wiebe, "Studying American Democracy" (paper delivered at the Cambridge American history seminar, 1992), and *Self-Rule: A Cultural History of American Democracy* (Chicago, 1995), pt. 3. According to Wiebe, American democracy in the twentieth century saw an uncoupling of majoritarian and individual ideals. Democracy became a rationalized hierarchical order in which the strategically located few worked through intermediaries to influence the amorphous many. The more participatory New Deal made little difference to that underlying new order.
3. Donald Bruce Johnson and Kirk H. Porter, eds., *National Party Platforms, 1840–1972* (Urbana, Ill., [1973]), 168–93, 469–522.

4. The Seventeenth Amendment still drew complaints from Ed Meese, Ronald Reagan's attorney general, as one of the two most disastrous wrong turns taken by Americans on the road to big government in the twentieth century. The Sixteenth Amendment, providing for a federal income tax, was the other. Ed Meese comment, Conference on Federalism, Institute of United States Studies, London, May 7, 1998.

5. The anti-communist strand was viewed as idiosyncratic in the 1960s but could not be dismissed so lightly in the age of Jesse Helms and Ronald Reagan. Michael J. Heale, *American Anticommunism: Combating the Enemy Within, 1830–1970* (Baltimore, 1990), 42–121; Michael J. Heale, *McCarthy's Americans: Red Scare Politics in State and Nation, 1935–1965* (Basingstoke, 1998), 79–276; Jonathan Bell, "The Cold War and American Politics, 1946–1952" (Ph.D. diss., Cambridge University, 2000); Alex V. Goodall, "The Enemies We Have Made: The State and the American Communist Party, 1919–1949" (Master's thesis, Cambridge University, 2000).

6. For World War I, see Neil A. Wynn, *From Progressivism to Prosperity: World War I and American Society* (New York, 1986). For the best and most recent analysis of the domestic impact of World War II, see John W. Jeffries, *Wartime America: The World War II Home Front* (Chicago, 1996). On race and World War II, see Daniel Kryder, *Divided Arsenal: Race and the American State during World War II* (Cambridge, 2000). For the impact on the infrastructure of the Sun Belt, see Bruce J. Shulman, *From Cotton Belt to Sunbelt: Federal Policy, Economic Development, and the Transformation of the South, 1938–1980* (New York, 1991), 88–134; Gerald D. Nash, *The American West Transformed: The Impact of the Second World War* (Bloomington, Ind., 1985); Carl Abbott, "The Federal Presence," in *The Oxford History of the American West*, ed. Clyde A. Milner II, Carol A. O'Connor, and Martha Sandweiss (Oxford, 1994), 469–500.

7. Robert Higgs, *Crisis and Leviathan: Critical Episodes in the Growth of American Government* (New York, 1987), 123–236; Wells quoted in Daniel T. Rodgers, *Atlantic Crossings: Social Politics in a Progressive Age* (Cambridge, Mass., 1998), 54. As one journalist had observed, "nobody would have thought of calling the sleepy, rather inconsequential Southern town that Washington was in Calvin Coolidge's day the center of anything very important." An economist noted, "The only business a citizen had with the government was through the Post Office. No doubt he saw a soldier or a sailor now or then, but the government had nothing to do with the general public" (William E. Leuchtenburg, *The FDR Years: On Roosevelt and His Legacy* [New York, 1991], 284; Matthew J. Dickinson, *Bitter Harvest: FDR, Presidential Power, and the Growth of the Presidential Branch* [Cambridge, 1996]).

8. Patricia Clavin, *The Failure of Economic Diplomacy: Britain, Germany, France, and the United States, 1931–36* (Basingstoke, 1996); Michael A. Butler, *Cautious Visionary: Cordell Hull and Trade Reform, 1933–1937* (Kent, Ohio, 1998); Alan Brinkley, *The End of Reform: New Deal Liberalism in Recession and War* (New York, 1995); Alan Brinkley, "The Antimonopoly Ideal and the Liberal State: The Case of Thurman Arnold," *Journal of American History* 80 (1993): 557–79; Philip Cullis, "Antitrust in America: The Scholarly Debate, 1910–1943" (Ph.D. diss., Cambridge University, 1993), pt. 2.

9. Anthony J. Badger, *The New Deal: The Depression Years, 1933–1940* (Basingstoke, 1989), 94–117.

10. Rodgers, *Atlantic Crossings*, 52–75.

11. Ibid., 56.

12. William E. Leuchtenburg, *The Supreme Court Reborn: The Constitutional Revolution in the Age of Roosevelt* (New York, 1995), 213–36; Mark Tushnet, *The NAACP's Legal Strategy against Segregated Education, 1925–1950* (Chapel Hill, N.C., 1987). For the revisionist view on the Court in the 1930s, see Barry Cushman, *Rethinking the New Deal Court: The Structure of a Constitutional Revolution* (New York, 1998).

13. Roger Daniels, *Coming to America: A History of Immigration and Ethnicity in American Life* (New York, 1990), 287–409; Richard Franklin Bensel, *Sectionalism and American Political Development, 1880–1980* (Madison, Wis., 1984), 147–74; Kenneth T. Jackson, *Crabgrass Frontier: The Suburbanization of the United States* (New York, 1985), 190–245.

14. Rosalind Rosenberg, *Divided Lives: American Women in the Twentieth Century* (London, 1993), 54–62, 69–73; Steven M. Buechler, *The Transformation of the Woman Suffrage Movement: The Case of Illinois, 1850–1920* (New Brunswick, N.J., 1986), 148–215.

15. Anna Harvey, *Votes without Leverage: Women in American Electoral Politics, 1920–1970* (Cambridge, 1998), 2–6; Kristi Anderson, *After Suffrage: Women in Partisan and Electoral Politics before the New Deal* (Chicago, 1996), 141–42, 159–60; Susan M. Hartmann, *From Mainstream to Margin: American Women and Politics since 1960* (New York, 1989), 7–17.

16. Harvey, *Votes without Leverage*, 6–9; Anderson, *After Suffrage*, 141–70; Susan M. Hartmann, *The Home Front and Beyond: American Women in the 1940s* (Boston, 1982), 143–62; Hartmann, *From Mainstream to Margin*, 7–17.

17. Paul Kleppner, "Were Women to Blame? Female Suffrage and Voter Turn-out," *Journal of Interdisciplinary History* 12 (1982): 621–43; Anderson, *After Suffrage*, 49–70; Hartmann, *From Mainstream to Margin*, 7; Gerald Gamm, *The Making of New Deal Democrats: Voting Behavior and Realignment in Boston, 1920–1940* (Chicago, 1989), 104, 149–50, 162–66. For conservative opposition to suffrage in the South, see Elna C. Green, *Southern Strategies: Southern Women and the Woman Suffrage Question* (Chapel Hill, N.C., 1997).

18. Harvey, *Votes without Leverage*, 1–22, 209–37.

19. Susan Ware, *Beyond Suffrage: Women in the New Deal* (Cambridge, Mass., 1981); Susan Ware, *Holding Their Own: American Women in the 1930s* (Schenectady, N.Y., 1982); Blanche Weisen Cook, *Eleanor Roosevelt*, vol. 2, *1933–1938* (New York, 1999); Doris Kearns Goodwin, *No Ordinary Time: Franklin and Eleanor Roosevelt: The Home Front in World War II* (New York, 1994); Hartmann, *Home Front and Beyond*, 143–86, 209–16.

20. John D. Buenker, *Urban Liberalism and Progressive Reform* (New York, 1978); Samuel Lubell, *The Future of American Politics*, 3d ed. (New York, 1965), 43–68; Lyle Dorsett, *Franklin D. Roosevelt and the City Bosses* (Port Washington, N.Y., 1977); Harvard Sitkoff, *The New Deal for Blacks: The Emergence of Civil Rights as a National Issue* (New York, 1978), 84–101; Mark Gelfand, *A Nation of Cities: The Federal Government and Urban America, 1933–1965* (New York, 1975), 23–70.

21. James T. Patterson, *Congressional Conservatism and the New Deal: The Growth of the Conservative Coalition in Congress, 1933–1939* (Lexington, Ky., 1967), 250–87; Tony Badger, "Local Politics and Party Realignment in the Late Thirties: The Failure of the New Deal," *Storia Nordamericana* 6, nos. 1–2 (1989): 69–90.

22. Patterson, *Congressional Conservatism*, 288–337.

23. Bernard Sternsher, "The Emergence of a New Deal Party System: A Problem in Historical Analysis of Voter Behavior," *Journal of Interdisciplinary History* 6 (1975): 127–49; Kristi Anderson, *Creation of a Democratic Majority, 1928–1936* (Chicago, 1979); Robert S. Erikson and Kent L. Tedin, "The 1928–36 Partisan Realignment: The Case for the Conversion Thesis," *American Political Science Review* 75 (1981): 951–62; Bernard Sternsher, "The New Deal Party System: A Reappraisal," *Journal of Interdisciplinary History* 15 (1984): 53–81; James E. Campbell, "Voter Mobilization and the New Deal Realignment: The Contributions of Conversion and Mobilization to Partisan Change," *Western Political Quarterly* 38 (1985): 357–76.

24. David B. Craig, *After Wilson: The Struggle for the Democratic Party, 1920–1934* (Chapel Hill, N.C., 1992), 112–204, 225–47.

25. Gamm, *Making of New Deal Democrats*, 161–82; Sternsher, "New Deal Party System," 53.

26. Lizabeth Cohen, *Making a New Deal: Industrial Workers in Chicago, 1919–1939* (Cambridge, 1990), 251–89; Meg Jacobs, "The Politics of Purchasing Power: Political Economy, Consumption, Politics and State-building in the United States, 1909–1959" (Ph.D. diss., University of Virginia, 1998), chaps. 2, 3.

27. Barry D. Karl, *The Uneasy State: The United States from 1915 to 1945* (Chicago, 1983), 155–81; Sidney Milkis, *The President and the Parties: The Transformation of the American Party System since the New Deal* (New York, 1993); John W. Jeffries, "A 'Third New Deal'? Liberal Policy and the American State, 1937–1945," *Journal of Policy History* 8 (1996): 387–409.

28. Alan Brinkley, "The New Deal and the Idea of the State," in *The Rise and Fall of the New Deal Order*, ed. Steve Fraser and Gary Gerstle (Princeton, N.J., 1989), 109; Alan Brinkley, *The End of Reform: New Deal Liberalism in Recession and War* (New York, 1995), 269; Numan V. Bartley, *The New South, 1945–1980: The Story of the South's Modernization* (Baton Rouge, 1995), 38–73.

29. Meg Jacobs, "'How about Some Meat'?: The Office of Price Administration, Consumption Politics, and State Building from the Bottom Up, 1941–1946," *Journal of American History* 84 (1997): 910–941; Jacobs, "Politics of Purchasing Power," chaps. 4, 5.

30. Bell, "Cold War and American Politics," chaps. 1, 2; Tony Badger, "Whatever Happened to Roosevelt's 'New Generation of Southerners'?" in *The Roosevelt Years: New Essays on the United States, 1933–1945*, ed. Robert A. Garson and Stuart Kidd (Edinburgh, 1999), 122–38.

31. Craig, *After Wilson*, 248–74.

32. Howell J. Harris, "The Snares of Liberalism? Politicians, Bureaucrats, and the Shaping of Federal Labour Relations Policy in the United States, c. 1915–1947," in *Shop Floor Bargaining and the State: Historical and Comparative Perspectives*, ed. Steven Tolliday and Jonathan Zeitlin (Cambridge, 1985), 148–91; Jacobs, "Politics of Purchasing Power," chap. 6; Richard Jensen, "The Last Party System: Decay of Consensus, 1932–1980," in *The Evolution of American Electoral Systems*, ed. Paul Kleppner et al. (Westport, Conn., 1981), 203–41.

33. David Potash, "The Origins of Conservative Republicanism" (Ph.D. diss., Cambridge University, 1998); Clyde P. Weed, *The Nemesis of Reform: The Republican Party during the New Deal* (New York, 1994).

34. Ronald L. Feinman, *Twilight of Progressivism: The Western Republican Senators and the New Deal* (Baltimore, 1980), 48–210; Nicol C. Rae, *The Decline and Fall of the*

8. The Rise of Rights and Rights Consciousness in American Politics, 1930s–1970s

James T. Patterson

Searching for a title to an essay on American politics between the 1930s and 1980, many writers might choose something like "From Roosevelt to Reagan: The Rise and Fall of American Liberalism in Mid-Twentieth-Century America." My title, however, has no presidents in it, and my essay tells a different story. It focuses less on presidents or political rhetoric than on long-term structural developments, notably the rise of interest groups—old as well as new—and of an ever-growing state and its bureaucracies and courts.

Reflecting a great increase in popular rights consciousness, these expanding institutions managed to protect a broad range of civil rights, civil liberties, and entitlements. As a result, many policies crafted by liberals, far from falling, were standing tall as bulwarks of a wide-ranging administrative state in 1980, though not always in the shape that their creators had anticipated.[1] To tell this story, I begin by sketching some of the major political changes and continuities during these fifty years and then backtrack to focus on the most important plot line of the narrative: the rise of rights and rights consciousness.

A Complex Picture of Continuity and Change

The changes are difficult to miss. They took place gradually, of course, but most dramatically in three bursts: during the mid-1930s, during World War II, and again during the mid to late 1960s. In all three periods, large structural developments—mainly economic or war-related—drove notable transformations, among them a considerable expansion of authority at all levels of American government. Most importantly, economic growth and unimaginable affluence after 1940 greatly widened popular rights consciousness, thereby encouraging the rise of numerous and clamorous interest groups and bureaucracies and bringing the courts into unprecedented activism in many areas of policy. My account of key changes, therefore, emphasizes the role of economic and international forces and stresses the increasingly pluralistic, bureaucratic, and litigious politics that emerged over time.[2]

Yet important continuities are also a major part of this tale. Generally, these can be called ideological and necessarily take us beyond primarily structural models of political change. Some of these ideological forces were—and are—conservative. Deeply rooted in the American historical experience prior to the 1930s, they are familiar to any student of American history: popular resistance to substantial growth of the state, especially when it seeks to expand welfare for the "undeserving"; distrust of authority, governmental and otherwise; and faith in localism, federalism, and the separation of powers as outlined in the Constitution. Amid all the change that transformed American politics in these years—and it was in many ways dramatic—these ideas remained strong, thereby ensuring that the United States continued to feature an unusually decentralized polity compared with most industrialized nations in the world.[3]

As Samuel Huntington argues, Americans have also been prone to display what he calls "moral passion" in a quest for a more egalitarian society. Rooted in the ideals of the Declaration of Independence, this passion (Huntington, like Gunnar Myrdal, labels it the "American Creed") exploded with special intensity during the 1960s, thereby exposing the limitations of consensus models of American politics that had captivated many scholars during the 1950s. Indeed, social and political conflict seemed for a time in the late 1960s to threaten basic institutions. But it was conflict within limits. Most of the protesters who agitated for change in the 1960s were neither anti-American nor advocates of social leveling. What they expressed was mainly a moral passion aimed at forcing the nation to live up to its democratic ideals.[4]

Anti-communism was another durable ideological continuity during much of this era. From the mid-1940s, when the cold war began, into the 1980s, when Ronald Reagan drew hurrahs for branding the Soviet Union an "evil empire," a bipartisan anti-communist center held with regard to foreign policy. Not even the enormous miscalculations that dragged the nation into the morass of Vietnam could shake these ideas, which drew much of their staying power from the anti-appeasement, "no more Munichs" mentality that arose after 1940. Even in 1968, when the disaster of Vietnam was easily apparent, two of the three major presidential candidates, Richard Nixon and George Wallace, devoted enthusiastic effort to deriding anti-war activists and to highlighting the dangers of international communism. The third candidate, Hubert Humphrey, never swam far from the big muddy wake of Lyndon Johnson.

Anti-communist pressures also influenced domestic policy making, especially during the most frenzied Red scare years between 1947 and 1954, when liberals dared not press hard for such "socialistic" programs as national health insurance. Moreover, the primarily right-wing forces promoting the Red scare did not disappear with the censure of Senator Joe McCarthy in 1954. They remained a lively presence in American politics in the 1960s—witness the enthusiasm that many voters showed for Wallace at the time—and into the Reagan years of the 1980s. At many points during these years, liberal office-seekers continued to cover themselves, lest they be knocked over by anti-communist rhetoric and activity.[5]

Perhaps the strongest ideological continuity during much of this era, however, was the staying power of liberal—not social democratic—ideas and policies.

These liberal ideas rested on that firmest of modern American faiths: although the federal government should be limited in size and scope, it should also help individuals to enjoy equal opportunity.[6] Franklin D. Roosevelt's New Deal in the 1930s determined that government must engage in this process. This idea took firmer root over time and flowered in the Great Society programs of Lyndon Johnson.

Some of this blossoming was too fast for people, prompting a backlash that seemed threatening to many liberal observers in the late 1970s and early 1980s. The journalist Theodore White, writing in the immediate aftermath of what he called Reagan's "landslide" presidential victory in 1980, concluded in 1982 that American politics—by which he meant liberal politics—had come to "the end of an era."[7] In retrospect, it seems that White exaggerated. But he expressed a generally accurate and widely held view concerning the strength of liberalism during the nearly fifty years before that.

Indeed, the long-range thrust of American political preferences between 1932 and the late 1960s—and of most public policies—was in a liberal direction. And liberal policies established in those years did not die in the 1970s.[8] Conservative efforts notwithstanding, the years from 1932 into the late 1970s were not an era in which liberal programs rose and then fell. Rather, these were years of considerable continuity, in which a growing number of federal efforts became bureaucratically well established and judicially well protected.

We may also consign political ideas on both the Right and the Left during these years to the somewhat dim edges of the political spectrum. Although political conservatives were frequently able to block new liberal legislation—notably, between 1937 and 1963, and again between 1966 and 1980—they never came close to dismantling the New Deal or its subsequent expansion. In 1964–1965, they were powerless before the legislative juggernaut that Johnson engineered. Thereafter, they could not stem the near-inexorable growth of public authority and of bureaucratic and judicial interventions on behalf of a lengthening list of rights and entitlements.

The Left between 1930 and 1980 was weaker still. As David Plotke emphasized, it is wishful thinking on the part of left-oriented scholars to think that FDR, for instance, missed an opportunity to restructure American economic relationships or political alignments in the 1930s.[9] On the contrary, socialist or social-democratic ideas and programs never had much of a chance during the Great Depression in the United States. The same may be said of the 1940s and thereafter.[10] Notwithstanding gusts of anti-corporate rhetoric that ruffled political life from time to time, most reformers from the 1930s into the 1970s did not call for social democratic programs that would have significantly expanded progressive taxation or redistributed income or resources. Instead, they expressed liberal ideas and called for the expansion of economic opportunity, so that the American dream of socioeconomic mobility might become a reality.

Liberals—and others—lamented a number of discouraging political trends during these years. Voting by eligible Americans plummeted after 1940, especially among the young.[11] Despite the great spread of educational attainment after 1945, even those who voted seemed as ignorant as earlier voters about many aspects of government, which was becoming more complex and harder to fathom.[12] Political parties fell apart in an age of electoral "dealignment," thereby (some thought) undermining orderly, productive policy formation.[13] Organized interest groups developed greater power. Alonzo Hamby bewails the power during these years of a "conglomerate of special interests . . . [that had] little support in the larger body politic and no compelling vision of a general public interest."[14] Reforms of these flaws in the 1970s had little practical effect.

Perhaps the most common scholarly lament about American politics and policies during these fifty years—a lament mainly from the Left—is that the United States only slowly and fitfully constructed a social safety net. There is no doubt that this was the case: although the New Deal ushered in the beginnings of an American welfare state, public spending for social welfare from all levels of government, education excepted, continued to be consistently lower as a percentage of gross domestic product than it was in most other industrial countries. By 1980, it was one-sixth below the average in such nations.[15] It also seems clear that income inequality remained more pronounced in the United States during this era than in most other industrialized areas of the world.

But without succumbing to romantic nostalgia—who can forget McCarthyism or Jim Crow?—liberals can find much to celebrate in the years between 1930 and 1970. For many marginal groups, notably African Americans, this was a time of extraordinary political as well as economic progress.[16] By the early 1970s, many Americans—blacks, the elderly, the welfare poor, political radicals, alleged criminals—enjoyed benefits, entitlements, legal protections, civil rights, and civil liberties that would scarcely have been imaginable in 1930, or even in 1960. In the early 1970s, other groups—environmentalists, women, the handicapped, and advocates of consumer protection—also secured greater protection and support from legislation, federal bureaucracies, and the courts.

This was also a time—notably, between World War II and the early 1970s—that huge numbers of people, especially in the rapidly expanding middle classes, developed grand and growing popular expectations about the future, both of the nation's salutary role in world affairs and of the socioeconomic possibilities of coming generations. For the millions of Americans who moved up the social ladder and came to enjoy the good life, these became realistic, achieved expectations. Economic growth drove many of these developments. As the pie enlarged, there was much more to share.

But, to repeat, less deterministic forces also mattered. For example, the surge of egalitarian ideas—many of them unleashed by the civil rights movement—was a key to the advance in the early 1960s of both liberal policies and a broader rights consciousness that gripped a host of claimant groups. So it was that a fortuitous combination of forces—of economic progress and moral fervor—worked together to promote significant, often beneficial changes for many previously marginalized people. The nation's political institutions, often maligned, ultimately proved capable of accommodating many of these changes.

The New Deal and the Rudiments of a Welfare State

The first of the three major bursts of political and policy change between 1930 and 1980 occurred during the outpouring of New Deal domestic programs, almost all of them enacted during Roosevelt's first term. These are well known and need no listing here.[17] Some of them, such as the Securities and Exchange Commission, Social Security, the Wagner Act, and the Fair Labor Standards Act, thereafter stood as bedrocks of American social and economic policy. Breaking significantly from the past, the United States began developing a welfare state.

Liberal and left-leaning critics of the New Deal have complained that New Deal policy making was excessively cautious and opportunistic. Looking at what was actually accomplished in the 1930s, these arguments at first seem persuasive. The New Deal did not enact more progressive taxation or focus on the claims of women, migrant workers, blacks, and other minority groups. Old-age pensions authorized under Social Security depended on regressive payroll taxes and were initially scheduled to start only in 1942. Roosevelt, a fiscal conservative, shrank from applying deficit spending on a large scale and did not end the depression.

A second and related criticism of federal policy in the 1930s deplores the paternalism, though mostly unintended, that stemmed from the creation of such landmark agencies as the National Labor Relations Board (NLRB). Workers, it is argued, gradually became overdependent on the NLRB and other forms of government protection, thereby losing much of the passion that had transformed the labor movement in the late 1930s.[18] Sidney Milkis, among others, has taken this argument further, concluding that although the New Deal increased the size and scope of the state in order to cope with the domestic crisis, the growth consisted of top-down, administrative-bureaucratic expansion and benefit allocation that weakened grassroots activism over time. "The New Deal's support for programmatic rights," Milkis maintains, "expanded entitlements at the expense of civic associations and practices."[19]

Michael Schudson adopted a similar position, emphasizing that the New Deal did much to promote the *electoral* success of the Democratic Party but in the long run weakened its *organizational* force. Thanks to the New Deal, the presidency and newly created federal agencies grew in importance, but the political parties, already fragile, began to fall into a long, ultimately near-fatal decline. What

Roosevelt created, in short, was a larger administrative state that sheltered growing numbers of bureaucrats who offered entitlements that made people dependent. Something vital—a face-to-face world of political activism—became a
long-run casualty of this process.[20]

Arguments such as these, enjoying the benefits of hindsight, are beguiling.
Many of the agencies and programs created in the 1930s indeed grew larger and
more entrenched over time.[21] People increasingly looked to Washington bureaucracies—and to the courts—for the maintenance and expansion of entitlements. The parties atrophied.[22] Moreover, the state did grow somewhat in the
1930s. Public spending for domestic purposes between 1925 and 1940 increased
from $650 million to $4 billion.[23]

But many of these long-range legacies of the New Deal were hardly apparent
in 1940. On the contrary, Roosevelt's policies seemed at the time to strengthen
the foundations of the Democratic Party. The social welfare policies of the New
Deal attracted to the party millions of working-class people and minorities who
had earlier voted Republican or (in most cases) had not voted at all. New Deal
patronage strengthened Democratic urban machines that stimulated larger
turnouts in many cities. The result of these changes was a new, more class-based
electoral realignment of political parties.[24] And the Republican Party, too, rallied
after 1937, becoming successful as early as the congressional elections of 1946. It
would have been difficult indeed in the 1940s, or even in the 1950s, to predict
the unraveling of political parties that was to escalate in the 1960s.

It would have been equally difficult in 1940 to credit—or blame—the New
Dealers for erecting a greatly expanded state. Lack of governmental administrative capacity, long a feature of the American system, continued to present
Roosevelt and his aides with formidable obstacles that they could not easily
overcome amid the crisis of the depression. The fate of the National Recovery
Administration, which collapsed in part because of administrative limitations,
amply demonstrated these obstacles. Defeat by Congress in 1938 of FDR's executive reorganization plan further revealed the administrative constraints
under which he was forced to operate. And Roosevelt never had much revenue
at his disposal; in the 1930s, only around 3 percent of the population paid personal income taxes. In comparison with other industrial nations, the United
States remained a highly decentralized polity before World War II.[25]

Although the constitutional revolution of the late 1930s legitimized considerable expansion of federal economic management in the postwar years, it is perverse to describe the New Deal as a major exercise in bureaucracy building. Conservatives exaggerated greatly when they sputtered about drowning in
"alphabet soup." In one such respect, however, Roosevelt was extraordinarily
bold: setting up large-scale work-relief programs to assist the unemployed. No
other nation traveled nearly so far along this path. But the Work Projects Administration (WPA) became the target of determined conservative opposition in

the late 1930s, and no president since then has dared to propose such a bold effort. Until 1940, when the state began expanding rapidly to promote military preparedness, America's public bureaucracies remained small.

It is also difficult to see the New Deal as a great exercise in entitlement giving. During World War II, Roosevelt issued a clarion call for an economic bill of rights. Everyone, he said, should have the right to a "useful and remunerative job," "a decent home," "adequate medical care," and a "good education." In calling for these blessings, he articulated an emergent rights consciousness that had grown in response to the New Deal. Later, these ideas gained strength in the United States. But in 1944, FDR was engaging mainly in wishful thinking: he did not expect people to demand a wide range of governmental entitlements.[26] Indeed, entitlements established in the 1930s were modest, consisting mainly of payments to large commercial farmers and of pittances that went to some of the indigent aged and blind and to a handful of mothers with dependent children. Given the extraordinary suffering that Americans endured during the 1930s, it is striking how little bureaucracy-building and entitlement-giving took place.

Still, if change seemed relatively modest as of 1940, it is clear in retrospect that the New Deal established the foundations of a welfare state and of bureaucracies that grew greatly in size and reach over time. Roosevelt, personifying the rise of humanitarian government, became a hero to millions of people. Core liberal ideas of the New Deal—that the state had a duty to help the needy and to enable people to achieve equality of opportunity—were to prove enduring in the years to come.

World War II and the Legitimization of Big Government

In some ways, the second burst of governmental change between 1930 and 1980—during World War II—altered relatively little. This was nowhere clearer than in social welfare policy. Thanks in part to collective suffering during the war, Britain greatly expanded its social safety net. In the United States, however, New Deal emergency programs such as the WPA and the Civilian Conservation Corps were terminated. Congress turned a deaf ear to proposals for federal health insurance, aid to education, or regional planning. Moreover, there were no important changes during the 1940s in the Social Security program enacted in 1935. Taxes to support old-age pensions remained low, at 1 percent for both employees and employers, and benefits failed to keep pace with inflation. Millions of needy people, notably domestic and agricultural workers, continued to be uncovered. Many of these people were African Americans, of whom more than 50 percent lived in poverty throughout the decade.

During the early 1940s, moreover, liberals seemed to lose a little of the fire they had breathed in the mid-1930s. I would not go as far as Alan Brinkley, who titled his book on liberalism between 1937 and 1945 *The End of Reform*. On the contrary, American liberals had never been as social democratic during the 1930s as his title implies, nor did they throw in the towel after 1940. I agree, however, that many liberals, especially after 1950, showed less interest in large-scale governmental planning, trust-busting, and public welfare policies than they had in the 1930s. Instead, they relied primarily on ideas about the capacity of fiscal policy—notably, deficit spending in hard times—to remedy economic ills.[27] These ideas, aptly labeled "growth liberalism" by some scholars, have dominated much liberal policy making in the United States since 1945.[28]

Liberals faced strong opposition from a bipartisan coalition of conservatives in Congress. This opposition was most determined among congressmen and senators from predominantly rural areas in both the North and the South, some of whom benefited from malapportionment into the mid-1960s.[29] But in urban areas, too, liberals often encountered resistance. As early as the 1940s, whites in cities facing huge in-migrations of African Americans fought tenaciously against desegregation of housing or schools.[30] The efforts of these and other people were largely responsible for holding back many liberal programs after 1937. During the 1940s and 1950s, conservatives grew feistier still. Although they never seriously sought to dismantle landmark New Deal programs such as Social Security, they succeeded in amending the Wagner Act in 1947, and they often frustrated liberal policy makers, at least until 1964.

During the 1940s, corporate-based programs moved into the vacuum caused by the absence of new public policies, thereby establishing for the rest of the century a private role in social welfare that was far greater than in western European nations. In 1940, only 8 percent of American firms offered companywide pension plans, and 36 percent offered some form of health insurance. By 1946, these percentages had risen to 23 and 68, respectively. The number of workers who subscribed to private health insurance leaped from 12.3 million in 1940 to 76.6 million in 1950.[31]

Still, the war years stimulated an enormous, unprecedented, and in some ways irreversible growth of the federal government, a growth that could not have been anticipated by even the most avid New Dealers in the 1930s. This expansion was most obvious in the realm of military policies, which also contributed mightily to the power of the presidency in American life. But the transformation was broad in a host of ways, bringing millions of Americans for the first time into direct contact with the federal government. The number of people who received Social Security, for instance, leaped from 220,000 in 1940 to 1.5 million in 1945 and to 3.5 million in 1950. The number who paid (federal) personal income taxes mushroomed from 3.7 million in 1930 to 14.6 million in 1940 to 49.9 million in 1945. Federal spending jumped from $2.9 billion in 1930 to $9.6 billion in 1940 to $95.2 billion in 1945. Federal expenditures as part of the gross national product (GNP) increased from 8 percent in 1939 to 47 percent in 1945, the highest percentage in U.S. history, then or since.[32]

Bartholomew Sparrow, who has written a book on the influence of World War II on the American state, concludes that the war worked a "virtual revolution in United States domestic policies."[33] Republican gains in 1946 did not succeed in reversing the tide. On the contrary, the Democratic national platform of 1948 was easily the most progressive in the party's history prior to 1964. It called for repeal of the Taft-Hartley labor law of 1947, asserted governmental responsibility for the stability of the economy, backed federal health insurance and aid to public education, and for the first time called for passage of civil rights legislation. Its foreign policy planks endorsed strongly internationalist policies aimed at blocking the Soviets in the cold war. The platform revealed a central legacy of the war years: the political legitimization of big government.

President Harry Truman did not manage to get many domestic goals approved during his seven years in office. Indeed, cold war issues frequently dominated America's political agenda until the early 1960s. Nor did Truman press much for redistributive goals; in the 1940s, as throughout the post-1930s era, liberals mainly stood for policies to promote greater opportunity, not greater equality of income. Moreover, reconversion to a peacetime economy shrank federal expenditures by more than half, from $95.2 billion to $43.1 billion between 1945 and 1950. But this sum was still many times higher than it had been in 1940. A good deal of the shrinkage between 1945 and 1950, moreover, occurred in military spending. The outlay for domestic purposes—much of it provided to veterans under the GI Bill of Rights of 1944—nearly tripled during these five years.[34] And in 1950, Congress finally liberalized Social Security: average benefits were increased by 70 percent, and 7.5 million new employees, including regularly employed domestic and farm workers, were made eligible for pensions. Gaps in the nation's social service net, at least for the elderly, were finally beginning to close.[35]

The expansion of Social Security, then and later the government's most far-reaching social program, revealed one more salient aspect of American politics that took firm hold by 1950 and became more obvious thereafter: without the support of strong interest groups, new social policies were not likely to get through Congress. As Daniel Rodgers has shown, enactment of Social Security in 1935 depended on the spread in the United States of transatlantic ideas dating back several decades.[36] It also owed its passage, however, to organized pressure from the elderly, many of them supporters in the 1930s of the Townsend movement for old-age pensions. Similarly strong pressure from the elderly, which became more intense over time, had much to do with the reform of 1950, as it did with many subsequent expansions.

Organized interest groups not only secured the political inviolability of Social Security. More generally, they helped prevent conservatives from paring back a variety of additional domestic programs—unemployment insurance, welfare, minimum wages, and the like—in the 1940s and 1950s. Accordingly, many of the liberal programs that had passed in the 1930s survived, even during the politically more conservative 1950s. They had become an apparently permanent part of a larger, more bureaucratized administrative state. No one made this reality more clear than President Eisenhower, who was personally very cool to most of these programs. He recognized, however, that he would assail them at his political peril. He explained to his conservative brother, "Should any political party attempt to abolish Social Security, unemployment insurance, and eliminate labor laws and farm programs, you would not hear of that party again in our political history."[37]

The Great Society and the Birth of a New Politics

As late as 1960, shortly before the third great burst of political change, two key, related political forces of the near future were still to achieve prominence. The first was the explosion of moral passion, driven strongly by the civil rights movement, which increased rights consciousness in the culture, helped to multiply the number of interest groups, and thereby transformed political activism. By 1970, for instance, not only African Americans but also women, gay people, environmentalists, consumer advocates, and various ethnic minorities had become well organized and were clamoring for governmental attention. For a brief time in the late 1960s and early 1970s, there was even a vocal, visible National Welfare Rights Organization.

Prior to 1960, however, these groups were scarcely to be heard in politics. As a sign of those earlier times, politicians, knowing that they need not fear retribution from the electorate or the media, casually referred to the homeless as "bums," "drunks," and "psychos."[38] Voters who had come of age in the 1930s, moreover, tended to retain durable loyalties to either the Democratic or the Republican Party. The percentage of voters who called themselves independents— mostly young people—rose slowly, from around 15 percent in the 1940s to 24 percent by the early 1960s.[39] As far as most politicians could tell in 1960, the great electoral realignment of the 1930s was holding fairly firm outside of a few western states. It seemed a serene, largely unchanging time.[40]

The second force that as of 1960 still lay largely in the future was structural: the fantastic performance of the economy. Following a recession that ended in 1961, the decade witnessed uninterrupted economic expansion. Economic growth between 1962 and 1965 was nothing short of sensational, at 5 percent or more per year. The poverty rate, at around 22 percent of the population in 1962, fell sharply to an all-time low of 11 percent by 1973. Liberal rhetoric to the contrary, these changes probably owed little to purposeful government policies. But liberal Democrats were naturally quick to claim credit for their expertise—it was an age of highly confident social science—and for the spread of affluence, which in turn prompted rising popular expectations about the government's capacity to ensure an even rosier future.

The combination of economic growth, moral passion, rising rights consciousness, and higher expectations from government played beautifully into the large and eager hands of Lyndon Johnson in the mid-1960s. Johnson, an extraordinarily skillful manager of Congress, proved that individuals can make a considerable difference in history. Driving hard for his so-called Great Society domestic programs, he secured from Capitol Hill a burst of liberal legislation that rivaled the output of FDR's first term: the War on Poverty, Medicare and Medicaid, immigration reform, and passage at last of general federal aid to public schools. Above all, Congress enacted two historic civil rights acts that did away with Jim Crow and guaranteed the voting rights of minorities. The Republican Party, damaged by the bizarre presidential candidacy of Barry Goldwater in 1964, seemed helpless before this onslaught of liberal policy making.

Johnson's programs, like FDR's, were generally liberal rather than redistributive in a social democratic sense. The War on Poverty, for instance, was a classic example of American liberal policy making; it aimed to enhance equality of opportunity, not establish equality of condition—to set up *doors* such as Head Start through which the poor might pass and move ahead, not *floors* of guaranteed income on which they could stand. The War on Poverty provided services, not cash, in the quintessentially American hope that services—and growth in employment—could, in the long run, render welfare almost unnecessary. The civil rights acts had immediate and lasting effects on American race relations. With Social Security, they rank as the most important domestic laws in the twentieth-century history of the United States. And most of the other Great Society programs remained on the books and expanded in the years ahead; it is highly misleading to label the years 1965 to 1980 as representing a sharp turn to the right or as a decisive repudiation of liberal programs.

Many of Johnson's laws, however, quickly aroused debate. Critics said correctly that Medicare and Medicaid would cost far more than had been anticipated, that public schools needed much more than money, and that the War on Poverty—never really more than a skirmish—was wildly oversold. All these laws, especially immigration reform (which resulted in great increases in the numbers of foreigners who came to America), thus had large and unforeseen consequences in later years.[41] Drawing on criticisms like these, the GOP scored major gains in congressional elections as early as 1966, and in 1968, Richard Nixon won the presidency.

By the 1970s, the faith in government that people had demonstrated in 1964–1965 had dissipated. In 1964, only 43 percent of Americans had thought that the federal government was "too big." By 1976, following the loss in Vietnam and Watergate, more than 58 percent thought so.[42] Even more skeptical responses concerning governmental competence greeted pollsters in later years. This decline of popular faith in the capacity of the state to do good things was one of the most lasting legacies of the 1960s and early 1970s.

President Johnson's mode of leadership contributed to a second lasting legacy: the remarkably rapid decomposition of the political parties. Eager to enhance his personal presidential power, he largely ignored the Democratic Party, which fell into disarray by 1968.[43] It grew so weak that in 1976, Jimmy Carter, a no-name, set up his own organization and grabbed the presidential nomination. The Republican Party too became less hierarchical. In the same year, former governor Ronald Reagan of California nearly took the GOP nomination away from incumbent president Gerald Ford.

Larger structural forces abetted this dramatic trend: the already decaying state of Democratic urban machines, whose access to patronage had fallen dramatically after dissolution of the WPA; intraparty polarizations caused by conflict over the Vietnam War; the escalating spread of highly rights-conscious, issue-oriented interest groups; and the growing tendency of voters, dismayed by both parties after 1965, to split tickets and to call themselves independents.[44] By the early 1970s, some two-thirds of voters split their tickets, compared with the one-fourth who had done so in the 1940s.[45]

The ubiquitous and powerful impact of television especially facilitated these changes. First of all, television promoted the rise of telegenic candidates such as John F. Kennedy, who could appeal beyond party. More significantly—neither Johnson nor Nixon could be said to be telegenic—television encouraged statewide and national candidates to ignore their party organizations and run their own campaigns, largely through ads and sound bites on the screen. Whether this was a good thing for American political life will forever generate debate; surely it was good for candidates with money.[46] But there is no doubt that television further weakened grassroots party organizing and accelerated the emergence of candidate-centered politics in the United States.

Changes in party procedures further advanced these tendencies. As the parties grew weaker, activists managed to substitute primaries for conventions; the latter had previously enabled party leaders to maintain some control over their tickets. By 1980, thirty states had true Democratic presidential primaries, and thirty-one had Republican primaries. These selected 76 percent of Democratic delegates and 65 percent of Republican delegates to the party conventions. By contrast, only seventeen states in 1968 had had Democratic presidential primaries, choosing 40 percent of the delegates, and fifteen had had Republican primaries, accounting for 43 percent of delegates.[47]

When the Democrats staggered forth from their fratricide in 1968, they also established new quotas for convention delegates that radically transformed their nominating base. Thereafter, the presidential Democratic Party became a shaky coalition of well-educated, upper-middle-class liberals—a "new class," they were called—and of blacks, Hispanics, feminists, environmentalists, and others on the left of the political spectrum. The more working-class-based Democratic electoral coalition of the 1930s and 1940s no longer held up well in presidential elections.[48]

The decomposition of parties did not, however, mean that the national party organizations atrophied. On the contrary, they professionalized and grew in size, hiring a wide range of consultants, pollsters, and media experts.[49] Using modernized money-raising techniques such as direct mailings, these professionals took advantage of the absence of meaningful controls on campaign expenditures and pulled in vast sums of money. In these ways, too, grassroots political activism lost importance.

Nor did the decomposition amount to a partisan realignment on the scale of those of the 1890s or the 1930s. Rather, it led to a *de*alignment, in which some groups—especially middle-class white southerners, religious conservatives and fundamentalists, and many working-class northerners—sheared off from the Democratic Party to vote Republican, principally in presidential elections. What realignment there was occurred mainly at this level, where Republican candidates for the White House scored well until 1992.[50] Democratic congressional candidates, in contrast, continued to highlight their support of social programs from the New Deal and Great Society, such as Social Security and Medicare; to employ the advantages of incumbency; and, in most cases, to outpoll Republican conservatives. They controlled Capitol Hill throughout much of the late 1960s, 1970s, and 1980s, thereby creating many years of divided, highly partisan government.

The Coming of a Rights Revolution

Arresting as these changes were, they were less significant than other dramatic developments during the late 1960s—a pivotal time of political transformation in recent American history. One key change involved the political agenda. As late as the 1960 election, the most contested national issues were familiar: the state of the economy and the cold war. In 1964, thanks to the civil rights movement, racial issues also rose to the top of the agenda. And by the early 1970s, a host of sociocultural issues—women's rights, environmentalism, prayer in the schools, rising crime, out-of-wedlock pregnancy, declining SAT scores, welfare dependency, concerns over rising immigration—greatly expanded the number of controversial items on the agenda of American politics. The salience of such sociocultural concerns was in some ways reminiscent of the Progressive Era, a time of high immigration when some of these same issues—mainly on the state level—had also preoccupied the public.[51]

Perhaps the most stunning changes during the late 1960s and early 1970s arose from the rights consciousness that had been growing rapidly since the early 1960s.[52] This rise sparked three big changes in American government. First, it led to what Hugh Davis Graham accurately called an "explosion in public law litigation," greatly broadening the role of the federal courts in American life.

Cases involving civil rights alone—affirmative action, employment set-asides, and the like—increased from 300 in 1960 to 40,000 by 1985.[53] Many of these cases reached the Supreme Court, which, following the landmark *Brown v. Board of Education* decision of 1954, issued a series of momentous rulings calling for the expansion and protection of rights. Blacks, political radicals, alleged criminals, welfare recipients, and many other out-groups hailed the liberalism of the Court under Chief Justice Earl Warren. Even under the more conservative Warren Burger, who succeeded Warren in 1969, the Court continued for a while along this liberal trail.

Between 1969 and 1973, it delivered a number of important decisions—favoring court-ordered busing to achieve racial balance in the schools, approving affirmative action in employment, and legalizing abortion rights, for instance— that the majority of democratically elected legislators would not have dared to support. Federal judges, indeed, sparked a due process revolution, interpreting vague legislative language in ways that led to the bureaucratic expansion of governmental activity on behalf of many well-organized groups. In so doing, these judges became eager partners in the growth of the administrative state.[54] Then and for many years thereafter, judges also oversaw the decisions of hundreds of school districts in order to prevent or curb racially discriminatory practices.[55] As conservatives were quick to point out, it was ironic at best that liberals, in the world's largest democratic system, had come to rely so heavily on nonelected, life-tenured, old men.

The rise in rights consciousness led secondly to a huge increase in federal regulation, as scores of well-organized groups—among them, governmental and public lobbies such as the National Governors Association, the United States Conference of Mayors, and the National Education Association—demanded federal protection and assistance. A raft of new social regulatory agencies came into being, such as the Equal Employment Opportunity Commission (EEOC), the Environmental Protection Agency (EPA), the Occupational Safety and Health Administration (OSHA), and the Department of Education. They joined ever-larger existing agencies and swelled the size of the federal bureaucracy. Although some deregulation—of transportation, banking, and communications— took place in the late 1970s, the spread of governmental activism was nonetheless relentless, continuing strongly into the 1980s as well.[56]

Indeed, federal spending for nondefense purposes increased, in constant 1972 dollars, from $130 billion in 1970 to $222 billion in 1980—from 14 percent of the GNP to 17 percent.[57] In the 1970s, the budgets of social regulatory agencies jumped from $1.4 billion to $7.5 billion. The number of pages in the *Code of Federal Regulations* leaped during the 1970s from 54,000 to 100,000. The regulators, far from protecting corporate groups, as many federal bureaucracies had done in the past, were normally proactive on behalf of the rights-conscious organizations that had helped bring them into being.[58] The EEOC adopted stances (in favor of affirmative action, for instance) that astounded congressmen who had voted for the supposedly color-blind Civil Rights Act of 1964. Even President Nixon, ostensibly a foe of such stances, made no serious effort prior to 1973 to prevent the spread of bureaucratic activism. Many of the new agencies, such as the EPA and OSHA, were created on his watch; others, such as the EEOC, greatly widened their ken during his first term.

The third consequence of the rights revolution was a large increase in categorical federal aid programs and unfunded mandates to states as well as to private employers. In 1960, these numbered 160; by 1970, there were 530. In part for this reason, state-local activism expanded considerably in the 1960s and thereafter; in fact, spending on these levels grew more rapidly between 1960 and 1980 than it did in Washington.[59] Legislation passed by a Democratic Congress in 1972 and signed by Nixon vastly expanded Social Security benefits and set up a generously funded federal program, Supplemental Security Income, for the needy aged and disabled. Congress also established programs—and regulatory bureaucracies—to promote bilingual education (1971) and to aid handicapped children (1974). It approved considerable growth in a food stamps program that had begun to increase during the late 1960s.

This expansion of federal programs, together with the growth in litigation and regulation, generally worked to the advantage of previously marginal groups and causes. Workers received better protection against accidents. Consumers hailed environmental laws concerned with water and air pollution. The welfare poor and the handicapped received more legal protection. Some blacks and women gained from affirmative action procedures. Bureaucratic and judicial administration such as this, often in the absence of legislation clearly authorizing such activity, broadened the reach and power of many federal programs in the United States. It transformed the American state, often confounding presidents, congressmen, employers, and state and local officials alike.[60]

It is common to label the 1970s an era of ascendant conservatism. Nixon overwhelmed George McGovern and his left-of-center followers in 1972. A Religious Right became much more politically active. The civil rights movement remained disorganized and badly fragmented. The Burger Court, with four Nixon appointees on it after 1971, moved in a more conservative direction after 1973. Articulate, well-funded "neoconservatives" assailed Great Society programs. Progressives despaired.

It is more accurate, however, to see the political world of the 1970s as one that featured many of the trends—not all of them "conservative," by any means— that had developed earlier, especially during the 1960s. Among these trends was the phenomenon of divided government—highly partisan Democratic Congresses and Republican presidents—which created a more fragmented legislative process. That fragmentation, in turn, led to the passage of many vaguely worded statutes that judges, as in the 1960s, often interpreted to expand the reach of the federal bureaucracy.[61] The bureaucrats, indeed, were intensely frustrating to Nixon, Ford, and Carter—all of them centrists in their political philosophies. They so irritated Nixon that after his reelection in 1972 he sought to bypass both Congress and the bureaucracy, thereby incurring the unremitting and effective vengeance of these institutions when the burglary at Watergate was exposed.[62]

The Enduring Nature of Rights Consciousness

Thanks largely to Watergate, Carter managed to win in 1976. But the agonies of his unhappy administration revealed with special clarity the continuing divisions within his own party, divisions that were further exacerbated by the ongoing racialization of politics, as featured in conflicts over busing and affirmative action. Many white Democratic voters, especially in the Sun Belt, which had grown more important politically since the 1940s, continued to abandon the old New Deal coalition at the level of presidential voting. So did many fundamentalist and evangelical Christians, who joined the armies of well-organized claimants that sought to influence policy making. Much had changed in the sociology and the geography of American presidential politics since 1932.

By the 1970s, the New Deal coalition suffered especially because of changes in the workforce. As late as 1954, 34.7 percent of nonagricultural workers in the United States had belonged to labor unions, most of which strongly supported the liberal domestic policies associated with the Democratic Party. That percentage was a postwar high. Even then, however, the manufacturing sector of the economy, where workers were most heavily unionized and often most militant, was beginning to falter. Thereafter, it was the service sector, usually low paid and difficult to organize, that demonstrated the most growth.

Many once-militant workers also moved into the middle classes and the suburbs. They left the ranks of the have-nots—and of the once-potent urban machines—and joined the ever-larger legions of the haves. By 1970, only 27.4 percent of nonagricultural workers belonged to unions, after which the percentage began to plummet. By 1990, only 11 percent of workers in the private sector remained as members of unions.[63] The decline of this important element in the Democratic Party deeply damaged the prospects for expansion of bread-and-butter liberal policies.

Governmental institutions in general seemed to be under siege during these years. Thanks to the disaster of American policies in Vietnam, which was fully apparent by 1968, the Establishment that had conducted foreign policy since the onset of the cold war lost much of its claim to expertise. When oil-producing countries imposed embargoes in the 1970s, American leaders had no effective response. When Iranian fundamentalists grabbed American hostages in 1978,

Carter seemed impotent. By then, some of the same people who had bewailed the rise of an imperial presidency during the Nixon years were pining for a reassertion of executive power, especially in the conduct of foreign policy. By 1980, Reagan was able to capitalize on a widespread sense that American foreign policy had no force or direction.

The media, meanwhile, became more intrusive and unforgiving during the 1970s. When Eisenhower bungled the U-2 affair of 1960, the press was easy on him. Once Kennedy had apologized for the Bay of Pigs fiasco—a stunning example of presidential incompetence—reporters rarely drew attention to his errors again. Washington insiders knew a good deal about his (and Johnson's) extramarital sexual activity, but they kept quiet. After Watergate, however, there was no holding the would-be Bernsteins and Woodwards back. An investigative journalism of exposure surged ahead and would not recede in subsequent years. This too was a major legacy of the politics of the 1960s and early 1970s.

The 1970s witnessed with special force the continuation of three additional trends that had become strong in the late 1960s. The first was the further decomposition of parties, accompanied by a more candidate-based, big-money-driven national politics. As *Time* complained in 1978, "taken together, the money, the media, the managers, and the computers may be turning American politics into a strangely lonely process. Candidates now buy what they need, pick their positions knowing in advance what is popular, and then spread those views widely on television and selectively by direct mail. Vanishing are the hosts of volunteers, the massive get-out-the-vote operations, and the need for help from established party organizations."[64]

The second trend in the 1970s was growing popular resistance to further governmental activism. A major political legacy of the late 1960s was the resurgence of anti-statist feeling in the United States. The "best and the brightest" among American liberals had not only dragged the nation into the Vietnam War; they had also erected a host of Great Society programs that—except for the civil rights laws—suffered from obvious flaws. And even the civil rights laws helped spawn such divisive issues as busing and affirmative action. When hard times descended on the nation in the early 1970s, persisting until the early 1980s, Americans were more certain than ever that politicians did not know what they were doing.[65] By the late 1970s, a full-flowered rebellion against taxes, on both the state and the federal levels, again brought to the fore an ever-present feeling among many Americans: the state must not be allowed to get too big.

The third trend, related to the first two, was the spread of cynical, near-corrosive, anti-authority feelings that affected seemingly all aspects of American life, but especially politics. By 1974, 66 percent of people said that government was run by the big interests, compared with only 25 percent who thought otherwise. Voting by eligible Americans dropped further in the 1970s, bottoming out at 38 percent in the election of 1978. So pervasive was this anti-government attitude that Hubert Humphrey exclaimed in 1975, "accountability is the cry of the day. A kind of consumerism is in the air, and neither the Congress nor the public is taking the President's nor anybody's word for anything. But there comes a time when suspicions can go too far. There comes a time when you have to trust someone."[66]

Reformers in the 1970s attempted to overcome the forces that had led to such anti-authority feelings. They passed a War Powers Act in 1973 and a Campaign and Elections Act and a Freedom of Information Act in 1974. They also succeeded in decentralizing congressional decision making so as to weaken the power of seniority in committees. For a variety of reasons, however, these efforts had little impact on most of the key trends of post–World War II politics: declines in grassroots activism and voting, party decomposition, candidate-centered campaigns reliant on enormous infusions of funds, exposure-oriented media, a cynical public, and (in foreign policy) presidential adventurism. Congress continued to be a highly partisan and more unmanageable institution than in the past. Cultural, ethnic, religious, and racial conflicts rent the polity. The social safety net, though considerably stronger than it had been in the 1950s, remained more porous than those in most other industrial nations. Income inequality persisted, increasing in the 1970s (and thereafter).[67]

Most discouraging of all to reformers, special-interest groups seemed increasingly powerful. Some, representing corporations and doctors, had long been influential. Others, proliferating amid the widening rights consciousness of late-twentieth-century America, made good use of "public interest" law firms, think tanks, activist federal judges, receptive congressional subcommittees, and federal bureaucracies that neither Congress nor the president could dominate. A powerful administrative state had emerged that answered to special-interest groups, federal bureaucracies, the courts, and key congressional committees. It bore little resemblance to the amateur government presided over by FDR in the 1930s.

Described in such language, many of the major political trends in the United States between the 1930s and 1980 hardly sound reassuring. Indeed, by the 1980s, a number of rights-conscious interest groups seemed almost wholly self-absorbed, unconcerned about groups other than themselves. Worried about these developments, the courts began backtracking a little, so as to hem in the power of the federal bureaucracy. By the early 1990s, many moderates joined conservatives in lamenting the expansion of group-based rights and the entrenchment of an entitlement-dominated political culture.[68]

But we can look at some of these developments from a less gloomy perspective. After all, there were good reasons, such as Watergate and Vietnam, why Americans became increasingly critical of their political representatives in the late 1960s and 1970s. To be more skeptical about officeholders, as engaged Americans had become, was hardly a vice. That people increasingly demanded rights, moreover, was understandable if not inevitable in an affluent world where rights seemed both affordable and attainable. Given the enormous advances in communications, it is equally understandable that groups often managed to organize effectively and succeed in their quests.

Further, are we to mourn the fragmentation and decomposition of urban machines and political parties, which often did little to represent politically marginalized Americans prior to the 1930s? Are these marginalized millions—not only African Americans, but also many other groups—not better off, at least in the short run, by relying on lawyers, lobbyists, and bureaucrats, arrogant though these officials may be?[69] From the special standpoint of groups such as these, the history of American politics between the 1930s and the mid-1970s—a period of considerable expansion of civil rights, civil liberties, and various governmental entitlements—can be seen in a somewhat happier light.

More important, perhaps, this history can be regarded as a time when a combination of developments—notably, wars, economic growth, and moral passions—intermittently but in the end decisively contributed to the swelling of an administrative state. At several points, especially from 1937 to 1963 and from 1966 to 1980, conservatives staved off the surge of liberal initiatives. But they could not turn back the tide. At other times, during the early New Deal and the mid-1960s, liberals achieved significant legislative triumphs. Meanwhile, World War II witnessed an especially dramatic and irreversible expansion in the size of the state, which in later years (especially during the 1960s and 1970s) acquired great bureaucratic and judicial reinforcement. As Reagan was to discover to his dismay after 1980, this reinforcement proved extraordinarily resistant to change.

Notes

1. Three important books dealing with this era stress the vicissitudes of liberalism: Gareth Davies, *From Opportunity to Entitlement: The Transformation and Decline of Great Society Liberalism* (Lawrence, Kans., 1996); Steve Fraser and Gary Gerstle, eds., *The Rise and Fall of the New Deal Order* (Princeton, N.J., 1989); and Allen Matusow, *The Unraveling of America: A History of Liberalism in the 1960s* (New York, 1984).
2. The number of paid civilian employees of the federal government increased between 1940 and 1980 from 1.1 million to 2.9 million. The number of state and local government employees rose even more rapidly during this period, from 3.3 million to 13.4 million. Department of Commerce, Bureau of the Census, *Historical Statistics of the United States* (Washington, D.C., 1975), 1100; *New York Times Almanac, 1998* (New York, 1997), 137–39.
3. Garry Wills, *A Necessary Evil: A History of American Distrust of Government* (New York, 1999).
4. Samuel Huntington, *American Politics: The Promise of Disharmony* (Cambridge, Mass., 1981), 4–30.

5. M. J. Heale, *McCarthy's Americans: Red Scare Politics in State and Nation, 1935–1965* (London, 1998), 281–301; Leonard Moore, "Good Old-Fashioned New Social History and the Twentieth-Century American Right," *Reviews in American History* 24 (December 1996): 555–73.

6. Alonzo Hamby, *Liberalism and Its Challengers: From FDR to Bush,* 2d ed. (New York, 1992), 395.

7. Theodore White, *America in Search of Itself: The Making of the President, 1956–1980* (New York, 1982), 7.

8. James Sundquist, *Dynamics of the Party System: Alignment and Realignment of Political Parties in the United States,* rev. ed. (Washington, D.C., 1981), 306–7.

9. David Plotke, *Building a Democratic Political Order: Reshaping American Liberalism in the 1930s and 1940s* (New York, 1996), 11–46.

10. For a different view, see Ira Katznelson, "Was the Great Society a Lost Opportunity?" in Fraser and Gerstle, *Rise and Fall of the New Deal Order,* 185–211.

11. Michael Schudson, *The Good Citizen: A History of American Civil Life* (New York, 1998), 294–301. Voting by registered voters, however, remained high throughout the era.

12. Ilya Somin, "Voter Ignorance and the Democratic Ideal," *Critical Review* 4 (fall 1998): 413–58.

13. Walter Dean Burnham, "The End of Party Politics," *TransAction* 27 (1969): 12–22.

14. Hamby, *Liberalism and Its Challengers,* 386.

15. Richard Rose, "Is American Public Policy Exceptional?" in *Is America Different? A New Look at American Exceptionalism,* ed. Byron E. Shafer (Oxford, 1991), 187–221. See also Desmond King, *In the Name of Liberalism: Illiberal Social Policy in the United States and Britain* (Oxford, 1999), 258–86.

16. Ably chronicled in Stephan Thernstrom and Abigail Thernstrom, *America in Black and White: One Nation, Indivisible* (New York, 1997).

17. For greater detail on the New Deal, see the essay by Anthony Badger in this volume.

18. Christopher Tomlins, *The State and the Unions: Labor Relations, Law, and the Organized Labor Movement in America, 1880–1960* (New York, 1985); Howell Harris, "The Snares of Liberalism? Politicians, Bureaucrats, and the Shaping of Federal Labour Policy in the United States, 1915–1947," in *Shop Floor Bargaining and the State: Historical and Comparative Perspectives,* ed. Steven Tolliday and Jonathan Zeitlin (Cambridge, 1983), 148–91. For a good analysis of this and other arguments concerning labor policy, see Nelson Lichtenstein, "From Corporatism to Collective Bargaining: Organized Labor and the Eclipse of Social Democracy in the Postwar Era," in Fraser and Gerstle, *Rise and Fall of the New Deal Order,* 122–52.

19. Sidney Milkis, *The President and the Parties: The Transformation of the American Party System since the New Deal* (New York, 1993), 312.

20. Schudson, *Good Citizen,* 205–33.

21. Tony Badger, "The New Deal without FDR," in *History and Biography: Essays in Honour of Derek Beales,* ed. T. C. W. Blanning and David Cannadine (Cambridge, 1996), 243–65.

22. Alan Ware, *The Breakdown of the Democratic Organization, 1940–1980* (Oxford, 1985).

23. Bartholomew Sparrow, *From the Outside In: World War II and the American State* (Princeton, N.J., 1996), 307–9.

24. Richard Jensen, "The Last Party System: Decay of Consensus, 1932–1980," in *The Evolution of American Electoral Systems,* ed. Paul Kleppner et al. (Westport, Conn., 1981), 203–241.

25. Tony Badger, "State Capacity in Britain and America in the 1930s," in *Britain and America: Studies in Comparative History, 1760–1970,* ed. David Englander (New Haven, Conn., 1997), 295–306.
26. Jeremy Rabkin, "The Judiciary in the Administrative State," *Public Interest* 71 (spring 1983): 62–84.
27. Alan Brinkey, *The End of Reform: New Deal Liberalism in Recession and War* (New York, 1995).
28. Robert Collins, *People of More: Economic Growth in Postwar America* (New York, 2000); Alan Wolfe, *America's Impasse: The Rise and Fall of the Politics of Growth* (New York, 1981).
29. James Patterson, *Congressional Conservatism and the New Deal* (Lexington, Mass., 1967).
30. See Thomas Sugrue, *The Origins of the Urban Crisis: Race and Inequality in Postwar Detroit* (Princeton, N.J., 1996); Arnold Hirsch, *Making the Second Ghetto: Race and Housing in Chicago, 1940–1960* (New York, 1983).
31. Sparrow, *From the Outside In,* 49–51. For conservative triumphs concerning health insurance in the 1940s, see Monte Poen, *Harry S. Truman versus the Medical Lobby: The Genesis of Medicare* (Columbia, Mo., 1979), esp. 88.
32. *Historical Statistics,* 1100, 1105; David Kennedy, *Freedom from Fear: The American People in Depression and War, 1929–1945* (New York, 1998), 624–25.
33. Sparrow, *From the Outside In,* 309, 276, 30.
34. Federal government expenditures for domestic purposes increased from $7.3 billion in 1945 to $19.9 billion in 1950 (*Historical Statistics,* 1120).
35. Sparrow, *From the Outside In,* 33–36, 276.
36. Daniel Rodgers, *Atlantic Crossings: Social Politics in a Progressive Age* (Cambridge, Mass., 1998).
37. Cited in Michael Schaller, *Reckoning with Reagan: America and Its Presidents in the 1980s* (New York, 1992), 11.
38. Aaron Wildavsky, "Resolved, that Individualism and Egalitarianism Be Made Compatible in America: Political-Cultural Roots of Exceptionalism," in Shafer, *Is America Different?* 116–37.
39. Jensen, "Last Party System," 220–21. The percentage of voters calling themselves independents then swelled, to nearly 40 percent by 1974.
40. Sundquist, *Dynamics of the Party System,* 218–74, 335–36.
41. See Steven Gillon, *"That's Not What We Meant to Do": Reform and Its Unintended Consequences in Twentieth Century America* (New York, 2000).
42. Huntington, *American Politics,* 216.
43. Milkis, *President and the Parties,* 181–83, 216–18.
44. A huge literature deals with the decomposition of parties in the late 1960s and early 1970s. Among the many useful sources are Walter Dean Burnham, *Critical Elections and the Mainsprings of American Politics* (New York, 1970), 106–19; Martin Shefter, *Political Parties and the State: The American Historical Experience* (Princeton, N.J., 1994), 86–94; David Broder, *The Party's Over* (New York, 1972); and Ware, *Breakdown of Democratic Organization,* esp. 6, 246–48.
45. Jensen, "Last Party System," 220–21.
46. Nicely summarized by Schudson, *Good Citizen,* 233–39, 281–87. Lamenting the "sound bite" culture promoted by politics on television, Schudson also notes the advantages that television ads—which are very expensive—give to wealthy office-seekers. Still, he welcomes the trend.

47. Byron E. Shafer, *Bifurcated Politics: Evolution and Reform in the National Party Convention* (Cambridge, Mass., 1988), 46–53.

48. For changes in the Democratic Party between 1968 and 1972, see Byron E. Shafer, *Quiet Revolution: The Struggle for the Democratic Party and the Shaping of Post-Reform Politics* (New York, 1983). See also Darrell West, *Air Wars: Television Advertising in Election Campaigns, 1952–1996* (Washington, D.C., 1997).

49. John Bibby, "Party Organizations, 1946–1996," in *Partisan Approaches to Postwar American Politics,* ed. Byron E. Shafer (New York, 1998), 142–85.

50. Joel Silbey, "Beyond Realignment and Realignment Theory . . . American Electoral Eras, 1789–1989," and Everett Carl Ladd, "Like Waiting for Godot: The Uselessness of 'Realignment' for Understanding Change in Contemporary American Politics," in *The End of Realignment: Interpreting American Electoral Eras,* ed. Byron E. Shafer (Madison, Wis., 1991), 3–23, 24–36.

51. Michael Lind, *The Next American Nation: The New Nationalism and the Fourth American Revolution* (New York, 1995).

52. Schudson, *Good Citizen,* 252–74.

53. Hugh Davis Graham, "Legacies of the 1960s: The American 'Rights Revolution' in an Era of Divided Government," *Journal of Policy History* 10 (1998): 267–88.

54. See R. Shep Melnick, *Between the Lines: Interpreting Welfare Rights* (Washington, D.C., 1994), 1016, 281–83.

55. Rabkin, "Judiciary in the Administrative State," 63.

56. Lou Cannon, *President Reagan: The Role of a Lifetime* (New York, 1991), 820. Some of the new agencies and departments established between 1965 and 1969 were the Department of Transportation, Department of Housing and Urban Development, Federal Highway Administration, Federal Railroad Administration, Federal Transit Administration, Equal Employment Opportunity Commission, National Endowment for the Arts, and National Endowment for the Humanities. Among the bureaucracies created during the 1970s were the Office of Management and Budget, Office of Science and Technology Policy, Minority Business Development Agency, National Oceanic and Atmospheric Administration, Department of Education, Department of Energy, Health Care Financing Administration, Drug Enforcement Administration, Occupational Safety and Health Administration, Pensions and Welfare Benefits Administration, Bureau of Alcohol, Tobacco, and Firearms, AMTRAK, Community Futures Trading Commission, Consumer Product Safety Commission, Federal Election Commission, National Credit Union Administration, National Transportation Safety Board, Nuclear Regulatory Commission, Office of Personnel Management, United States Postal Service, and Environmental Protection Agency.

57. Bureau of the Census, *Statistical Abstract of the United States, 1981* (Washington, D.C., 1981), 245–48, 421.

58. For one case study, see R. Shep Melnick, *Regulation and the Courts: The Case of the Clean Air Act* (Washington, D.C., 1983).

59. State-local spending in current dollars increased from $61 billion in 1960 (compared with $90 billion in federal spending) to $432 billion in 1980 (compared with $526 billion in federal spending), or from $339 per capita in 1960 (compared with $502 per capita in federal spending) to $1,909 per capita in 1980 (compared with $2,324 in federal spending). Bureau of Census, *Statistical Abstract, 1981,* 275.

60. Graham, "Legacies of the 1960s"; Milkis, *President and the Parties,* 253–55. The growth of the state also led to a considerable rise of voluntary organizations,

which delivered many of the services called for by this federal legislation. The result was the development of a substantial government-nonprofit partnership. See Donald Critchlow, "Implementing Family Planning Policy: Philanthropic Foundations and the Modern Welfare State," in *With Us Always: A History of Private Charity and Welfare,* ed. Donald Critchlow and Charles Parker (Lanham, Md., 1998), 211–40; and Peter Dobkin Hall, *Inventing the Non-profit Sector and Other Essays in Philanthropy, Voluntarism, and Non-profit Organizations* (Baltimore, 1992), 7.

61. Melnick, *Between the Lines,* 10–16.
62. For comments on Watergate that stress these institutional aspects, see Shefter, *Political Parties and the State,* 86–87.
63. Nearly 40 percent of workers in the public sector belonged to unions in 1990. Their presence contributed further to the rise of lobbying, rights consciousness, and the growth of the administrative state.
64. *Time,* November 20, 1978, 35.
65. Ironically, many policy makers—thanks to sophisticated managerial methods imported from the corporate sector—did have a slightly better idea of what they were doing after 1960. Creation of the Office of Management and Budget in 1970 is thought to have improved the formulation of fiscal policies. The point, however, is that Americans were less inclined to believe what public officials told them.
66. Cited in Huntington, *American Politics,* 175, 104.
67. *New York Times,* September 5, 1999.
68. Melnick, *Between the Lines;* Mary Ann Glendon, *Rights Talk: The Impoverishment of Political Discourse* (New York, 1991).
69. See Jack Walker, "Interests, Political Parties, and Policy Formation in American Democracy," in *Federal Social Policy: The Historical Dimension,* ed. Donald Critchlow and Ellis Hawley (University Park, Pa., 1988), 145–70.

9. The Two Majorities and the Puzzle of Modern American Politics

Economic Development, Issue Evolution, and Divided Government, 1955–2000

Byron E. Shafer

In their own time, the surface upheavals of American politics during the immediate postwar years might reasonably have suggested a major political shift, the coming of a new political era with different issue contents and different supporting arrangements. Yet with hindsight, the immediate postwar period, for all its undeniable fluctuations, still appears politically of a piece with the ongoing New Deal era. Elite partisan combatants of the day variously hoped or feared that 1956 would mark an effective end to this era. The election of 1956 would instead confirm its continuation, albeit in a form modified from its substantive and structural heyday. Participants could not know that the central substantive concerns of that era had a full postwar generation to run, nor that its central structural supports had a full postwar generation in which to be key shaping influences. But it *would* be a full generation from the end of the Second World War before evident and dramatic issue shifts came together with glacial but irresistible social changes, explosively, to demand a different political dynamic.

Similarly, when that explosion finally arrived in the late 1960s, few participants could be confident that it represented lasting change. Both the fearful and the hopeful were naturally inclined to focus on surface manifestations of disruption that almost could not, in principle, form the underpinnings of an extended era. Few observers at the time failed to notice the extensive anomalies of the 1968 election— anomalies, that is, when viewed within the confines of the New Deal order. None missed the fact that these led to Richard Nixon's narrow victory as president, while the Democratic Party retained solid control of both houses of Congress. Yet none could know that the latter was to become the diagnostic partisan outcome for a new political era. And none could know that the surface anomalies of 1968 were best seen not as idiosyncratic events in their own right but as crystallizing vehicles for the emergent issues and long-term forces that would terminate the late New Deal.

The Era of the Late New Deal

None of this seemed inevitable when the postwar era began. Indeed, a reasonable reading of immediate postwar politics would have suggested that some new era was already in the process of being born. In the first fully postwar election, that of 1946, the chaos of economic and social reconversion produced the first Republican Congress since 1928. Harry S. Truman then spiked hopes (or fears) that the New Deal era had been just a Roosevelt interregnum when Truman held the presidency in his own right in 1948 and regained control of Congress. But the Republicans were back in 1952, in control of both the presidency and Congress this time, making that a potential turning point in their hopes for a new political order. By 1956, however, what Dwight D. Eisenhower, his voters, and Americans in general were entitled to deduce from all this superficial upheaval was only that they were living in a modified extension of the existing political world, in what can rightfully be called the "late New Deal era."

Afterward, the world of the 1950s would be widely understood as an extension of the political world of Franklin D. Roosevelt and the New Deal. The great and dominating substantive concern of both ends of this era was social welfare, as befitted an agenda called into being by economic catastrophe. By the time an Eisenhower presidency was under serious discussion, the policy content of this dominant economic-welfare dimension included all the hallmark programs of the Rooseveltian New Deal: unemployment compensation, Social Security, industrial recovery, farm price supports, labor-management regulation, rural electrification, and so on. By the time Eisenhower was actually president, the policy content of the same dimension had expanded to include full employment plus the "missing pieces" of the original New Deal agenda: health care, housing assistance, poverty amelioration, higher education, and, last but not least, civil rights.[1] The staying power of these programs, as items for partisan conflict, would prove remarkable.

The great and dominating secondary concern of this period was foreign affairs, again befitting an era forced within a painfully few years to confront the catastrophe of total war. In the years when Eisenhower was becoming both an international leader and a household name, this major secondary focus involved proper pursuit of World War II, through a huge buildup of defense manpower and industry. In the years of his full celebrity, it involved proper pursuit of a cold war, with its mixture of international alliances, military support, and conventional foreign aid.[2] The United States had been drawn reluctantly into the worldwide conflicts capped by the Second World War; it was to be a principal architect of the succeeding international environment, so that this environment would remain an ever-present substantive concern.

Lest such continuity seem dependent on simple substantive interpretation, it is worth noting that it was accompanied by—was part and parcel of—a parallel extension of key structural influences. Thus there were social coalitions to go with these programmatic directions, coalitions that were in fact integral to them. By 1946, two of these, robustly constructed, dominated the political landscape. Both were built principally on social class, unlike the geographic basis of the previous political world, albeit with important ethnic and regional twists. The larger was a blue-collar coalition, aligned with the national Democratic Party, that featured working-class Americans generally, a few key multiclass minorities (especially Jews), and the entire (the "solid") South. The smaller was a white-collar coalition, aligned with the national Republican Party and essentially reliant on middle-class Americans.[3] Truman confirmed the incentives for racial minorities (especially blacks) to shift toward the Democratic coalition. After his reelection, as the urban orientation of the Democratic Party was also confirmed and as the role of organized labor in party councils increased, farmers as a group and rural areas generally, outside the South, shifted in turn toward the Republican coalition.

These social coalitions were buttressed by organized interests of a highly partisan sort in which labor-management divisions were critical. There were some undeniable ironies to this divide. From one side, industrial recovery as fostered by the Democrats, along with a wartime boom, had restored profitability to corporate business. From the other side, corporate gigantism was especially good at producing organizational gains for union labor. But regardless, organized labor became an increasingly important adjunct to the Democratic Party in legislative and then in electoral politics, to the point where it actually substituted for the party in more and more places. By contrast, although corporate management provided some funding and the occasional "blue-ribbon" candidate for the Republicans, it was really small business—the Chamber of Commerce, not the National Association of Manufacturers—that carried the load for the minority party among the interest groups.[4]

Policy positions and social coalitions were then knit together and connected to the institutions of national government by the political parties. By 1956, however, these were not just mirror images within a two-party system; they had become parties that were different in organizational kind. The Democrats were an amalgam of urban machines in the North, courthouse rings in the South, and volunteer activist branches scattered throughout the country. New Deal programs had actually helped extend the life of the organized (the "regular") Democratic Party within this mix. The Republicans, still paying a high price for incumbency when the Great Depression hit, had already moved to become the kind of organizationally amorphous, activist-based political party that both would become in the second postwar era, relying on ideology and issues to motivate party workers. For them, this was not so much modernization as simple survival. Although they retained some rural rings in the North, New Deal programs had essentially wiped out the Republican machines present in the pre-depression years.[5]

There was, in consequence, a diagnostic partisan dynamic to this mix of policy conflicts, social coalitions, and organized intermediaries—a distinctive character to political competition in the late New Deal era. Seen by way of ongoing policy conflicts, the party on the Left, the Democrats, was widely perceived as more in tune with public preferences on social welfare. By contrast, the party on the Right, the Republicans, was widely perceived as more in tune with public preferences on foreign affairs. The crucial fact was that the public ordinarily gave a much higher priority to social welfare. Seen by way of ongoing social coalitions instead, the dominant fact about partisan politicking from 1932 through 1968 was that the unity and vitality of the Democratic coalition remained the central story of electoral and institutional politics.[6] The election of 1946 had signaled an adjustment to this dominant fact. Before, Democrats won, full stop. Afterward, Republicans could win if Democratic policy assets were devalued, as they were in 1946, or if Republicans had special assets of their own, as they would in 1952. But this was still an adjustment, not a change.

As happened so often in American history, the basic institutional structure of American government channeled this partisan dynamic in important ways. Because president and Congress were separately elected, there had to be, in effect, *four* institutional parties within the American two-party system: a presidential and a congressional Democratic and Republican Party. But here, it was the response of the minority Republicans that was most revealing. In a presidential contest, all those state Republican Parties that found themselves in either competitive or Democratic states—at that time, the Republican Parties of states representing the majority of Americans—needed an economic moderate as their nominee. And for more than a generation, they got one: Wendell Willkie in 1940, Thomas Dewey in 1944, Dewey again in 1948, Dwight Eisenhower in 1952, Eisenhower again in 1956, and Richard Nixon in 1960. Which is to say, the presidential Republican Party did accept the social welfare consensus.

In congressional contests, however, the situation—with its incentive structure—was strikingly different.[7] Many seats remained reliably Republican and thus had no need for social welfare accommodation. Many of the rest were reliably Democratic, such that accommodation (or not) was irrelevant. Lacking much incentive, then, few successful Republican Parties moderated at the congressional level. Moreover, just to make the partisan picture more stark (and Republican problems more severe), it should be noted that an institutional arrangement that helped hobble a minority Republican response to party competition presented no counterpart difficulties for the majority Democrats. For them, differing presidential and congressional parties, both dominant, could comfortably go their separate ways under the Democratic label. If they needed to reconcile for policy purposes, they could always do so in government, in Washington.

Those facts made the Eisenhower interlude especially good at showing the political dynamic of the late New Deal in its full complexity. Eisenhower, the Republican presidential candidate in 1952, was the most popular living American. If Roosevelt had beaten the depression, "Ike" had won the war—and Roosevelt was dead. Yet Eisenhower largely accepted the strategic imperatives that FDR had bequeathed him, featuring foreign policy issues but emphasizing that he was a "modern Republican," at home with popular social welfare programs. This was sufficient not just to earn him the presidency but also to draw a Republican congressional majority into office with him. His fellow officeholders, however, those Republican beneficiaries of his presidential coattails, had not begun to make their peace with the New Deal. Accordingly, the public threw them out at its first opportunity, in the midterm elections of 1954, and even Eisenhower could not drag them back with him when he was reelected (by a landslide) in 1956.[8]

More lastingly, Eisenhower would accomplish one great partisan task and fail at another, and the two together would influence party competition until after 1968. In the first, Eisenhower ended the Korean War while simultaneously cementing his fellow Republicans into the cold war consensus. This was one policy realm about which he really cared, and he would be lastingly successful in it. What he failed to do was bring the Republican congressional party into the social welfare consensus too. Indeed, Eisenhower himself actually moved closer to Republican dissidence on these issues as his administration aged. As a result, the human icon could still be comfortably reelected; there was no counterpart figure on the political landscape. But his party, despite the fact that it increasingly *was* his party, could not.

The Foundations Crumble

The year 1956 was noteworthy for a much less obvious fact about American society, albeit a fact with substantial implications for American politics. This was the first year in American history that the Census Bureau declared a white-collar majority for the nation as a whole.[9] The political implications of this massive subterranean fact were indirect and complex. Indeed, the next round of elections, the congressional elections of 1958, would bring one of the largest *Democratic* gains of the postwar years; it would be almost two generations before the Democratic Party gave these back. Yet American society was changing in glacial but irresistible ways that were utterly uncharacteristic of the world of the depression and the Second World War, and hence unlikely to underpin a continuing New Deal order.

The great if undifferentiated engine for this change was the postwar economic boom. From the late 1940s through the mid 1960s, the American economy provided explosive growth. Appearing all the more remarkable from the viewpoint of the other developed nations, each more seriously damaged by the Second World War, economic growth in postwar America remained remarkable in its own right, and it represented a complex of further changes. It was not just total income—and median income and average income—that grew apace in the postwar years. Such wealth was the product of a hugely different economy, in which a long-term trend away from agriculture became a huge movement into manufacturing and industry and then eventually into service provision and information technology. A different structure to the economy also meant, by definition, a different occupational structure for American society. And a different occupational structure meant a different *class* structure as well.[10]

The partisan implications of this change, as it moved closer to an impact on politics and public policy, were not straightforward. The great decline in national economic fortunes of the late 1920s and 1930s *had* shifted the social base for American politics from a geographic to a class alignment. By the end of the Second World War, there was one party rooted in the working class, facing another party rooted in the middle class, with many cross-currents but with a clear societal majority for the former. Had these sharpened class lines held in anything like their midcentury incarnation, the implication of postwar economic change would have been obvious: as the middle class grew, so should the Republicans. Yet the hidden breakpoint of 1956 was early evidence that this was not to be the case. The middle-class majority had already arrived; Republican prospects continued to lag. Indeed, the share of society identified with the Democratic rather than the Republican Party actually continued to grow. And very little of this further partisan drift resulted from any additional working-class increment to the Democrats.[11]

What was happening instead was a major change in the class base of both parties, but especially of the Democrats, with powerful implications for subsequent politics. By inexorable extension, the Democrats too were becoming a more middle-class party. One implication of this change, in turn, was that a growing segment of the party would be less concerned with the old redistributional issues that had underpinned the New Deal Democratic coalition and more concerned with an aggregate of social, cultural, and behavioral issues—less with the "quantity of life" and more with the "quality of life" instead.[12] Middle-class Democrats, representing the more liberal elements of the American middle class, would never turn their backs on the social welfare gains of the New Deal, and this fact would remain important. But new priorities almost had to follow from their new and growing partisan presence.

Because the Republicans would remain the minority party throughout the ensuing generation, their story was less consequential to American politics as a whole. Once, they would have acquired the liberal middle class by means of class identifications. If they no longer did, then this party too was becoming a very different social coalition (and ideological vehicle) just under the surface. If anything, its commitment to economic and welfare conservatism was being strengthened. But so was the potential for a newly fashioned conservatism on those quality-of-life issues. This particular subterranean fact would be masked for another generation, while the liberal Republicans of the Northeast, the industrial Midwest, and the West Coast remained an important minority faction within the minority party. But by 1956, these liberal Republicans were already, had they known it, an endangered species.

Such grand and gross partisan transitions were hardly the end of the roster of political impacts from economic development. The major interest groups of American politics were being reshaped as well, again indirectly but forcefully. One of the great stories of the New Deal era had been the rise of organized labor generally and then its integration into the Democratic coalition. Economic decline and resurgent class conflict would have been stimuli toward union resurgence on their own. But this time, the government had been actively supportive of labor organization, union recognition, and collective bargaining, and this legislative support was a powerful contributor to the explosive growth of the labor movement in the immediate postwar years. Unlike earlier periods of union growth, however, organized labor this time came quickly to establish a huge overhead agency, the AFL-CIO, and to affiliate it, informally but effectively, with the national Democratic Party.[13] The result was important for keeping social welfare issues at the center of American politics and for forging the policy link between welfare liberalism and cold war anti-communism.

There had been a parallel development on the other side of the organizational aisle, for the immediate postwar years were also the heyday of the giant corporations, massive corporate entities characteristic of a booming postwar economy. The form itself had emerged by the 1920s, before the Great Depression had choked off its spread. Its growth merely resumed in the immediate postwar years. Yet this was to be the era of corporate gigantism, and that fact too had implications for the New Deal order. Much more than small business, big business was prepared to make its peace both with union labor as an organized interest and with the main policy substance of the New Deal. This remained a practical, not a principled, peace; the great corporations would hardly become another element of the Democratic coalition. Yet they did accept labor-management relations as a normal part of economic life. Moreover, because they tended to be concentrated in states where big labor was also particularly strong, corporate Republicans came to accept basic social welfare programs as a normal element—that is, a normal imperative—of the political landscape.[14]

The postwar economic boom then undermined both these developments, which is to say, in undermining both these great organized interests, economic change undermined their policy contribution as well. The membership of organized labor peaked in the early 1950s and declined gradually from then on. It peaked as the sectors of the economy that were most easily unionized—those same great corporate manufacturing sectors—peaked themselves as a share of the economy. Thereafter it declined, as manufacturing gave way to service provision as the growth sector of the economy. Labor remained a crucial element of the Democratic coalition, in triumph through the mid-1960s and in adversity thereafter. But it would never again walk the halls of Congress, much less the corridors of the White House, with the confidence it had in the 1950s and early 1960s.[15]

Once more, there were parallel developments on the other side of the labor-management divide, for corporate gigantism also peaked in the 1950s. Ironically, just when social thinkers were beginning to set out the character of an organizational world built around these giant economic units, they began to recede.[16] This too was a response to the growth of the service and knowledge sectors of the economy, as opposed to the industrial and manufacturing sectors. It meant that a number of other social phenomena associated with the rise of what Eisenhower designated "modern Republicanism"—accepting of organized labor, at ease with social welfare—also began to change. Eventually, this more liberal wing of the Republican Party would be folded into the regular party structure.

These economic changes, in their final indirect contribution to politics, naturally began to affect the structure of the political parties. Among Democrats, the result was huge policy tensions within the dominant Democratic coalition, followed by extensive procedural reform. The key impetus to both was the explosive rise in the share of college-educated Democratic identifiers. At the end of the Second World War, although there was an unavoidable "intellectual wing" to the Democratic coalition, the share of college graduates was minuscule. During the 1950s, courtesy of the economic boom generally but also of the GI Bill as a conscious policy intervention, not only the share of college-educated Americans but also the share of college-educated Democrats grew apace.

There were problems as well as prospects in this growth. The new (middle-class, college-educated) Democrats were not normally members of the main organized constituency groups of the national Democratic Party—namely, organized labor and the growing civil rights organizations.[17] They resided in areas where the orthodox party organization, the "regular" Democratic Party, was frequently enfeebled—namely, the burgeoning suburbs. They were also equipped and inclined to participate in politics as independent actors, often motivated by specific causes, rather than as devoted members of basically partisan organizations. Eventually, they would have their way through a stream of participatory procedural reforms, from extending the reach of primary elections into presidential politics to extending a bill of rights for individual members of Congress.

The Republican version of this story was inevitably related, though with the main elements reversed. The Republican Party had long since achieved the organizational character that the Democrats were only just approaching, courtesy of the death of the old Republican machines and the debilitating effect of protracted minority status. More to the practical point, as the New Deal era aged and as the Democratic Party grew but became more internally divided, the Republicans at first appeared to shrink and become more homogeneous. Liberal Republicans, the main dissident faction, had always been heavily dependent on deference from the regular party. When corporate gigantism receded and the party structure became more skeletal and hence more dependent on the Old Guard, this more liberal faction just disappeared into the regular party structure.

As the liberal middle class also became more Democratic, there was a more evidently homogeneous social base, a more socially but especially a more economically conservative social base, left to be reflected in this more skeletal Republican Party structure. What prevented this from becoming a long-running extension of the old order was a different and even more indirect fallout from economic growth, capped by a conscious elite reaction to developments inside the Democratic Party. Said differently, as educated Democrats began to secure their policy wishes within the Democratic Party, a less-educated segment of society, reacting against these policies, became increasingly available to the Republicans. And this development brought both counterpart opportunities and counterpart tensions to the other side of the partisan aisle.

This new target population was the evangelical—the pietistic—Protestants, and they were strong conservatives on the very cultural and national questions that were central to the rise of middle-class Democrats.[18] Economic development contributed to their leadership too, producing new seminaries that paid special attention to the latest technology for reaching their followers. It was these leaders who would forge an informal but strong relationship to the Republican Party. As with the coming of corporate Republicans in an earlier era, however, this potential for numerical gain came at the cost of increased intraparty tensions. From one side, the evangelicals were much more socially conservative than the remainder of the party. From the other, they were much less economically conservative, resting well inside the national social welfare consensus.

Flash Fires and Crystallizing Issues

The issue substance of American politics was likewise undergoing an evolution during the late New Deal years. But here, the surface manifestations of change were insistent, even intrusive. Each great underlying dimension to public policy—social welfare and foreign affairs—generated a dramatic and extended substantive conflict. Although both these conflicts were inevitably shaped by the changing contours of the society in which they occurred, neither was directly a product of these changes. Rather, both grew logically out of the policy positions and social coalitions of the New Deal era. By the time they played out, however—and both were not just dramatic but also long running—they had helped refashion the entire nature of substantive conflict in American politics.

The greatest and most dramatic of these new issues was civil rights, culminating in a veritable civil rights revolution. In playing his part in constructing the New Deal order, Franklin Roosevelt had consciously avoided this issue area.

For him, a central task in building a liberal coalition behind the social welfare programs of the New Deal had been attracting and then holding southern Democrats. The problem was that they were both numerically essential and the most conservative elements in this aspiring coalition. What made the American South "solid" in the Democratic coalition, despite this instinctive conservatism, was a multiclass white majority united by racial segregation as public policy. Roosevelt recognized that civil rights as a policy priority would challenge this arrangement, stress his coalition, and thus potentially imperil his economic and welfare gains. He chose social welfare and allowed civil rights to languish.[19]

In partisan terms, not much changed with the passing of Roosevelt. A focus on civil rights still seemed likely to reduce the policy advantage that the national Democratic Party derived from economic and welfare issues, perhaps in a major way. Nevertheless, liberal activists in the postwar years set about redressing this otherwise curious hole in their overall policy program, a move in which they were powerfully reinforced by an increasingly aggressive and mobilized civil rights movement. The Civil Rights Act of 1957 and then the far more consequential Civil Rights Act of 1964 and Voting Rights Act of 1965 were the main substantive products. Huge new constituencies for the Democratic Party were their most immediate structural result, in the form of newly mobilized black voters in the South but also in the North. Huge new stresses in the northern Democratic coalition and major cracks in its southern counterpart also followed.[20]

The other great, partially autonomous, substantive contribution of the late New Deal era, one that had a curious parallel to that of civil rights, involved what was to become the Vietnam War. There had been an earlier attempt to draw the United States into combat in Southeast Asia, when the French were defeated at Dien Bien Phu and Vietnam was partitioned. But President Eisenhower, with Korea as a powerful recent analogy—that is, mindful of the fact that *ending* the Korean War remained a major policy asset for the Republican Party—failed to respond. By contrast, John F. Kennedy, an orthodox product of a Democratic coalition that melded pursuit of social welfare with prosecution of the cold war, and needing personally to neutralize foreign policy issues by appearing no less firm than his Republican opponents, took the opposite tack.[21]

Lyndon Johnson then brought both aspects of the Democratic policy inheritance from the New Deal to their postwar zenith. He launched the Great Society, including Medicare, Head Start, and the War on Poverty. And he escalated the war in Vietnam by means of a manpower draft that ultimately reached into the collegiate middle class. The partisan consequences, by way of stresses inside the Democratic coalition, were cataclysmic. The new college-educated Democrats were not stressed by the Great Society; it was not what principally motivated them, but they were supportive. They were, however, deeply unhappy with the Vietnam War, and the baby-boom generation, in college at the time, would provide them with expressive "shock troops" for their unhappiness.[22] In the process, dramatic public protests also elevated the issue realm of foreign affairs in the public mind, a realm where Republicans retained the policy advantage.

These two issue areas, separately and together, were to draw an array of others onto the substantive agenda of American politics. The violent aftermath of the civil rights revolution, along with the extensiveness of student protest, fueled an associated concern with public order. More tellingly, so did an explosion of crime in general within American society. Murder, robbery, burglary, rape, and assault all jumped alarmingly in the 1960s, most with the greatest decadal increase since statistics were collected. If legal desegregation was the most intensive substantive development of the time, and if student protest was the most symbolically dramatic, increased criminal activity was both more extensive than the former and more tangible than the latter. No party would be able to seize any continuing advantage from being better able to handle crime, but the perception of being tolerant of it would thereafter always be extremely harmful.[23]

A cluster of other, lesser concerns also claimed their place on the policy agenda, and if most of these had been seen before, in earlier historical incarnations, they inevitably reappeared in a manner appropriate to the structural character of contemporary politics. Thus the natural environment came back as a matter for political debate, but in a way that reflected the postwar boom and the new social composition of the political parties. Historically, it had been the more middle-class Republican Party that was the vehicle for conservation and environmental concern, while the Democrats focused on redistribution and concrete benefits. Now, it was the middle-class wing of the Democratic Party—the liberal middle class—that focused on conservation and environmental activism. Feminism moved onto the agenda as well, with the same social and partisan relationships. Historically, feminism had fit most comfortably with the Progressivism of the Republican Party. Now, it fit most comfortably in the college-graduate wing of the Democratic Party instead.[24]

It jumps ahead of the story to note that all these latter concerns—Richard Nixon would first summarize them simply as "permissiveness"—fueled a backlash by Protestant evangelicals to what they viewed as inescapable evidence of moral and cultural decline. But what was already much in evidence by the early 1960s was the role of one particular *institution* of American national government in further propelling and then holding these cultural and social concerns at the center of the American policy agenda. That role was to be large and recurrent. It was also a particularly good example of the way in which partially autonomous (and thoroughly unintended) structural changes could shape the substantive content of a national policy agenda.

This institution was, of course, the U.S. Supreme Court. The Court under Chief Justice Earl Warren had already, in the 1950s, been a critical actor in vastly upweighting the importance of civil rights as a policy realm. Beginning in the 1960s, the Court then turned to a string of essentially cultural conflicts, once more elevating their public importance as it did so. Moreover, the Warren Court—ending an era in which economic regulation dominated the agenda of the Court and beginning an era characterized by civil liberties instead—reliably offered one side, the progressive position, on cultural issues such as busing, school prayer, abortion, capital punishment, criminal justice, homosexual rights, and so on, often in clear contraposition to public preferences.[25]

The key point, however, did not involve the individual substance of any of these issues, great or small. The key point instead was that civil rights as a new twist on social welfare, along with Vietnam as the latest twist on foreign affairs, was only the flash point, however dramatic, for a much larger evolution in the central substance of American politics. There are many ways to distinguish the substantive core of the new era. But at bottom, the old political world had featured partisan division and issue conflict over the (re)distribution of material goods, around economics and social welfare. The new political world added—and often featured—partisan division and issue conflict over the character of national life, over the behavior operationalizing a national culture, from the family hearth to the international stage.

This first set of concerns was essentially distributional, involving the proper share of divisible goods allocated to various sectors of society. The second set was essentially valuational, involving the proper behavioral norms within which social life should proceed. The older economic-welfare concerns hardly went away, and their continuing presence remained central to the substantive character of the new era. But they were joined by the new cultural-national concerns on secondary, equal, or superior footing, depending on the context of the day. In that sense, the key substantive characteristic of this successor era was the vigorous presence of *two* great (and, as we shall see, cross-cutting) dimensions to political conflict.

Given that its substantive and structural foundations were shifting—crumbling over much of the postwar period—the New Deal era managed to last and last. Nevertheless, it could not last forever, and it came apart, with an explosion, in one disruptive year. At the time, it was possible to chalk up the disruptions of 1968 to peculiar—horrible—acts of fortune, such as the assassination of Robert Kennedy, or to dramatic but idiosyncratic personalities, such as the quixotic emergence of George Wallace. For some years afterward, it was still possible to chalk up the presidency of Richard Nixon to the specific events of 1968, events disastrous enough to bring a defeated former vice president to power with only a plurality vote, and an exceedingly narrow one at that.[26] In such a context, it was still reasonable to believe that the American political sequence might feature a Nixon interregnum, as it had earlier featured an Eisenhower interregnum, followed by restoration of unified Democratic control of national government.

Yet with hindsight, what those disastrous events did was to crystallize a set of long-running developments, developments that had been undermining the late New Deal Era since at least the mid-1950s. The crystallizing events would, of course, go away. Their underlying developments would not. Said differently, the constituent elements of a new political era, in both its substance and its structure, were all incipiently present by the time of the 1968 election. It may have *seemed* that some simple strategic correction could neutralize that fact. But when political orders shift, this is a common (temporary) misperception. In the nature of politics, the passage of time is required for a new political dynamic, appropriate to these substantive and structural contours, to be consolidated. And this dynamic necessarily acquires its operational impact through the details of politicking on particular events. But all that would not just occur. It was effectively prefigured by 1968.

The Era of Divided Government

When it first arrived, the substantive breakup of the old era was easiest to recognize in foreign affairs, where the cold war consensus disintegrated. Now, nationalists who continued to support the containment of Communism faced off against accommodationists who felt that containment was an increasingly sterile doctrine and that it was time to move on to acceptance and engagement. Yet while the Vietnam War gave this division its initial edge, a panoply of security issues, from arms control through defense budgets, would be available to keep the division alive.[27] And foreign affairs was now to be joined with a much broader array of essentially cultural concerns, helping to bring them to the fore while simultaneously reducing its own role within this evolving cluster.

Vietnam *protest* was still a useful route into the remainder of this valuational dimension, within which foreign affairs was only one large but supporting element. Anti-war protest as behavior had been borrowed, most centrally, from civil rights protest. And anti-war protest was to lead to a general round of reform agitation in politics. But protest was linked from the start in the public mind to other, essentially cultural divisions—over that burgeoning crime wave, for example, where the question was whether crime was a socioeconomic product to be understood (the progressive position) or a moral breakdown to be countervailed (the traditional view). Vietnam protesters themselves often underlined this link by insisting that they were part of a "counterculture," and this was as good an introduction as any to the larger valuational division that eventually included the public role of religion, community prerogatives, patriotism and national integration, educational orientations, public deportment, and even the proper attitude toward human life, especially at its beginning and end.[28]

In one sense, the structure of politics at the social base for any era characterized by ongoing *dual* concerns—the social coalitions to go with substantive divisions over both social welfare and, now, cultural values—had long been incipiently familiar. At least it had long been understood that economic liberals, those most concerned with the welfare essence of the New Deal program, were often social conservatives, emphasizing family, neighborhood, community, and country, just as it had long been known that economic conservatives, especially the highly educated and occupationally prestigious among them, were often cultural liberals, emphasizing the autonomous management of social life—their own and others'.[29] What changed, then, was only the arrival—most of the contributors to this volume would say the reappearance—of a second great dimension, the cultural dimension, at a position of equal prominence in national politics.

This seemed surprising only because the presence of these relationships—especially the presence of a traditionalist cultural majority within them—had always been intuitively accepted by party operatives and candidates for public office, indeed, understood to be so overwhelming as to make this dimension the "third rail" of American politics. Events of the late 1960s made this no longer so self-evident. At a minimum, a huge postwar generation had grown up without the need to consider economic security. For them, there was mainly the long postwar boom, and there were the social insurance programs of the New Deal whenever it hesitated. In that light, cultural traditionalism and orthodox social controls could seem not so much the glue holding society together as the residue of a time-lag in social thinking.

Changes in the structure of political parties then institutionalized these divisions. In fact, both American political parties now shared the dominant structural characteristics of the immediate postwar Republicans. That is, both were now effectively networks of issue-oriented political activists, not individuals for whom partisan solidarity displaced ideology.[30] The New Deal program had sustained the organized Democratic Party for another generation after the inception of that program, actually funneling some fresh resources through party channels. Yet the institutionalization of these benefits was principally through formal governmental machinery even then. Beyond that, continuing civil service reform was joined by the gradual unionization of government—the greatest success of a union movement in decline—taking far more resources out of the hands of either party than the government had given back. The gradual passing of a New Deal generation of partisans, where no subsequent generation could achieve the same programmatic fervor, was topped off by institutional reform of presidential selection, the last holdout against reform generally. And the old structure of the political parties was gone.

In its place were individual activists whose support was now essential to mounting campaigns and gaining public office: they *were* the party in the operational sense. More to the practical point for a new political order, they were also the key to institutionalizing a partisan connection between the economic-welfare and cultural-national dimensions. They had not abandoned the old social welfare basis of the party system. Republican activists remained conservative, and Democratic activists remained liberal on these matters. They had merely expanded the foreign affairs dimension to cultural issues more generally, in a way that they found to be ideologically consistent. Republican activists were thus traditionalist in social matters and nationalist in foreign affairs, Democratic activists were progressive in social matters and accommodationist in foreign affairs.[31]

Had these increasingly consequential activists not been naturally inclined toward this particular combination of positions, they might have been driven to it anyway by the nature of the new (ideological and issue-oriented) organized interests that joined one or the other party coalition. For the Democrats, these included environmentalists, peace groups, feminists, and homosexuals. For the Republicans, they included anti-abortionists, gun owners, tax reformers, and religious fundamentalists. But in truth, there was no need for "pressure" from these groups to secure these two opposing partisan programs. Party activists were now the natural product of membership in precisely these organizations.[32]

Once again, there was a characteristic political dynamic to go with this mix of issue conflicts, social cleavages, and altered intermediaries, a dynamic to characterize partisan competition in the era of divided government. Now, there was not just a heightened interparty conflict inherent in this tension, between what had become consistent liberals and consistent conservatives among those who did the work of the political parties. Now, there was an intraparty conflict, an elite-mass conflict as well, between these activists and their own rank and file. Among Republicans, this latter conflict was at its most intense between economically conservative but culturally liberal identifiers and their leaders. Among Democrats, it was at its most intense between economically liberal but culturally conservative identifiers and their leaders.[33]

Yet the institutions of American government again provided a simple resolution for these tensions, and it was this resolution that would provide not just the context for public policy making in our time but also the name for the time itself. At bottom, there were now two opposing majorities simultaneously present in the general public—more liberal than the active Republican Party on economic and welfare issues, more conservative than the active Democratic Party on cultural and national concerns. The obvious solution was to colonize one elective branch of national government with one majority and one elective branch with the other. Split partisan control was what this solution contributed practically. "Divided government" was what it came to be called, and the era of divided government had been born.

There was only one serious effort to configure this era differently, to make it work differently rather than just to triumph within it, and that effort came right at the start. Having arrived at the White House courtesy of the social upheavals of the 1960s, Richard Nixon attempted, in effect, to make the new political order a Republican counterpart to the old—with Republican majorities in the general public and Republican control of all the main institutions of national government, presumably to be punctuated by the occasional Democratic interlude. In order to do this, he needed not just to capitalize on foreign affairs and cultural values, where the Republican Party already possessed major latent assets. He needed to neutralize party disadvantages on economics and social welfare, which meant accepting Keynesian fiscal interventions and making some final peace with the welfare state.[34]

Once more, however, if this made great sense for the presidential Republican Party, it had few obvious attractions for sitting congressional Republicans, who were already successful without any such adjustment. Worse still, it had little attraction to the active Republican Party in the states and localities, whose volunteers were increasingly active in politics precisely because they were conservative on both major dimensions; that was the point of their participation. As a result, Nixon failed to transform the era of divided government into a period of unified Republican dominance, an opposite partisan successor to the New Deal era. His efforts, always powerfully constrained by his own party, crashed completely with the coming of the Watergate crisis. His successors, Ronald Reagan and George Bush, albeit hugely successful in other respects, never really tried.

In the particular sequence in which this era initially arrived—led off by Vietnam, race, public order, and countercultural protest—the logical opening resolution was a Republican presidency stapled onto a Democratic Congress. Yet other issue sequences were easily capable of other results in a political dynamic with these enduring characteristics. All that reliably followed was that unified partisan control of national government had become the deviant outcome, in effect requiring strategic disasters or public miscalculations.

One of these happened immediately after Nixon, when circumstances allowed Jimmy Carter to appear simultaneously as the economic liberal *and* the social conservative in the aftermath of Watergate. Such a resolution, however, could not last. Carter was not interested in being an economic liberal, and a Democratic administration was not going to be culturally conservative.[35] Unified government was thus swept away. Indeed, if the Carter adventure is chalked up to these miscalculations, courtesy of the fallout from Watergate (it is hard to imagine Carter being elected president in its absence, and he was defeated at the public's first opportunity), then split partisan control of national government was the uniform natural state of American politics from 1968 through 1992. Bill Clinton was able to stave it off again, but only for a brief and unhappy two years before it came back dramatically.

Substance, Structure, and Public Policy

That still understates the scope and constraints of the modern era, however, for electoral outcomes themselves were merely a kind of shorthand—a register—

for what was going on in the larger society. There was an established political dynamic, developing gradually and indirectly during the late New Deal, crystallizing explosively in 1968, and running relentlessly through all of politics thereafter. And this dynamic was in turn the product of an ongoing interaction between continuing substantive conflicts and continuing structural influences. Such an established order should have been shaping legislative struggles too, and hence policy making, as indeed it was. Beyond that, electoral contests and legislative struggles should have been more or less seamlessly joined, linked by the larger political environment in which they occurred, as of course they were. A quick tour of recent politics, leading directly to the year 2000, can exemplify both.

The last gasp for an argument that there was no *era* of divided government, but only a sequence of idiosyncratic events and personalities leading, among other things, to split partisan control, was provided by the election of 1988. The two presidential candidates were genuine moderates within their parties: Vice President George Bush as the moderate Republican, and Massachusetts Governor Michael Dukakis as the moderate Democrat. Moreover, the issue environment for their contest was distinguished by the absence of pressing concerns in either economics and social welfare or culture and foreign affairs. This was thus the perfect context for a campaign typical of its era, with the Republicans focusing on foreign affairs and cultural values and the Democrats countering with social welfare and economic benefit.[36]

A stereotypical campaign was probably sufficient to produce a stereotypical outcome, although the Republicans did hit hard on cultural issues and benefited from generally good economic conditions, while the Democrats wasted time on the theme of neutral competence before settling on their mainstay issues of social welfare and group interest. The outcome was footnotable as the first victory by a vice president seeking to succeed his president directly since Martin Van Buren in 1836. Yet in essence, it was just another quintessential product for an era of divided government. Republicans retained the presidency, and Democrats managed to pick up seats in both houses of Congress. The result was thus the (re)enshrinement of two contrasting majorities, forced to colonize different institutions with different parties, courtesy of party programs that would not comprehend both.[37]

This result was also, of course, the partisan context for the policy struggles that followed during the Bush administration. Two great struggles characterized this administration and thereby inevitably reflected that context. First was the budget battle of 1990, demonstrating anew the disastrous potential of a social welfare priority for a Republican president. By early 1990, governmental economists, including those at the White House, could see a recession looming a year or so down the road, at the most inopportune political (that is, electoral) time. In an effort to ameliorate this, the president went so far as to abandon his vow of "no new taxes" and moved for a series of policy summits with the Democratic congressional leadership. Initially, the product looked promising, as Bush succeeded in getting his preferred slant on cuts, expenditures, and taxes from the Democrats.

The situation changed radically when this package was torpedoed *by his own party* in Congress. If a Republican president needed to compromise on taxes in order to secure reelection, and if a Democratic Congress needed to compromise on spending in order to save programs, Republican congressmen needed to promise tax *cuts*, which were their main defense in the social welfare realm. They were joined by liberal Democrats, who had always objected to the president's preferred slant, and the budget plan was killed. To resurrect it, Bush had to cede its legislative content to the Democratic leadership and then merely sign the result.[38] Along the way, what was, on the surface, a public humiliation for the president became, in a deeper sense, a key example of the process by which a public majority more liberal than the active Republican Party could manage to work its will through a government characterized by split partisan control.

To add injury to insult in the case of President Bush, the resulting package would prove insufficient to stave off a deep recession. Yet what appeared likely to salvage his personal fortunes was victory in the second great conflict of the Bush presidency. Iraq had invaded Kuwait during the heart of budget negotiations in 1990. To respond, the president had to do something with a major legislative legacy of the Vietnam War, the War Powers Act, which limited his authority to commit troops without congressional support. In order to commit those troops without acknowledging the act, Bush sought direct legislative approval. As a result, the crucial opening skirmishes of what became the Gulf War were fought not between the Allied forces and the Iraqi army but between a Republican president and his Democratic Congress.

The House of Representatives was once again the key theater for this conflict. And there, Democrats, characteristically for the era of divided government, opposed the use of force. But the issue was Republican territory, and an almost unanimous majority of Republican congressmen voted for the key resolution— and gave the president his win. In the process, a public majority more conservative than the active Democratic Party again managed to work its will through a government characterized by split partisan control. Thereafter, given a short and crushing military victory with minimal casualties, George Bush achieved the highest public approval rating ever registered by an American president.[39] Assuming that cultural-national issues could be kept at the center of public debate, he seemed destined for a comfortable reelection.

Within a remarkably few months, however, it became clear that they could not be kept at the center. The predicted recession proved deeper than expected, and economics became the dominant concern of the 1992 election campaign. Moreover, by separating many Americans from job-based health care plans (and appearing to threaten the same for many more), the recession moved a classic social welfare concern to the top of the policy agenda. This was a propitious context for any Democrat, and the actual candidate, Arkansas Governor Bill Clinton, would benefit profoundly from it. Ironically, he had already benefited from Bush's success in the Gulf War, in the sense that it had scared all the other major Democratic contenders out of the race for the nomination.

Clinton had to endure an ongoing stream of scandals and character revelations over his military service, sexual promiscuity, and personal honesty. All that these ultimately did, however, was to set up, yet again, the usual partisan confrontation in an era of divided government. Republicans were once again able to emphasize cultural values and foreign affairs. Democrats were once again able to emphasize economic benefits and social welfare. In 1992, it was the latter that received public priority; as a result, there was a Clinton presidency, and split partisan control formalistically disappeared.[40] But it would be less than a single term of Congress—less than two years—before it was clear that the practical contours of divided government were as alive and functioning as ever.

Campaigning as a "New Democrat"—moderate on economics and moderate on culture—Clinton was encouraged by his party to govern as an old Democrat, solidly liberal in both realms. In this, he far overshot the national consensus on economics and social welfare, leading with economic stimulus rather than deficit reduction, and following with a health care proposal that would have been difficult to secure at the height of the New Deal. Moreover, he managed to combine the wrong side of cultural values and foreign affairs in one highly explosive issue when he symbolically inaugurated his administration with protracted conflict over gays in the military.[41] Yet the policy conflict that capped all this, and that testified most forcefully to the continuing contours of an era of divided government, was the final major one before the 1994 elections, over an omnibus crime bill.

The original draft bill had been carefully crafted to restore the president's credibility as a cultural moderate. What it ran into was a partisan counterpart to the fate of the Bush plan for a revised 1990 budget, illuminating, this time, the disastrous potential of a cultural-values priority for a Democratic president. As Bush had been undone by the extreme wing of his own party, by conservative Republicans, so Clinton was undone by the extreme wing of his, by liberal Democrats, when they joined conservative Republicans to scuttle his crime bill. By the time he regained their support with some progressive amendments and had essentially purchased the backing of moderate Republicans, he was left with a legislative centerpiece that looked like the stereotypical Democratic bill of Republican oratory: culturally liberal and full of "pork."[42]

The Democrats thus went into the 1994 midterm election having failed to deliver on those items that the public had favored in 1992, in the realm of economics and social welfare, but having dramatically reconnected itself to those items that the public had never favored, in the realm of cultural values and foreign affairs. The result was a genuine disaster, in the form of the first uniformly Republican Congress in forty years, the first Republican Congress without a president at the head of the ticket in fifty. This is only a different way of saying that the result was the return of split partisan control—orthodox divided government—but the other way around this time, with a Democratic president and a Republican Congress.

That Congress, especially the newly Republican House, proved remarkably united in programmatic terms, centered around a set of legislative proposals entitled the "Contract with America." As a policy agenda, that document remained a classic Republican program of its era, stiffly conservative on both economic-welfare and cultural-national matters. In the abstract, it was hugely successful, not just in securing floor votes for its propositions in the House but also in effectively becoming the national policy agenda for 1995. Concretely, in getting actual legislation, it was much more marginally successful, given a less committed Senate and a hostile president.[43] Nevertheless, in the full flush of its success in at least seizing control of the national policy agenda, the Republican congressional leadership moved at the end of 1995 to tackle the deficit itself, by tackling the keystone social welfare programs of the United States: Medicaid, Medicare, and even Social Security.

Moreover, in an effort to force a resolution, to make the president meet them halfway, the Republican leadership shut down the national government twice, over the Christmas and New Year holidays in 1995–1996. They were never to recover. The line of presidential preferences, so closely balanced across 1995—where a close balance is usually a warning light for an incumbent president—diverged sharply in early 1996 and never converged again. In effect, Bill Clinton was allowed to run for reelection as the defender of bedrock social welfare programs, without having spent a dime on them and without having to promise to do so. In return, the Republican campaign had to focus on the president's character and on its alleged policy implications, for drug use and criminal activity generally, and for sexual morality and personal honesty once again.

There was plenty to talk about on these latter dimensions. Nevertheless, what inevitably resulted was the classic campaign for an era of divided government, with the Democrats emphasizing economics and social welfare and the Republicans hammering cultural values and foreign affairs. In a booming economy, where the Republicans had just underlined their role as opponents of the old—consensual—social welfare basics, those facts were easily sufficient to overwhelm the character concerns that were also widely acknowledged by the general public. Receiving less emphasis from analysts this time, however, was the rest of the picture, of split partisan control. Republicans held both houses of Congress—for the first time since 1926–1928—and support for Republican congressional candidates actually rose late in the campaign, when it became clear that Democratic President Clinton would be reelected.[44]

Millennium

One other result of the 1996 elections was even easier to miss: neither side returned to Washington with anything resembling a policy agenda this time. No one could have foreseen that by 1998 it would be possible to campaign by arguing over what should be done with a budget surplus. That was to be the unforeseen product of continuing economic expansion plus, crucially, the budgetary compromises enforced by split partisan control. No one could have foreseen the degree to which the president's problems with the "character issue" would explode into a formal impeachment process, although the place of this issue within the contours of an era of divided government had a good deal to do with its subsequent course, being a natural Republican counter to a Democratic emphasis on social welfare.

Anyone, however, might have noticed that there was no further agenda, and hence no conscious contribution to any new political era. When the Democrats then picked up a few congressional seats in the 1998 elections, they aggressively celebrated a midterm pickup for the presidential party, a pickup last seen in 1934. In return, Republicans mourned and shook up their congressional leadership.[45] Within the contours of its political era, however, the result was really a wash, and neither party should have credited it for much. The Democrats still held the presidency, and the Republicans still held Congress. And neither party had any new agenda for the closing years of the second millennium.

This meant that active Democrats were still very liberal on both major substantive dimensions of American politics, and active Republicans were still very conservative on both. The general public remained left of those active Republicans on economics and social welfare, just as it remained right of those active Democrats on cultural values and foreign affairs. And the institutions of American government still accommodated these divisions easily, through the device of split partisan control. The era of divided government was no doubt being undermined by changing social structures and emerging substantive concerns as all this occurred. But it was safely enough ensconced to extend into the next millennium as the framework for American politics and policy making.

Notes

1. For social welfare in the early New Deal years, see Arthur M. Schlesinger, Jr., *The Coming of the New Deal* (Boston, 1959), and William E. Leuchtenberg, *Franklin D. Roosevelt and the New Deal, 1932–1940* (New York, 1963). For social welfare in the late New Deal years, see Alonzo O. Hamby, *Beyond the New Deal: Harry S. Truman and American Liberalism* (New York, 1973), and James L. Sundquist, *Politics and Policy: The Eisenhower, Kennedy, and Johnson Years* (Washington, D.C., 1968).

2. For foreign affairs in the early New Deal years, see James MacGregor Burns, *Roosevelt: The Soldier of Freedom, 1940–1945* (New York, 1973), and John Morton Blum, *V Was for Victory: Politics and American Culture during World War II* (New York, 1976). For foreign affairs in the late New Deal years, see John Lewis Gaddis, *The United States and the Origins of the Cold War, 1941–1949* (New York, 1972), and Seyom Brown, *Faces of Power: Constancy and Change in U.S. Foreign Policy from Truman to Johnson* (New York, 1968).

3. For the forming of these two great social coalitions, see James L. Sundquist, *Dynamics of the Party System: Alignment and Realignment of Political Parties in the United States* (Washington, D.C., 1973), esp. chaps. 10–12, and Everett C. Ladd, Jr., with Charles D. Hadley, *Transformations of the American Party System* (New York, 1975), esp. pt. 1. See also David Burner, *The Politics of Provincialism: The Democratic Party in Transition, 1918–1932* (New York, 1968).

4. For organized labor and partisan politics, see Robert H. Zieger, *American Workers, American Unions, 1920–1985* (Baltimore, 1986). For corporate business and partisan politics, see Nicol C. Rae, *The Rise and Fall of the Liberal Republicans: From 1952 to the Present* (New York, 1989). See also Byron E. Shafer, "Partisan Elites, 1946–1996," in *Partisan Approaches to Postwar American Politics*, ed. Byron E. Shafer (Chatham, N.J., 1998).

5. For the Democrats, see Alan J. Ware, *The Breakdown of Democratic Party Organization, 1940–1980* (Oxford, 1985). For the Republicans, see George H. Mayer, *The Republican Party, 1856–1964* (New York, 1964). More generally, see David R. Mayhew, *Placing Parties in American Politics* (Princeton, N.J., 1986).

6. The "ownership" of these issues is documented initially in Angus Campbell, Philip E. Converse, Warren E. Miller, and Donald M. Stokes, *The American Voter* (New York, 1960), esp. chap. 5. The lasting character of this arrangement is developed in Aaron B. Wildavsky and Nelson W. Polsby, *Presidential Elections: Strategies of American Electoral Politics* (New York, 1964). On the electoral model developed to embody party competition in these years, see Angus Campbell, "Surge and Decline: A Study of Electoral Change," *Public Opinion Quarterly* 24 (1960): 397–418.

7. For an indication that the framers of the U.S. Constitution would have been unsurprised, see Paul Eidelberg, *The Philosophy of the American Constitution: A Reinterpretation of the Intentions of the Founding Fathers* (New York, 1968), chaps. 4, 5, 9. For the evolution of this difference between congressional and presidential parties, see Wilfred E. Binkley, *President and Congress* (New York, 1937). For the Republican Party amidst this difference in the late New Deal era, see Charles O. Jones, *The Republican Party in American Politics* (New York, 1965).

8. On Eisenhower in particular, see Stephen E. Ambrose, *Eisenhower: Soldier and President* (New York, 1990). For the effort in 1956, see Charles A. H. Thomson and Frances M. Shattuck, *The 1956 Presidential Campaign* (Washington, D.C., 1960).

9. For the statistic in its larger context, see Richard B. Freeman, "The Evolution of the American Labor Market, 1948–1980," in *The American Economy in Transition*, ed. Martin Feldstein (Chicago, 1980). William H. Chafe treats this as part of a larger shift from "industrial" to "post-industrial" America in *The Unfinished Journey: America since World War II* (New York, 1991), 114. All such interpretations are rooted in U.S. Department of Commerce, Bureau of the Census, *Statistical Abstract of the United States* (Washington, D.C., various years).

10. Ralph E. Freeman, ed., *Postwar Economic Trends in the United States* (New York, 1960), and Feldstein, *American Economy in Transition*. See also Richard A. Easterlin, *Growth Triumphant: The Twenty-first Century in Historical Perspective* (Ann Arbor, Mich., 1998).

11. Summary statistics can be found in Warren E. Miller and Santa A. Traugott, comps., *American National Election Studies Sourcebook, 1952–1986* (Cambridge, Mass., 1989), table 2.1, "Party Identification," as updated in National Election Studies, Center for Political Studies, University of Michigan, "Party Identification 3-Point Scale 1952–1998, in *The NES Guide to Public Opinion and Electoral Behavior*, at http://www.umich.edu/~nes/nesguide.htm. For some of the class-based cross-currents underneath this summary, see Miller and Traugott, *American National Election Studies Sourcebook*, table 2.18, "Party Identification of Occupation Groups" (and update), plus, especially, Jeff Manza and Clem Brooks, *Social Cleavages and Political Change: Voter Alignments and U.S. Party Coalitions* (Oxford, 1999).

12. Michael Barone, *Our Country: The Shaping of America from Roosevelt to Reagan* (New York, 1990), esp. pt. 4; James T. Patterson, *Grand Expectations: The United States, 1945–1974* (New York, 1996), esp. chaps. 19–24. Compare John Patrick Diggins, *The Proud Years: America in War and Peace, 1941–1960* (New York, 1989), with John Morton Blum, *Years of Discord: American Politics and Society, 1961–1974* (New York, 1991).

13. Vivian Vale, *Labour in American Politics* (London, 1971); Graham K. Wilson, *Unions in American National Politics* (New York, 1979). See also Derek C. Bok and John T. Dunlop, *Labor and the American Community* (New York, 1970).

14. Alfred D. Chandler, *The Visible Hand: The Managerial Revolution in American Business* (Cambridge, Mass., 1977); Sanford M. Jacoby, ed., *Masters to Managers: Historical and Comparative Perspectives on American Employers* (New York, 1991). See also Edwin M. Epstein, *The Corporation in American Politics* (Englewood Cliffs, N.J., 1969).

15. Robert Price, *Profiles of Union Growth: A Comparative Statistical Portrait of Eight Countries* (Oxford, 1980); Thomas A. Kochan, Harry C. Katz, and Robert B. McKersie, *The Transformation of American Industrial Relations* (New York, 1986).

16. For example, see John Kenneth Galbraith, *The New Industrial State* (Boston, 1967). Compare that with the actual situation for the mid-1950s to the mid-1960s in Feldstein, *American Economy in Transition*.

17. For the social coalitions, see Byron E. Shafer, *Quiet Revolution: The Struggle for the Democratic Party and the Shaping of Post-Reform Politics* (New York, 1983); for the attitudes associated with them, see Everett C. Ladd, "Liberalism Upside Down: The Inversion of the New Deal Order," *Political Science Quarterly* 91 (winter 1976–1977): 577–600.

18. See especially J. Christopher Soper, *Evangelical Christianity in the United States and Great Britain: Religious Beliefs, Political Choices* (Basingstoke, 1994). See also George M. Marsden, *Fundamentalism and American Culture* (New York, 1980), and James Davison Hunter, *American Evangelicalism: Conservative Religion and the Quandary of Modernity* (New Brunswick, N.J., 1983).

19. Frank B. Friedel, *FDR and the South* (Baton Rouge, 1947); Harvard Sitkoff, *A New Deal for Blacks: The Emergence of Civil Rights as a National Issue* (New York, 1978).

20. For the movement itself, see Thomas R. Brooks, *Walls Came Tumbling Down: A History of the Civil Rights Movement, 1940–1970* (Englewood Cliffs, N.J., 1974), and Harvard Sitkoff, *The Struggle for Black Equality, 1954–1980* (New York, 1981); for its legislative conflicts, see Hugh Davis Graham, *The Civil Rights Era: Origin and Development of National Policy, 1960–1971* (New York, 1990).

21. For these early years of a long-running conflict, see especially George C. Herring, *America's Longest War* (New York, 1979). See also Larry Berman, *Planning a Tragedy: The Americanization of the War in Vietnam* (New York, 1982), esp. chap. 2.

22. For Johnson in both regards, see Eric F. Goldman, *The Tragedy of Lyndon Johnson* (New York, 1968), and Doris Kearns, *Lyndon Johnson and the American Dream* (New York, 1976). On postwar demography, see Richard A. Easterlin, *Birth and Fortune: The Impact of Numbers on Personal Welfare* (New York, 1980); on student "shock troops," see James Miller, *Democracy Is in the Streets: From Port Huron to the Siege of Chicago* (Cambridge, Mass., 1994).

23. On the issue and its place in a growing complex of cultural-national concerns, the key text remains Richard M. Scammon and Ben J. Wattenberg, *The Real Majority* (New York, 1970). On the issue in its own right, see James Q. Wilson, *Thinking about Crime* (New York, 1975), and Kathlyn Taylor Gaubatz, *Crime in the Public Mind* (Ann Arbor, Mich., 1995).

24. On environmental politics, see Michael J. Lacey, ed., *Government and Environmental Politics: Essays on Historical Developments since World War Two* (Baltimore, 1993), and Samuel P. Hays, *Beauty, Health, and Permanence: Environmental Politics in the United States, 1955–1985* (New York, 1990); on gender issues, see William H. Chafe, *The Paradox of Change: American Women in the Twentieth Century* (New York, 1992), and Cynthia E. Harrison, *On Account of Sex: The Politics of Women's Issues, 1945–1968* (Berkeley, Calif., 1989).

25. For this particular point about the Court in postwar politics, see Richard L. Pacelle, Jr., *The Transformation of the Supreme Court's Agenda* (Boulder, Colo., 1991); for the Court in politicking more generally, see David M. O'Brien, *Storm Center: The Supreme Court in American Politics* (New York, 1986).

26. Theodore H. White, *The Making of the President 1968* (New York, 1969); Lewis Chester, Godfrey Hodgson, and Bruce Page, *An American Melodrama: The Presidential Campaign of 1968* (New York, 1969).

27. Most directly, see Ole R. Holsti and James N. Rosenau, *American Leadership in World Affairs: Vietnam and the Breakdown of Consensus* (Boston, 1984); more generally, see Everett C. Ladd, Jr., and Charles D. Hadley, *Political Parties and Political Issues: Patterns in Differentiation since the New Deal* (Beverly Hills, Calif., 1973).

28. An even grander framework for the same basic division is Seymour Martin Lipset and Stein Rokkan, "Cleavage Structures, Party Systems, and Voter Alignments: An Introduction," in *Party Systems and Voter Alignments: Cross-National Perspectives*, ed. Seymour Martin Lipset and Stein Rokkan (New York, 1967). A different take on the same matters is Ronald Inglehart, *The Silent Revolution: Changing Values and Political Styles among Western Publics* (Princeton, N.J., 1977).

29. Research on "working-class authoritarianism," an otherwise puzzling phenomenon to its authors, often shares this basic perception. T. W. Adorno and associates, *The Authoritarian Personality* (New York, 1950); Seymour Martin Lipset, *Political Man: The Social Bases of Politics* (New York, 1960), chap. 4.

30. A powerful summary of the change is the conclusions of Ware, *Breakdown of Democratic Party Organization;* the more general phenomenon is discussed in James Q. Wilson, *Political Organizations* (New York, 1973), chaps. 1–6.

31. Gareth Davies, *From Opportunity to Entitlement: The Transformation and Decline of Great Society Liberalism* (Lawrence, Kans., 1996); Allen J. Matusow, *The Unraveling of America: Liberalism in the 1960s* (New York, 1984).

32. Kay L. Schlozman and John T. Tierney, *Organized Interests and American Democracy* (New York, 1985); Jack L. Walker, *Mobilizing Interest Groups in America: Patrons, Professions, and Social Movements* (Ann Arbor, Mich., 1991).

33. Byron E. Shafer and William J. M. Claggett, *The Two Majorities: The Issue Context of Modern American Politics* (Baltimore, 1995). See also Ladd with Hadley, *Political Parties and Political Issues*.

34. Robert J. Mason, "The New American Majority: The Challenge to Democratic Dominance, 1969–1977" (D.Phil. diss., Oxford, 1998). See also Daniel Patrick Moynihan, *Maximum Feasible Misunderstanding: Community Action in the War on Poverty* (New York, 1969).

35. Betty Glad, *Jimmy Carter: In Search of the Great White House* (New York, 1980); Charles O. Jones, *The Trusteeship Presidency: Jimmy Carter and the United States Congress* (Baton Rouge, 1988).

36. See, especially, Jean Bethke Elshtain, "Issues and Themes in the 1988 Campaign," in *The Elections of 1988*, ed. Michael Nelson (Washington, D.C., 1989); more generally, see Gerald M. Pomper, ed., *The Election of 1988* (Chatham, N.J., 1989).

37. Paul R. Abramson, John H. Aldrich, and David W. Rohde, *Change and Continuity in the 1988 Elections* (Washington, D.C., 1990).

38. The best way to follow the 1990 budget fiasco, week by week, is *Congressional Quarterly Weekly Report* (CQWR). See, especially, George Hayer, "Defiant House Rebukes Bush; New Round of Fights Begins," *CQWR*, October 6, 1990, 3183–88, and George Hayer, "One Outcome of Budget Package: Higher Deficits on the Way," *CQWR*, November 3, 1990, 3710–13.

39. An easy way to follow the Gulf War is through the *New York Times* (NYT) from August 1990 to March 1991: from R. W. Apple, Jr., "Invading Iraqis Seize Kuwait and Its Oil; U.S. Condemns Attack," *NYT*, August 3, 1990, to Andrew Rosenthal, "Bush Halts Offensive Combat; Kuwait Freed, Iraqis Crushed," *NYT*, February 28, 1991. But see, especially, Special Report, "Deciding on War," *CQWR*, January 5, 1991, 7–44.

40. Paul R. Abramson, John H. Aldrich, and David W. Rohde, *Change and Continuity in the 1992 Elections* (Washington, D.C., 1994); Gerald M. Pomper, ed., *The Election of 1992* (Chatham, N.J., 1993); Michael Nelson, ed., *The Elections of 1992* (Washington, D.C., 1993).

41. Kenneth S. Baer, *Reinventing Democrats: The Politics of Liberalism from Reagan to Clinton* (Lawrence, Kans., 2000).

42. See, especially, Holy Idelson, "An Era Comes to a Close," *CQWR*, December 23, 1995, 3871–73.

43. On the outcome, see Tim Hames, "The US Mid-term Election of 1994," *Electoral Studies* 14 (June 1995): 222–26; on the "Contract," see Ed Gillespie and Bob Schellas, eds., *Contract with America* (New York, 1994); on its legislative trajectory, see Donna Cassata, "Republicans Bask in Success of Rousing Performance," *CQWR*, April 8, 1995, 986–1005.

44. For the outcome, see Byron E. Shafer, "The American Elections of 1996," *Electoral Studies* 16 (September 1997): 394–403; for analysis, see James W. Ceaser and Andrew E. Busch, *Losing to Win: The 1996 Elections and American Politics* (Lanham, Md., 1997).

45. Special Report, "Election 1998," *National Journal*, November 7, 1998.

AFTERWORD

Differences abound in these grand overviews of American politics, differences of specific interpretation but also differences of fundamental approach. Indeed, the reader is submerged in—grabbed by—both sorts of differences by the time a second chapter has arrived. In opening the volume, Ron Formisano focuses on the machinery of American government and its evolution (or not) as the central dynamic of American politics in the early years. By contrast, David Waldstreicher, covering much the same territory, focuses on the cultural expressions of politics, "the political" in the largest and most amorphous sense, for a picture of that same dynamic.

Formisano sets out his perspective from the start. "I argue that the issue of state power—how much government, and with what degree of capacity for action—pervaded the major ideological and partisan conflicts of the early Republic and conditioned the party battles of the Federalists and the Republicans, as well as the sectional and partisan struggles that came later." In this perspective, a political culture of popular participation, born in the Revolution, was coupled with a widespread distrust of government, born of the colonial experience. The result was a government that did not work, and the first great domestic political conflict was really over the attempt to create a national government in the largest sense—a state—that did.

Thereafter, however, the successful constitutionalists split, and the two sides (plus their inheritors) can be traced through American history for a long time. One side sought national greatness, built necessarily on economic management and institutions to guarantee public order; it could only hope to inculcate this through a native population brought up in its norms and responsibilities, and it feared an opposition built not just on unsympathetic social groups but on irreligion and immorality. The other side sought individual—and therefore local—autonomy; it welcomed the continuing replication of these values through migration and immigration, and it necessarily saw state building as authoritarianism, militarism, stasis, and immobility.

Waldstreicher is equally forthright in a different approach. "Even while artfully triangulating the story of class, ethnic, religious, gendered, and even regional social formations in particular places, many scholars have left the story of national politics to others, sometimes even while continuing to accept the periodizations paced by national politics. . . . In important ways, racism proved to be democratic nationalism's crucial supplement, only to emerge in the end as its Achilles' heel." For this approach, telling explicitly that "national story," Waldstreicher blends the (changing) situation of the country as a single entity with the (changing) cultural rituals that characterized individual life at the local level. Along the way, a public life celebrating the birth of a nation gave way to a public life focusing more and more on issues of race, adapted to particular sectional (not national) needs and views.

In the process, a *national* politics, built inevitably on pulling together in response to a hostile outside world, likewise gave way to a continental politics, built instead on sectional divisions and interests. The opening national concerns were powerful enough in their time to cause Thomas Jefferson, a president who represents Formisano's anti-statists, to add the Louisiana Purchase. The subsequent racial concerns, though Waldstreicher would insist that they were always there, began their move to diagnostic status as just one more grand "wedge" in the attempt to disrupt the Virginia dynasty, which arrived to control continental politics for a generation, before these concerns moved to the center of public ritual—and inevitably, public politics—in a way that was ultimately impossible to compromise.

It is possible to take these first two chapters, and their approaches, as representing polar opposite perspectives, and their authors do occasionally try to put each other in a context that could be considered evidence of just such a fundamental difference. The first approach begins with the organizational institutions of a government; the second with the anthropological institutions of a culture. The first is thus built around certain key structural facts: around social coalitions interacting with a government that begins to make a partially autonomous contribution to the character of politics. The second is built instead around the grand substantive contents of politics: around first national and then continental issues.

Yet this badly overdraws the difference. Formisano's evolving American state is, simultaneously, a key intermediary in an explanation of the character of an extended period in American history. That is, it responds both to an outside world that contributes the concerns (the substance) a political system must address and to the main alternative views (again, the substance) of what a government ought to do. Likewise, if Waldstreicher's evolving public life responds centrally at one level to the main substantive concern of its time, it is also powerfully influenced by two giant structural facts: first, by the basic structure of an international order, in which the new United States is a weak and apparently vulnerable player, and second, by the less evident structure of a continental order, in which sectional divisions of economy and society become increasingly dominant.

Both analysts are thus in some sense focusing on one of the grandest issues in all of American political development—namely, the fundamental scope of government, the size of the state and its role in national life. Or, rather, they are addressing the issue of the state versus the culture, the issue of the degree to which this will be—and must be looked at as—a "civil society." The two authors come at this concern from opposite sides, yet they cannot escape being ultimately focused on it. Formisano argues that a political culture, a party system, and a governmental structure can (and do) evolve on partially separable tracks, whereas Waldstreicher sees these as much more intrinsically connected. Yet the grand question that their essays formulate can still be recognized in both.

So can some inescapable views on the next major interpretive question, about the nature of the American politics that succeeded this opening era and then lasted throughout the whole nineteenth century, as well as about the roots of its greatest individual crisis, the Civil War. Joel Silbey, who opens both this exposition and its intrinsic set of major debates, focuses most centrally on the main intermediary institution in the American politics of the time. For him, this is not just the simplest way to pull together a variety of substantive issues and structural influences. It is also a major autonomous influence in its own right, even providing the name—the familiar shorthand—for arguments over this era, the "party period."

"The years after 1820 were a time of remarkable political innovation and energy in the United States. The ideological and cultural assumptions undergirding politics changed; new values and outlooks came to dominate the scene. And at its center were critical new forms of political organization. . . . Political parties shaped, clarified, and gave coherence to the socioeconomic forces so vigorously in play. . . . Their triumph was remarkable." Silbey and Waldstreicher agree on the break point separating the immediate postcolonial world from the party period: the years after 1819, when the economic and geographic attachments of an older Atlantic political system became instead the economic and geographic attachments of a newer continental system. They also differ profoundly on the centrality of political parties to the change, as evidenced in the subtitle of Waldstreicher's original chapter, "Before, Beneath, and Between Parties."

For Silbey, the fundamental economic transformation of American society, now frequently summarized as the "market revolution," unleashed a set of forces that effectively called forth the first mass political parties (and hence the first mass party system). From above, these new parties were the sole available means for making policy in the face of sweeping change. From below, they were the obvious means of linking citizens with government, again in the face of those worrying or exhilarating changes. Either way, they represented something very different from the perspective on politics shared by major actors in the earlier period, a new view in which social division and policy conflict were inherent and inescapable, and thus needed to be managed.

The two parties that emerged gave a new incarnation to the original division first set out by Formisano, in his postconstitutional division. The old postconstitutional side associated with Thomas Jefferson became the Democratic Party, epitomized now by Andrew Jackson, with his deep hostility to market relationships. And the old postconstitutional side associated with George Washington became the Whig Party, looking for commercial development to provide im-

well-being, social mobility, and national greatness. Formisano would th Silbey on the extent to which these two parties really penetrated and organized society and its politics. Formisano leaves more room for anti-party sentiment and extraparty organizations; Silbey's view is summarized by the title of his chapter, "To One or Another of These Parties Every Man Belongs"—an argument that these other forces did not seriously nuance politics.

Both analysts encounter yet a third view from Michael Holt, who emphasizes the malleability and perceived impermanence of these parties and their party systems. "People's awareness from personal experience of the ease with which new parties could be created in part fostered this sense of uncertainty and precariousness. But it sprang as well from social, economic, inter-sectional, constitutional, and political changes during those years that generated demands among some groups for a shift in the substantive issue agenda on which politics and governance focused."

Looking at the nature of American politics on either side of the Civil War, Holt is additionally struck by the amount of change. And in this, he goes back to the central focus developed by Formisano—namely, the partially autonomous role of a changing state, plus, for him, the partially independent influence of prior public policies themselves. "With regard to economic policies and much else, there was a significant change between the 1830s and the 1880s in the allocation between the national and state governments of jurisdictional authority over different policy areas of public life. One of the most striking omissions from the literature on the party period, and from the recent debates about it, for that matter, is any serious consideration of Federalism and its evolution over time in the nineteenth century."

The power of the synthesis summarized in the notion of a party period, drawing together much of the nineteenth century (or not), explains a lot of the phraseology and some of the content of these disputes. But at another level, what Formisano, Waldstreicher, Silbey, and Holt are all arguing about is a second grand issue in American political history: the degree to which political actors, in their wishes and through the institutions shaped most directly by them, managed to control their environment by directing its politics, or the degree to which their wishes and initiatives were instead determined overwhelmingly by forces effectively outside their management. And nothing raises that issue more starkly, highlighting interpretive differences among these authors in a different way, than the question of the causes of the Civil War.

For Waldstreicher, the conflagration was an inescapable result of forces present from the beginning of the nation. The failure to resolve issues of freedom and slavery in the Constitution, and the partial (and ultimately inflammatory) form of the requisite compromise, could be forestalled by the great national issues based on international threats in the immediate postrevolutionary years. But when those threats were resolved and those issues receded, freedom and slav-

ery—and race—became inevitably enmeshed in the cultural life of
Americans, to the point where there was no resolution possible, short
For him, in essence, the Civil War begins at the beginning.

For Formisano, by contrast, the turning point came around 1820. Before that,
state development was proceeding sufficiently that, had it continued, a national
state might have found a way around and through these huge sectional conflicts,
or it might at least have lasted until economic change overwhelmed them. Moreover, the first crack in this development, the attempt to bring Missouri into the
Union as a free state, was begun largely as a political gambit rather than a principled initiative. But the South was alarmed, and this alarm reinforced an effort
to bring states' rights—and anti-statism—to the center of politics. This brought
a halt to state development and resulted in a deadlock that was resolvable, in
hindsight, only by force of arms.

For Silbey, at the other extreme, it was not the state but the party system that
staved off growing sectional division, and for a remarkably long time. Both
major parties had serious organizations in all major regions. Their leaders believed that other issues—economic development versus local autonomy, and all
the cultural attachments these represented—constituted the core of politics.
Moreover, the interaction of the structural fact of widespread two-partyism with
this substantive ideology about the core of politics provided additional reasons
to resist sectional division. The resulting, explicitly political, consciously desired
resolution lasted through 1852, so that it was only in 1854 (and after) that the
resolution broke down and the Civil War inexorably loomed.

In that sense, the three authors treat parties very differently: Silbey as an independent variable, Formisano as an intervening variable, and Waldstreicher as
a dependent variable—to stereotype their positions only a bit. By the same token,
they take the reverse view of the balance between human actors and social
forces: Waldstreicher the most socially determined; Formisano seeking a clarified middle ground in which prior conscious decisions become embedded in
government arrangements, which then acquire an influence of their own; and
Silbey the most deliberately autonomous, in which human actors look consciously at, and try to find some organized way through, the forces around them.

Holt is the most conditional of the four, though in making himself least easy
to stereotype on the first question—the place of political parties—he carves himself the most extreme position on the second—the role of individual and, here
especially, elite actors. By arguing for the plasticity of the political environment
throughout the middle of the nineteenth century and by emphasizing the malleability of human actions in response, Holt really argues for the importance of
conditional interactions. There were structural encouragements for this, for example, in the ease with which third parties could be formed. And there were substantive stimuli to change, as public policies moved to different institutional the-
aters. But political leaders were not necessarily just responding to structural

elements in their environment, though in responding individually, they were contributing influences that did not necessarily work in the fashion their creators had intended.

This perspective makes it easier to accept the major change in the character of American politics that arrived in the late nineteenth century, one that is arguably still in place in the modern era and that both Peter Argersinger and Richard Jensen address explicitly. As such, these two chapters—and their major interpretive differences—are the pivot between the four that precede them (Formisano, Waldstreicher, Silbey, and Holt) and the three that follow them (from Anthony Badger, James Patterson, and myself). Yet it is Argersinger who sets out most systematically the nature of the change, and it is he who locates the engine for this change most centrally inside the political system, inside the substance and structure of practical politics.

His account of "The Transformation of American Politics" begins, in the years after the Civil War, with the "before" condition. Present were those same political parties that both Silbey and Holt show as surviving the war. But beneath them, there were now social groups identifying with these parties through cultural values. And above them, there was a government that had fallen back, after the war, to a (familiar) state of fragmentation and restriction. Split partisan control of national government at frequent points only exacerbated this. So did the character of the major policy issues of the time—the money question and the tariff, but even land policy and pensions—which cross-cut rather than unified these parties.

In the 1890s, all this came apart, and the new world—our world—succeeded it. A regionally based party system replaced a highly competitive one. Mass partisanship declined, but interest groups multiplied. Administrative agencies began to rival party organizations in the distribution of governmental benefits. Congress lost primacy, and the presidency began a century-long rise. The last bastion of indirect election, the Senate, fell to what was now a less mobilized and less partisan electorate, further facilitating the rise of independent entrepreneurs as candidates. "Partisanship came to be identified less with party organizations and hoopla than with particular leaders and policy issues. New party leaders, as James Wright wrote, were often 'less political strategists than they were issue-oriented political activists. Their approach to politics held that issues made coalitions; the older political practice tended toward the opposite approach.'"

For Argersinger, the big change was most centrally the product of several interrelated developments in policy and politicking, and the centering of this change on politics writ large is a distinctive part of his argument. "Indeed, the machinery of government powerfully shaped both political conduct and public policy. But if constitutions, legislative and executive institutions, and electoral rules shaped politics, they were themselves the legacies of past political actions, products of what one scholar has aptly described as the continuing 'dialectical interplay of meaningful decisions and structural constraints.'"

Thus an unexpected Republican sweep of national offices in 1888, underpinned by various forms of gerrymandering and overrepresentation, forced a policy response, which was then massively rejected by the public in 1890. The Democrats moved to greater partisan dominance in the 1892 election, only to have the depression of the 1890s fall on their watch. Thus, 1896 became a watershed, sweeping the Republicans back into office and, this time, sweeping the old system away with the Democrats.

Argersinger buttresses this in an additionally intriguing way, in his framing of the arrival of women's suffrage. This was the era when women got the vote, and their change in tactics on the way to doing so—away from a nineteenth-century feminism and toward womanly influences on reform—was entirely consistent with the larger political argument. But so is the point that suffrage as a whole was not a response to some generalized national dynamic. For example, as the vote was being extended to women, it was being withdrawn from blacks and often from low-income whites as well, first in the South and then nationwide.

Although Holt and Silbey do not explicitly address this particular argument, they do present an implicit alternative. Holt too locates a political shift in political factors, but for him, this shift was powerfully influenced by changes in the rules of the game. Ballot reforms, for example, sharply reduced the plasticity in the system that third parties provided until the late nineteenth century. Simultaneously, registration reforms reduced the competitiveness of the two main political parties, along with their ability to mobilize voters and coordinate government. Silbey does not cover the postwar years in his chapter, but prior work that contributed to that chapter certainly does. There, he attributes special influence to the ongoing economic transformation that, if it called forth the new political parties in the 1820s, ultimately overwhelmed them in the 1890s instead.[1]

By contrast, Jensen locates the essence of this change in a sweeping shift of intellectual climate, and he takes the world of ideas—the spirit of an age—as far as any of the contributors as a basic mainspring of political transformation. He begins with the centrality of a set of ideas that came to be grouped as Progressivism. "The centrality of ideas helps explain why social, demographic, and economic correlates of voting behavior were much weaker in the Progressive Era than in the Gilded Age. . . . If everyone was progressive, correlations would necessarily be low—precisely because the importance of the phenomenon was so correspondingly high." Yet he goes even further, making the rise (and ultimate fall) of Progressivism a major incarnation of an ongoing dynamic in American politics, in which the core value of republicanism needs constant rescue from corruption—that is, constant purification—by way of modernization and efficiency in the case of the late nineteenth and early twentieth centuries.

This ideational approach applies even to the subelements of this shift. "A party system dies when its core issues are resolved and new issues surge to the fore." Hence the Civil War system died as the passage of time inevitably weakened the partisan reach of the war, reinforced by "purification" (that is, restriction) of the southern Democratic electorate and by "modernization" (that is, enactment) of the northern Republican agenda, especially in federalizing the judicial system. What arose as a replacement was a national search for efficiency, to go with a burgeoning new economy, and a national search for ways to moderate and regulate the most dramatic manifestations of that economy, such as the trusts.

Evidence of the shift surfaced everywhere: in the engineer as hero, in an emphasis on education as the solution to nearly any social ill, in reforms aimed at rooting out corrupt partisan practices. This does not imply that the political machinations of the day were irrelevant. The sequence of elections from 1888 to 1896, along with the policy responses to each in turn, was critical to forcing the ultimate triumph of the new mentality in 1896, when Republicans were able to align support for the new economy with the rescue of individual citizens from the depression. William McKinley then seized on the outcome of 1896 to replace the old cultural basis of a decaying party system with ethnocultural pluralism. Thereafter, Progressivism as an organizing philosophy was secure, and subsequent conflicts were over who truly represented it and how far it should go—until the Great Depression shifted the public philosophy once again.

Badger, in moving the larger story on, acknowledges—and disagrees with—the main explanations put forward by both Argersinger and Jensen. He notes that the substance of policy issues changed in major ways between the late Progressive Era and the immediate period after World War II. The tariff, trusts, banking, and currency were all gone by the postwar years. Social welfare, foreign affairs, and civil rights had arrived as staples of substantive conflict. But he also argues that policy outcomes in these realms changed considerably less, and that the political structures underlying these substantive issues changed even less—less than is usually argued, and less than the coming of a self-conscious New Deal era would suggest. "What emerges is both more stasis and more contingency than the two leading alternatives usually provide."

The coming of the New Deal, as reinforced by the war emergency, resulted in a remorseless expansion of the power of the federal government; that was certainly a structural difference. The restarting of the economy moved workers out of agriculture, and the postwar boom moved Americans generally out of the cities and into the suburbs. None of those developments would be reversed. But whereas Jensen treats the Great Depression (and the subsequent New Deal) as the end of one party system and the beginning of another, and Argersinger points to a longer-running trend in the nature of American politics in which the New Deal is only a perturbation (however major), Badger looks for a different interpretation that is more effectively structural than Jensen's and less explicitly political than Argersinger's.

For him, the key facts are that several major alleged transformations of political structure actually went less far than is commonly supposed, so that a different (and older) structural influence on American politics reasserted itself—remained dominant, really. Those alleged transformations include women's suffrage, which was never a dramatic electoral influence; partisan realignment, which was always far from complete in its ideological coherence; and a short-lived coalition of working- and middle-class Americans behind welfare statism, which came apart quickly in the postwar years. What remained important, then, both before and after the New Deal, was an anti-statist coalition—once anti-Prohibition and now anti-welfare, once anti-*Teddy* Roosevelt and now anti-*Franklin* Roosevelt—with a lineage running even further back into American history.

Patterson accepts many of the same developments as tools for extending the postwar analysis, but he weighs and balances them in a different manner. He too notes the relatively modest welfare state imparted by the New Deal, but he emphasizes the huge and irreversible growth of the federal government by the end of World War II, not just in welfare and defense but also in taxing and spending, as well as in programs and public bureaucracies. He too credits an enduring resistance to state growth and distrust of authority on the part of the general public, but he brings back the periodic outbursts of moral passion that this same public has been capable of. And through this framework he squeezes the monumental economic expansion of the postwar years, producing general economic progress plus "the increasingly pluralistic, bureaucratic, and litigious politics that emerged over time."

Patterson has written elsewhere about the conservative coalition,[2] but he differs from Badger in regarding a resurrected anti-statist alliance as effectively unable to roll back much (if anything) of the New Deal and little of the Great Society to follow. He adds the civil rights movement, as the great embodiment of moral passion for the postwar years. The result is a swelling of rights consciousness that, along with its institutional embodiments, was perhaps the critical development of this period. There was an explosion in public-law litigation; there was a surge in federal regulation as more and better-organized groups demanded (and got) federal protection; there was a huge increase in categorical aid programs from the national level, along with unfunded mandates for states and private employers.

By 1980, Patterson is returning to the main themes of the opening chapters in this volume: the racialization of politics and, especially, the growth of the state—not so much its deliberate development as its automatic and inescapable growth. Divided government reinforced this, by neutralizing the control of elected governmental institutions within which political parties were additionally declining. Yet if continuing fragmentation, a growing public distrust of government, and a growing public cynicism about politics brought an end not just

.ew welfare legislation but to most examples of rights legislation as well, "this ..story can be regarded as a time when a combination of developments—notably, wars, economic growth, and moral passions—intermittently but in the end decisively contributed to the swelling of an administrative state."

I also take the New Deal era as a substantive starting point, along with postwar economic growth as the critical structural engine. But whereas Badger treats this growth principally as an incentive for increased conservatism, and Patterson treats it instead as a force for rights consciousness and a rights-based state, I squeeze it through the social coalitions left on the political landscape by the New Deal. The result is two cross-cutting social majorities whose contents and preferences go a long way toward creating an extended period of split partisan control of national government—of "divided government," the hallmark of modern American political life.

"None could know that the surface anomalies of 1968 were best seen not as idiosyncratic events in their own right but as crystallizing vehicles for the emergent issues and long-term forces that would terminate the late New Deal." The decomposition of political parties was important, as they increasingly became networks of independent issue activists. The rise of new interest groups, especially in the realm of cultural values and social causes, was another important factor. So was the onward substantive march of the New Deal, as civil rights was added to the cluster of issues involving social welfare, and the Vietnam War was added to the cluster involving foreign affairs.

In the end, it was the fact that economic development did not directly benefit the more conservative party, but instead added wealthier and better-educated cultural liberals to the Democrats, along with less-educated cultural conservatives to the Republicans, that explained the peculiar pattern of electoral combat and policy output in our time. Richard Nixon tried to change the resulting constraints, to create a unified Republican government. Jimmy Carter tried to escape these constraints, believing that he could present himself apart from them. And Bill Clinton initially failed to understand the need to address these constraints, producing the first modern instance of divided government in the other direction, with a Democratic president facing a Republican Congress. But none could successfully overrule the substance and structure of their time.

Badger, Patterson, and I also deal differently with those great questions raised initially by Formisano and Waldstreicher and then by Silbey and Holt—namely, the parameters of a civil society as opposed to a state, and the slack available to individual actors as opposed to social forces. For Badger, leaders had that slack but failed to take full advantage. For Patterson, their actions were just one more element of a contingent mix. And for me, they were largely dependent—either shaped or defeated by an enduring mix of substance and structure. For Badger, the civil society ultimately constrained the state, even at the apparent moment of the greatest prospect for some other outcome. For me, society and state interacted in complex ways to produce a continuing pattern of outcomes. And for Patterson, the state actually grew and achieved increased autonomy, quite apart from the direct wishes of the general public or even of its elected government.

Those are some of the similarities and differences across time that are implicit in the preceding chapters, above and beyond their own particular substance. Some of these contrasts are surely facilitated by the interpretive approaches used to produce them. Thus, cultural approaches probably add emphasis to the place of society, whereas statist approaches add emphasis to the place of electoral rules and governmental arrangements. Yet this only begs the question, at bottom, of the appropriate approach for the particular time. In any case, it is surely possible to roll the same comparative analysis on and on, subject only to the limits of the imagination of the analyst.

To take only one example, consider the ongoing interaction between social coalitions and policy preferences in all these chapters. In the beginning, the great substantive issues of American politics involved domestic economics and foreign affairs, and although these were closely linked in the immediate postindependence years, as both Formisano and Waldstreicher emphasize, it is also true that the "court" party was consciously interventionist on both issues, the "country" party consistently anti-statist. In the early party period, by contrast, domestic economics and moral regulation became the important concerns of politics. Yet the two interventionist positions remained linked, although this time, the anti-interventionists, the Democrats, were usually dominant.

After the Civil War, in the Gilded Age, domestic economics and cultural values remained dominant concerns, with the latter acquiring substantial importance. They remained connected in the same way—interventionist on both for the Republicans, anti-statist on both for the Democrats—and the conjunction led to an extremely competitive, even politically unstable, historical era. This was succeeded in the Progressive Era by an upweighting of economics and a downweighting of culture, so that the interventionist party, the Republican Party, was able to sustain an extended period of one-party domination, interrupted only by a party split in 1912.

The New Deal era in one sense only extended this pattern: cultural concerns did not entirely disappear—the Democrats repealed Prohibition, for example—but economics became even more overwhelmingly dominant, thereby extending the substantive priorities of the Progressive Era. But in a second sense, the New Deal brought perhaps the most fundamental change of all, for this time—and really for the first time in any extended fashion—the parties switched their positions on domestic economics, with the Democrats becoming interventionist, and the Republicans becoming anti-statist. Previous Democratic administrations, in power, had not always been as militantly anti-statist as their ideology implied, just as previous Republican administrations had not been as active as they appeared to promise. But this was still arguably the largest such change in all of American history.

It appeared to shift again for a time, when World War II and then the cold war made the Democrats interventionist on both dimensions. But the era of divided government restored these positions in lasting fashion—at least as this is written. Cultural values once again became the main substantive alternative to domestic economics in American politics, through crime and punishment, abortion and euthanasia, civil liberties and public order, and so on. And this time, one party, the Democrats, was interventionist on economics and anti-statist on culture, while the other, the Republicans, was the reverse.

That is merely one more apparent and speculative pattern that might be drawn from the preceding chapters. Regardless, all these chapters, individually and collectively, surely draw out a chain of social consequences of immense import. This seems self-evident when they are focused on the grand questions implicit in any comparison: the scope of the state and the question of conscious impact and control. The scope of the state versus the role of society is often at issue in these political syntheses, whatever the specific substance of politics may be. The question of the ability of individuals, alone or as collectivities, to shape the social forces of their time rather than be shaped by them lurks constantly under the surface of these syntheses—and never more than in analyses focused on government, one of the few great levers putatively intended to allow individuals to manage those forces.

But the lesser substance, the specific substance of these individual chapters, also encompasses developments of major consequence. The substance of their politics is often large and always of interest. Symbolic investment is often intense, sometimes with real impact on daily lives. And there are larger and not just smaller shifts in these patterns as well. In particular, the nature of American politics—the place of the individual participant, the form of intermediary organization, the rules of the game itself—appears to change substantially during the Progressive Era, producing a great "before" and a great "after" to American political life, as Argersinger and Jensen successfully suggest, albeit in different ways.

For me, the centrality of politics to politics—that is, the number of times that the nature of politics is powerfully influenced by formal governmental rules or explicit policy disputes—remains striking. Apportionment, for example, appears in most of these stories, from the three-fifths rule before the Civil War to the "rotten borough" states of the West afterward, from the fact of two seats for all in the Senate to the refusal of many states to reapportion their House districts, and so on. Holt is especially good at adding to this roster, with both a shift in electoral rules and the varying placement of policy decisions under Federalism being central to his account.

Tariffs and the "money question," among partisan issues, likewise had a remarkably long run, especially given the (limited) change in their application that actually occurred. But that is a matter of personal taste and curiosity. It is better to close by noting the sweep of these chapters both individually and collectively, the force of their syntheses one after another, and—most especially—the prospect that others can go on from here to do other things, related but inevitably different.

—B. E. S.

Notes

1. Joel H. Silbey, *The American Political Nation, 1838–1893* (Stanford, Calif., 1991), esp. chap. 12.
2. James T. Patterson, *Congressional Conservatism and the New Deal: The Growth of the Conservative Coalition in Congress, 1933–1939* (Lexington, Ky., 1967).

CONTRIBUTORS

Peter H. Argersinger is professor of history at Southern Illinois University. Among his books on American political history are *Populism and Politics: W. A. Peffer and the People's Party* (Lexington: University Press of Kentucky, 1974), *Structure, Process, and Party* (Armonk, N.Y.: M. E. Sharpe, 1992), and *The Limits of Agrarian Radicalism* (Lawrence: University Press of Kansas, 1995). He is currently working on two books—one dealing with the politics of apportionment in the Midwest during the 1890s, and the other a larger analysis of American election laws in the late nineteenth century.

Anthony J. Badger is Paul Mellon professor of American history at Cambridge University and vice-master of Sidney Sussex College. Among his works are *Prosperity Road: The New Deal, Tobacco, and North Carolina* (Chapel Hill: University of North Carolina Press, 1980); *The New Deal: The Depression Years, 1933–1940* (New York: Hill and Wang, 1990); and, with Brian Ward, eds., *The Making of Martin Luther King and the Civil Rights Movement* (London: Macmillan, 1996). He is currently finishing a book on FDR and the 100 Days and writing a biography of Lyndon Johnson.

Ronald P. Formisano is Bryan chair of History at the University of Kentucky. His books include *The Transformation of Political Culture: Massachusetts Parties, 1790s–1840s* (New York: Oxford University Press, 1983) and *The Great Lobster War* (Boston: University of Massachusetts Press, 1997), along with numerous articles, including "The Concept of Political Culture," *Journal of Interdisciplinary History* (winter 2001). His current research focuses on populist movements from the American Revolution to the 1990s.

Michael F. Holt is Langbourne M. Williams professor of American history at the University of Virginia. His published works include *The Political Crisis of the 1850s* (New York: W. W. Norton, 1983); *The Rise and Fall of the American Whig Party: Jacksonian Politics and the Onset of the Civil War* (New York: Oxford University Press, 1999); and, with David Herbert Donald and Jean H. Baker, *The Civil War and Reconstruction* (New York: W. W. Norton, 2001). His current research focuses on Reconstruction.

Richard Jensen is professor of history, emeritus, at the University of Illinois at Chicago. He has written *The Winning of the Midwest: Social and Political Conflict, 1888–1896* (Chicago: University of Chicago Press, 1971), and *Illinois: A Bicentennial History* (Champaign: University of Illinois Press, 1977), along with numerous articles on historiography, social history, and political history. The founder of the H-Net network of e-mail discussion groups, he is now involved in creating on-line historical teaching methods.

James T. Patterson is Ford Foundation professor of history at Brown University, where he teaches courses in late-nineteenth-century and twentieth-century U.S. history. He is the author of *Grand Expectations: The United States, 1945–1974* (Oxford: Oxford University Press, 1996), which won a Bancroft prize in American history. His most recent book is *Brown v. Board of Education: A Civil Rights Milestone and Its Troubled Legacy* (Oxford: Oxford University Press, 2001). He is now working on a history of the United States, 1975–2000, which is expected to become a volume in the *Oxford History of the United States*.

Byron E. Shafer is Andrew W. Mellon professor of American government, Oxford University, and acting warden of Nuffield College. His published work includes *Quiet Revolution: The Struggle for the Democratic Party and the Shaping of Post-Reform Politics* (New York: Russell Sage Foundation, 1983); *Bifurcated Politics: Evolution and Reform in the National Party Convention* (Cambridge: Harvard University Press, 1988); and, with William J. M. Claggett, *The Two Majorities: The Issue Context of Modern American Politics* (Baltimore: Johns Hopkins University Press, 1995). He is currently working on a book on social structure and postwar politics with Richard G. C. Johnston; a book on issue evolution in the postwar years with William Claggett; and a book on public opinion as a strategic landscape, introducing new opinion measures, with Richard H. Spady.

Joel H. Silbey is President White professor of history at Cornell University. He has written, among other books, *The Shrine of Party: Congressional Voting Behavior, 1841–1852* (Pittsburgh: University of Pittsburgh Press, 1967), *The Partisan Imperative: The Dynamics of American Politics before the Civil War* (New York: Oxford University Press, 1985), and *The American Political Nation, 1838–1893* (Stanford, Calif.: Stanford University Press, 1991). He has just completed a biography of Martin Van Buren, the founder of the American political party system.

David Waldstreicher is professor of history at the University of Notre Dame. His published work includes *In the Midst of Perpetual Fetes: The Making of American Nationalism* (Chapel Hill: University of North Carolina Press, 1997), which won the Jamestown Prize of the Omohundro Institute of Early American History and Culture. He is currently working on a study titled *Runaway America: Benjamin Franklin, Slavery, and the American Revolution* and is coediting, with Jeffrey L. Paisley and Andrew Robertson, a collection of essays called *Beyond the Founders: New Approaches to the Political History of the Early Republic*.

INDEX